Politics and Change
in the Middle East:
Sources of conflict
and accommodation

Politics and Change in the Middle East: Sources of conflict and accommodation

ROY R. ANDERSEN
ROBERT F. SEIBERT
JON G. WAGNER
all of Knox College

Prentice-Hall, Inc., Englewood Cliffs, N.J. 07632

Library of Congress Cataloging in Publication Data

ANDERSEN, ROY R.
    Politics and change in the Middle East.

    Bibliography
    Includes index.
      1. Near East–Politics and government.   I. Seibert, Robert F.
II. Wagner, Jon G.   III. Title.
DS62.8.A5   320.956   81-11998
ISBN   0-13-685057-X   AACR2

Printed in the United States of America

10   9   8   7   6   5   4   3   2   1

Cover design by Maureen Olsen
Manufacturing buyer: Edmund W. Leone

ISBN   0-13-685057-X

Prentice-Hall International, Inc., *London*
Prentice-Hall of Australia Pty. Limited, *Sydney*
Prentice-Hall of Canada, Ltd., *Toronto*
Prentice-Hall of India Private Limited, *New Delhi*
Prentice-Hall of Japan, Inc., *Tokyo*
Prentice-Hall of Southeast Asia Pte. Ltd., *Singapore*
Whitehall Books Limited, *Wellington, New Zealand*

Contents

Maps

To our children:
Brynn, Eric, Kyla, and Nicholas

Preface

This book has grown out of the authors' conviction that a proper understanding of present events in the Middle East requires a knowledge of the cultural, social, and economic, as well as the political background of these events. It is, more specifically, an outgrowth of the authors' attempts to develop an undergraduate course sequence aimed at such understanding. We found that despite the abundance of excellent scholarship on the Middle East, there was a paucity of works which brought together the diverse disciplinary perspectives in a way suitable to our pedagogic aims. It is our belief that this book, with its combination of historical and contemporary materials and its integrated perspective, will provide something of value that is not elsewhere available to the undergraduate student or educator.

We have directed our writing to an undergraduate audience not specifically acquainted with the Middle East. In addition, we have made every effort to avoid disciplinary jargon, arcane theoretical concepts, or other devices that would necessitate a sophisticated background in any of the social sciences. This is not to say that we do not introduce any special concepts or terms, but we do so only as necessary, and we do it as painlessly as possible.

One of the characteristic problems in writing about another culture involves the use of language. The words used by Arabs, Turks, or Persians to describe institutions and concepts fundamental to their civilization usually have no direct equivalent in English. One is faced with the dilemma of whether to translate them (which necessarily introduces our own cultural bias), or to use "native" terms (which places on the reader the burden of learning a new vocabulary). Added to this problem is the more technical matter of how to transliterate Arabic or other languages into the medium of the English alphabet. Our solution has been one of compromise; we have used foreign words when there is no English equivalent or when the nearest English equivalent would be awkward or misleading. Despite our efforts to minimize foreign words, the text has unavoidably made use of a number of them—

especially Arabic terms. All these are explained in the text, and whenever possible the explanation accompanies the first appearance of a term, which is indicated by the use of italics. As an extra aid to the student, we have also included these terms in a glossary. The terms explained in the glossary are in boldface type the first time they appear in the text. As for the spelling of Arabic and other foreign words, we have omitted the diacritical marks that scholars use to render their transliterations technically correct. We do so on the assumption that the limited number of terms we use can, for the reader's purposes, be determined without these marks. Nearly all Arabic terms appear in several different English forms in the literature; we have tried to hold to those forms which reflect the most frequent current usage among informed scholars who write for a general audience. In personal names especially, we have often departed from the technically correct forms and employed instead, the forms used in English news reportage and popular historical writing.

The authorship of this book is genuinely a joint affair; there is no "senior" author. The order of our names on the list was randomly chosen. One of the authors is an economist with a long-standing interest in economic development, one is a political scientist specializing in political development in the Third World, and the third is a cultural anthropologist specializing in religion and culture change. Each chapter was largely the work of a single author, but each reflects a dialogue that began long before the book was conceived and has continued throughout its preparation.

We cannot hope to name all the persons and institutions that have made important contributions to this writing. We are grateful to those at the University of Chicago's Center for Middle Eastern Studies, whose help has been offered repeatedly and in a variety of ways. We also wish to thank Knox College for its material and moral support during the preparation of this work. In particular, we are grateful to Nicholas C. Dvoracek and Paul G. Irvin of the Knox College Audio-Visual Department for their efforts in preparing original maps for this book. We are especially indebted to the United States Office of Education, which made it possible for the three authors to observe at first hand, the phenomena of social change in two Muslim countries, Egypt and Malaysia, during 1976 and 1977. We also thank those at the American University in Cairo, Cairo University, the American Research Center in Egypt, the American Friends of the Middle East, and the Center for Egyptian Civilization Studies, as well as other individuals and organizations in the United States and other countries who helped to make this book possible. Above all, we take this opportunity to express our appreciation to our wives and children for suffering bravely through what is, as every author knows, the seemingly endless task of transforming a set of ideas into a finished book.

R. R. A.
R. F. S.
J. G. W.

Politics and Change
in the Middle East:
Sources of conflict
and accommodation

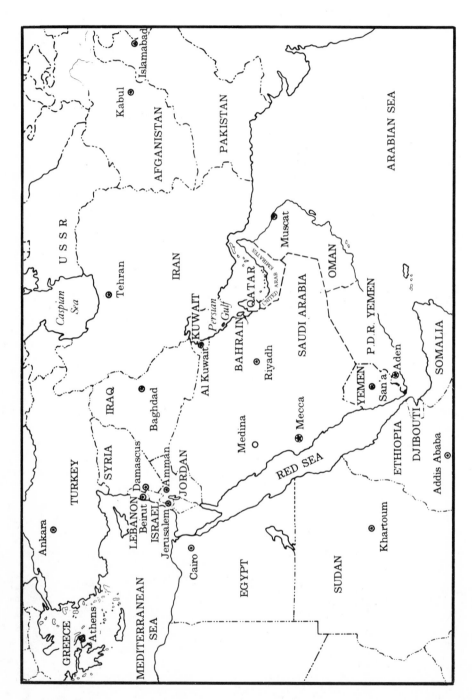

The Middle East

Introduction

The impact of the dramatic increase in petroleum prices during the 1970s laid to rest the notion that any single industrialized nation could exist in "splendid isolation." The industrial activity of the developed countries of the world was disrupted, inflation ripped through their economies, and the distribution of real income changed markedly. Industrial societies cannot function smoothly without a steady flow of energy, and through the 1950s and 1960s an increasing percentage of their energy consumption was in the form of petroleum. Therefore, it is not surprising that the fact of world interdependence was driven home so forcefully by the price increases directed by the Organization of Petroleum Exporting Countries (OPEC).

Since the strength of OPEC is centered in a few Middle Eastern nations, their actions will continue to be of considerable interest to the rest of the world regardless of how the region's current military conflicts are resolved. Saudi Arabia, for example, has more international financial reserves than most countries of the world. Even if the Saudis' remaining reserves of petroleum were to vanish, they would continue to have a substantial influence on the international financial scene. The influence of Iran, also a major petroleum-producing state, runs along somewhat different lines. Under the Shah, Iran's oil revenues quickened the pace of modernization and created the sixth largest military force in the world. However, Iran's modernization caused tremendous social changes and led to a revolution and a dramatic shift in policy. Libya has used some of its petroleum revenues to finance various "peoples' revolutions" around the world and to provide a safe haven for several revolutionary or terrorist groups. Thus, politics in the Middle East directly and substantially affect politics in Bonn, London, Tokyo, and Washington—and ultimately in Hometown, U.S.A.

The Middle East's geographical position alone—lying as it does between Africa, Asia, and Europe—is ample reason for it to command the world's attention. A sign in the Cairo airport proclaims it the "Crossroads of the World," a slogan that rings true for several reasons. Three great monotheistic religions—Judaism, Christianity, and Islam—arose from the same society and culture; the Western and Muslim intellectual heritages have much more in common than is generally recognized. Although the roots of Western thought can be traced to Greece, much Greek philosophy and science was preserved and transmitted to the West through the writings of Muslim scholars. In fact, the Middle East served as a repository of Greek thought while Europe languished in the Dark Ages. Also during this time, a great intellectual and cultural florescence occurred in the Islamic world. The development of algebra (from the Arabic, *al-jabr*), fundamental advances in the sciences of optics and medicine, and many other intellectual achievements originated in the Middle East. Furthermore, concepts from the Far East were melded into Middle Eastern intellectual and cultural patterns. "Arabic" numerals, the decimal system, and the use of zero—all brought to the Middle East from India—paved the way for profound advances in quantitative thinking. The role of the Middle East in trade and conquest, no less than its intellectual activity, made it a crossroads in every way.

Although the success of OPEC alone gives ample reason to study the region, there are other less spectacular but just as important reasons for educated persons to study the Middle East. The Middle East is not a desert devoid of high culture and rich history; the religion of its peoples is not characterized by wild-eyed fanaticism. The Middle East should not be viewed as an exotic area of intellectual inquiry, but rather as integral to our understanding of the world.

A serious study of the relationship of the Middle East to the rest of the world must include a welter of diverse information—"facts," assumptions, hypotheses, and theories—which for the average student will truly be of an introductory nature. Similarly, although Egypt, Saudi Arabia, Iran, Lebanon, and other Middle Eastern states share a common heritage, particular influences—historical, geographic, and economic—have produced substantial individual variation. Thus the Middle East cannot be viewed as a monolithic entity; its constituent elements must be studied carefully in order to identify points of commonality and divergence.

A maze of facts usually generates more confusion than understanding, more tedium than excitement. We have therefore selected two themes—conflict (and its resolution) and modernization—to make the task more manageable for the beginning student. Although we focus on political systems in the Middle East, we carry our themes across disciplinary lines into other social sciences. However, we have not attempted a systematic coverage of Islamic art, literature, science, and theology, although such coverage would indeed lend richness and subtlety to the topics covered in the text. We encourage the student to explore these topics.

Politics and Conflict

The first theme centers around the definition of politics employed: the study of conflicts between groups of people and how those conflicts are resolved in formal human institutions. Conflict is present in all societies and is caused by competing demands for scarce resources. The demand for resources embraces a wide variety of valued things, but may include such ordinary things as money, land, and water or more abstract things such as deference, prestige, or occupational status. The propensity of human beings to demand such things in greater quantity than the supply allows leads to conflict over distribution or consumption. When formal organizations make socially binding decisions regarding such things, they are engaging in the political resolution of social conflict. To sum up, *conflict* arises out of the inevitable competition for scarce resources; *politics* involves the resolution of these conflicts through the formal and informal processes and institutions that constitute government. We consequently equate politics with the formation and resolution of conflict in social life. Although there are many alternate definitions of politics that could be employed, the one given here is widely used and fits into the major plan of this book.

Conflict and conflict resolution occur at various levels of social organization. For example, conflict over water resources can take place at the local level (which fields are to receive how much water?), or the regional level (should a dam be constructed in region A or region B?), or the national level (should a country rely on its existing water sources or explore the feasibility of desalination of ocean water?). Although all of these decisions involve the provision and allocation of scarce resources, the people, institutions, and style of decision making will vary from one level to another. Conflict resolution involving personal discussion among those affected is more likely to occur at the local level than at the national. The political processes employed depend on the level and arena of conflict.

In this text, we discuss political conflict in terms of the applicable arenas. For example, in a discussion of the elite structure of a given government, we distinguish between the qualities and styles of national and local elites. This is a convenient way of analyzing a nation's political system. However, no nation consists of neatly layered conflict arenas; any given arena interacts with other arenas potentially higher, lower, or equal in level. The arenas of conflict in a nation resemble the composition of a multiflavored marblecake in which various colors and flavors dip and swirl irregularly.

The complex interaction of arenas can be seen in the decisions that led to the construction and operation of the Aswan High Dam in Egypt. Egypt is, as Herodotus said more than two thousand years ago, the "gift of the Nile." Almost all its arable land lies in the Nile Valley and Delta. Over thousands of years the cultivators of the land have adapted their agricultural techniques and timing to the annual flooding of the river. Regulating the flow of the Nile through the construction of a large dam, it was theorized, would free the farmers from dependence on the caprice of the river, minimize flood damage, and maximize agricultural production.

However, the project brought to light many unanticipated conflicts—some of which had been simmering below the surface of day-to-day events, and some of which were created by the construction and operation of the dam. The major themes of conflict were as follows: (1) The financing and construction of the dam involved superpower interests: the United States had first agreed to finance the project, but backed out of the agreement; the U.S.S.R. then stepped in to fill the breach. (2) The determination of water rights between Egypt and the Sudan had to be resolved, since the lake formed by the dam crossed the border dividing the two countries. (3) Thousands of families had to be relocated from the lake site into existing or new villages and towns. (4) A system for allocating irrigation water to Delta farmers had to be developed. (5) Drainage problems induced by the operation of the dam required individual, village, provincial, national, and finally World Bank intervention. The relationships between various groups involved had to be reworked, sometimes drastically. The Aswan Dam was—and is—the focal point of conflict in several arenas; it is an example of the tendency for solutions in one arena to generate new problems in another in a complex cycle of cause and effect.

Modernization

Modernization presents some of the same problems of definition as politics and conflict. Economists, for example, generally describe modernization in terms of sustained growth of per capita income. To some sociologists, modernization consists of changes in value structures and the building of the "modern person." Political scientists often define it according to the changing behavior of the public and the institutions of government. Despite the lack of a universally shared definition, almost everybody agrees that each perspective is a legitimate starting point for analysis, and that in fact the modernization process involves complicated interactions of economic, political, social, and intellectual phenomena. There is no *premium mobile* to be found—no single perspective or cause sufficient to explain the process except on a highly generalized level.

Most observers would agree that a modernizing society attempts to provide a higher level of material well-being for its population, usually by building an industrialized economy. Such a society seeks a new social and political consensus, often by broadening the basis of political participation. And it attempts to develop a higher level of personal competence in its population through higher levels of literacy, health, and education. All of these characteristics involve the pursuit of an enhanced quality of life and increasing levels of efficiency. All of these characteristics, as they change, produce new forms of conflict and strain, providing new grist for the mill of politics. Moreover, contemporary governments must contend with the *revolution of rising expectations*, which means that populations of less modern countries are increasingly aware of their "right" to the supposed benefits of modernization. Since governments often fall short of the public's expectations, strains and conflicts arise between social classes as well as between the general public and the government.

The general characteristics of the modernization process do not constitute a definition; they are the result of a more fundamental set of forces. Although we shall wait until Chapter 6 to develop a formal definition of modernization, we shall point out some of the basic intellectual problems of the modernization process.

One source of difficulty is that the terms *traditional* and *modern* imply two discrete and static conditions. But one would have to look long and hard to find a society that is statically traditional or statically modern. All societies are, and have always been, constantly changing. The problem in traditional societies, then, is not that of introducing change, but rather one of assessing those elements of change which induce modernization or a quickening of the modernization process. The scope and acceleration of these changes should be measured against what previously was being achieved in the country under consideration, the rate of change in the more modern countries, and the stated or implied goals of the country. That is, the modernizing task is generally judged on the basis of at least three admittedly foggy standards: (1) the rate of change relative to that of the past; (2) the gap between the more and the less modern sectors, which may be increasing or diminishing; and (3) popular goals and expectations. Needless to say, anyone who tries to comprehend all of this will face some profound problems. And since political leaders often act on notions of modernization that are based on myth, history, and the work of academic scribblers, the intellectual problem is readily transformed into policy dilemmas and political realities.

By describing groups of societies as being either traditional or modern, one lumps together highly heterogeneous traditional societies and contrasts them with more homogenous modern nations, including Europe and its offshoots as well as Japan. One runs the risk, then, of defining "modern" as Western (or Japanese). But there is precious little evidence to suggest that the only forms of modernization possible are those which the Western world has experienced to date. Indeed the remarkable increase in the economic strength of several nonindustrial oil-rich countries has presented students of the modernization process with a novel and perplexing case in point. The modernization processes in the already developed countries occurred over centuries. The popular notion of the "miracle" of Japanese growth, for example, holds that the process started only after World War II; more sophisticated accounts, however, place the turning point in the late nineteenth century, during the Meiji Restoration. Recent work has even suggested that one should go back to the Tokugawa period (twelfth through seventeenth centuries) to appreciate properly the changes that paved the way for the twentieth-century "miracle" of Japanese growth. Western scholars often claim that such profound changes inevitably take long periods of time to incubate—often many centuries, as was true for Europe and Japan. But the sudden overflowing of some national treasuries may fundamentally transform several key Middle Eastern countries over a period of decades rather than centuries. For example, Saudi Arabia, the most powerful of the oil-rich countries, has been increasing the material well-being of its citizens at a breakneck pace; however, the traditional institutions of government, family, and clan, an apparently nonsecular attitude among the populace, and the uneven distribution of wealth all raise troublesome questions with respect to the path of modernization. Are Middle Eastern attitudes and institutions sufficiently flexible to be molded into Western political and economic forms, or will the economic forces be blended into the more traditional social and political patterns? Whatever the track of the modernization process, will it be self-sustaining or will it eventually lead to stagnation and decay? Attempts to answer these questions are necessarily speculative, but important nevertheless.

Other problems must be explored if one is to understand the modernization process. It is not clear, for example, to what extent strategically placed and timed external forces are able to trigger or to frustrate modernization. The debate over the effect of multinational corporations provides a ready example of this kind of issue. Multinational firms provide needed technology and management skills, earn foreign exchange, and provide employment; however, they may also present the host country with severe constraints to modernization.

In this book special attention is paid to the relation between religion and modernization, a matter of particular importance in the Middle East. Some aspects of modernization—especially the growing acceptance of scientific knowledge—may challenge the existing influence of religious leaders and institutions. Religious reactions to increasingly secular sources of authority may create intense, extended conflicts. Many religions, including Islam, have been able in certain circumstances to embrace and encourage modernization; they may also fight it bitterly, with mixed results. In any case we must pay close attention to Islam as a potentially powerful influence in the modernization process.

The puzzle presented by the modernization process in general and the Middle East in particular has shaped the format of this text. Two elements of the format should be made clear at the outset: First, we shall heavily emphasize the historical forces that have shaped the Middle East. To understand what the Middle East is and what it might be requires that one know what it was. The chapters dealing with the history of past centuries, therefore, are best viewed as part of the present landscape and not as a separate story. Second, since the politics of the Middle East are woven together with general social and economic forces, a multidisciplinary approach has been adopted, an approach facilitated by the diversity of the authors' academic training in political science, economics, and cultural anthropology.

Political affairs in the Middle East are treated here as the product of the interaction among social organization, secular values, religion, and the control and allocation of authority and resources at all levels. While the variables must sometimes be isolated for analysis, to remove them permanently from their context is to invite misunderstanding.

One further matter that deserves mention here is the definition of the Middle East itself. The term *Middle East* raises some problems, for it originates in recent Western military usage and utilizes present national boundaries that cut across historically significant cultural and geographical divisions. Furthermore, the reference to the region as part of the "East" reveals a European bias; from the larger perspective of the whole civilized area stretching from Western Europe to East Asia, the so-called Middle East is located somewhat toward the West and has close cultural ties with the Mediterranean region as a whole. Despite these problems, we shall follow the (more or less) established convention and define the Middle East as the region bounded on the northwest by Turkey, on the southwest by Egypt, on the southeast by the Arabian peninsula, and on the northeast by Iran. At the same time, it must be remembered that this division is somewhat arbitrary, and that bordering regions like Afghanistan, the Sudan, and North Africa have much in common with their "Middle Eastern" neighbors. For this reason, we shall include them in our discussions whenever appropriate.

1

Traditional Cultures of the Middle East: The cradle of civilization and politics

In dealing with "exotic" peoples and cultures, we often form stereotypic images, founded on some grain of truth but containing enough distortion and error to make them at least useless and often harmful. Popular images of the Middle East are a case in point.

The Middle East is no stranger to the Western imagination. It is the setting of the Jewish and Christian Holy Scriptures. We derive our images of the Middle East partly from these Scriptures and the Sunday-school images spun around them, and from the news reports of current events. The Middle East is often seen as the primeval wilderness from which our civilization sprang, which has since lapsed into timeless stagnation. In the popular imagination it is inhabited mainly by fierce desert nomads who, driven by a childlike attachment to tradition and the fiery narrowness of the barbaric "Mohammedan" faith, spend most of their time menacing each other and impeding peace and progress. Hollywood films depict the "Arab" as a violent and sinister figure, while news coverage highlights "terrorism" and the ineffectuality of Arab unity and military prowess. Thus we have a composite picture of the Arab (and all native Middle Easterners are thought to be Arabs) as an evil buffoon. However, the popular notion of the Middle East as a geographical and cultural backwater inhabited by ignorant fanatics is incompatible with even the most elementary knowledge of Middle Eastern culture and history.

The most significant historical features of the Middle East are not marginality and simplicity, but centrality and diversity. The centrality of the Middle East in history is partly the product of its strategic location at the juncture of three continents (Africa, Asia, and Europe) and its consequent pivotal role in trade, conquest, communication, and migration.

Middle Eastern cultural diversity is aided by local geography and by the complexities of cultural adaptation in the region. The geographical diversity of the Middle East, which depends largely on the relative availability of water, is striking.

Although the "desert" image is correct insofar as the region is predominantly arid, there are sharp contrasts. The Nile Valley and the "fertile crescent" of the Tigris-Euphrates region and Mediterranean coast were the sites of the first known farming civilizations and the sources of the images of Eden and the Land of Milk and Honey. These geographical contrasts have also led to diverse but interlocking ways of life suited to different strategies of survival and adaptation.

Another factor contributing to diversity in the Middle East is the region's long and complex cultural evolution. Prior to about 10,000 B.C., all the world's peoples were gatherers of wild foods; the domestication of plants and animals—which set human culture on its path of increasing complexity—originated in the Middle East at about that time. During the ensuing twelve millennia, the Middle East has ranked in the vanguard of social and technological evolution more consistently than any other region of the world. It is from the Middle East that Europe received not only its basic agricultural crops and techniques, but indeed all the most fundamental social and cultural elements we associate with "civilization," including literacy, urban life, and occupational specialization. It is especially interesting, in view of this book's political theme, that the Middle East is the site of the earliest states and formal governments. Due partly to the organizational requirements of irrigation systems, the independent villages of the region were soon encompassed in regional forms of political organization, in which the village-dwelling farmers became "peasants" dominated by a nonfarming urban ruling class. This ruler-producer split is the foundation of the state, since it facilitates, through various forms of taxation, a substantial amount of *surplus production*—that is, production that exceeds the subsistence needs of the farming population. This surplus subsidizes the power of the state and ultimately allows the existence of an urban population engaged in various occupations not directly associated with agricultural production, a necessary condition for the specialized accomplishments of "civilized" peoples. The necessity of enforcing peasant taxation and protecting the prerogatives of the ruling classes, regulating trade and exchange, and generally mediating social relationships in an increasingly complicated society, gave rise to what we now take for granted as the political apparatus of the state: legal codes, police and military forces, courts, and other instruments of "law and order." The role of the Middle East in political innovation did not end with the early civilizations; the region was also the birthplace of three world religions, each involving unique contributions to social thought. Yet, despite the leadership of the Middle East in political and social development, the region has long been characterized by social conservatism. The ancient lifestyles of individual peasants, nomads, and townspeople have until recently been little affected by intellectual and organizational advances in the larger society; instead, these lifestyles have been woven into the fabric of an increasingly complicated plural society.

FOUNDATIONS OF SOCIAL DIVERSITY

While the American "melting pot" ideology views cultural diversity as an accidental and temporary byproduct of history, such diversity has been an enduring and valued part of life in the Middle East. Middle Eastern culture is characterized not only by diversity but by *pluralism*—the maintenance of diversity as a significant aspect of the social system. The use of cultural diversity, or pluralism, as a structuring principle in society has led some writers to characterize social life in this region as a "mosaic." This mosaic character is particularly difficult to discuss because it follows no simple pigeonhole scheme but includes many dimensions, levels, and criteria of variation that cut across one another. These include six important dimensions of variability and identity which together determine much of the character of traditional life in the Middle East: (1) ecological pluralism, (2) regional and local ethnic pluralism, (3) religion, (4) family and tribe, (5) occupational groups, and (6) class distinctions. Although it is useful to discuss each of these in turn, the reader should remember that in practice these dimensions are partly dependent on one another.

Ecological Diversity

Of the many elements that contribute to social diversity in the Middle East, the most basic is the relation of people to the land. The vicissitudes of wind patterns, rainfall, and river courses, combined with effects of irrigation systems, often lead to stark contrasts in the land and its potential uses. In parts of Egypt, for example, a railroad track divides a verdant field producing two or three crops a year from a desert so barren as to discourage even Bedouin herders. Although these arable regions constitute less than ten percent of the land in the Middle East, their role in the economic and social order of the region has been of the utmost importance since prehistoric times. For several thousand years, since the origin of the state and associated intensive agricultural techniques, a large portion of Middle Eastern farmland and an even larger portion of the farming population and agricultural produce have depended on irrigation systems.

The nonagricultural lands that make up the bulk of the Middle East are by no means uniform in character. Some of these are forested mountain slopes; others are arid steppes capable of supporting nomads with their herds of camels, sheep, or goats; still other regions, like the "empty quarter" of Arabia or Egypt's Western Desert, support virtually no human populations at all. Water is the crucial resource in all these regions, and the utility of a territory inhabited by a group of camel nomads, for example, may change from year to year, day to day, and mile to mile according to the availability of rainfall or ground water. The importance of water is illustrated by the fact that a permanent well, hardly worth noticing in more watered parts of the world, determined the location of the early Arab trading settlement of Mecca, later to become the birthplace of Islam and the spiritual homeland of Muslims around the world.

The geographical division between the desert and the arable lands is a recurrent phenomenon throughout the Middle East, and it is accompanied by a threefold social division that also spans the entire region: the division between peasants, nomads, and townspeople. Peasants, who comprise as much as three quarters of the population, are engaged directly in agricultural production and live in the small, simple villages that dot the cultivable countryside. Nomads are also engaged in primary economic production, based on the husbandry of camels, sheep, goats, or cattle, usually in those regions that are incapable of supporting agricultural production.

Townspeople, on the other hand, are engaged not in primary food production but in other, more specialized occupations ranging from government, scholarship, or priestly functions to crafts, peddling, and begging.

Nomads

Nomadic herders captivate the imaginations of Middle Easterner and foreigner alike, and often tend to be seen by both (and by themselves as well) as the "purest" expression of the region's cultural tradition. In fact, the nomads for the most part are economically and politically marginal. While nomads have traditionally been the sole inhabitants of the region's nonarable land, their population has never been more than a small fraction of the total for the region (in recent times nomadic or seminomadic herders have made up less than fifteen percent of the population). Nomadic herding is not practiced in the farming regions, and in transitional regions it is combined with village farming. The forms of nomadism vary according to the capacity of the land, which in turn depends on water. Semi-arid steppes support cattle, sheep, and goats, while the true desert supports only camel nomads such as the **Bedouins** of Arabia. The camel nomads, for all their aristocratic self-adulation, are confined to the most marginal lands, those unusable to anyone else. And if Bedouins are admired even by the townspeople for their independence, virility, and simple virtue, it is also true that the nomads as such have only rarely been influential in the political affairs of the states that dominate the region. The ruggedness and apparent simplicity of nomadic life have led to the widespread misconception that it is the oldest and most primitive lifestyle of the Middle East and that it involves complete independence from the more settled and sophisticated life of the towns and villages. This is not strictly true, for nomadic herders depend on villages and towns to a varying degree for manufactured items and agricultural products which they obtain by trading their animal products, and in the old days, by raiding the villages. When drought makes herding less feasible, some nomads are liable to shift temporarily or permanently to a more settled life in town or village. The camel nomadism of the desert has existed only since the introduction of the camel in about 2,000 B.C. Even the herding of sheep and goats, which originated much earlier, depends to some extent on the existence of settled populations and probably does not predate them as a general stage of development.

Of all the nomads in the Middle East, the Arab Bedouin occupies a special position. The Bedouins are Arabian camel nomads who constitute only one of the many nomadic groups in the Middle East, yet they play a curious and significant role in the cultural consciousness of the region. Prior to the birth of the Prophet Muhammad, the Arabs (that is, the original speakers of Arabic) were a group of tribes occupying central Arabia. Many were camel nomads, and the rest were sailors, caravaneers, and townspeople who acknowledged descent from nomadic herders. Islam facilitated the spread of Arabic as the daily language of much of the Middle East and the holy language of all Muslims, and with it came some measure of identification with the Arab Bedouin heritage. Thus, despite the ambivalence which the townspeople sometimes feel for the "barbarians" of the desert, the Bedouins are acknowledged as the "truest" Arabs. (In Arabic the term "Arab" refers, in the strictest usage, only to the Bedouin.) Even an Egyptian shopkeeper, descendent of generations of peasants and townspeople, might boast to the European visitor of being "an Arab from the desert."

Peasants and Townspeople

Despite the common perception of pastoral nomadism as the primeval Middle Eastern lifestyle, peasants and traditional townspeople carry on an equally old and well-established pattern of life, one which has its roots in the early civilizations of Egypt and Mesopotamia. The relation between village-dwelling peasants and townspeople depends, as we have seen, on a political organization that taxes the village-dwelling farmers, thus subsidizing the ruling class in particular and the nonfarming town populations in general. The development of the state, then, entails two divergent ways of life, the urban and the rural, each of which exists as a result of the other.

From the perspective of the traditional Middle Eastern state, the peasant village existed only for the purpose of delivering its tax quota in the form of agricultural produce, money, labor, or some combination of these. For their taxes the villagers rarely if ever received such government services as police protection, education, or public works. As long as the village headman delivered the taxes, the village was left to govern itself. Internally, the village was relatively homogenous, consisting only of peasants who had little influence on the politics of the state that governed their lives, and little chance for social mobility within the larger context of the state and the urban civilization.

Although modern Middle Eastern states are generally committed to changing these conditions, life in peasant villages retains a continuity with the past. Many villagers are still small landholders, share croppers, or landless laborers. Each village is divided into families and blocks of related families, and is headed by a patriarch of the most influential family, whose authority is shared with other village elders. Like the nomads, the peasants have been led by the conditions of their lives to a distinctive philosophical outlook. Unlike the nomads whose values emphasize militant independence, peasants are typically fearful of authority, distrustful of the world outside the village (and often of their own neighbors), and pessimistic with regard to social change. The unenviable position of peasants has led the traditional townspeople and nomads alike to despise them as "slaves of the soil" while continuing to depend on them for the production of basic foodstuffs.

If popular conceptions of the Middle East give undue attention to the nomads because of their romantic image, "historical" treatments of the region are liable to place great emphasis on the towns and cities as the locus of rulers and their "high" culture, the source of written documents on which historical scholarship depends. The life of urban dwellers in the Middle East does not lend itself easily to general description, because townspeople are involved in a great variety of occupations and modes of living. The traditional Middle Eastern town is, among other things, a seat of government. As such, it is the home of the rulers and their retinue, which include military leaders, civil and legal authorities, and religious leaders. In addition to these few relatively favored and affluent political elites, traditional urban life also involves a middle class of merchants, artisans, professionals, and petty officials. The least affluent and prestigious townspeople are peddlers, laborers, and sometimes beggars. In addition to its role in political and religious leadership, the town is a center of crafts and trade, with the suq, or bazaar, serving as a distribution point for manufactured wares as well as the products of the farmers and nomads. Many traditional towns also became producers of wealth in their own right by virtue of their profitable involvement in the trade between Europe, Asia, and Africa. Although Middle Eastern town life is every bit as "traditional" and ancient as that of the villages and deserts, it is here that the sophistication and diversity of culture reaches its peak. Some of the cities mentioned in the Jewish and Christian scriptures, such as Jericho and Damascus, are among the oldest in the world and were already ancient in Biblical times. Others, like Baghdad and Cairo, were founded over a millennium ago as seats of Muslim government, and represent notable efforts in urban planning.

Ethnic Diversity

The ecological pluralism of nomads, peasants, and townspeople is only one dimension of cultural diversity, the others being ethnic, religious, familial, occupational, and social class distinctions. Ethnic differences, or differences in historical descent and cultural heritage, occur both between and within regions. Vast regions of the Middle East are set apart from others by their distinctive language and culture; the most prominent example being the division between the speakers of Turkish, Persian, and Arabic. Each of these groups occupies a major contiguous portion of the Middle East, and each correctly conceives of itself as having different cultural roots. The extent of their historical divergence is suggested by the languages themselves, which are classified into different families and differ from one another more than English does from Persian. These regional groups are also characterized by some differences in values, outlook, details of social organization, and to some extent, religion.

The ethnic diversity of the Middle East would be relatively easy to discuss if it were confined to regional divisions, but the vicissitudes of history have brought about a more complex situation, since migrations have created much of the cultural diversity. It is difficult to say whether the Middle East has seen more migrations than other regions or whether these are simply better documented due to the region's long tradition of literacy. Waterways and seafaring, land trade, the nomadic ways of some of the inhabitants, and the existence of highly organized states bent on conquest have all contributed to the physical mobility of peoples. We find, for example, the Sumerians appearing rather suddenly more than six thousand years ago in the lower Mesopotamian region, creating the world's first literate civilization, and then fading from the scene to be displaced and eclipsed by peoples of other backgrounds. The Jews historically occupied several parts of the Middle East, including Egypt and Palestine, and then many dispersed from the region only to return in this century. During the long career of the Islamic state, Arab ruling classes spread their influence from Spain to Persia; Egyptians were ruled by resident Turks; and much of the region found itself under the sword of Asian Mongols, while the ethnically diverse elites of the Islamic world sought refuge in Muslim India. While such migration resulted in a considerable amount of cultural assimilation, it also gave rise to multiple ethnic communities within regions.

What is most striking about local ethnic diversity, from the viewpoint of the outsider, is that these ethnic distinctions have been such a stable feature of traditional Middle Eastern life. The reason for this is that ethnic distinctions are reinforced by two other major kinds of traditional diversity: descent and occupation.

Descent, Occupation, and Social Stratification

The importance of family, kinship, and common descent in the Middle East is difficult for a Westerner to appreciate. While the European or American considers the individual to be the basic functioning unit of society, the individual has relatively little autonomous importance in the traditional Middle East, or for that matter in most traditional societies. Instead, the individual's status, privileges, obligations, identity, and morality are inextricably tied to the descent group. The minimal descent unit is the extended family, whose structure we shall discuss in the following section. The extended family is part of a larger group of related families, the **hamula** or lineage. The families of a nomadic hamula pitch their tents together, and among sedentary villagers the hamula is also likely to be represented by a clustering of residences. The hamula is, among other things, a political unit that serves to resolve internal disputes between families and to represent their interests to the outside world. Sometimes the lineages are further united into a "tribe." Each of these units is based on the notion of common "blood,"—that is, shared ancestry from some patrilineal founder. The idea of common descent extends to larger groupings: all Arabs consider themselves as having a common descent, and for that matter the Jews, Christians, and Muslim Arabs together are thought to share common ancestors in the Biblical patriarchs. The more specific and immediate the common descent, the more relevant it is to one's personal obligations and identity. It is hardly surprising, in view of this descent orientation, that ethnic groups within a particular region are in no hurry to obliterate their distinctive ancestry.

Perhaps an even more important factor in maintaining ethnic distinctions is their integration with occupational divisions. In the traditional Middle East one's occupation was often determined by family background. Of course, the matter of occupation was relatively simple for the child of a Bedouin or peasant family, but scarcely less so for the son of an urban artisan. Membership in organizations that controlled crafts and trades was frequently passed from father to son, as was the requisite training. Since occupation was largely ascribed rather than achieved, it frequently became associated with certain ethnic groups. This fact was brought home in practical terms when, after the formation of Israel, the exodus of the Jewish population of Yemen* left the country virtually bereft of blacksmiths, bricklayers, and practitioners of certain other trades dominated by this ethnic group.

Ethnic differences thus are often associated with religious affiliations. Regions may differ in their predominant religions, as in the case of the Shiite division

*"Yemen" is a modern nation-state; "*the* Yemen" is a region.

of Islam, which is the majority religion in Iran and parts of Iraq. Many minority religions are concentrated in specific regions, as with the Christian Copts of Egypt. The integrity of separate religious communities has been reinforced on the local level by the traditional Muslim practice of allowing these communities protection and self-government in return for their recognition of the existing Islamic governments.

A final type of social pluralism is class distinction. Since the origin of the earliest states, Middle Eastern society has been stratified into classes that enjoy varying degrees of privilege and wealth. These distinctions are subdued in the countryside, but quite apparent in the cities where lifestyles range from poverty to opulence. Distinctions of class are of course tied in various complex ways to family background, ethnicity, occupation, and ecological situation.

Examples of Diversity

As we have seen, the immense cultural diversity of the Middle East depends on factors such as ecological situation, ethnic background, family and tribe, occupation, and social class. The complex way in which these dimensions intertwine can be seen in two different examples of traditional life: the city of Mecca in Muhammad's day, and the Bedouin camp.

The town of Mecca as the young Muhammad knew it, at about A.D. 600, had been founded a couple of centuries earlier by a tribe of Bedouins who had moved from nomadism to trading and had located their settlement at the site of a permanent water supply and the junction of two major trade routes. Their social organization and world view still bore the stamp of Bedouin life, yet even this budding town had begun to manifest a more urban complexity. The formerly egalitarian founding tribe had differentiated into richer and poorer divisions, and the more favored displayed the trappings of aristocracy. Some families of this tribe had begun to control and monopolize religious worship, in which shrines played a large role. Attached to the ruling tribe were subordinate "client" groups, and below them were slaves. The range of occupations was considerable, and many were interwoven with specific ethnic backgrounds. One author makes reference to "Syrian caravan leaders; travelling monks and curers;... Syrian merchants; foreign smiths and healers; Copt carpenters; Negro idol sculptors; Christian doctors, surgeons, dentists and scribes;... Abyssinian sailors and mercenaries."[1] It should be kept in mind that Mecca was at this time a relatively new and modest-sized trade settlement, a mere upstart in comparison with the more established seats of Middle Eastern government.

Even the traditional Bedouin camp was hardly the simple affair one might expect. In fact, such a camp was liable to include representatives of as many as half a dozen non-Bedouin groups, each performing a separate function as defined by various criteria of descent and cultural tradition. While the Bedouin kin group owned the livestock, the camel herders themselves may have come from another, less "noble" group which lent its services as a form of tribute to the Bedouin, who in turn took the responsibility of fighting to protect the herds from other Bedouin

---

[1] Eric R. Wolf, "Social Organization of Mecca and the Origins of Islam," *Southwestern Journal of Anthropology*, VII (1951), 336-337.

raiders. Members of another ethnic group, the Sulaba, whom some anthropologists recognize as the most ancient inhabitants of the desert, served as desert guides, coppersmiths, leatherworkers, and in various other specified functions. The Sunna, members of a group said to be of partly African origin, served as blacksmiths. African slaves were also part of an affluent Bedouin household; well-dressed and well-fed, they were reputed to be fierce fighters in defense of their masters' herds. Two sorts of traders were also likely to be found in the Bedouin camp. One of these was the Kubaisi, an ambulatory shopkeeper who supplied the camp with a variety of merchandise; the name is derived from a town on the Euphrates from which at least some such merchants traditionally came. Finally, the 'Aqaili, usually a member of the tribe of 'Aquil, bought camels on behalf of urban firms, in return for cash and rifles. In this complex scheme, the Bedouin served primarily as soldier and protector, engaging in raids against other Bedouins, defending the group against such raids, and granting safe conduct across his territory.[2]

UNITY IN DIVERSITY

As we have seen, the cultural pluralism of the Middle East is set within a context of unity and integration. The ties that bind diverse segments of society into an integrated whole are based on two principles: the functional interdependence and complementarity of unlike parts; and the overarching similarities of culture, social organization, and religion.

Nomads, peasants, and townspeople are by no means autonomous groups, nor are they separated by competition, although conflicts of interest certainly do occur between them. Bedouins often depend on peasants for agricultural products and on townspeople for manufactured goods. In the past, Bedouins have exploited helpless villagers for tribute, sold protection to caravans, and acted as middlemen in trade. The existence of villages is a further convenience when climate or other factors force Bedouins into settled life, just as the opposite movement may occur when conditions are reversed. Although the Bedouins were rarely, in traditional times, subject to the sort of control and taxation the state would have liked to impose, neither were they entirely exempt from state control. The peasants, on the other hand, were under the direct state control, which set the conditions that governed their lives. Despite local village self-government, all peasants were not only expected to fill their tax quotas but to obey all laws of the state, over which they had little say. The peasants were also subject to raiding and tribute demands from nomads. It is difficult to say in what ways the peasants depended on others, since exchanges between them and townspeople or Bedouins were typically out of their control and somewhat in their disfavor. Just the same, the towns did provide manufactured items and markets where certain of the peasant's needs could be provided for, and the state provided, in principle, military protection.

Because they were not engaged directly in food production, the townspeople were in a sense the most dependent of all. (Urban populations ultimately depend on

[2]Carleton S. Coon, *Caravan: The Story of the Middle East* (Huntington, N.Y.: Robert E. Krieger Co., 1976), pp. 191–210.

rural surplus production directed into the towns through taxation and trade.) In the Middle East the situation was complicated by the presence of the Bedouin, since the Middle Eastern marketplace served as an intermediary between two modes of rural production. Clearly the divisions among occupational specialties, like those of ecological situations, have been characterized by economic interdependence and complementarity.

We must also not forget that the Middle East possesses an overarching culture that in some measure unites all its people. If one's identity as an Arab, for example, implies separation from Persians, Turks, Berbers, and Kurds, it also implies a unity of outlook and identity with many millions of other Arabs. Cultural similarity, however, transcends even these broad regional and ethnic groupings; significant features of culture and social organization have traditionally united all Middle Easterners. A list of these features would be very long and would range from the threefold ecological system mentioned above to particulars of material culture like the use of the black hair tent among nomads throughout the entire region. Most significant, however, are similarities in social organization, structure, and values that underlie all three ecological types.

Family, Kinship, and Marriage

In all parts of the Middle East, for example, the family has had almost the same structure and function. It is patrilineal—that is, it traces descent only through the male line. Wives are expected to take up residence with their husbands after marriage. The family is strongly patriarchal, and it remains intact until the father dies, at which time each of the sons becomes a family head. Typically, then, such a family consists of three generations of men and their wives, and any unmarried daughters or sisters. The preferred form of marriage among Muslims is between a man and his father's brother's daughter. Although there are conflicting reports on the actual frequency of such cousin marriages, marriage in the Middle East seems to be exceptional in its tendency to favor close patrilineal relatives. The family serves as the basic unit for holding property in the form of farmland, herds, or smaller business enterprises; it thus acquires a fundamental economic significance.

The importance of kinship does not end with the family. Peasant villagers, townspeople, and nomads alike recognize larger kin groupings among related families. Among the nomads these groupings are extended to a tribal organization. Tribes vary in size from a single wandering band to a powerful and influential group encompassing numerous bands. Relations among the men of each tribe are relatively egalitarian, leadership being based on the primus inter pares (first among equals) principle. There are frequently, however, marked differences of social standing, or "nobility," among tribes, to the extent that marriage to members of lesser tribes may be forbidden. It is in the nomad bands and their tribal organizations that one frequently finds blood feuds, collective responsibility, group honor or "face" (Arabic: **wajh**), and strict rules governing hospitality and sanctuary. (These will be discussed further in the following chapter.)

Traditional marriage and sex mores are similar throughout the Middle East. Marriage is often arranged by parents; it is more a relationship between kin groups than between individuals. An effort is usually made to match mates in terms of social prestige and background. The traditional position of women is definitely subordinate; great emphasis is placed on female chastity, purity, modesty, and even complete seclusion and veiling—particularly among the traditional urban elites (veiling was uncommon among peasants and nomads). The conduct of women has always been thought to reflect on the honor of the patrilineal family, and even today some Middle Easterners claim the right to kill a sister or daughter (but not a wife) if she is caught in a compromising situation. Muslim law permits as many as four wives, but while multiple marriages are a sign of affluence they are infrequent in actual practice. Traditionally, males could initiate divorce more easily than women. Despite these inequalities, Islamic law allows remarriage of divorced women, insures women a share in the inheritance of property, and protects their right to own property separately from their husbands.

Religion

Of all the factors that unify Middle Eastern culture, none is so fundamental as religion. The Middle East is the birthplace of the three major monotheistic religions: Judaism, Christianity, and Islam; the vast majority of Middle Easterners today, however, are Muslims, or adherents of Islam. This is significant not only because of the ubiquity of a single religion, but also because that religion has a remarkably pervasive influence on social and cultural life. Islam permeates the daily life and social norms of the 95 percent of the Middle Eastern population which is Muslim. It is a religion whose stated aim at the time of inception in the early seventh century was the unity of all people into a single social and spiritual community, and it succeeded to a noteworthy degree. Islam brought unprecedented political, intellectual, and spiritual unity to the Middle East and made the region a hub of world power for a thousand years. How and why this happened is the subject of the following chapter.

2

The Foundations
of Islam

Through the dusty streets of a middle-class residential neighborhood in Cairo echo the sounds of dawn: The first vendors are calling their wares, their chants accompanied by the clopping of hooves and the rattling of cartwheels. Blended with these is a more haunting but equally familiar sound, a singsong of Arabic from the loudspeakers on the minaret of a small local **mosque**:

> God is most great.
> I testify there is no deity but God.
> I testify that Muhammad is the Messenger of God.
> Come to Prayer;
> Come to Salvation . . .

It is the same message which five times daily has called the faithful to prayer in Cairo and its predecessors for more than 1,300 years. That same message, in the same Arabic, emanates from mosques as far away as West Africa and Indonesia, calling one-seventh of the world's population (only a minority of whom are Middle Easterners or Arabs) to pray toward their spiritual homeland in Mecca. The religion of Islam, signified by this call to prayer, is central to an understanding of the Middle East's most salient features—its historical and contemporary influence on other parts of the world, the unity of belief and commitment that counteracts some of its bitterest political divisions, and the religious vitality that infuses every aspect of its social, cultural, and political life.

Ninety-five percent of all Middle Easterners are Muslims, followers of the faith of Islam. For them, religion is not a matter separable from daily life or confined to certain times and places; it is the foundation of all ethics, morality, and family life—ultimately, the blueprint for a righteous and satisfying life. Dismayed by the secularism of both the capitalist and the communist ideologies, Muslims see

Islam as an essential element that gives direction to their social aspirations and saves them from the dissipation and immorality they see in the West. They are also keenly aware of Islam's success as a world religion, a religion that has always aimed at the social unity of the entire community of believers, that has led the Middle East to a position of considerable historical influence, and that provided the foundations of a civilization which for many centuries surpassed Europe.

CENTRAL BELIEFS OF ISLAM

For the Muslim, Islam is at its root nothing more nor less than the complete acceptance of God and submission to His will. The very word "Islam" means "submission," and "Muslim" means one who submits. The most important step toward this submission is the recognition that there is only one God, the God of Abraham and Moses, of Christians and Jews as well as Muslims, whose name in Arabic is Allah. Muslims believe that they alone have accepted God completely, and that all their beliefs follow from this acceptance. According to the teachings of Islam, a complete acceptance of God entails recognition of His absolute oneness; a Muslim must reject not only other gods but all alleged "associates" of God, including offspring and other semidivine personages. Christians, they feel, have compromised their monotheism by mistaking one of God's prophets for the "son" of God. The acceptance of God also requires belief in all of God's messages through all His appointed messengers, including not only Jesus and the Old Testament prophets, but also—and most significantly—the seventh-century Arab prophet Muhammad. It is through Muhammad, the "seal of the prophets," that God has sent His final and most comprehensive revelations, placed on the lips of Muhammad by God and recorded in the holy scripture, the **Koran**. Since true belief in God means acceptance of His final revelations, the Muslim declaration of faith (the **shahada**) testifies that "There is no God but Allah, and Muhammad is His prophet." Such a declaration is sufficient to make a person a Muslim, but the conscientious pursuit of the faith demands much more.

The Five Pillars of Islam

Muslims recognize five fundamental ritual obligations which make up the "pillars" of their religion. The first and most important of these is the declaration of faith mentioned above. The second is prayer, which ought to be performed five times a day (before dawn, just after noon, in late afternoon, just after sunset, and in mid-evening), facing in the direction of the **Kaaba**, the holy shrine in Mecca. Prayer may be performed anywhere, but the preferred situation is with other Muslims in a special place of worship, the mosque. Prayer involves a complex series of preparations, prescribed movements, and phrases. The most important prayer time is Friday noon, when Muslims participate in a formal service under the direction of a prayer leader (**imam**), who reads from the Koran and may also deliver a sermon and discuss matters of public interest.

The third pillar of Islam is the giving of alms, either in the form of **zakat**, a fixed amount used to meet the needs of the religious community and provide for the welfare of its members, or as a voluntary contribution (**sadaqua**) which brings religious merit to the donor.

The fourth pillar of Islam is fasting during the daylight hours of the month of **Ramadan**. While Islam is not an ascetic religion, Muslims view the abstention from food, liquids, smoking, and sexual relations as a celebration of moral commitment, healthy self-discipline, and religious atonement. Since Ramadan is a lunar month, it rotates through the seasons; and the abstention from food or water from dawn to dusk of a summer day is no small sacrifice. At the same time, it is typical of Islam's relatively practical orientation that the very young, the elderly, the sick, and even the traveler are exempted, at least temporarily, from this obligation.

The fifth and final ritual obligation of Islam, the pilgrimage to Mecca, falls only on those members of a Muslim community whose health and resources permit them to fulfill it. It is a great honor to make the **hajj**, or pilgrimage, and those who have done so carry the honorific title of **hajji**. The center of the pilgrimage is a shrine in Mecca said to have been founded by Abraham. The pilgrimage draws together, both physically and spiritually, persons from various national and cultural backgrounds who represent the farthest reaches of Islam. During the pilgrimage, however, all participants shed the marks of their nationality and social position and don the plain white cloak, which signifies the equality of every Muslim before God.

The Koran and the Hadith

The ritual obligations of Islam, important as they are, are only the outward expressions of the system of belief that underlies Muslim life. When Muslims accept the oneness of God and the validity of Muhammad's revelations as the word of God, they also accept certain sources of authority for religious truth. Foremost among these is the written record of Muhammad's revelations, the Koran. The Koran is said to be the exact word, and even the exact language, of God. Approximately as long as the New Testament, the Koran is composed of a series of chapters, or **suras**, of varying length. If we were to compare it with the literary forms familiar to the American reader, it more closely resembles a book of poetry than a narrative or a continuous essay. In fact, the Koran in the original Arabic (the form in which Muslims of all nations know it) is regarded as a masterpiece of poetic literature as well as religion. Its subject matter ranges from terse warnings about the Day of Judgment to long discourses on marriage, inheritance, the treatment of non-Muslim minorities, and the duties of each Muslim in spreading the faith. Of the Koran's message on these points we shall have more to say later in this chapter.

A second source of divine authority is the collection of sayings and practices attributed to the prophet. The prophet's personal utterances were not, like the Koran, a direct recitation of God's words, but they are thought to have been informed by the prophet's divine inspiration. Muslim religious scholars recognize that not all these reports (**hadith**) about the Prophet are equally reliable, and much effort has been devoted to tracing their sources and evaluating their accuracy. Even so, there exist various hadith which can, like the holy texts of other religions, be used to support widely differing positions on many issues. There are several recognized schools of Muslim law that differ on the degree to which analogy, scholarly interpretation, social consensus, and established custom might be used to supplement the Koran and the hadith, but all agree that the latter are the most fundamental basis of the Muslim social and legal code **(Sharia)**. In principle, they apply to every life situation that a believer might encounter, and provide a guide for every sort of decision.

The Ulema

Since Islam teaches the equality of every believer before God, there is, at least in orthodox **Sunni** Islam, no clergy to act as intercessors with the divine. On the other hand, the emphasis on written texts has given rise to an important class of religious scholars, the **ulema**, who collectively advise the community and its political rulers according to God's word. To the extent that most traditional education in Muslim societies is religious in nature, the ulema have filled the role of academics and teachers; to the extent that Islam recognizes no ultimate division of religion and state, the ulema have been not only legal and political thinkers but a political force in their own right. This is true in the contemporary Muslim world, where Cairo's Al-Azhar, the center of Muslim high scholarship, is also an international forum for the discussion of contemporary issues of Muslim politics and social values.

Unlike most Far Eastern religions, which generally try to divorce themselves from the flow of historical events, Islam resembles Judaism and Christianity in its explicit involvement with society and history. Although it is the ultimate concern of every Muslim to prepare himself for the Day of Judgment, that preparation takes worldly form in the pursuit of a just and righteous social life. Perhaps even more than Judaism and Christianity, Islam is intimately concerned with specific social relations and institutions. Our discussion of Islam will therefore take the form of a historical account. Islam arose in a particular social setting, and it directly addressed social problems related to that setting. One of the paradoxes of Islam is that while it goes beyond most other religions in specific references to the cultural institutions of its original setting, it has spread to encompass an astonishing variety of peoples and cultures without sacrificing the relevance of its original precepts. In so doing it has followed a remarkable path of adaptiveness balanced with continuity, operating in some contexts as a revolutionary force and in others as a source of stability and cohesion, or, when its practitioners have seen fit to use it so, a source of deep conservatism. None of these uses is inherent in the religion itself, but each is the outcome of particular human communities applying Islam to particular historical situations. Because Western readers are likely to see Islam as an essentially conservative ideology, let us consider the radical transformations that Islam brought to its original social setting.

PRE-ISLAMIC ARAB ETHICS

Unlike the Persian, Byzantine, and other empires that were the heirs of thousands of years of urbanization and central government, the Arab urbanites of Muhammad's time were in a process of transition to settled life, and their society was still organized on the ethical principles that had served their nomadic Bedouin forebears. It is this traditional Arab ethic, or rather the conflict between it and urban life, that provided the backdrop for Muhammad's teachings. Islam at its inception constituted both a revitalization and a radical reform of the old ethic. For these reasons, it is worthwhile to take a closer look at traditional Bedouin society.

As is usually the case with nomadic peoples, the Bedouins did not have a centralized government or political authority. Such authority would have been impossible to maintain, not only because no centralized power can easily impose itself on peoples of such mobility, but also because there was no economic foundation to support one. Yet the Bedouins were by no means isolated in the desert wastes; they were in frequent contact with other Bedouin and non-Bedouin groups, and had need of some measure of political order to regulate cooperation and resolve conflict. In such situations, political organization tended to be built from the bottom up—that is, groups were arranged in a hierarchy of levels that acted to deal with whatever conflicts or common interests were at hand. There is a saying attributed to the Arabs, "I against my brother; my brother and I against my cousin; my brother and cousins and I against the outsider." The saying signifies a hierarchy of loyalties based on closeness of kinship that ran from the nuclear family through the lineage, the tribe, and even, in principle at least, to an entire ethnic or linguistic group (which was believed to have a kinship basis). Disputes were settled, interests were pursued, and justice and order maintained by means of this organizational framework, according to an ethic of self-help and collective responsibility. If a member of one nuclear family was injured or offended by a member of another family, it was the right and obligation of all members of the injured family to settle the score. If the disputants were members of different lineages, all members of both lineages became involved (in varying degrees, depending on closeness to the offended and offending parties). In the same way, a whole tribe or allegiance of tribes might have been moved to defend its interests against another group. The collective duty to take up the disputes of a kinsman meant also that someone might legitimately be killed in atonement for the crimes of a relative. An "even score" might take the form of a life for a life or a theft for a theft, or it might be sought in a negotiated settlement. An inherent weakness in the system emerged, however, when the disputing sides were unable to agree on what constituted an even score; and the situation developed into a blood feud that involved whole tribes and their allies and lasted for generations.

Yet the revenge ethic was not the unbridled play of impulse, but a system designed to keep a modicum of order in a society without centralized legal authority. Since the individual's kin group answered collectively for his transgressions, it exercised considerable power of restraint over impulsive acts. Restraint was required even in revenge, which if excessive could initiate a new cycle of offense and counter-revenge. Revenge could, as already noted, be mitigated through an arbitrated settlement that preserved both the system of order and the honor of the disputants while keeping violence to a minimum. In the end, however, it was the ever-present threat of violent reprisal that acted as the chief deterrent against crime.

Every form of social organization requires a particular kind of value commitment, and the central value of the Bedouin ethic was (and still is) the honor and integrity of the various groups, or rather the concentric circle of groupings, with which the individual identified. Group honor was often referred to as "face," (wajh) the maintenance of which was a central concern of every member of a given group. (It is, incidentally, the enduring concern for the purity of the group through its patrilineal kin line, and the belief that sexual misconduct of its women is one of the greatest blows to a family's honor, that contributes today to the seclusion of Arab women.) The other side of the Bedouin's fierce unity against outsiders was his hospitality toward those who entered his domain with permission and were therefore under his protection. Hospitality, as much as revenge, was the measure of a group's willingness and ability to protect its interests and those of its allies and was thus a reflection on its honor.

Despite its harshness, the Bedouin ethic had its benign side as well. Not only was hospitality highly valued in Bedouin society, but so was generosity. Arab traditions point to the existence, from pre-Islamic times to the present, of a strong belief in the virtue of generosity and sharing, even toward strangers. Generosity to outsiders was a gesture of hospitality that reflected favorably on the strength and honor of the group. The sharing of wealth within the kin group provided for the needy, reinforced the sense of general equality and cooperation essential to the members' mutual commitment, and supported the leader's prestige by emphasizing his benevolence.

Although the Bedouin Arab's system of law and politics was based on the patrilineal kin group, it could be extended in various ways to adapt to varying circumstances. Alliances could be established between tribes, and geneologies might consciously or unconsciously be altered to reflect the new relationships. Other pseudo-kin relations were, in pre-Islamic times, established through adoption. Through the payment of tribute and obedience one group could become the protected client of another, a status which connoted social inferiority and was therefore undertaken only when necessary. Slavery, a widespread practice throughout the ancient Mediterranean and Middle East, provided yet another set of human relationships that supplemented the family and tribe, and that carried its own set of customary regulations.

In sum, then, the Bedouin system of political and legal organization centered on kin groups and their dependents. Ultimately it depended not on authority imposed from the top, but on the individual's sense of honor which was invested in an ever-widening series of kinship groupings. While such a system was well adapted to the needs of a decentralized society, it resulted in a relativistic morality, which placed loyalty to the group above all abstract standards guiding human conduct. A deed was evaluated in terms of kin loyalties rather than ethical merit; even the deities were often tied to territories and groups and thus provided no means for moral transcendence. The outlook thus created has sometimes been called "amoral familism" because it equated ethics with family interests; it might be better thought of, however, as a moral system centered on kinship, a system which was functional in certain circumstances but carried with it some severe limitations in uniting people under a more inclusive morality.

We have examined the pre-Islamic Bedouin social ethic in such detail for several reasons. It is important to realize that the organizational and moral aspects of the system have persisted not only among Bedouins but also to a more limited extent among settled Arabs to the present time, and that this ethic has influenced Muslim society in a number of ways. It is even more important to realize that the ministry of Muhammad revolutionized the Arab society of its time by subordinating the old familistic ethic to a transcendent system of morality, facilitating a moral and political transformation in Arabia and beyond.

THE SOCIAL SETTING OF MECCA

At the time of Muhammad's birth in about A.D. 570, Arabic-speaking peoples occupied the central Arabian peninsula; they were subject to the influences of several powerful empires. Most Arabs were either Bedouin nomads or their settled descendents who occupied themselves with trade and agriculture. Agriculture in the area did not compare with that of the more fertile regions of the Tigris-Euphrates and Mediterranean coast to the northwest, or of the Yemen to the southeast. Consequently, neither the wealth nor the political organization of the Arabs matched that of their neighbors. At that time Syria (the traditional name for the fertile part of the Middle East bordering the Western Mediterranean) was under the control of the Byzantine Empire, while the Iraq* (the farming region along the Tigris and Euphrates) was controlled by Byzantium's principal antagonist, the Sassanian Empire with its ties to the Iranian highland. The Yemen, home of an urban agricultural and trading civilization, was losing its former power and was under the threat of domination by the Christian Abyssinian Empire in Africa, which had already intervened in the region on one occasion. Placed in a delicate situation between several more powerful forces, the Arabs were gradually developing their own urban economy and their own political strategies. Arab groups near the areas of Byzantine, Sassanian, and Yemeni influence benefited from an arrangement in which the empires sponsored and subsidized them as "kingdoms" in return for military protection of their borders against the rival empires and their Arab clients. Away from these "buffer" Arab kingdoms, equidistant from the contemporary superpowers, most Arabs remained nomadic while some others were beginning to develop a different source of strength.

Located astride some of the most important trade routes that connected Europe, Africa, and Asia, Arabia moved much of the world's long-distance trade. For several centuries prior to Muhammad's time, Arabs had been assuming an increasingly active part in the trade that crossed their region. The Arab tribe of **Quraish** had founded the trade settlement of Mecca in the **Hijaz** (the mountainous region of Arabia's Red Sea coast) at the juncture of several major trade routes.

Although the Meccans were relatively sophisticated urbanites who were several generations separated from Bedouin life, their society was essentially structured by the Bedouin ethic, with some modifications. The backbone of Meccan organization was the Quraish tribe and its constituent lineages, which had successfully man-

*The term, "*the* Iraq" distinguishes the historically recognized region from the modern nation of the same name, Iraq.

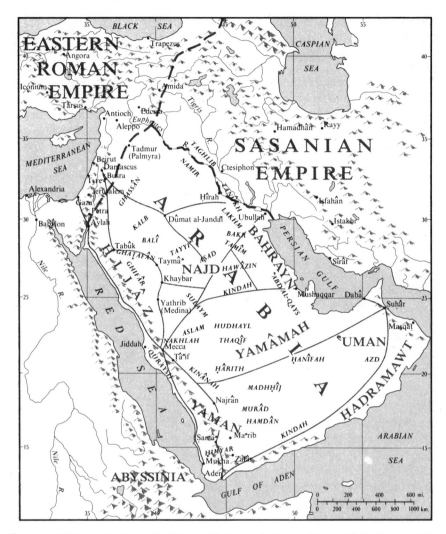

Towns and Tribes in Arabia in the Time of Muhammad. *Source*: Marshall G. H. Hodgson, *The Venture of Islam*, Vol. I. Chicago: University of Chicago Press.

aged to avoid blood feuds only by emphasizing tribal loyalties over more divisive ones. The leadership of the community was vested in the tribal elders, who, as among the Bedouins, had limited powers of enforcement. In order to insure the much-needed security of the regions through which their trade passed, it was necessary to enter into alliances with surrounding desert tribes, alliances which obliged them to take part in costly disputes with their allies' respective enemies. Meccan trade was sanctified and protected by pagan religious practices, particularly by the Meccan holy shrine of the Kaaba, which drew pilgrims from much of Arabia. By establishing times and places of truce connected with religious observances, the

Meccans were able to protect trade from the threat of feuds among the tribes. Thus through the selective use and modification of Bedouin organization, the Meccans established a viable urban-mercantile economy. The system brought considerable affluence to the Meccans and allowed them to win influence and respect among other urbanites and merchants in the Yemen and Syria as well as the Hijaz.

Even so, the Bedouin ethic as applied to an urbanized mercantile society was beginning to show its limitations in Muhammad's time, with accompanying strains on Meccan life. Economic inequality had increased between the various lineages of the Quraish, leading to a conflict of vested interests and a growing social stratification that was difficult to reconcile with familial unity. Non-Quraish minorities who had become clients of the Quraish were now reduced to little more than debt slaves. The town of Mecca held a wide range of occupations practiced by several resident ethnic groups including Copts, Syrians, Africans, and Jews; these also did not fit comfortably into a social structure based primarily on kinship, pseudo-kinship, and slavery. In addition to the problems of inequality and diversity, the Meccans were faced with the ever-present threat of feuding should the unity of the Quraish become disturbed; there was no binding, authoritative central leadership. Located between warring empires and in the midst of feuding tribes, the Meccans lacked convincing assurances that their military strength could always be concentrated against outside threats rather than internal squabbles. In adapting the Bedouin social ethic to their needs, the Meccans were straining it to its limits.

The Confessional Religions

The religious as well as the social life of Mecca were hovering on the brink of significant change. The previous centuries had seen the rise from Asia to Europe of a variety of religious traditions which, unlike their more ancient counterparts, "looked to *individual* personal adherence to ('confession of') an explicit and often self-sufficient body of moral and cosmological *belief* . . . which was embodied in a corpus of sacred *scriptures*, claiming *universal* validity for all men and promising a comprehensive solution to human problems in terms which involved a *world beyond death.*"[1] Although these "confessional religions" included such widely divergent traditions as Christianity and Buddhism, the forms native to the Middle East exhibited some general similarities. The Zoroastrianism of Persia resembled the major Semitic religions, Christianity and Judaism, in its belief in the oneness of God and of transcendent truth, a single universal standard for righteous conduct, a historical struggle between good and evil, the necessity of practical social action and individual responsibility, and a final divine judgment that holds every person accountable for the actions of his or her lifetime. The implications of such religions are quite different from those of a pluralistic, relativistic, kinship-centered paganism.

These confessional religions had political implications as well as spiritual and intellectual influences. The major political entities of the time were associated with confessional religions—the Persian Sassanian Empire with Zoroastrianism, the Byzan-

---

[1] Marshall G. S. Hodgson, *The Venture of Islam* (Chicago: University of Chicago Press, 1974), p. 125.

tines and Abyssinians with Christianity, and the Yemen with both Christianity and Judaism. These last two religions in particular had been making inroads in central Arabia, and some Arab groups had already converted to them. The cohesiveness which these religions offered was an attractive alternative to pagan pluralism, and it might have seemed in A.D. 600 that many more Arabs would eventually become Jews or Christians.

Inner developments as well as outer pressures were moving the Meccans toward religious change. The Meccans had found it expedient to promote the centralization of worship in pilgrimages such as that of the Kaaba, and that change carried with it the seeds of a more fundamental religious transformation. In Arab tradition, the minor deities of places and social groupings had been the most important forces in daily life. Allah, the God presiding over relations between tribes—and therefore over intertribal pilgrimages, shrines, and truces—began to assume a greater importance as the intertribal character of worship developed. In Muhammad's time the Kaaba was associated primarily with Allah, but the Meccans still recognized a plurality of gods, rites, and cults that separated them from the monotheistic religions by a wide gulf.

MUHAMMAD'S MINISTRY

Muhammad was born into a minor but respectable branch of the Quraish. His father died shortly before his birth, and in keeping with the custom of some Meccan families he spent the first few years of his life in the desert under the care of a Bedouin wet nurse. Muhammad's mother died when he was six, after which he was placed in the care of his uncle, Abu Talib. The young Muhammad tended sheep and sold goods in the marketplace, and by the time he reached adulthood he had gained a reputation as a capable businessman and a person of good character (in Mecca he was known as *al-Amin*, "the trustworthy"). At the age of twenty-five he married Khadija, a wealthy widow fifteen years his senior, for whom he had been managing business accounts. She remained his only wife until her death some twenty-five years later. During their marriage she bore him three sons, all of whom died before reaching adulthood, and four daughters.

One might have expected Muhammad to settle into a life of secure prosperity; in fact he might have done so had he not been preoccupied with the moral and religious problems of his time. Like many of his contemporaries, Muhammad was dissatisfied with the religious climate around him. He often returned to a cave on the outskirts of town, where he meditated. During one of these retreats he received the first of a series of visions in which the Angel Gabriel called upon him to become the Apostle of God. According to his biographers, Muhammad at first doubted the visions, but accepted his calling after Khadija and a Christian relative of hers pronounced them genuine. These first visions came in about A.D. 610, but it was several years before he began his public preaching. Khadija became his first convert; she was quickly followed by Ali, a younger cousin being raised in his household, and Zayd, a former slave of Khadija. During the first few years of his ministry, Muhammad's converts were to span the social scale from slaves and tribeless persons to wealthy merchants; for the most part, however, they tended to be young men occupying the less favored positions within the more respected families.

When Muhammad began his public preaching, his revelations were simple and direct: there is but one God, Allah the Creator, and those who ungratefully turn away from Him to the pleasures of this world will be held accountable on the Day of Judgment. Wealth and social position will count for nothing in the Final Judgment, while justice, piety, and righteousness will count for everything. Every person is equal before God, and righteousness is a matter between the individual and God, not a striving for power and position among kin groups. Pride, the mainspring of the Bedouin ethic, was a vice to be replaced by humility before the Creator.

It seems that another central theme in the earliest revelations was the Meccans' excessive pride in wealth and their unwillingness to share with those in need. Through Muhammad, God accused the Meccans:

> ...you honor not the orphan,
> and you urge not the feeding of the needy,
> and you devour the inheritance greedily,
> and you love wealth with an ardent love.
>
> (Koran, 89:18–21)

There is no evidence that Muhammad supported a communistic system in which all wealth was to be made public, but only that he advocated more compassion and sharing and less stinginess and pride, than was common among the Quraish. In this, evidently one of the earliest ethical messages in Muhammad's preaching, there is considerable continuity with the Bedouin ethic. The most favored Meccan families had succeeded in cornering a growing portion of the community's wealth and privilege, and they had all but abandoned the traditional obligations of sharing. By attacking the Meccans' greed and calling on them to share their wealth, Muhammad was reasserting a moral principle recognized in the Bedouin tradition, but now in a new context and with new ramifications. In a mercantile society where success depended more on opportunism than kinship, the power of the kin group over the individual was often too weak to enforce such sharing. In the Koran these obligations therefore came to be represented as sacred duties for which the individual will answer to an all-powerful God on Judgment Day. In this way, Muhammad's reassertion of a traditional value had a radical twist.

In some respects the revelations of Muhammad were perfectly in tune with the developmental course of Meccan society. As has already been pointed out, the Meccans were in need of a unifying moral-religious system not only to serve their need for internal cohesion, but also to meet the challenge of the other monotheistic religions and the political forces with which they were associated. Yet in other ways, the teachings of the Prophet ran against the grain of the prevailing cultural beliefs and the vested power interests in Mecca. In particular, the Quraish saw in Muhammad's budding sect a challenge to the values that legitimized their own power, and a denunciation of the religious observances which they had so carefully structured to serve their political and economic interests. Furthermore the Prophet himself, as God's appointed leader of the righteous, appeared to be making a personal bid for power that might encroach on their own. Not too surprisingly, the Quraish led the way in persecuting Muhammad and his followers, to the extent that part of the Muslim community (but not the Prophet) sought temporary asylum in Abyssinia. Relations between Muslims and non-Muslims were tense in Mecca, and became more so as the Muslims made it increasingly clear that they sought the conversion of all Meccans. The tide seemed to turn against Muhammad in 619 when Khadija, his most intimate personal supporter, and Abu Talib, who had insured the support of his lineage against the rest of the Quraish, both died.

The Hijira

Muhammad's followers were saved from an increasingly threatened existence in Mecca by what was to become a turning point in the growth of Islam. In 620 the Prophet was approached by a handful of converts from the town of Yathrib, 200 miles to the north of Mecca. Yathrib had been founded (or revived) as a farming oasis by several Arab Jewish clans, who had later been joined by other families of pagan Arabs. The problems of family ethics in the city had eventually reached a level of crisis, in which blood feuding was so widespread that the community had little peace. The Muslims and others at Yathrib saw in Muhammad an arbitrator whose religious commitments and sense of justice would serve them well; therefore they promised obedience to Muhammad and safety to the Muslims if the Prophet would agree to relocate in their city. After negotiating during the two following years with a growing delegation of Muslims from Yathrib, the Muslim community emigrated in the year 622.

The year of the migration, or **Hijira**, subsequently became the first year of the Muslim holy calendar, and the city of Yathrib became thereafter known as Medinat al-Nabi ("city of the Prophet") or simply Medina ("the city"). There is more than a ritual meaning to the Hijira date as a demarcation. It was in Medina that the Muslims, cut off from previous kinship ties, established their independent political existence based on the principles of Islam. It was also in Medina that Muhammad was presented with the opportunity to construct a new social order among his followers, based on the principles of Islam. If Mecca was the birthplace of Islam as a religion, Medina was its birthplace as a state and a way of life.

The Koran's Social Regulations

The social problems of Medina had some parallels to those of Mecca, but the differences were considerable. Medina was based on farming rather than trade, and the kinship groups there were still relatively strong. Unlike Mecca, where the domination of the Quraish had given some measure of unity and had helped avert blood feuding, Medina was torn by violent strife among its many kin groups. The predominantly Arab population of Medina was not entirely pagan but included a substantial and influential Jewish faction, a fact which was to complicate Muhammad's ministry there. While some of the most basic ideas of Islam—including the oneness of God, Final Judgment, humility and generosity—were first preached at Mecca, the longer suras containing the most detailed social regulations came to Muhammad while he was judge-arbiter at Medina, and were first addressed to the people of that city.

For the most part the social regulations of the Koran do not define political institutions as such (even the leadership of the Muslims after the Prophet's death was left unprovided for), but they do emphasize the moral responsibility, autonomy, and dignity of the individual by providing detailed rules by which the righteous could guide their daily lives with a minimum of dependence on the old sources of authority, particularly the tribe and lineage. The required abstention from pork, wine, and gambling was, for example, a matter to which any individual believer could adhere without outside support or resources, thereby placing himself in the community of believers and setting himself apart from tradition by these simple and very personal acts of choice. The blood feud, one of the most sacred duties of the old order, was outlawed; in its place equal penalties were set for specified crimes, regardless of the social status of the parties involved. Similarly the zakat, the alms tax collected by the Muslim community on behalf of the needy, transferred certain duties and powers from the lineage and tribe to the religious leadership, and at the same time gave the powerless a more secure status independent of their kin groups.

Many of the Koran's social regulations concern marriage and the family, and here again the tendency was to favor the rights of the individual and the immediate family over those of tribe and lineage. Numerous forms of marriage prevailed in Arabia prior to Islam, some of which were nothing more than casual relationships in which each partner remained under the control of his or her respective family, and others which made wives little more than slaves. The status of marriages and their participants was determined more by family connections, power, and social position than by any universal rules. The Koran universalized marriage forms and family obligations; it discouraged casual forms of quasi-marriage and gave equal status in law to all marriages between free persons. The Koran limited the number of wives a man may take to four, and counseled that all wives must be treated equally. Inheritance remained within the immediate family rather than becoming diffused into the larger kin group. The rights of the husband-father (including the right to divorce) were strengthened, not so much at the expense of the wife, who had never enjoyed much power, as of his and her lineages. The husband's rights included the ultimate custody of children after divorce.

In tune with the theme of personal autonomy and responsibility, the Koran showed its recognition of individual rights in other ways. For example, the right to life was affirmed in the prohibition of infanticide, a practice that had often been used to eliminate girl babies. The Koran held strongly for individual property rights, urging respect for the property of even the most vulnerable members of society, including women and orphans. The bride wealth traditionally paid by a husband to the wife's family was to become her personal property, and a woman's property was protected from the husband during marriage and retained in the event of divorce.

Slavery was a firmly entrenched practice in the Middle East (and until recently, nearly everywhere else where economic organization permitted it). Nevertheless the Koran allowed slaves greater rights than those granted in, say, nineteenth-century America, and taught that it is meritorious to free a slave. Muhammad set an example by freeing his own slave, who later became a prominent Muslim.

It has been suggested by some writers that the conception of fairness, individualism, and equality implied in Koranic teachings is derived more from the cultural outlook of the marketplace than from the temple or the palace. If this is true, it may be more than coincidence that such an innovation originated not in the older and more civilized centers of power, but in the new mercantile communities of the Hijaz. In any case, it is difficult to deny that Islam was, in the context where it originated, a major step toward the forms of morality most widely recognized in the modern world.

The Spread of Islam

While Muhammad's position in Medina was that of judge-arbiter and did not necessarily depend on the conversion of the populace, the pagan Arab population of the city increasingly became Muslim. The pressure to convert came from several sources including not only the attractiveness of the teachings and the prospect of inclusion in a cohesive social entity, but also an increasingly aggressive self-identification on the part of the Muslim community.

A central concept in the Koran is that of the **Umma**. Originally the term referred to the people to whom a prophet is sent, but it soon came to refer to the believers in Islam as a community in themselves. It is to this community that a Muslim's social responsibilities were ultimately directed, and loyalty to the Umma came to be seen as inseparable from loyalty to God. The idea of the Umma expresses Islam's radical departure from the past in a most fundamental way, for membership in this community of believers cut across all traditional distinctions of family, class, and ethnicity. In principle, the Muslim owed allegiance unconditionally to another Muslim, even a foreigner or a person without social standing, against even a sibling or parent if they were unbelievers.

It does not seem that Muhammad at first had in mind the creation of a new religious community to oppose Judaism and Christianity. Rather, he saw himself as a reformer of those religions, who in the tradition of previous prophets would lead Jews, Christians, and pagan Arabs out of error and thereby revitalize the religion of Abraham. Muhammad at first prayed in the direction of Jerusalem and observed the fast of the Jewish Day of Atonement. He was soon to be disappointed, however, by the unwillingness of most Medinese Christians and Jews to convert to Islam. During the Medina period the religion of Islam came to be defined in a manner increasingly distinct from the other monotheistic religions. Muslim prayer was reoriented in the direction of Mecca, where the Kaaba was eventually to become the central shrine of Islam. The fast of the Day of Atonement was replaced by the month of Ramadan. The Koranic revelations outlined a general policy toward the other religions in Arabia that later came to be applied in other contexts as well. If the message of the prophet is God's holy word it applies equally to all who will accept it. Because of Islam's emphasis on the creation of a divinely guided community whose religion is expressed in ethics and justice, the dedicated Muslim cannot rest content with personal enlightenment or salvation.

Jihad and the Djimmi System

The extension of the faith is a holy duty and a struggle from which a conscientious Muslim should never retire. This struggle is represented in the concept of **jihad**, or "holy war." Just what is entailed in the Koran's support of jihad has always been subject to various interpretations by Muslims, but the Koran did make it clear that Christians and Jews were "people of the book" who, though in error, ought not to be converted against their will. As long as they did not oppose the hegemony of the Muslim community in Arabia, they were to be placed in the status of protected communities, or **djimmis**. Following the Arab traditions of client-patron relationships, these communities were expected to pay a tribute tax and to show deference to the Muslims; but they were protected from harsh treatment, exploitation, and attack by either outsiders or Muslims. The pagan Arabs were a different case: Muhammad was above all a prophet sent to them, for they had strayed the farthest from God. The conversion of all pagan Arabs, including not only most Meccans but also most Bedouin tribes, was so important that it was to be implemented by whatever use of force proved necessary.

The conversion of the Arabs proceeded apace during the Medina years. After the Hijira, Muhammad and his followers began to attack the Meccan caravan trade and to clash in a series of skirmishes and battles with Meccan forces. The success of some of these early engagements, sometimes against unfavorable odds, was widely interpreted in Arabia as evidence of divine favor toward the Muslims. Muhammad offered all converts a share in the booty of war, and the Muslims began to gather a following of Arab tribes that posed a growing threat to the Meccans and their own Arab allies. Under Islam, much of the amorphous realm of the Arabs was crystallizing into a community united by a divine purpose and a sense of community.

The Meccans had been obliged to make so many concessions to the growing power of the Muslims that when the Prophet's army reentered the city, some eight years after the forced emigration, it encountered only token resistance. Muhammad was a benign conquerer, so much that his veteran followers complained of the material rewards granted the Quraish in return for their support. Mecca became a Muslim city almost overnight. The Kaaba, following the destruction of pagan idols and its "restoration" to Allah as Abraham's temple, became the focal point of Muslim prayer and pilgrimage.

Two years later, in A.D. 632, Muhammad, the messenger of God, died. Unlike most prophets, he had lived to see the basic fulfillment of his mission. The word of God had been delivered and heard, and the pagan tribes of Arabia had become at least nominally converted to Islam. The religion of Muhammad's childhood had become virtually extinct. Islam was established as a coherent set of beliefs, ritual practices, and social ethics that had swept much of the world known to Muhammad. This in itself is a remarkable enough accomplishment, and it is unlikely that Muhammad could have anticipated that Islam was to spread its influence farther and more deeply than did the Roman Empire, or that within four generations people from Spain to Western China would be praying toward Mecca.

FIVE POPULAR MISCONCEPTIONS ABOUT ISLAM

According to popular notions widespread in the West, Islam is an exotic religion of the desert nomad, a religion characterized by fanatical intolerance of the "infidel," spread "by the sword," and dedicated to an ultraconservative view of human social existence. Such a picture is founded on misconceptions about the nature of Islam and of its historical role in Middle Eastern society.

Islam as an Exotic Religion

Viewed from the perspective of Jews and Christians, Islam is by no means an exotic religion. Each of these three religions embodies many of the same notions of society, history, divine will, and personal responsibility—especially compared with the nonhistorical, other-worldly orientation of many Eastern religions. Each recognizes the same God, the same early patriarchs, and many of the same prophets; and each originated among Semitic-speaking peoples of the Middle East. There are differences, to be sure, but in the perspective of cultural history the three religions must be seen as very closely related. In some respects the Muslim might see more continuity among the three religions than does the Jew or Christian, since Muhammad's prophecies are believed to be merely an outgrowth of the same tradition that encompasses Jesus and the Old Testament prophets. Muhammad had come into contact with Jews and Christians and was familiar with their own verbal renditions of their scriptures. While there is no direct written connection between Judeo-Christian and Muslim scriptures (Muhammad was said to have been illiterate) and certain scriptural events have become altered and elaborated in the Koran, there can be no question that Islam views itself as the culmination of the Judeo-Christian religious tradition.

Insofar as Muhammad was an apostle to the Arabs, and the Arabs identify ultimately with their Bedouin heritage, there is some truth to the picture of Islam as a "religion of the desert." In fact, Islam draws selectively on certain ancient Bedouin values such as sharing wealth and caring for those in need. Nevertheless, at its core Islam is an urban and cosmopolitan religion that in its day undermined the tribal system of ethics and religion and replaced it with a rationalized, universal set of beliefs. Its main thrust is at one with the other confessional religions, and not with "primitive" religions centered on nature and the family. Therefore to represent Islam as merely an extension of the Bedouin outlook, as is so often done, is fundamentally false.

Islam as a Militant Religion

One often encounters the assertion, even among some historians, that Islam is a particularly militant and intolerant religion, and that it was spread mainly through the use of force—or as the phrase goes, "by the sword." Historically, Islam no more deserves such a reputation than does Christianity. It is true that the scriptures of

Islam do not advise believers to turn the other cheek, and that the Koran actually praises those who go to war in defense of the faith. The very concept of jihad, the holy struggle against the unbeliever, seems to the Westerner to suggest a program of ruthless suppression of other religions. It should be kept in mind, though, that the concept of jihad is a complex one for Muslims, and that the idea of struggle can be interpreted and implemented in various ways. In some sense, the duty of spreading the faith and the idea of universal brotherhood and equality before God are but two sides of the same coin. If the message of God is good for all people, then one does humankind a disservice by leaving the infidel to his disbelief. This, however, does not and never has meant that the Muslim community sanctions random acts of aggression against non-Muslims. On the contrary, the djimmi system protected the rights of religious communities that rejected Islam entirely.

As for conversion by the sword, the Western accusation against Islam has an exceedingly weak foundation. The Koranic stand on forced conversions is ambiguous, and one can find hadith that seem to forbid it as well as those that seem to support it. Muhammad took a hard stand toward pagans, the nonmonotheistic Arab tribes, but opposed the forced conversion of adherents of the confessional religions in Arabia. In later times other communities, including the Hindus in India, were extended formal protection as djimmis. As we shall see in the next chapter, the millions who converted to Islam did so for a variety of reasons. Even the pagan Arabs probably converted more often for the sake of various material, social, and spiritual advantages than out of fear. The Muslims of the Far East, whose population today rivals that the Muslim Middle East, were generally converted through the influence of peaceful merchants. The reader should not forget that despite the teachings of Jesus, Christianity was quite often spread at the point of a sword in much of Europe and the Western Hemisphere. We suspect that if the historical record is examined carefully, it will show that the spread of Islam depended no more consistently on the use of force than did the spread of Christianity.

Islam as an Intolerant Religion

As for religious intolerance, it is instructive to compare the attitudes of Christians and Muslims toward the Jews, who were a religious minority in both the Muslim and Christian worlds. Tensions have often existed between Jewish communities and the politically dominant Muslims or Christians. One reason for this tension lies in the very nature of the Jewish existence as a religious and cultural minority, with all the conflicting loyalties, suspicions, and persecutions that frequently accompany minority status. Second, the presence of an unconverted population seems to thwart the universalistic claims of both Islam and Christianity. Finally, the historical connections of both Christianity and Islam with Judaism has given rise to more specific allegations against the Jews: Christians have traditionally blamed them for betraying Christ, while Muslims have accused them of spurning Muhammad's ministry. Indeed, tension between Muslims and Jews became severe even at Medina, where early attempts to convert the Jewish Arabs of that city came to nothing. The Prophet eventually expelled two of the major Jewish clans and sanctioned a blood bath against the third for their alleged intrigues against him. During this period, the

Koranic revelations upbraided the Jews for their supposed errors and their lack of faith in God's prophet.

Despite the ever-present potential for conflict, the actual history of Jewish minorities in both Christian and Muslim worlds has been quite variable, and it would be difficult indeed to portray the differences in terms of Christian love versus Muslim intolerance. While interethnic relations in both contexts had their ups and downs, the Christian and Jewish minorities under Islam ultimately enjoyed the status of protected communities as defined in the Koran. To be sure, this djimmi status carried obligations of civil obedience, special taxation, and limitation of political independence, but it also exempted minorities from the requirements of jihad and zakat. It can be argued that Jewish minorities in Christendom labored under equally severe restrictions and held a less secure legal status. It is interesting to note that when the Muslims were expelled from Spain in the twelfth to fifteenth centuries, the Jewish communities which had previously thrived under Muslim rule were subjected by the conquering Christians to persecution, forced conversion, and banishment. Putting aside the ecumenical spirit that has recently accompanied modernization in the Christian world, there is little in the historical record to support the Western image of Islam as an essentially fanatical and intolerant religion compared with traditional Christianity. Neither is there much support for the idea that active enmity between Muslims and Jews (or Christians) is inevitable.

Islam as an Ultraconservative Religion

Many Westerners believe that Islam is a more socially conservative religion than is Judaism or Christianity. Some have even referred to the recent revival of religious commitment in Muslim countries as a "return to the seventh century" (as though, unlike Christians and Jews, a Muslim must choose between religion and modern life). It is true that Islam's scriptures are notable for their detailed pronouncements on the conduct of social life, a fact that poses a special challenge to the Islamic modernist. However, Judaism and Christianity are by no means lacking in specific social rules; and the scriptures of these religions date to an even earlier period than the Koran. The social ideas presented in the Koran were in many respects radical departures from the prevailing customs of the time, and must be seen in their historical context as innovative.

Islam as a Sexist Religion

Since Islam's position on women's rights has sometimes been used as an example of Muslim conservatism, let us examine this subject more closely. Like Judaism and Christianity, Islam reflects the patriarchal character of traditional Middle Eastern society. Many of its social regulations presuppose a family in which the male is the chief authority and economic provider, as well as a descent system traced through the husband and father. We therefore find a variety of sexually differentiated rules; for example, men but not women may take more than one spouse, a woman receives only half a man's share of an inheritance, and divorce is easier for a man than a woman to initiate. In each of these matters, however, Islam may not be as conservative as it first appears. Plural marriage was permissible among pagans,

Jews, and Christians until long after Muhammad's day, and the effect of Islam was therefore not to originate plural marriage but to regulate it, to set limits upon it, and to define the rights and obligations of each partner. Under Islam a man is allowed no more than four wives, and only one if he is unable to treat several wives equally. Men are counseled to treat their wives with kindness, and hadith even criticize men who behave selfishly in sexual intercourse. The Koran advises those with marital difficulties to seek arbitration by representatives of both the wife's and the husband's families, indicating not only that the preservation of a marriage is desirable but also that a woman's grievances ought to be taken seriously. As for property and inheritance, the most significant innovations of Islam were in securing for women the right to inherit property and to receive the bride wealth formerly paid to the bride's family, and in protecting her full rights of property ownership even in marriage and divorce. This right of a woman to control her own property after marriage, established by the Koran in the seventh century, is still being sought by women in some parts of the Western world.

The veiling and seclusion of women, for which Islam is often criticized, is more a matter of folk practice than an intrinsic part of Islam. While the Koran advocates sexual modesty on the part of women, it makes the same requirements of men. The social custom of keeping women veiled or behind closed doors is not specifically Muslim, but reflects traditional Middle Eastern concerns. The purity of the women in a family guaranteed its honor and insured the integrity of the male line. Furthermore, the impracticality of keeping women in extreme seclusion has caused the practice to be concentrated in, and symbolic of, the traditional urban upper classes (including many Jews and Christians). It is traditional public opinion in favor of female seclusion which, contrary to the practice of Muhammad and the early Muslims, has kept women out of the mosques and away from active religious practice. Over the past century, many Muslim intellectuals have objected to the seclusion of women on the grounds that it is contrary to Islam.

The Koran echoes the sentiments of traditional Middle Eastern society and of Judeo-Christian thought in saying that "men are the managers of the affairs of women, for that God hath preferred in bounty one of them over the other" (4:50–52). However, Islamic scriptures do not go as far as the Judeo-Christian in asserting the moral inequality of women and men. We do not find in the Koran anything corresponding to Paul's pronouncement about the "shame" of women for having brought sin into the world (in the Koran both Adam and Eve are tempted equally), or the Christian idea that man is the image and "glory of God" while woman is "created for man." If anything, the Koran goes out of its way to emphasize the moral (as distinct from social) equality of the sexes. Repeatedly it makes clear the fact that its pronouncements stand alike for every believer "be you male or female."

If we can separate the essential religious teachings from social customs that have grown up around them, we will find in Islam no more basis for sexist attitudes than is present in the scriptures of Judaism and Christianity. It is true that a relatively large portion of Muslims retain close ties with the customs of a premodern age, while many Christians and Jews living in the West have all but forgotten some of the more conservative social customs upheld in their scriptures. Nevertheless, there is no reason to assume that Islam is inherently less compatible with modernization and change than its sister religions. Many Muslim modernists, in fact, view Islam as an essentially progressive religion with regard to sex roles and other social issues, and chide conservative Muslims for allowing custom and prejudice to distract them from the true principles of their faith.

In this chapter we have endeavored to portray Islam as a religious faith and as a product of human history. In so doing we have introduced the reader to the interplay between religion and society. At any given point in history, the relationship between religious thought and social practice is likely to be a complex one, with religion acting as both a conservative force and an invitation to social change. As a society develops through time, that relationship is subject to constant revision and reinterpretation, sometimes in differing ways by different members of society. While every religion has fundamental themes and values that ultimately guide its development, the range of possible circumstances, applications, and interpretations is often astonishing.

A fundamental challenge to any religion is to address the universal problems of human existence in a way that transcends the narrow limits of time and place, while retaining enough particularity to give its message substance and social relevance. Islam originally addressed the problems of a very specific society in an exceptionally particular and detailed way, and yet it has subsequently presided over a dozen centuries of cultural development among peoples spanning three continents. While readers should be sensitive to the unifying features of Islam, they should also keep in mind the many contradictions and conflicting interpretations that have occurred within other religious traditions as they adapted to varying circumstances and interests, and expect no more consistency from Islam than any other living religion.

3
The Political Legacy of Islam, A.D. 632–1800

Accustomed as Westerners are to the ideal of separation of politics from religion, it is easy to overlook the extent to which political thought and action throughout history have been expressed in religious terms. In traditional Christianity no less than in Islam, questions of justice, public obligation, class privilege, and even revolution have been inseparable from religious issues. Some writers see this as evidence that until recently humankind was driven by religious urges at the expense of practical considerations; others have concluded that the religious impulse is nothing more than a cloak for self-interest. A more moderate interpretation, which we prefer, is that religion has provided the concepts and the language by which human beings have pursued their immediate interests and defined their ultimate values. For this reason, a religious outlook never remains static. It is, indeed, a continuous dialogue; and the form of that dialogue bears the stamp of general human concerns, the changing circumstances of history, and the special qualities of vision that characterize the particular tradition.

While the social thought of Islam is in itself neither more nor less important than that of other world religions, it is especially significant for the study of Middle Eastern politics. Islam has had a decisive influence on state politics throughout the region since the death of Muhammad, and today the Islamic heritage is present in new ways. To be sure, Islam is not immune to the influence of contemporary events, and its current political role is different from the one it played in previous centuries. Nevertheless, Islam has a personal and social significance that most contemporary Middle Easterners take seriously; and there is no doubt that the present restructuring of Middle Eastern societies and their interrelations will continue to be based on a common Islamic cultural heritage. Even those who wish to minimize the role of religion in politics must pursue their programs with an acute consciousness of the Islamic milieu.

The revelations of Muhammad introduced a new framework within which to work out the problems of social life. Yet no matter how consistent a statement one makes about the human condition, the attempt to apply it to actual conditions will always lead to contradictions and conflicts, and to resolutions that raise new problems in turn. The difficulties are compounded even further as a religious tradition encounters cultural variation and historical change. As human communities over the past thirteen centuries have explored the implications of the Islamic vision, they have uncovered numerous conflicts and paths of resolution. No simple generalization can do justice to this rich heritage of thought, nor is it possible to catalogue fully the many outlooks that have developed under the auspices of Islam. It is possible, however, to sample some of the issues that Muslims have most often raised, and to indicate the characteristic ways in which these issues have been approached within that tradition.

The ministry of Muhammad had a dual character that arose from his role as a civic leader and a religious visionary. Muhammad made it clear that Islam can be realized only by the creation of a religiously guided community, the Umma. At the same time, such a community exists only insofar as it is defined by Islam. Thus, neither the religion nor the Umma can exist except in terms of each other. Islam requires, by its very nature, a social order that is both politically sound and divinely guided. But the requirements of political efficacy and divine guidance are not always easy to reconcile, at least in the short run; and the problems arising from this contradiction have stimulated much of the political dialogue in Islamic thought. This problem of mediating the demands of faith and politics has manifested itself in more specific conflicts such as power versus justice, privilege versus equality, guidance by the community versus the conscience of the individual, and the need for adaptive innovation versus the enduring vision of Muhammad's model community.

THE ESTABLISHMENT
OF THE ISLAMIC STATE

The teachings of Muhammad, concentrating as they did on individual obligations, left unanswered a great many questions vital to the future of his community. Most pressing was that of leadership, for which Muhammad had made no provisions. After the Prophet's death, the community at Medina made preparations to choose its own leadership and expected the Meccans to do the same. Many Bedouin "converts" considered themselves to be personal clients of Muhammad and believed that their obligations ended with his death. At this critical moment in history, the initiative was seized by Abu Bakr and Umar, two of Muhammad's closest associates who were to become the first two **caliphs**, or representatives, of the Prophet. Under their strong leadership, the unity of the Muslim community was aggressively asserted. They declared that there would be no prophets after Muhammad, and that the Umma must unite under a single authority. Bedouins slipping away from the Islamic fold were brought back by force in the **Riddah** Wars ("Wars of Apostasy"); and even as these campaigns were being completed, the energies of the newly united Arab armies were turned against the faltering empires of Persia and Byzantium, thus launching Islam on its fateful course.

The Muslim campaigns against the neighboring empires were phenomenally successful. Weakened by decades of indecisive warfare against one another and by internal strains, the exhausted, stalemated Sassanian and Byzantine empires encountered the greatest threat where they had least expected it. The old Arab buffer states, no longer subsidized by the empires, joined with the Muslim Arab conquerers; other local populations, often religious minorities long persecuted by the established state religions, were less than enthusiastic in defending the hegemony of their old masters. Under Umar's guidance (634-644), the terms of conquest were lenient, even attractive. Establishing a pattern for subsequent conquests, Umar allowed life to go on protected and undisturbed in those cities that submitted willingly; they were subject only to a tax. These taxes, along with revenues from lands won in battle and one-fifth of all other booty, went to the Muslim state, which in turn distributed much of it to its soldiers. Under Umar's leadership Egypt, the fertile crescent, and much of Iran came under Muslim domination; the Sassanian Empire was toppled, and the Byzantines were driven back into Anatolia.

The Muslim Empire, as it took form in the early period, was an Arab military state. Using Bedouin military experience and turning its energies from internal raiding and feuding toward fighting the infidel, the Muslim state rapidly gained power. Under capable administrative leadership, the Arab conquerers instituted an orderly process for collecting revenue and for distributing it by means of the army register, or **diwan**. Conquered people were guaranteed their civic and religious freedom as djimmis in return for their submission to Muslim rule and taxation (often a more attractive arrangement than the older empires had afforded). The Arabs themselves lived in garrison towns segregated from the conquered populace; they had no intention either of blending into the local life or of inviting their new subjects to become like them. Forced conversion of the djimmis was rarely an issue, since the Muslims considered their religion, their Arab background, and their privileged status as conquerers and tax recipients as inextricably connected. In order to promote religious unity and to safeguard against any possible deviations from the faith, Umar did much to establish the forms of worship and to promulgate knowledge of the Koran in the garrison towns. The center of social life in such towns became the mosque, and the military leader himself emphasized the religious character of the community by personally leading the people in prayer.

The caliph Uthman (644-656) continued Umar's policies, but with less success, for the Muslim community was now confronting some of the social and moral problems arising from the transition of a religious movement into an organized state. Many malcontents saw Uthman as a symbol of what they thought was wrong with the community: a turning from faith to secular power. For them it was particularly galling that Uthman's kinsmen the **Umayyads**—who unlike Uthman himself had long opposed Muhammad—were now being favored in administrative appointments. Opposition to Uthman was particularly strong in the Iraq at Kufah, and in Egypt. In 656, Uthman was murdered by a group of his opponents from the Egyptian garrison, and the Prophet's cousin and son-in-law Ali was immediately proclaimed caliph. The rebels, who supported Ali's accession, claimed that Uthman had betrayed Islam and that his murder was therefore justified; Uthman's supporters and others

THE SPREAD OF ISLAM

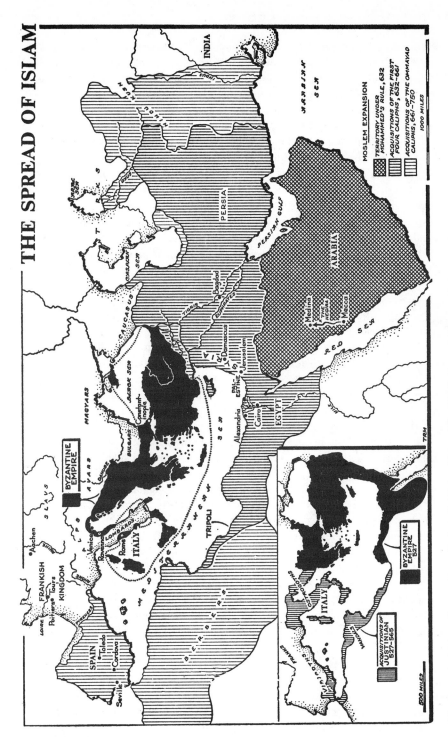

The Spread of Islam. *Source:* From Sydney Nettleton Fisher, *The Middle East: A History*, 2nd ed. New York: Alfred A. Knopf, 1969.

horrified by the killing accused Ali of condoning it, and demanded that he punish those responsible. The situation quickly developed into civil war, with Ali's supporters in the Iraq pitted against Muawiyah, the Umayyad governor of Syria. After initial successes, some of Ali's men persuaded him to submit to arbitration as demanded by Muawiyah, whereupon a faction of Ali's army, the **Kharijites** (see p. 54), turned against him for abandoning the cause. His supporters' loyalties were split, the arbitration was indeed damaging to his position, and Ali's fortunes declined until his death at the hands of a Kharijite in 661.

The death of Ali was a turning point for Islam. The last of the Prophet's close personal followers was now gone. The initial unity of Islam was forever shattered, and the issue was raised—an issue which was to trouble Islam until the present—of whether civil order within the Umma is more important than the divinely mandated legitimacy of its leadership. The accession of Muawiyah established a dynasty of rulers whose ultimate recourse was to secular power, and the religious idealists took on the function, which they have generally had ever since, of a moralistic oppositional force.

THE GOLDEN AGE OF THE CALIPHATE

If Islam had lost some of its purity in the eyes of its more idealistic adherents, it was also entering into its own as a civilization and an empire. Under the Umayyads (661–750), Islam spread across North Africa to Spain; in the East, it spread to the Indus Valley. The structure of the empire remained essentially that of an Arab conquest state, in which Islam remained primarily the religion of a segregated Arab elite. Other trends, however, were beginning to appear.

Despite the ethnic biases of the Arabs, the universalistic, cosmopolitan facets of Islam were beginning to surface as the empire embraced highly sophisticated peoples who were both willing and able to take an active part in Muslim civilization. At first, non-Arab converts to Islam were given only marginal status as Mawalis, or clients, of influential Arab families. Indeed, their existence posed economic problems since the empire was set up on the assumption that Arab Muslims would collect taxes from their subjects on the basis of religious affiliation. In practice, non-Arab converts to Islam often found themselves excluded from Muslim economic privileges despite their conversion. But the forces of change were at work. The Arabs with their Bedouin and mercantile backgrounds were now heirs to ancient agrarian traditions, and the conditions associated with agrarian life came to have more and more sway over them. The Arab ruling class came increasingly to look like any other local gentry, and the caliphs took on the aspect of semidivine emperors ruling at their court in Damascus.

Throughout the period of Umayyad rule, a gathering variety of factions promoted a growing antigovernment spirit. Some disliked the favoring of Syrians over other Arabs; some opposed the distinction of Arabs from other Muslim converts; and some disliked the centralized control over the distribution of revenues, which they felt worked to their disadvantage. Many Arabs despised the pretentions of the caliphs and chafed under the spirit of imperial rule, so incompatible with traditional

Arab values. Whatever the specific sources of discontent, the criticisms tended to converge on the accusation that the government was impious, that it had made irreligious "innovations" instead of following the way of the Prophet, and that it had forgotten its communal obligations in favor of material advantages for the few. What was needed, they agreed, was true Islamic guidance for the community. In the 740s a coalition of interest groups and sects, including the **Shiites** (literally, "partisans" of Ali who still bore their grudge against the Umayyads), launched a civil war that ended with the establishment of the **Abbasid** dynasty in 750.

Many of those who had supported the overthrow of the Umayyads were soon to be disappointed. It is true that the bases of the empire were considerably broadened by the change, for the new order with its capital at Baghdad was much more open to the participation and influence of the Iraqi Arabs and especially the non-Arab Persians. Some writers have even gone so far as to characterize the change as one from Arab to Persian domination, because of the decisive participation of Persians at the highest levels of government as well as the increasing influence of Persian language, literature, and culture. Yet in these changes lay the seeds of bitter disappointment for the old opposition. Far from returning to charismatic rule by Ali's inspired descendents, as the Shiites had hoped, or even a return to a purer life modeled on the early Umma, as others had advocated, the caliphate continued on its evolution toward agrarian absolutism. Under the Abbasid caliphs, the power of the court reached its peak, with the caliph exercising his own law at his whim, which was enforced on the spot by his ever-present executioner.

The city of Baghdad, which the Abbasids built for their capital, symbolized the trends in government. Unlike the Arab garrison towns located on the edge of the desert, Baghdad was built on the Tigris River on a site that commanded key agricultural lands in the Iraq and principal trade routes. It was laid out in a circle; and instead of emphasizing Arab tribal divisions as the garrison towns had done, the entire city was oriented toward the government complex and the caliph's huge palace. The court of the caliph was the center of an aristocratic high culture marked by strong Persian influences, and Baghdad came to play a dominant economic, political, and cultural role reminiscent of the older Persian and Mesopotamian seats of government.

While absolute despotism was as repugnant to the Bedouin and the ulema as it is to modern taste, it by no means hindered Abbasid civilization itself. Such a monarchy protected the powerless—especially the peasants—against the more grotesque abuses frequently visited on them by decentralized oligarchies and competing petty rulers, and it also brought a degree of order that set the stage for unprecedented material prosperity in the Muslim world. Trade and agriculture flourished, banking and communications were effectively organized across the empire, and government was carefully regulated under a *vizier* (comparable to a prime minister) and an established bureaucracy.

This was the Golden Age of Muslim civilization, to which Muslims in later times would look for inspiration. Muslim power was unparalleled anywhere in the world, while Islamic art, architecture, literature, and poetry—drawing on Arabic, Persian, Greek, Indic, and other traditions and supported by the courtly high culture—reached their peak of development. Arabic works from this period on mathematics ("algebra" and "logarithm" are Arabic-derived words), chemistry, optics, and medicine put these sciences at such a high state of development that Europeans were still consulting them five hundred years later. The Crusaders who entered the Middle East at the end of the eleventh century, after the decline of the Abbasid caliphate, were seen with some justice as uncultivated barbarians.

Ironically, the Golden Age of Islamic civilization also signaled the beginning of the decline of the caliphate. For reasons not altogether clear, the Abbasid caliphs began to lose their hold on the vast empire after their first century of rule. In an attempt to bolster their own power against competing factional loyalties, the caliphs by 850 had begun to use private armies. These guards were usually slaves obtained from the Turkic-speaking nomadic tribes of the Eurasian steppes; they were kept totally dependent on the caliph and were loyal, presumably, only to him. The caliphs, however, soon found themselves at the mercy of their own palace guards; by the middle-to-late ninth century, most caliphs were puppets of a Turkish soldier class that was in one form or another to dominate most of Islam for the next thousand years. In the ninth century, some provinces started to assert their independence, and the empire began to devolve into a decentralized civilization with the caliph as figurehead. Under various dynasties, multiple centers of power developed, and their political control decreased with distance; in some areas there was little more than local civic government. Yet the social unity of the Umma and the norms that governed Muslim life did not depend on a central government and therefore did not decline with the caliphate. Instead, the political disintegration of Islam was accompanied by the continued development of a common, international pattern of Muslim social life that was based on Islamic Sharia law and was overseen by the formally educated ulema.

MONGOL DESTRUCTION
AND THE REBIRTH OF EMPIRE

The period from the mid-tenth to the mid-thirteenth centuries saw the militarization of political power. This tendency was brought to an extreme by the Mongol conquests and afterward in the period of the Ottoman and other late empires. Before the thirteenth century, the overall tendency toward decentralized rule by local emirs was reversed only a few times—as in the case of the Seljuk Turks during the eleventh century. The Mongols, however, were able to consolidate pure military power on an unprecedented level. The Mongol invasions were joint efforts involving Turkic-speaking armies recruited among the nomadic tribes of the Eurasian steppes and a Mongol military elite originating in Asia. Due to a complex of historical and technological factors, during the thirteenth and fourteenth centuries the Mongols and their armies were able to conquer most of the civilized world from China to Eastern Europe and place it under the centralized administration of military chieftains. With the fall of Baghdad in 1258 and the execution of the last Abbasid figurehead caliph, political control passed into purely military hands. Although non-Muslim in origin, the Mongols and their Turkish forces converted to Islam;

subsequently some of the severest Mongol campaigns under Timur (Tamerlane) were fought in the name of Islamic purity. Destructive as their terrorist techniques were, once established the Mongols became patrons of Islamic high culture and rebuilders of public works. One of their most enduring influences, however, was the establishment of efficient, highly organized states based on the army. In these states, ultimate control was in the hands of a supreme military ruler whose succession was determined by armed contest within the ruling dynasty; the army organization included not only combat troops but the entire governmental apparatus. So centered on the army were these empires that their capitals were wherever the army and its supreme leader happened to be, and government records were carried into the field on campaigns.

Eventually the effects of Mongol conquest gave way to more home-grown military empires, which in some respects benefited both from the destruction of the old order and from the Mongol military system. Equally important in these new empires was the use of gunpowder, which favored the technically advanced urban populations over the Eurasian nomads and allowed greater concentrations of power to develop. The most important post-Mongol concentrations of power in the Middle East were the Safavid Empire, centering approximately in what is now Iran, and the Ottoman Empire, originating in what is now Turkey. Each arose and achieved much of its glory during the sixteenth century, and each was dominated by a Turkic military elite but used Persian or Turkish as a literary language and Arabic as the religious language. Each followed somewhat similar paths of development, but it is the Ottoman state that is of the greatest interest here, partly because it most directly confronted the growing power of Europe, and partly because it continued as an active force in world politics until the twentieth century.

The Ottoman Empire

The **Ottoman Empire**, named after its original ruling family of Osman Turks, had its roots in Anatolia during the pre-Mongol period. Located on the frontier of the Byzantine Empire, the Ottoman state had long been associated with the continuing struggle against the infidel; accordingly, it held a prestigious position within Islam and attracted many would-be **ghazis**, or defenders of the faith. A turning point for the Ottomans came with the long-sought conquest of Constantinople in 1453, which they renamed Istanbul and made their capital. Ottoman power grew rapidly as Islamic territories expanded into Hungary and even to the gates of Vienna, which the Ottomans unsuccessfully besieged in 1541 and again in 1683. To the south, Ottoman power encompassed the Levant, Syria, the Iraq, the Hijaz, and Muslim North Africa as far west as Algeria. Rivalry between the Ottomans and Safavids took on religious overtones as the Safavids became more militantly **Shiite** (see p. 52) and the Ottomans increasingly Sunni, a conflict that has left the Middle East religiously divided to this day along former Ottoman-Safavid boundary lines.

Like other Muslim empires before it, the Ottoman Empire developed features of an agrarian state with its social stratification and its absolute monarchy, but the Ottoman form remained distinctive. A military ruling family presided over a vast army of **Janissaries** recruited as slaves and loyal only to the rulers. These slaves were

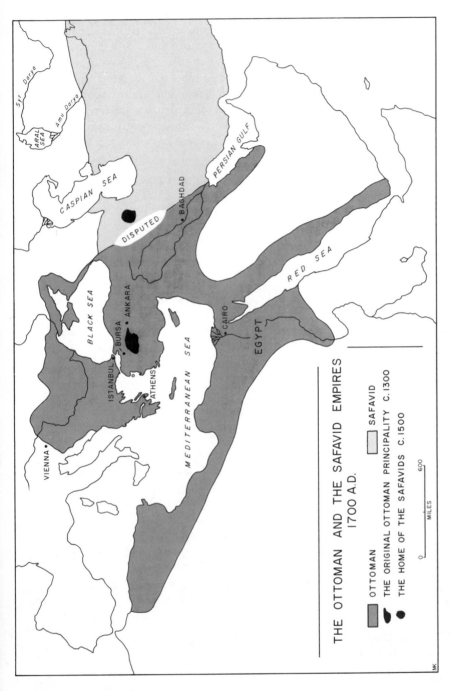

THE OTTOMAN AND THE SAFAVID EMPIRES
1700 A.D.

OTTOMAN

THE ORIGINAL OTTOMAN PRINCIPALITY C.1300

THE HOME OF THE SAFAVIDS C.1500

SAFAVID

0   600
MILES

The Ottoman and Savavid Empires, 1700 AD. *Source:* Yahya Armajani, *Middle East Past and Present*, © 1970, p. 161. Reprinted by permission of Prentice-Hall, Inc., Englewood Cliffs, N.J.

recruited as children from non-Muslim populations, often Christian, and were brought up and trained as Muslims. They formed a class that made up not only the military component of the army but the bureaucracy as well. At first they were not allowed to marry. When marriage was permitted, the offspring of slaves were free-born and therefore disqualified from government service, and so there was little opportunity for the formation of privileged classes or loyalties at odds with Otto-man interests. The machinery of Ottoman government was remarkably efficient. Furthermore, the Ottomans accomplished what few Muslim governing powers had done before them: they successfully allied themselves with the ulema. Ottoman success with the ulema was related to the empire's origin as a ghazi state and its de-votion to defending the faith against not only the Christian powers but the Shiite Safavids as well. It should also be kept in mind that a career as a religious scholar was one of the few paths of prestige open to the freeborn sons of the military-bureaucratic slave class. Under the Ottoman system, the ulema came to relinquish much of their traditional oppositional role with regard to the ruling powers, and came instead to identify with those powers. In return, the government supported the ulema's authority and that of Shariah law, and submitted to some token checks on its power; for example, the ulema could in theory depose the Ottoman sultan if they judged him unfaithful to Islam.

A certain amount of pluralism was built into the Ottoman system. The djimmi communities, or **millets**, were allowed military protection, religious free-dom, and self-government under their own chosen leaders, subject as always to a kind of second-class citizenship in the Muslim state. Ottoman provinces relatively distant from Istanbul, such as the Hijaz and North Africa, were also allowed some degree of self-govenment. For example the **Mameluks** of Egypt, a Turkish slave class that had ruled Egypt from 1250 until their defeat by the Ottomans in 1517, were allowed to continue in power under minimal Ottoman supervision.

By the eighteenth century, the empire had long since stopped increasing its territories and was beginning to take note of the rapidly growing European threat. Some attempts were made to modernize the Ottoman army, but these were thwarted by more sweeping weaknesses that plagued the empire. The military ruling class had gradually become civilianized, had suffered a loss of discipline, and had begun to lose even its former structural integrity (army bureaucrats, for example, began to pass their status on to their children). Corruption and demoralization became wide-spread in government, a condition which many Western observers of the time assumed to be a universal trait of "oriental" governments. When the Western powers began in earnest to move in on the Middle East around the turn of the nineteenth century, they found the Ottoman Empire ill prepared to resist them.

GROWTH AND DECLINE
IN THE ISLAMIC STATE

Many observers have noted that Muslim civilization and Muslim political power seem to have gone through an early period of phenomenal growth and vitality that was followed by a long era of "decline," or "stagnation," ending finally in Western dominance. Often, the rapid growth is attributed to military force driven by religious fanaticism, while the "decadence" that followed is said to reveal either the defects of the "oriental mind" or of Islam itself, both of which are often accused of authoritarianism and resistance to innovation. Such a view is misleading not only because there is no such thing as an oriental mind, but also because the problem of "growth" and "decline" is much too complex to lend itself to such easy generalizations. The Muslim world, like any civilization that endures for centuries or millennia, experienced many different kinds of growth and decline. Indeed, what is decline from one point of view may be growth from another—for example, the decline of centralized government was accompanied by a strengthening of Muslim law that reached across political boundaries. Furthermore, decline in one local region may be offset by growth in another.

The original growth of Islamic civilization actually involved two processes that reinforced one another: the spread of Islam as a religion, and the extension of Muslim political rule (or ties with the centers of Muslim power). The reasons for the spread of Islamic influence varied with the circumstances. In Medina, conversion to Islam was a matter of civic convenience as well as personal conviction. Among the Bedouins of the Arabian peninsula, political advantage and later the threat of force encouraged conversion. The subjects of the Sassanian and Byzantine empires yielded to a well-organized conquering army, but at the same time they were attracted by the promise of being better off as djimmi communities than as Byzantine or Sassanian subjects. Under the Umayyads, non-Arabs converted despite Arab discouragement in order to benefit from the advantages of Muslim social status. In India political conquest preceded conversion, while conversion itself resulted more often from the attractiveness of Muslim institutions and the personal appeal of **Sufism** (Muslim mysticism) than from the threat of force. In Southeast Asia, which now includes some of the world's most populous Muslim nations, Islam spread peaceably as part of an international mercantile culture, again aided by the appeal of Sufism.

The difficulties encountered by the various Muslim political powers after their establishment were due to a variety of causes, but none of these involved turning away from Islam as such. It appears that the Middle East may have been suffering some long-term adverse effects on its ecology, as a result of the ancient and intensive agricultural exploitation of the land. Many Islamic governments followed a policy of assigning "tax farms" as rewards to the military; these temporary revenue assignments were often exploited with little regard for the welfare of the peasants or the condition of the land and irrigation works, thus contributing to the decline of productivity. Coupled with the Mongol invasions and the Black Death during the thirteenth and fourteenth centuries, these trends may have reduced the vitality of agriculture, urban life, and even trade. There is some indication that population may have declined and that nomadism may have increased during the age of the Muslim empires. In addition to the economic factors, certain political processes seem to involve a dynamic of growth and decline. In agrarian societies, an existing order tends to accumulate vested interests, tax exemptions, and special privileges to the detriment of the overall functioning of the polity, until at last the weakened governmental power is overthrown and the accumulated commitments wiped away (as happened in the Arab conquest of Byzantine and Sassanian domains). This and other political processes may have contributed to cycles of political disintegration and revitalization both before and during the age of Muslim power.

As for intellectual development, it appears that the creative exploration of new ideas reached a peak during the Abbasid caliphate; afterward the legal, moral, and theological conceptions of the ulema prevailed and became increasingly hostile to innovation, especially after the ulema were integrated into the Ottoman order. While some see this as further evidence of the stagnation of "oriental" civilizations, one could just as easily see it as the natural consequence of the refinement of the Sharia, and particularly of its institutionalization in the madrasah schools where the ulema were trained—features that in turn provided much of the strength of Islamic law. The spirit of conservatism that prevailed after the collapse of the caliphate did not in itself cause political decline, nor was it very different from the conservatism that prevailed in Europe before the eighteenth century. This pattern of peaks and valleys in political power and social strength has been common to both regions throughout most of history.

LEGITIMACY IN GOVERNMENT

As stated earlier, the teachings of Muhammad stressed the righteous community that was structured to realize the demands of justice and piety. Since the early caliphate, a central problem in Islam has been to reconcile the demands of political reality and those of faith. The champions of Islamic values needed a workable government in theory, but rarely approved of what they found in practice. The Islamic governments needed the approval of Islam to make them legitimate, but while the Muslim rulers were devout men they were willing to make only limited concessions to Islamic ideals in government.

In some respects, the first caliphs were able to avoid many of the inherent difficulties of legitimizing Islamic political power. They were personal followers of the Prophet and were intimately acquainted with his words and deeds and ruled largely by virtue of that knowledge. Like traditional Arab leaders they also depended largely on their own personal qualities and reputation, and on their close acquaintance with the community (that is, with the core of Muhammad's following). They also acquired much legitimacy through their military leadership (Umar preferred to be called the "commander of the faithful" rather than caliph), a role well established in Arab tradition, and which carried with it the notion of leadership among men who were essentially equals.

The Political Role of the Ulema

Under Uthman a gap began to develop (or to become apparent) between Islamic ideals and the realities of political power and privilege. The issue of Uthman's murder and Ali's accession became symbolic for Muslims of the conflict between communal loyalty and religious purity. Although the Umayyads won on behalf of political solidarity, they had to face renewed challenges first from Ali's sons and later from a coalition of factions who wished to see Islamic government guided by uncompromising religious ideals. When this coalition failed to reverse the tendency toward secular power, Muslims were obliged to choose between remaining loyal to the protest against government, or to the powers that governed Islam regardless of their faults. While the Shiites took the former course, the bulk of the community, later called *Sunni*, chose in favor of the political unity of the Umma. As the pious, learned men of the Islamic world began to form into a coherent body of ulema, this body became a kind of loyal opposition, aloof from and critical of the government but not overtly disloyal to it. The ulema generally recognized the legitimacy of the caliphs, even though criticizing their ways. As the caliphs became powerless, they were still invested with theoretical legitimacy as the arbiters of any affairs concerning all Islam, and as the source of authority to the various emirs, or local rulers. After the fall of the caliphate, the ulema were inclined to grant at least some legitimacy to the emirs on the grounds that they provided the political order necessary to the community. This trend culminated in the Ottoman theory that whoever can rule the Muslim community according to the Sharia is entitled to be considered the caliph. The Ottoman interpretation completes the transition from the original theory in which secular power is derived from religious legitimation, to one in which religious legitimation is derived from secular power.

The unique political role of the ulema in Islam deserves special comment. Many traditional agrarian societies have a priesthood, a privileged group of religious practitioners who mediate ritually between the common people and the supernatural, and who tend to be intimately connected with—and supportive of—the political ruling class. The Muslim ulema, however, are scholars rather than priests; and their training in subsidized institutions was open, in theory, to anyone showing promise. Under the protection of Islam, the ulema traditionally presented a voice of opposition that attempted to hold political figures accountable to the principles of Islam, principles opposed to privilege and self-indulgence. Even today this heritage influences the relations between the Muslim religious leadership and state politics. The ulema in Saudi Arabia, for example, retain the right to declare a king unfit to govern, and they exercised this right in 1964 when they approved the deposing of King Saud.

THE SHARIA LAW

The Koran did not provide a complete guide for social life, and after the death of Muhammad the question arose as to how it was to be interpreted and how Muslims should deal with problems it did not directly anticipate. It soon became evident that the secular values of the conquered agrarian states, not to mention the old Arab ways, might reassert themselves unless Islam provided more detailed codes. By gradual steps, religious scholars developed a complex, cumulative set of guiding rules for Muslims that came to be known as the *Sharia*. At the core of the Sharia is the Koran, but it was necessary to supplement the Koran with reports (hadith) about the sayings and practices of the Prophet and his community. Later, as Sharia thinking attacked more complex problems, the Koran and the hadith were extended by means of the principle of analogy, by reference to the consensus of the Umma (or more specifically, its recognized religious leaders), and by reference to the welfare of the Umma. The relative importance of these various avenues of **fiqh**, or understanding, was debated by leading scholars and by the ninth century several major schools of legal thinking had developed. Each of these was accorded equal validity, and although they differed somewhat on the methods of arriving at legal codes, their results were similar. Muslims were expected to adhere consistently to one or another of these schools, usually according to the common practice of the locality. Today there are four such recognized schools in Sunni Islam.

Formal training in Sharia law became institutionalized in the **madrasahs**, Islamic schools supported by privately endowed religious foundations (**waqf**, plural *awqaf*) where any capable person could study free of charge. Such schools helped to determine who was qualified to interpret the tradition, and to standardize the Sharia against indiscriminate reinterpretation. They also made it possible to broaden the Sharia beyond the strict limits of the Koran and hadith without sacrificing its coherence or throwing it open to uncontrolled change. The Sharia, thus broadened and codified, provided a universal law that applied to every Muslim and to diverse aspects of life ranging from the settlement of political and business disputes to the regulation of family life. The application of this code and the qualifications of its administrators were valid in all Muslim nations regardless of political boundaries, which allowed Islam to prosper as an international social order even in times of political decentralization.

Based on the mercantile and Arab values of Mecca and Medina, the Sharia embodied a social philosophy that was opposed to social class or other privilege; it tended to support individual rights and individual social mobility and to protect the weak against the strong. Along with an uncompromising concern for Islamic principles of social justice, however, went a distrust of innovation and of the deviant or the outsider—an inclination that became more and more established in the madrasahs after the fourteenth century. In the madrasahs the methods of teaching became extremely conservative and were aimed at discouraging innovation. Any question that had once been decided upon and accepted by the ulema was no longer open for discussion, and new issues were to be resolved insofar as possible in exact accordance with previous decisions. Even the number of errors was determined—there were six dozen false sects of Islam, and every new heresy could be classified with those already known. Yet without this careful regulation the Sharia probably could not have served its vital function in Muslim life.

The sway of the Sharia was never absolute. Because monarchs often found the Sharia incomplete, irrelevant to certain questions, or excessively "soft" on criminals, they typically established their own courts and legal codes. The peasants and townspeople, on the other hand, sometimes found it in their interest to follow customary law, even (as in the case of some inheritance rules) when it contradicted the Sharia. Despite these auxiliary legal systems, however, the Sharia stood as the supreme expression of legitimacy. It was the core of Islamic social life, to which every Muslim ultimately owed allegiance. Safe from random innovation, local cultural influence, and the tampering of political interest groups, the Sharia provided a means of integrating an international civilization.

THE SHIA

The conflicting demands of political unity and religious purity, which became apparent so early in Islamic history, gave rise to the great sectarian split within Islam—that of the Sunnis and the Shiites. While the majority of Muslims are Sunnis, who place loyalty to the established order of the Umma above religious disputation, the Shia, a substantial minority, believe that only a divinely inspired political leadership is worthy of a Muslim's loyalty. The historical split between the two groups is difficult to discuss because the key events of the past have been imbued subsequently with complex symbolic significance. At the time of his death, Ali stood for the protest against the supposed corruptions of Uthman's rule, and his defeat was viewed by many Muslims—particularly those in the Iraq—as an unfortunate triumph of worldly power over true Islamic piety. Those loyal to Ali, and to what he stood for, came to be known as the *Shia* (party) of Ali. A turning point in the history of the Shia was an insurrection in 680 against the Umayyads under Ali's son Husayn, in which Husayn, abandoned by the bulk of his supporters, was killed. With the rise of the Abbasids in 750, Shiite hopes that the new political unrest would lead to a reinstatement of Ali's line were dashed, and the Shia assumed the posture of a minority opposition to the political establishment. Under the Abbasids the division between the Shiites and the Sunnis became more distinct. The Sunni position, even among those who sympathized with Ali's protest and despised Uthman and the fallen Umayyad dynasty, was that devotion to the solidarity of the Umma and obedience to its recognized leadership should transcend religious dissension. By the tenth century, the Shiites had developed into a distinct and very influential group which proposed, in opposition to the Sunni view, that Muslims should follow only those authorities who were rightly guided. In the Shiite view, this gift of divine guidance (what sociologists call "charisma") was possessed only by a small number of the elect, descendents of the Prophet through his daughter Fatima and his son-in-law Ali. While Husayn was the last of these to make an open bid for power, the Shiites believed that secret knowledge and divine inspiration had passed through Ali's line to a succession of rightful leaders. The Shiite movement eventually split over differing interpretations of this line of succession. The largest faction was the "Twelvers," who believed that the twelfth imam in the succession had gone into hiding from the wicked world, where he would remain until his eventual return as the **Mahdi**, or Muslim Messiah. In Twelver Shiism, which predominates in Iran, it has occasionally been possible for religious leaders to claim sweeping powers as representatives of this "Hidden Imam." Another major faction, the **Isma'ilis**, emphasized the esoteric knowledge of a secret religious elite, a knowledge revealed to the pious follower only by degrees as he ascends in the religious hierarchy. Isma'ili Islam reached the peak of its influence in the Fatimid dynasty in Egypt (696-1171), which was renowned for its achievements in government, commerce, art, and learning.

The Shia came to see the majority of Muslims as betrayers of their faith, and temporal power as essentially illegitimate. In this atmosphere of resistance they developed the practice of denying their true beliefs in public when necessary, as well

as the idea that the inward truth of the Koran (as opposed to its outward or superficial meaning) is unknown to the community at large and must be interpreted by
the Imams or their agents. (The use of the term *imam* can be confusing, since it can
refer to a variety of roles ranging from a leader of Muslim prayer to—in Shiite
thought—a leader of all Islam. Generally, we have capitalized Imam only when it
refers to the latter or to a specific historical personage such as the Imam Ayatollah
Khomeini.) Another strong current in Shiite thought is the tragic view of the fate of
the righteous man in an unrighteous society, and a deep sense of guilt over the betrayal and martyrdom of Husayn. Once a year, during the month of **Muharram**,
commemorating Husayn's martyrdom, these sentiments are celebrated in an outpouring of grief, self-flagellation, and resentment toward the Sunnis. If the ulema of
Sunni Islam looked askance at the political establishment, the Shia simply regarded
it as illegitimate, to be tolerated only for the time being. Despite the differences in
outlook, Sunni and Shiite Islam actually developed remarkably parallel institutions,
parallel Sharia codes, and even parallel debates over similar issues. Mystical Sufism,
which was largely a Sunni phenomenon, developed its Shiite counterpart in a particularly inward-turning brand of personal devotion to Ali and Husayn.

Even in Ali's day the Iraq was a center to proto-Shiite resistance. It remained
so under the Umayyads as part of the protest against Syrian power; and even after
the fall of the Umayyads, Shiism remained strong in the old Sassanian domains—so
much that some historians characterize Shiism as a Persian movement against
Arabism. Shiism was even more radically localized, however, during the rivalry between the Sunni Ottomans and the Shiite Safavids, when nonconforming minorities
in each domain were persecuted or driven out. Today Shiism is largely confined to
the Middle East, where more than a fourth of the Muslims are Shiites, most of
whom live in Iraq or Iran.

SUFISM

If the Sharia was uncompromisingly oriented toward history, justice, and practical
responsibility, other elements of Islam addressed very different facets of religious
life. Mysticism, that brand of religious awareness that emphasizes the clarifying and
enlightening inward experience over conventionalized and verbally communicated
ideas, is pervasive in human cultures and was well established in the Middle East before the rise of Islam. Like Christianity and Judaism, Islam has developed its own
distinct tradition of mysticism. In early times the mystically inclined Muslims, or
Sufis, were a small minority hardly distinguishable from other Muslims, but after
1100 they became more prominent and influential. The Muslim philosopher-theo-
logian Ghazali (d. 1111), though not a Sufi himself, aided the rise of Sufism by arguing that it was not only consistent with the Sharia but was a valuable complement
to it.

Sufi mystics used classic techniques of posture, breathing, meditation, music,
and dance to induce states of extraordinary awareness which they regarded as closeness to God. In their philosophical writings they emphasized love and cosmic unity,

even posing Jesus as the ideal sufi. Like the Sharia, Sufism was populistic—it took little notice of traditional lines of privilege and was open to all who would pursue it. Unlike the ulema, who were oriented strongly toward the Sharia, the mystics tended to be tolerant of local cultures and customs, of human weakness, and of different levels of understanding. They even interpreted the jihad, or holy war, as an inward struggle for enlightenment. Even so, Sufism had its outward, institutional side. After the tenth century, Sufis began to organize themselves into separate orders, or **tariqahs**. Each of these recognized a different line of communication of mystical knowledge, beginning with the private communications of Muhammad to certain followers, and going through a known line of teachers **(pirs)**. One could become a pir only by studying under another recognized pir, so that the body of knowledge within each order was preserved and controlled. These Sufi orders had social and political uses, for they often became the organizational core of guilds, young men's military clubs, or even some governmental organizations. One ambitious caliph, shortly before the Mongol invasions, even sought to restore the power of the caliphate through the judicious use of Sufi tariqahs.

Because of Sufism's tolerance, its association in folk religion with local "saints" and their tombs, and its abuse by wandering charlatans or extremists who considered themselves outside the Sharia, the ulema often took a dim view of Sufism. However, despite occasional outbursts of anti-Sufi reaction, as in the thirteenth century, Sufism was established as legitimate by the Sharia principle of consensus. Some ulema scholars were Sufi pirs themselves, and Sufism came to dominate the inward side of religious life in Islam, especially among the Sunnis. The personal appeal of Sufism supplemented the social appeal of the Sharia and contributed greatly to Islam's spread as a religion, and thus indirectly to the political sway of Islam. Furthermore, Sufism remained another potential counterbalance to the outward authority of any "Islamic" government.

ISLAM AND RADICAL POLITICS

Muhammad's ideal of religiously based law and government contained the seeds of religious support for the establishment and of religious opposition to it. The tradition of religious opposition is represented in one way by the ulema, and in quite another by the many radical movements in Islam's history. It is not possible to mention all the major movements that have arisen in Islam, but a few examples will suffice for illustration: the Kharijites, the Ismailis, the Sudanese Mahdi, and the Wahhabi movement.

The Kharijites

Islam's first civil war began with an insurrection of Egyptian soldiers who murdered the caliph Uthman and justified the act with the accusation that he had departed from Islam and was therefore a usurper. Ali's supporters accepted this line of reasoning, while his opponents accused him of condoning the murder of a believer and of attempting to disrupt the community. When Ali agreed to submit the issue to arbitration, his most extreme supporters turned against him to become *Kharijites* ("seceders"). The Kharijites embodied a radically anarchistic interpretation of Islam, in which personal piety was held to be not only the sole measure of a person's right to lead the community, but the only criterion for membership in the Umma itself. Thus, the impious Uthman was not only a false caliph, but an unbeliever falsely professing Islam; it was therefore the duty of a believer to kill him. In Kharijite eyes, anyone who had committed a "grave" sin was excluded from the Umma, and the most extreme Kharijites did not hesitate to kill non-Kharijites indiscriminately when the occasion presented itself. Even among the Kharijites themselves no leader was to be trusted on principle, and their "caliph" could be deposed for the slightest transgression. Ali found it necessary to suppress the Kharijites by force, and he was eventually assassinated by one of them. There were more than a score of Kharijite rebellions during Ali's and Muawiyah's reigns, and small Kharijite communities have continued to exist down to the present. In their extreme approach to the issue of piety versus political order, the Kharijites severely crippled their own political strength and assured themselves a marginal role in Islamic society.

Ismailis and Qarmatians

The Shiites went in a direction opposite to that of the Kharijites by elevating the charismatic leader to an exalted status, the Ismaili Shiites going to the farthest extreme. Their central belief was that a highly esoteric knowledge of the all-important inner meaning of Muhammad's teachings was transmitted through secret communication from the Prophet to certain elect followers. The Ismailis gave rise to a number of movements, but none more fascinating than the **Qarmatians**. Originating in the desert between Syria and the Iraq in the late ninth century, the movement designated its leader as an emissary of God. The Qarmatians were dedicated to the overthrow of the wealthy and privileged, and the Bedouins and peasants who joined the sect apparently held all goods in common. After its suppression by the Abbasids, the movement reappeared in Bahrain where it became established as an egalitarian, communistic state that lasted well into the eleventh century. It is said that the Qarmatians spurned the Sharia and orthodox forms of worship, and that one of their leaders who was thought to be Mahdi, or Muslim Messiah, set himself above Muhammad (this, however, may be hostile propaganda). In any case, the Qarmatians seem to have regarded other Muslims as unbelievers, and in 930 they succeeded in abducting temporarily the Black Stone from the shrine at Mecca, on the grounds that it was an object of idolatry.

The Mahdi

The Qarmatians were by no means the only Muslims to believe in a Mahdi. Running sporadically throughout Islam is a chiliastic orientation, which holds that the world will eventually be delivered from its wickedness into an age of justice and piety, and the wicked will suffer vengeance from the righteous. The idea of a deliverer, or Mahdi, appears repeatedly in this chiliastic thinking. Of the many persons hailed as Mahdis, one of the most recent and striking examples is the Sudanese

Mahdi of the late nineteenth century. Arising in opposition to the inroads of the modernizing Egyptian ruler Ismail, whose stated intention was to make Egypt part of Europe (and the Sudan part of Egypt), the Mahdi drove the Egyptians out of the Sudan and preached a program of Islamic moral reform, not only for the Sudan but for all Islam. The Mahdi appointed his own caliph. Publicized among pilgrims at Mecca, his program seemed to many Muslims an attractive alternative to the weakened and discredited Ottoman leadership until the British finally succeeded in crushing the movement in the 1890s.

The Wahhabi Movement

In Arabia during the late eighteenth century, a former Sufi teacher Muhammad Ibn Abd-al-Wahhab came under the influence of the conservative Hanbali school of Sunni Muslim thought, which rejected the role of ulema consensus in the interpreting of the Sharia. He called for the purification of Islam from the influence of evil innovations, which he believed was responsible for the decadence of the Ottoman world. With the aid of Ibn Saud, a local ruler who had converted to the movement, Ibn Abd-al-Wahhab set about to promote an extremely puritanical reform of Islam, which opposed all forms of Sufism and pre-Islamic custom and denounced most Muslims as idolators and infidels to be killed. Even after decades of Ottoman attempts to suppress the movement, Ibn Saud's grandson was able to seize Mecca and Medina, to destroy many of Islam's holy shrines, and to massacre the residents of these cities. The movement was temporarily suppressed in 1818 only to reappear in the twentieth century among other members of the house of Saud and to become the foundation of the modern state of Saudi Arabia. Thus the deep-lying conservatism of contemporary Saudi Arabia, far from being a survival of some ancient Islamic heritage as the popular press might lead one to believe, is in fact the result of a relatively recent political-religious movement which by usual Muslim standards can only be regarded as ultraconservative and radically puritanical.

As these examples show, Islamic political-religious movements have a long history and can take many forms. Like similar movements in Christianity, they tend to adopt a "restitutionist" outlook—that is, they see themselves as restoring the original purity of the religion. The exact nature of that restoration, of course, tends to be partly a projection of the values of the reformers. Despite their unswervingly religious tone, such movements tend to display an acute consciousness of social problems, and to support political programs—some more practical than others—to remedy them. Some such movements bear significant political fruit, as in the case of Wahhabi influence in Saudi Arabia. The sociology of religion shows that such religious movements often center around charismatic leaders who are thought to have special knowledge of transcendent order and purpose, and they often arise in times of cultural, social, political, and economic upheaval. It should not be surprising then, if the last decades of the twentieth century see a succession of charismatic religious movements within Islam, propounding various avenues toward the revitalization of the faith, and providing the vehicles for an assortment of social and political reforms.

DIVERSITY IN ISLAMIC POLITICAL THOUGHT

The Ayatollah Ruhollah Khomeini, leader of Iran's 1979 revolution, was quoted as saying "We Muslims are of one family even though we live under different governments and in various regions." While the statement is an accurate reflection of the Muslim ideal of a united Umma, it should not be taken to mean that Islam represents a single, monolithic bloc with a fixed perspective on every significant issue. The recent upsurge of Islamic revival can only be expected to revitalize discussion and controversy among Muslims on the many issues that have always occupied the dialectic of Islamic thought. It is not easy to say, once and for all, what constitutes the Islamic vision of society, law, and government. Almost from its beginning, Islam has had its factions, particularly the Sunnis and the Shiites. It has manifested an inward, mystical side as well as an outward set of codes and institutions. Muslims have tried to mediate between the heritage of Middle Eastern civilization with its despotism and social privilege, and the principles of social equality enunciated in the Koran. Islamic civilization has been deeply influenced in various times and places by diverse cultural traditions, secular philosophies carried on from the Greeks, the aristocratic high culture of the royal courts, and the folk practices that preceded Islam and were independent of formal theology. Cosmopolitan and universalistic in its core outlook, Islam has had to deal with those who chose not to join the brotherhood of Islam. Each one of these conflicts has engendered not one but numerous solutions, depending on historical circumstance.

Yet it would be misleading, despite the change and adaptability of Islam, to see it as entirely amorphous or plastic, lending itself indifferently to every possible interpretation. Throughout the Islamic dialogue run certain recurrent themes that have their roots in the fundamental principles laid out in Muhammad's ministry. One of these is the interdependence of religion and the sociopolitical order, which is built more deeply into Islam than in most world religions. It would be harder for a serious Muslim to accept the separation of church and state than for a traditional Christian, even though the possibility of such a separation is suggested by Egyptian President Sadat's admonition that there should be "no religion in politics, and no politics in religion." Furthermore, Muslim law involves a detailed pattern of everyday life that regulates such matters as alcohol consumption and marriage. Such personal moral regulations existed more informally in traditional Christianity, but in Islam they are part of a literate tradition that will be relatively difficult to change or to separate from political issues. The Sharia is not easily circumvented; strictly speaking it is open only to interpretation, not legislation. The arrangements that gave the Sharia and the ulema such independence in the past will probably continue to insure Islam's role as an active challenge to the political status quo. Westerners observing the dialogue in contemporary Islamic political thought may mistakenly assume that Islam is "waking up" and examining these issues critically for the first time, but nothing could be further from the truth. Whatever the solutions toward which Muslims move, they can be expected to show the influence of previous dialogue within the tradition, a dialogue that will continue to allow for diverse possibilities.

4

Western Imperialism
1800–1914

"Imperialism" is a familiar word that seems at first to have a clear and straightforward meaning, but on closer inspection becomes blurred and indistinct. It may mean any one of three relationships in which a relatively powerful country dominates the political, economic, or cultural affairs of a weaker one. In political imperialism, the powerful country controls the major governmental decision making of the weaker, either directly or by proxy through pliant, cooperative officials of the weaker country. Economic imperialism denotes a situation in which a weaker country becomes dependent on stronger countries for income. Cultural imperialism means a situation in which a weaker country adopts the language, manners, and lifestyle of the stronger.

All three kinds of imperialism occurred in the Middle East in the nineteenth century. It is difficult to assess the full consequences of these relationships since many aspects of them have not yet been fully played out and are still active today, but many writers feel that the negative effects of imperialism will ultimately outweigh the positive. The study of imperialism, however, contains many difficulties in concept, definition, and measurement, and a final positive or negative assessment is far from certain. For example, it is often difficult to say whether certain commercial transactions between weak and powerful countries benefit only the powerful or whether they work to the mutual benefit of both. And while a weaker, less developed country may chafe over being dependent on a stronger one, its very dissatisfaction may spur it to make some positive reforms that it might not otherwise have made. The effects of imperialism on the weaker country may be shallow or deep. One country may survive a period of imperial stewardship and keep most of its social, cultural, and economic fabric intact. Imperial domination in such a case is only a kind of veneer. In other cases, imperial domination may deeply disrupt a country's social, economic, and political structures.

"Nationalism," like imperialism, is another term that most people understand immediately, but on closer study find difficult to apply exactly. Nationalism is not just a matter of simple patriotism born of deep loyalty to an ethnic group, religion, homeland, leader, or set of institutions, although nationalist movements frequently contain a mixture of all these elements. Nationalistic movements give the appearance of solidity because they are often bound together by resentment toward the imperial power. Once the imperial power is removed, the seemingly solid and cohesive nationalist movement often disintegrates into perhaps scores of factional conflicts. We must study such root factions and forces if we are to gain a deeper understanding of a particular country or region.

In this chapter, therefore, we shall examine how European imperialist powers penetrated the Middle East in the nineteenth century, just before the various nation states in the region emerged. The Europeans did so in a series of powerful, deep-reaching thrusts, and we shall examine how certain areas responded to such battering.

SETTING THE STAGE

For thousands of years, most areas of the world were fairly equal in technology and economic well-being. Major inventions and technological innovations occurred at irregular intervals and in widely separated regions. An innovation that arose at a certain time or in a certain region had little influence on a technology that was being developed in another place or time. It took centuries, even millennia, for ideas and innovations to become uniformly diffused over the large areas of Asia, Europe, and the Middle East. Regions that were late to adopt a particular innovation or bit of technology from abroad had a comfortably long time in which to achieve parity with other regions before the next innovation came along.

During the period from about 1400 to 1700, however, a set of institutions and cultural forms was developed in Europe that promoted and regularized the flow of innovations. The most important advances occurred in organization and administration, weaponry, and communications. The process of how these innovations were accepted and how a continuing need for them was institutionalized is still not well understood. The result, however, is clear: technical innovation became a continuous, irreversible, steadily accelerating process. The process of regaining parity because of slow diffusion was at an end; Western Europe achieved technological dominance over the rest of the world, and other regions had no time to catch up.

It is difficult to say just when the West began to penetrate the Middle East or when it finally achieved political and economic dominance. One very important date, however, is 1498. It was in this year that the Portuguese navigator, Vasco da Gama, sailed around the southern tip of Africa and to India, thus opening up an important new trade route to the East. Although Europeans had gradually taken control of the Mediterranean sea trade for the past two hundred years, the opening of this new ocean route to India now assured them of total control over most of the world's maritime trade. The Middle Eastern overland trade routes began to decline. European control of the Mediterranean had already begun to shift the middleman functions from the Arabs to the Venetians and Genoese. Furthermore, Western technical and manufacturing innovations were resulting in the production of better products. As a consequence, Middle Eastern handicraft production, especially that along the south and east Mediterranean coasts, also began to decline. These developments tore wide rents in the economic and social fabric of the region. For example, Middle Eastern handicraft production was loosely organized in guilds—groups of craftsmen whose taxes provided a source of revenue for the various local governments, and whose presence contributed vitally to the social life of the area. Many of the ulema were either guild members or were supported by them. European dominance in commerce and production was accompanied by advances in military technology. European armies became powerful instruments of national will. After four centuries of successful expansion, the Ottoman Empire began to lose territory to the Europeans.

Some writers claim that the Europeans' technological superiority also gave them a sense of moral superiority. While this may or may not be true, Europeans, in their quest for control of the Middle East, often clothed their political and economic motives in the vestments of religion. A belief in the inherent decadence and wickedness of Islam provided several generations of Europeans with a strong rationale for imperialistic ventures in the Middle East, and this belief had a strong impact on the various cultures with which they associated.

THE OTTOMANS

By 1800, the decline of the Ottoman Empire was well under way and was to accelerate over the next hundred years. Western technology and military power were having an increasingly powerful impact. The Ottoman elite, long used to thinking that Western knowledge was not worth having, realized that it could no longer maintain its sense of superiority. An early sign of this change of attitude is the so-called Tulip Period (1718-1730), during which the Ottoman elite succumbed to a fad for everything Western. It built French-style pleasure palaces, wore Western clothes, sat on Western chairs, and cultivated Western gardens. It developed a mania for tulips and sent prices of tulip bulbs to absurd heights, high offices being sold for particularly exotic strains.

Aside from these extravagances, the period also saw the tentative beginnings of a new intellectual atmosphere; previously rejected reforms were now being seriously entertained. Most of them were shallow and aimed only at making institutions in the existing framework—especially the military—more effective. Selim III (1789-1807) attempted more fundamental reforms; and while most of these failed or were only partially successful, they did lay the groundwork for later reforms in the nineteenth century. Once antireformist resistance was overcome, particularly that from the traditional military corps, the Janissaries, reform activity quickened, culminating in the **Tanzimat** period. The Janissaries represented the most important group of the nonmodernized army. They viewed the building of a modern army and bureaucracy as a threat to their power and, therefore, were at the forefront of the coalition resisting reform. But Sultan Mahmud II (1808-1839) cleverly built a new coalition loyal to him and had the Janissaries killed when they rebelled in 1826. This event is called the "Auspicious Incident" because it allowed the sultan to initiate a period of significant reform. The Tanzimat period is the name given to the reform period.

The Tanzimat Period (1839–1876)

The Tanzimat reforms were achieved with no clearly defined master plan other than a mostly unstated desire for greater government centralization. During previous centuries, the empire had expanded successfully by means of policies that favored extreme decentralization. By giving local governments large measures of autonomy, the *millet system* had kept the provinces reasonably satisfied. However, the military in remote areas had begun to look more to its own interests than those of the empire. Within limits, local authorities had the power to tax the population as they saw fit, as long as they remitted a negotiated amount to the central government; the sultan consequently had little control over the size of the royal treasury. As the empire declined and the booty of conquest stopped flowing into the capital, the Ottoman sultans tried to make up the difference by increasing taxes. However, the provincial authorities, having become used to self-rule for several generations, felt no great loyalty to the sultans and firmly resisted them. The sultans therefore saw that it was crucial to reorganize the empire around a strong central authority.

The Tanzimat reforms were many and far-reaching. Ministries were established to impose uniform regulations all over the empire. The military was completely reorganized along Western lines, and its incentive system was restructured to create greater commitment to the empire. The tax collection system was streamlined to allow revenues to flow directly to the royal treasury; local governments had their powers reduced.

Although many Tanzimat reforms failed and many others did not work out exactly as intended, they marked a turning point in Ottoman history. And although the empire continued to lose territory in the nineteenth century, the reforms were a sign of considerable lingering vitality. The Ottoman Empire was far from being the "sick man of Europe," as was said at the time and was commonly believed well into this century. To be sure, the empire was beset by internal and external difficulties of massive proportions, but there was also substantial positive change. The entrenched powers were understandably opposed to the reforms, but in time they were either accommodated or suppressed. Modern organizational forms and military technology spread to other areas, especially communications and education.

Although the reforms' impact on cultural life was not a central concern during the early years of the Tanzimat period, they had a pervasive and enduring result. Many reforms required that administrators undergo specialized training and education. A new generation of technocrats arose who began to respect the West, for it was there that the needed knowledge was stored. Along with technical knowledge, this new class also absorbed the political philosophies of nationalism and democracy. The lack of qualified personnel within the empire, and the increasing encroachments of European governments and commercial interests also brought an influx of powerful and active Europeans to the center of the empire.

The Tanzimat reforms were surrounded by international intrigue. England,

France, and Russia (and later Germany) had vital interests in the Middle East which they tried to protect and enlarge. For most of the nineteenth century, the Ottoman Empire had to defend itself against European powers who were pushing and shoving among themselves for competitive advantage. Europe generally did not want to see the Ottoman Empire collapse; the scramble for spoils afterward would have certainly ended in a bloodbath and much destruction. So, first one European power and then another supported the empire. But while the Europeans wished the Ottoman Empire a long life, they did not want to see it strong. On the contrary, they chipped away at its edges and blunted many of the effects of the Tanzimat reforms. There is no question that nineteenth-century Ottoman administration was corrupt and inept, but it is questionable whether a smoothly functioning modern organization would have done much better. The European powers had the empire pinioned. The Tanzimat reforms were a significant attempt to adapt to technological realities, and they represented a skillful attempt to resolve the empire's internal conflicts while playing off European interests. But in the end, the Ottomans could not escape the debilitating entanglements imposed on them by Westerners.

As the European powers increased their leverage, responsible parties in the empire grew increasingly dissatisfied with the course taken by the sultan and his inner circle. Various changes of policy were demanded, the most important being representation in the legislative bodies, the adoption of a constitution, and the formation of an Ottoman ideology. Some favored a wholesale adoption of European ways, some sought a return to a past era of Islamic purity, and others advocated a host of intermediate positions. The restive attitude of the new technocrats and the role of the Western powers presented the sultan with a problem common to most reforming autocrats—how to control the demands of a new class of people who possess the technical knowledge on which the empire depended. Since the military and commercial presence of the competing Europeans prevented any return to past ways, and since the Europeans could not be expelled, a long series of struggles and partial accommodations took place; this process resulted in the granting of a constitution in 1876 by the shrewd Sultan Abdulhamit (1876-1909). The constitution was suspended shortly thereafter, but was reinstated with significant changes in 1908.

The Young Turk revolution (1908), which prompted the sultan to reconvene the legislative body and activate the constitution, had its ideological roots in various sources of discontent. A significant pan-Islamic and then pan-Ottoman movement, supported by the sultan, arose in the last third of the nineteenth century. The pan-Islamic movement championed the rights of all Muslims. The pan-Ottoman movement was broader; it called for more-or-less equal rights for all (including non-Muslim) subjects of the empire. But these movements contained many contradictions. Increasingly, waves of ethnic and geographical nationalism developed in reaction to Ottoman hegemony at the same time the sultan was reaffirming the equality of all his subjects. This led to discontent among the military forces who were asked to support the call for equality while being attacked by the supposed beneficiaries of the call. The ideological reaction was pan-Turkism, the notion that the ethnic identity of the empire deserved first consideration. Turkish greatness and the virtues of the Turkish people were celebrated in a large number of literary works.

By the turn of the twentieth century, the calls for a Turkish nation, military discontent, millet terrorism, and European pressures put Sultan Abdulhamit in an increasingly defensive position. He responded with many repressive measures. He paralyzed the bureaucracy by insisting on personally approving the smallest changes in policy. A financial crisis sparked a widespread revolt. The revolution of 1908 forced the sultan to agree to demands for a constitution and representation.

The period after World War I was particularly devastating for the empire. The positive effects of some of the modernizing reforms were undone by a series of crippling conflicts. Furthermore, the Ottoman Empire had aligned itself with the Central Powers during the war; when they were defeated, the empire was dismembered. The Allied forces divided the empire among themselves and imposed a particularly harsh rule on Turkey. But the Turkish nationalist forces who had been successful in 1908 rose to defend the homeland. Led by Kemal Atatürk, they repelled the Europeans and established an independent Turkish state. A remarkable series of reforms followed that would ultimately transform and secularize Turkey.

EGYPT

Long-standing corruption and generally ineffective rule had led to centuries of decay in Egypt. But the power of this weak Ottoman province was to change markedly during the nineteenth century. For the Ottomans of the nineteenth century, Egypt was something to be both feared and imitated.

In the last decade of the eighteenth century, the French were looking on Egypt with increased interest largely because of their struggle with the British. Egypt could be France's grainery, control Middle Eastern military and commercial traffic, and provide a base from which to threaten the British in India. Napoleon invaded Egypt in July, 1798, and with remarkable ease destroyed the Mameluk forces who ruled Egypt under loose Ottoman control. Napoleon presented himself to the Egyptians, and especially the ulema, as a liberator from foreign rule. But his call for cooperation went unheeded, and he was forced to quell a rebellion in Cairo in October, 1798.

As all rulers of Egypt knew, control of the Levant was vital to Egyptian security. Consequently, Napoleon invaded Palestine and Syria in 1799. He met with failure, however, as Ottoman forces halted the French advance, and the British navy attacked the French fleet. Since the security of Egypt could not be maintained, Napoleon quickly reassessed his position and quit Egypt in August, 1799. The last French forces withdrew by 1801.

The brief French presence in Egypt gave advance warning that European powers would be drawn into Middle Eastern affairs on a much larger scale than before. It also served as a lesson to the Ottoman rulers and to the future Egyptian ruler, **Muhammad Ali (Mehemet),** that European organizational and technical skills were superior to those of the Ottoman Empire—so superior that the rulers would have to adapt quickly if the empire was to remain secure.

Muhammad Ali had fought against the French in Syria. Born in Albania, and serving in the Ottoman army, this "selfish, illiterate genius" slowly eliminated his Ottoman rivals in Egypt and assumed control in 1805. He was to rule Egypt until his death in 1849. The lessons of French military superiority were not lost on him. He also realized that the key to building a similar kind of force required a fundamental reordering of the Egyptian economy; the material requirements of a strong military depended on an economy that could supply the needed goods. Although officially confirmed as governor in 1806, it was only after beating back a half-hearted British invasion in 1807 and massacring the last serious Mameluk rivals to power in 1811 that Muhammad Ali achieved a secure hold in Egypt. He then began in earnest to modernize Egypt's military. Egyptians were sent to France to learn modern military technology; and foreign advisors, particularly French, were brought to Egypt. Technical knowledge was diffused throughout Egypt by means of training institutes and translations of technical treatises.

Because a strong military was necessary for retaining and expanding power, much of the early effort was directed to meeting its basic needs. An army of over 100,000 men, if it was to be modern, needed munitions, communication systems, clothing, and food. Since there was no established industrialist class in Egypt, the government financed and managed its own factories. European industrialists and financiers were invited to provide capital and expertise to supplement the effort. In addition, Egyptian soldiers—drafted into military service in 1823 for the first time in centuries—were "forced" to learn technical skills. To guard against foreign domination of key positions, European factory managers and technical personnel were required to train their Egyptian counterparts.

To mount this ambitious drive, the government needed a strong financial base. The 1811 massacre of the Mameluks gave the state control of their vast landholdings. All land rights were subsumed by the government, and the system of tax administration was altered. The traditional system had allowed local leaders to pay a sum to the government in return for the right to tax the **fellah**; under the revised system, the government collected the taxes directly. The government also assumed control of most agricultural marketing, especially export crops. These policies increased revenues, lessened the power of reactionary local leaders, and partially circumvented an Anglo-Ottoman treaty that limited import and export taxes to 3 percent.

Long-staple cotton was introduced to the Nile Delta in 1821. Although this superior strain of cotton stimulated local textile production, it also tied Egyptian economic fortunes to the vagaries of the international market. Cotton soon became Egypt's leading export, accounting for 75 percent of all receipts by 1860. The Delta, capable of producing a food surplus from a variety of crops, was transformed into a cotton monoculture designed to sustain the textile mills of England. Egyptian dependence on cotton earnings forced more and more land to be turned over to its production, and the country that Napoleon saw as a grainery for France was now forced to import food.

Muhammad Ali grew increasingly independent of the Ottoman authorities. The empire saw little harm in this during the early years of his rule. Before Muhammad Ali, Egypt had been a corrupt and militarily weak entity and of little value beyond the taxes paid by Cairo. Under him, Egypt seemed to be undergoing constructive change and developing a credible military force. Muhammad Ali's armies waged various campaigns under the Ottoman banner, the most important being the successful campaigns against the Wahhabis, the conservative expansionist tribal movement in Arabia.

Muhammad Ali's independent actions finally led to a crisis in 1832. Under the pretext of insufficient payment for Egyptian aid in the empire's unsuccessful attempts to stem the Greek rebellion, he invaded and occupied Syria—making Egypt an all but independent political and military force. In 1838, he declared his intention to become king of Egypt. The antiquated military force that the empire sent to displace the Egyptians from Syria was no match for Muhammad Ali's modern troops. After defeating the empire's forces, he toyed with the idea of invading Anatolia proper, but European interests, especially the British, defused the crisis. The British did not want to see Egypt, an ally of France, grow powerful; nor did they relish the possibility of Russia dominating a weakened Ottoman Empire. When Mehmut II died in the midst of the crisis, it seemed that Russian influence in the imperial court would be expanded significantly. The admiral of the Ottoman navy sailed the fleet to Alexandria to be put in the service of Muhammad Ali rather than run the risk of being controlled by the infidel Russians. As it was, the empire weathered this "Russian threat."

British and Ottoman pressures effectively halted the reformist and expansionist actions of the Egyptian ruler. Muhammad Ali retained his role as governor of Egypt and was given the right to hereditary rule, but he lost much in the bargain. He relinquished the Ottoman fleet, pulled out of Syria, reduced the size of the army from 130,000 men to 18,000, and accepted the 1838 Anglo-Ottoman Commercial Code. The 1838 Commercial Code enlarged the preferential treatment afforded to foreigners doing business in the Ottoman empire and made state monopolies illegal. The aggressive economic policies of the preceding thirty years had changed the face of Egypt. Some ventures had been successful, but many operations were wasteful and inefficient. Although Egypt may not have been able to sustain these at such a pace, it was unquestionably shaking off its mordibund status of the previous centuries. Acceptance of the 1838 Commercial Code both sealed the fate of Egypt's economic experiment, and assured foreign control of most Egyptian commerce and industry.

The story behind the building of the Suez Canal under the direction of the remarkable Ferdinand de Lesseps illustrates European dominance in a spectacular fashion. The terms of the contract to build the canal (1854), the methods used to construct the canal, and subsequent European actions serve as a model of imperial deceit and connivance at its worst. Essentially, Egypt supplied all of the labor, about 20,000 men, and gave the shrewd de Lesseps free access to the Egyptian treasury through various contract provisions, bribes, and bullying. In return, Egypt retained $\frac{7}{16}$ ownership but surrendered most of its rights to the profits until the canal was completed (1869). Other smaller ventures proposed by Europeans and accepted by the weakened heirs to Muhammad Ali's governorship were similarly one sided. The granting of concessions to Europeans ended in a financial crisis that opened the way to total European control.

The financial chaos that engulfed Egypt in the 1870s was not, however, due exclusively to European chicanery. The Civil War in the United States brought a trebling of cotton prices and also deprived English mills of cotton grown in the Southern states. The Egyptian governor of this period, Ismail Pasha, in an attempt to Europeanize Egypt, constructed a large system of canals, railroads, bridges, harbors, and telegraph facilities, and brought over a million acres of land back into cultivation. He did much of this on the assumption that cotton prices would remain high. Many of the contracts with foreign construction firms were made on highly unfavorable terms, the Egyptian administration being very corrupt. The spending extravaganza, coupled with the end of the U.S. Civil War and the consequent dive of cotton prices, put Egypt in an impossible position. The external debt of Egypt had reached over £70 million by the time the Suez Canal opened, as opposed to about £3 million six years earlier. Thus, an increasing proportion of the government's revenue went directly to foreign debt repayment—about 60 percent in 1875. In that year the British government bought the Egyptian shares in the Canal for £4 million, in what amounted to a liquidation sale. Egypt was now bankrupt and faced with the prospect of total foreign ownership of the Suez Canal. By 1876 British and French officials were overseeing Egyptian and Ottoman finances in order to protect European interests.

To improve Egypt's finances, the puppet governor Tawfiq imposed an austere fiscal policy that led to an army rebellion in 1882. This gave the British ample excuse for drastic action to protect their investments. At the "official request" of Tawfiq, British forces invaded Egypt, crushed the rebellion, and settled in for the next seventy-five years. The official British position in Egypt was awkward, however. Although they had been invited to enter at the governor's request, they nevertheless owned the Suez Canal, which in turn was situated in a province of the Ottoman Empire. This ambiguous situation was to persist until Egypt was declared a British protectorate in 1914.

Britain had an excellent reason for wanting to control Egypt: the Suez Canal shortened the route between England and India by 4,000 miles. The occupation of Egypt, however, burdened the English with the usual geopolitical anxieties. The security of the Red Sea, and thereby the Arabian peninsula, became vital. The Levant and the Sudan also had to be dealt with if security was to be assured. The latter two problems were solved by convincing the Ottoman sultan to cede the Sinai peninsula to Egypt (1906) and by establishing a joint Anglo-Egyptian force to reimpose rule over the Sudan (1898). Britain entered the twentieth century with a firm foothold in Egypt.

THE LEVANT

Muhammad Ali's control of the Levant during the 1830s forms a watershed in the history of the area. The reforms introduced and the subsequent European penetration has been aptly called "the Opening of South Lebanon." In the decades before the Egyptian incursion, the population of the interior, if not the coast, looked eastward when they were looking outside their immediate area at all. European trade had been on the decline, and Europeans were treated with a xenophobic hostility when they did manage to gain access to the area. The area had a relatively sparse population (about 1,300,000), rapacious Ottoman governors, and a highly insecure hinterland. However, the urban population, about half of the total, had learned to live with the situation by developing a relatively closed system of production and distribution.

The modernized, Western-oriented Egyptian army radically altered this situation. Security of travel was greatly enhanced; life in the cities became more secure; and most important, a wave of European commercial interests quickly entered and dominated economic life. By the time of the Egyptian withdrawal, Syria was looking to the West for trade; the indigenous craftsmen had to shoulder the brunt of the change because their nonstandardized, low-quality, high-priced goods could no longer find a local market. The process continued after the Egyptian departure.

Western ascendency was given a further boost in 1858 when the Maronites created a crisis in Lebanon by declaring it a republic. Under Ottoman rule, the **Druze**, Sunni Muslims, and **Maronite** Christians had achieved an uneasy balance. The Tanzimat declaration of equality for all non-Muslims in the empire had already aroused Muslim antipathy. In 1860 the situation worsened and erupted into large-scale religious massacres. Because they had long-standing interests there, the French landed troops under the pretext of giving aid to the Ottomans and calmed the situation. An autonomous Lebanon, limited to the mountains and not including the coastal areas, was established. A Catholic Christian governor was to administer the area and maintain a local militia. The Ottomans maintained only titular control and effectively abandoned the area. Thus the French, and a host of Christian missionaries, gained a base of operations in the Middle East.

THE ARABIAN PENINSULA

In the history of the world's major religions, circumstances occasionally allow strong revivalist movements to form and flourish. The Middle East in the nineteenth century provided the right circumstances for Islam. The **Sanussi** movement in Libya, the rise of the Mahdists in the Sudan, and the Wahhabi movement in Arabia were three of the most important.

Muhammad Ibn Abd-al-Wahhab (1691-1787) spread his message during the latter part of the eighteenth century. He was convinced that the strict, austere Hanbali law was superior to the other three sanctioned Sunni schools of law and that Islam had deviated from its true path. He criticized especially the Sufi (and pre-Islamic) custom of venerating saints by worshipping at their tombs, which he thought to be idolatry. Abd-al-Wahhab spread his word throughout the **Najd** region of Arabia; in time he converted a powerful tribal ruler, Ibn Saud, who spread the doctrine and his rule over great stretches of Arabia.

The Ottomans long had controlled the coastal Hijaz and the holy cities of Mecca and Medina. From there, Ottoman rule arched out over what is now Jordan and extended south to the al-Hassa area of Arabia on the Persian Gulf. It is likely that the Wahhabis would have been left undisturbed in the great desert areas if their religious beliefs had allowed them to adhere to geopolitical boundaries. But this was not to be the case. They declared that those who practiced the idolatry of saint worship were infidels and, as such, deserved death. By 1803 the grandson of Ibn Saud controlled the Hijaz, including Mecca and Medina. The tombs were destroyed, and many worshippers were put to death. The Ottoman authorities, of course, could not tolerate a renegade force holding two of the most holy cities of Islam, but lacked the means to expel them. It was not until Muhammad Ali consolidated his strength in Egypt that an attempt was made to beat back the Wahhabi movement. The first Egyptian forces were dispatched to Arabia in 1811; however, the armies of Ibn Saud were not pushed deep into the interior, until the Egyptian campaign of 1818–1820.

For the remainder of the century the interior of Arabia passed back and forth between the authority of the Ottoman-backed Rashids and the forces of the Saud family. It was only in 1902 that a small band of Saudi forces raided Riyadh, the seat of Rashid power, and began to assume control of most of what is now Saudi Arabia (with the exception of the Hijaz, which remained under Ottoman control). Saudi power was more or less consolidated by the beginning of World War I.

Nineteenth-century European interests in the Arabian peninsula centered on trade and communications; therefore they concentrated on securing the safety of the coastal areas. The British were seeking greater control in the area in order to defend India from possible encroachments by the French, Russians, and Germans.

Napoleon's invasion of Egypt in 1798 brought a swift reaction. In addition to Nelson's destruction of the French fleet off Alexandria, the British took Perim Island (1799), which lies between Africa and Arabia in the narrow southern inlet to the Red Sea. Because they lacked supplies, especially water, they were quickly forced to abandon the island and withdraw to Aden, a port area long known and used by the British in their East India dealings. The British reluctantly made Aden a permanent outpost as event after event dictated their presence; they would retain control of Aden until 1967.

What Westerners call the Persian Gulf (and the Arabians call the Arabian Gulf) came early under British control with the taking of the Straits of Hormuz in 1622. (A glance at a map reveals that whoever controls the Straits of Hormuz controls all traffic in and out of the Persian Gulf. Since about 50 percent of the world's petroleum now passes through the strait, the area is vitally important.) To the British in the seventeenth century, the security of Hormuz and the ability to insure safe passage through the Gulf was important because they needed a quick line of communications to India. The route around the Cape of Good Hope was long and risky, and the Red Sea was under uncertain Ottoman control until the British intervened in Egypt in 1882. The next best route from India to England was to sail to what is now Kuwait and then travel overland through Basra and Baghdad.

By the 1830s the British had largely suppressed piracy on the Persian Gulf through military forays and treaties with the coastal powers. Later in the century they thwarted other European trade schemes in the Middle East by entering into treaties with local rulers which prohibited trade or other dealings with any other foreigners without British approval. The most notable of these agreements was the one made with Kuwait in 1899.

In the nineteenth century, then, British Gulf policy changed from simply establishing a line of communications within the empire to defending it. British control of Egypt and the Suez Canal relieved them from having to penetrate the interior of Iraq in order to protect their communication lines. German influence in the Ottoman Empire gave them reason to go on the defensive. The Germans gained a concession in 1899 to build a railroad through Ottoman territories in the Middle East. By the beginning of World War I, the Constantinople-Baghdad portion of the line was complete. But by as early as 1900, the ruler of Kuwait, in accordance with the recent British treaty, had refused the Germans permission to build a terminal on the Gulf.

Events, however, finally forced the British to push into Iraq. In 1907 petroleum was discovered in the Abadan area of Iran, and there was some evidence that nearby Iraq would hold equally important fields. Another chapter of Middle Eastern history was beginning to unfold.

IRAN

Although all of the nation states in this area are special cases in many ways, Iran stands apart from them all. Because of its political, social, and cultural differences, and because of its geographical position, Iran's relationship with the Middle East proper has waxed and waned over the centuries.

During the eighteenth and nineteenth centuries, Persia was subject to less European influence than Egypt or the Levant. European commercial interest, of course, had become well established during the preceding centuries, but the full-scale economic, military, and philosophical thrusts of the West had not yet penetrated to the heart of the Persian system. Yet Persia's nationalist sentiments—generally reactions against foreign domination that are expressed in mass movements—in some ways presaged those in other parts of the Middle East. This seeming contradiction is not yet fully understood, but it is clear that important aspects of Persian society included such elements as official social classes, power relationships designed to increase insecurity and mistrust, and the central place of the Shiite clergy.

From Sassanian times on, the social structure of Iran has consisted, with some exceptions, of four major groups: (1) the royal family, (2) the political and military bureaucracy, (3) the religious establishment, and (4) the masses. Although some outstanding individual cases helped promote a popular belief in easy social mobility, shifts from one class to another were relatively infrequent. Widespread belief in the possibility of upward mobility, of course, enabled the ruling class to promise the less fortunate a chance to enjoy a better life. But in such a system, downward mobility is just as possible; favored positions were therefore jealously protected. Desirable posts were usually procured by some form of money payment, or bribe, indicating that accumulated wealth was generally a prerequisite for entering and retaining a high position. Since the accumulation of wealth depended on having a good position, the system not only reduced mobility but promoted class tensions. The bureaucracy also suffered, since considerations of individual merit were often set aside. The shah presided over this system that was frought with class rivalry and predatory competition. The ruling class could move social inferiors about with relative ease and frequency as if they were chess pieces, thereby limiting any individual's or group's power and influence.

Iran had long had a Shiite majority. Traditionally, the Shiites had opposed any secular authority because of their belief that the betrayal of Ali had given rise to a series of illegitimate rulers. While waiting for the return of the Hidden Imam, who will set the world on the correct path again, the Shiites believed that the clergy had an obligation to examine all secular actions and make them consistent with Islamic thought. Since interpreting the correct path of state and religious affairs depended on specialized scholarly wisdom and knowledge, a loose hierarchy of clerical authority developed in Iran that was lacking in Sunni Islam. Since most secular authorities are unwilling to submit to higher authorities, an understandable tension developed between government officials and clergy. And since the clergy had the ear of the masses, any secular ruler had to be careful and restrained in dealings with the clergy.

Bazaar merchants have traditionally been important sources of discontent and have led opposition movements in the Middle East; but in Persia, they were subject to the same insecurities that shackled the bureaucrats and the military. The clergy, through their spokesmen, the **mujahids** (learned religious leaders with successful ministries), were the only group not under the shah's direct control.

The Qajar Dynasty

The Qajar dynasty (1779–1925) came to power about fifty years after the fall of the Safavid Empire. At first, the Qajars were extremely brutal in their attempts to consolidate power. Once they had established a reasonable degree of control over the various tribes, however, they then had to face the emerging threat from the West. By the 1850s, two major Western actors—England and Russia—had forced Persia into the arena of Western politics. The British feared that a Russian advance southward would ultimately threaten India. The Russians had long desired access to the Indian Ocean—as they still do today.

The Qajars seem to have seen the need for radical bureaucratic and military reforms, but their actions were no more than superficial palliatives. Shah Nasiruddin's rise to power (1848–1896) roughly marks the beginning of the reform movement; the Persian elite began to realize that the Western powers could not be banished but would have to be accommodated. The last half of the century saw numerous intrigues between the British, Russians, and occasionally the French, as they entered into agreements over their respective roles in Persia, broke the agreements, and then hammered out new ones. The shah, meanwhile, in order to maintain Persian independence, was attempting to play off one power against the other and create a stalemate between them.

To accomplish this, and to build up the treasury, the Qajar rulers during this period began to grant concessions to Europeans. In essence, a European adventurer-entrepreneur would pay a sum of money to obtain a monopoly in some sphere of economic activity. The concessionaire would then return home to sell shares in the new company to speculators and thereby turn a profit. The rulers granting these concessions welcomed European money because it absolved them from having to impose heavier taxes on an already restive population. They also hoped that they could check European power by granting concessions to individuals of different nationalities, that the Europeans would see the need for political security and stability in Persia so as to protect profits, and they would also introduce some industrial development to boot. To be successful, such a policy called for a finely tuned balance of forces. The concessionaires, however, often played fast and loose with contracts, and the ruling elite were increasingly concerned with shoring up royal revenues.

The 1872 concession drawn up by the grand vizier for Baron Julius de Reuter, a British citizen, is a spectacular example of the sorry state of Qajar affairs. The concession gave de Reuter a monopoly over railways, mines (excepting precious metals and stones), irrigation construction, and all future factories, telegraph lines, road construction, and for twenty-five years, the proceeds of customs collections. In return, the royal purse was to be increased by a small flat payment and a share of the profits of the various ventures. In short, the country had been sold, and sold very cheaply. The reaction against this outrageous concession was swift in coming. Protests erupted from the Russians, members of the royal court, the clergy, and nationalistic groups. The combination of international pressure and internal discontent forced the shah to cancel the concession on a technicality.

This was not the end of concession granting, however. The British continued to make inroads, the most significant being the rights to form a national bank and to navigate the Karun River and the granting of a tobacco monopoly. The tobacco concession (1890), following on the heels of the bank and river navigation concessions, was to be complete—from the growing of the tobacco to export sales. Again, Russian reaction was strongly negative. Internal reactions led by a domestic coalition (which was to surface periodically throughout the twentieth century) signaled the beginnings of the drive for a constitution.

Under the inspiration of the remarkable **Jemal al-din al-Afghani**, who was active all over the Middle East as a proponent of pan-Islamic policies, a coalition was formed of merchants, clergy, and intellectuals, many of the latter having a Western orientation. The intellectuals and mujahids were able to set aside their fundamental disagreements in the face of their common hatred of what they viewed as the selling of Persia. The Russian government gave material and moral support to the coalition.

As this dissatisfaction grew into a countrywide protest—ironically coordinated through the use of the British telegraph system—and tottered on the brink of revolution, it became clear that the reaction against the tobacco concession was part of a larger hatred toward all foreign concessions and, thereby, the policies of the Qajar regime. Facing the prospect of revolution, the shah canceled the tobacco concession in 1892.

The "tobacco riots" and the cancellation of the tobacco concession had far-reaching implications for the subsequent history of Persia. For the first time, a nationwide protest against the policies of the regime, spearheaded by the relatively independent and very powerful clergy, had immobilized the government. The internal coalition formed the backbone of the movements that later resulted in the granting of the 1906 constitution and the overthrow of the Pahlevi dynasty in 1978-1979. More immediate effects included a decade of Russian ascendancy in Persia, the slowing of concession-granting to foreigners, and the beginnings of the same kind of disastrous debt policy that brought so many woes to Egypt and the Ottoman Empire in previous decades.

The shah was forced to pay a sizable compensation to the tobacco concessioners. Because he lacked requisite funds, the British provided a loan. The Russians, fearing a reassertion of British influence, also provided loans, thereby tightening the financial noose. In this respect, Persia was closing the gap between it and other Middle Eastern countries by the beginning of the twentieth century. On the other hand, it received little benefit from foreign intrusion due to the conditions of the intervention, the corrupt, obsolete government structure, and the relationship between the various social classes.

Further British inroads were made with the award of a petroleum concession in 1901, the discovery of petroleum in 1908, and the British government's purchase of most of the shares in the resulting oil company in 1913, a few weeks before the beginning of World War I. The weakness of the Qajar dynasty, and growing fears of expansionist Germany, also led the British and Russians to formalize an often-breached agreement that divided Persia into spheres of influence: the Russians were to have the North and the British the South, with a neutral strip in between.

The Qajar dynasty limped along until the conclusion of World War I, but its power rested on a weak base. Riots in 1905-1906, led again by the mujahids with the support of modernizers and merchants, forced the granting of a constitution (1906) and the formation of a consultative assembly, the *Majlis*. Although the assembly initiated a series of reforms, intrigues by the rulers and international powers, internal dissension in the Majlis, and economic recession mitigated against a full-blown democratic and modernizing movement.

During World War I the Allies viewed Persia as a vital conduit through which to supply materiel to Russia. Due to the success of the Russian Revolution of 1917, the Bolsheviks renounced the Tsarist claims in the 1907 Anglo-Russian agreement. The British then moved northward and assumed almost total control of Persia. Shortly after this, they withdrew from the Caspian Sea area, and the Soviets invaded the port of Enzeli. The Iranian Soviet Socialist Republic of Gilan was formed in 1920, but the Soviet Union withdrew its support for it less than a year later and the republic failed. In this chaotic swirl of events, Reza Shah came to power.

Reza Shah led the Russian-trained Cossack Brigade, one of the few, if not the only, effective military units in the Persian army. He assumed power on February 26, 1921, named himself commander-in-chief of the military, and appointed an intellectual ally as prime minister. As Reza Shah gathered more power, he dismissed the prime minister in 1923. In 1925 he ascended to the throne and took the ancient and kingly Persian name of Pahlevi.

Reza Shah was an extraordinary modernizer and autocrat who faced the formidable tasks of establishing internal order, lessening foreign domination, and establishing Iran as a modern nation. The Majlis continued to function under his rule. Indeed, his taking of the Peacock throne was confirmed by a vote of the Majlis and by an amendment to the constitution, but the Majlis failed to fulfill the hopes of those opposed to autocratic rule in that it merely rubber-stamped Reza Shah's policies rather than evolving into an independent legislative body. The shah promoted divisiveness among those on the periphery of power. This created insecurity, fragmented the opposition, and convulsed the machinery of government. Acting along the lines of Muhammad Ali in Egypt a century earlier and his contemporary Atatürk, the shah developed a series of reforms to lessen the power of the clergy and increase his own. He also laid the foundation for a modern economy by constructing an improved communications network and instituting educational reforms.

Because of the shah's flirtation with Germany during the 1930s, culminating in his refusal to join the Allied cause at the outset of World War II, the 1907 Anglo-Russian accord was renewed, the British protecting their petroleum interests in the South and the Russians controlling the North. To save the throne, Reza Shah abdicated to his son, Mohammed Reza Pahlevi.

CONCLUSION

Nineteenth-century Middle Eastern history was dominated by the tidal wave of European power that swamped and distorted every society it touched. Although the procedures and timing of European penetration differed in the specific countries, there were some common features.

First, most Western inroads were made with reference to European geopolitical rivalries. It was not until the twentieth century that the Europeans (and the United States) seriously considered the economic prizes to be gained from the Middle East. During the nineteenth century the various European powers generally tried to avoid the financial and political headaches associated with direct rule; rather, they sought to establish client relationships.

Second, the general process of Western dominance had a certain inevitability due to the technical superiority and advanced organizational structure of the West. The technical revolution had been largely institutionalized in the West after centuries of cultural and scientific preparation. Military might was the most obvious manifestation of this superiority, but it was perhaps no more important than the organizational and cultural modifications that supported the technical revolution.

Third, European involvement in Middle Eastern affairs dramatically disrupted the area's society and culture. Some countries attempted to modernize themselves; others completely rejected all Western influence. All countries, however, generally recognized the technical superiority of the West and tried to avoid Western domination; however, all of them failed. The peoples of the Middle East fought a rearguard action; their policies and pronouncements tended to be protective, not affirmative. Much of the history of the Middle East in the twentieth century can be viewed as an unraveling of the consequences of nineteenth-century European domination.

5

The Rise
of the
State System
1914-1950

The period after World War I saw the decline of Western political hegemony in the Middle East. However, many events during the preceding decades paved the way. For example, the defeat of the Russians by the Japanese in 1905 was greeted with much satisfaction in the non-European world. A Western power had been humiliated at last by an Asian power. The news of the Russian defeat, together with other events, provided a needed catalyst for action in the unsettled Middle East. In Persia, the revolts of 1905-1906 severely weakened the Qajar dynasty and resulted in the establishment of a consultative assembly. In Turkey, the Young Turk revolution of 1908 sealed the fate of the Ottoman rulers. In Egypt, an incident in 1906 sparked a nationalist movement.

Each change in Ottoman policy over the decades—from pan-Islam to pan-Turkism—had a strong impact on other Arab lands. After 1908, the ethnic nationalism of the Turkish leaders became openly imperialistic. Under the millet system, an individual's nationality was not defined by geographic boundaries. An Ottoman Muslim could identify equally with all Muslims of the empire—members of his own millet. Ottoman Muslims did not consider themselves to be Turks, Iraqis, or Syrians: the words existed as historical terms or identified administrative districts. As pan-Ottomanism and then pan-Turkism weakened identification with the empire, and as Western influences filtered into the Middle East, the Arabs of the provinces began to search for a new set of symbols on which to base their identity. The Ottoman Middle East, then, was in a state of political and intellectual flux at the onset of World War I.

The strong ties between Germany and the Ottoman Empire that had developed over the preceding quarter century led to an alliance in war. The Allies had good reason to fear Ottoman entry into the war: the Ottoman military forces were reasonably strong and the truncated Ottoman Empire still posed a considerable threat to what the Allies, especially the British, perceived as their national interests. The Suez Canal and the petroleum fields of Persia were of particular importance.

Egypt was still nominally part of the Ottoman Empire until the outbreak of the war, even though British forces had occupied the country since 1882. Egypt was made a British protectorate in 1914, after England declared war on the Ottoman Empire. There was little fear for the security of Egypt from the west and south. Libya (then Tripolitania and Cyrenaica) had been invaded by the Italians in 1911 and declared a possession of Italy. However, the Italians faced continual tribal resistance, especially after their entry into the war on the Allied side prompted the Central Powers to aid the guerrillas. After members of the Sanussi, a largely rural religious movement, were beaten back after moving to attack Egypt, the fractious Libyan resistance became ineffective. The Sudan had been administered by the joint Anglo-Egyptian condominium since 1898-1899 and caused little concern.

The Arab lands of the Hijaz and (Greater) Syria posed the most significant threat to the security of Egypt and the Persian Gulf. Two basic concerns faced the Allies: The Ottoman military threat and the closely related, but distinct, question of the attitudes of the local Arab leaders.

The military concern was realized early on both the Egyptian and Persian Gulf fronts. By early 1915 Ottoman forces had reached the Suez Canal and Ottoman supporters had disrupted the flow of petroleum from Persia. There followed a long and bitter struggle by the British to beat back the enemy. After sustaining very heavy losses the British entered Baghdad by March, 1917. The British pushed through Palestine, taking Jerusalem in December, 1917. An armistice was reached only in October, 1918. By then the British had pushed toward Homs and Aleppo. The "sick man" of Europe had waged a brave and tenacious battle.

With the military balance in doubt until the end of the war, the Allies sought aid from every available quarter. This led to a series of secret agreements and overt pledges that helped swing the outcome in their favor; but these same pacts contained fundamental contradictions, some of which have not yet been resolved.

The McMahon-Husein Correspondence

At the onset of the war an immediate Allied concern was how the people in the Ottoman provinces would react to the coming call for a jihad by the sultan-caliph. Obviously, an Arab revolt against the Ottomans would aid the Allied war effort in the Middle Eastern front. There were reasons to suppose that conditions were ripe for such a revolt. The key figure to be won over was Sherif Husein, sherif of Mecca and emir of the Hijaz. The British high commissioner in Egypt, Sir Arthur Henry McMahon, contacted Husein, hoping to persuade him to sever his already strained relationship with the Ottoman Empire.

The McMahon-Husein correspondence (July 14, 1915, to January 30, 1916) set the terms for an Arab revolt. In return for entering the war on the Allied side, Husein was assured that a large stretch of Ottoman-Arab territory would be made independent under his leadership at the conclusion of the war: it included the Hijaz and what now is Syria, Iraq, and Jordan. He had first demanded that other territories be included, but allowed his claims to lapse on what now is the non-Hijaz portion of Saudi Arabia, Lebanon, and areas extending northward into Turkey. The fate of Palestine was left somewhat ambiguous in the correspondence: After the war, the British seized this ambiguity to press their claim that Palestine was not part of the agreement.

Husein's silence to the call for a jihad was transformed into a call for an Arab revolt. Although the revolt did not produce anything resembling a mass movement, it brought relief to the Allies. The crack Ottoman troops stationed in the Yemen were isolated in Medina and between the Hijaz and British-dominated Aden, and the people of Syria found cause to retaliate against the brutality of their Ottoman rulers.

The British also made an agreement with Ibn Saud, recognizing his rule in the non-Hijaz area of what is now Saudi Arabia, allowed for a formal recognition of Kuwait, and entered into agreements that essentially called for the Persian Gulf peoples to cooperate with the British without forcing them to take up arms in the actual conduct of the war.

British success in promoting the Arab revolt by promises of independence did not prevent them from completing negotiations with the French and the Russians (who repudiated its claims after the 1917 revolution) that created a new division of Western influence in the Middle East. The Sykes-Picot Agreement (1915–16) allowed the French control of the Levant coastal area and the right to oversee the interior of Syria. The British were to receive what is now most of Iraq and Jordan. Palestine was to become an international zone. The terms of this agreement were revealed to Husein by the Russians during the war, but the British managed to calm his fears by minimizing the document's importance. However, this agreement formed the basis of the postwar division of British and French areas of domination. The Allies entered into other agreements that defined areas of influence or rule throughout the rest of the region. As with the Sykes-Picot Agreement, the Allies were able to dictate terms that would expand their influence after the war. These agreements were to cause much frustration and bitterness.

The Balfour Declaration

Although the disposition of Palestine was unclear under the McMahon-Husein agreement, it seemed most likely that it would become an independent Arab state. The Sykes-Picot agreement called for Palestine to become internationalized. After the British issued the famous Balfour Declaration on November 2, 1917, the fate of Palestine was unclear. The declaration, sent by Lord Balfour to Lord Rothschild, must be quoted in full:

> I have much pleasure in conveying to you on behalf of His Majesty's Government the following declaration of sympathy with Jewish Zionist aspirations, which has been submitted and approved by the cabinet:
> His Majesty's Government view with favor the establishment in Palestine of a National Home for the Jewish People, and will use their best endeavors to facilitate the achievement of this object, it being clearly understood that nothing shall be done which may prejudice the civil and religious rights of existing non-Jewish communities in Palestine, or the rights and political status enjoyed by Jews in any other country.
> I should be grateful if you would bring this declaration to the knowledge of the Zionist Federation.

The carefully constructed ambiguity of the statement was designed to elicit Jewish support for the Allies without alienating the Arabs. It succeeded in the former but failed in the latter, and thus added another layer of misunderstanding to the growing dilemma.

Palestine, the Holy Land of the Bible, had always had Jews among its population. But it was not until the last two decades of the nineteenth century that substantial numbers of Jews emigrated to Palestine from Europe. Many European Jews were motivated by the ethnic nationalism that had spread throughout Europe in the nineteenth century and was now beginning to take hold in other areas. But wherever they lived, the Jewish people were a small minority, a minority that had frequently endured extreme physical brutality and systematic social and economic discrimination. While their situation was not always desperate in Christian Europe, it was always insecure. Whether or not the Jews could or should be assimilated into their European countries of residence, therefore, was a central question for Jewish leaders. Many of them began to believe that the Jews were entitled to self-determination. However, to enjoy this, the Jewish people would have to have their own political entity, a separate state. The trickle of Jews who settled in Palestine before the turn of the century came primarily from Russia and Poland (the great majority fled to Western Europe and the United States). Those who emigrated to Palestine did so for many reasons—religious, secular, socialistic, and personal. All, however, sought a better life.

The World Zionist Organization

The idea of creating a special homeland for the Jewish people originated with Theodor Herzl (1860-1904). After covering the Dreyfus trial (1895) as a correspondent, Herzl became convinced that as long as they remained a minority people, Jews would always suffer periods of deprivation. His book, *The Jewish State* (1896), aroused enough interest to warrant calling the first World Zionist Congress, which was held in Basel, Switzerland, in 1897. The congress created the World Zionist Organization and called for the formation of a Jewish homeland in Palestine. The movement spread quickly throughout Western and Eastern Europe. However, Palestine had not been a unified area under the Ottomans; rather, it had been divided into two provinces, with the area around Jerusalem enjoying a special status.

During the nineteenth century, millions of Europeans were emigrating to new lands in various parts of the world; the Jewish call for a homeland in Palestine was therefore not unique in that regard. Zionist leaders, however, believed mistakenly that hardly any local people would be displaced since most of Palestine was relatively empty. Moreover, they believed that what people were there were of such a low culture that they could only benefit from contact with sophisticated Europeans.

The World Zionist Organization financed and organized a substantial wave of immigration to Palestine in the decade before World War I. By 1914, about 85,000 Jews were living in Palestine, three times the number thirty years earlier; however, they comprised less than 15 percent of the total population, most of which was Arab. Jews were still a small minority even in Palestine, but they were a highly organized and growing minority. A settler's life was often difficult, and a number of settlements failed for lack of farming experience, harsh agricultural conditions, and a host of other conditions. But the settlements generally succeeded. It should be remembered that, however loosely it was controlled, Palestine was still part of the Ottoman Empire, and the settlers were subject to Ottoman law and administration. For example, Ottoman law did not always allow noncitizens to own land. A complex system of third-party land ownership had to be worked out. Also, Russian Jews were often singled out for harsh treatment because Russia was an Ottoman enemy.

With the beginning of World War I, the Ottomans imposed systematically harsh treatment on all Jews in Palestine. Wartime dislocations and a failed harvest compounded the woes of all residents—Muslim, Christian, and Jewish alike. By the time of the Balfour Declaration, the Jewish population had declined to about 55,000. Given these deteriorating conditions, Zionist leaders saw their vision of an independent Jewish state rapidly recede. The war posed difficult problems for them. Jewish leaders were not sure that supporting the Allied cause would improve the position of world Jewry or further the goal of creating a Jewish homeland. Germany, in fact, had recently improved conditions for Jews and created a better environment for them than had any other country in Europe. Seeing that Jews would have a difficult time wherever they lived, and seeing widespread anti-Semitism in the Allied countries, the Zionist leaders gave the Allies only half-hearted support.

The Allied powers, however, were facing enormous difficulties during the war and needed Jewish financial support. Dr. Chaim Weizmann, a Manchester University chemist with connections to high-ranking officials in England (due to his war-related research) and a Zionist leader, pressed the Zionist cause with the British. Zionists in other Allied countries were doing the same. Finally an agreement was reached which culminated in the Balfour Declaration.

THE MANDATES

The Allies were well aware that the contradictory agreements made during World War I were going to be difficult to resolve. After the war, the British and Americans urged the formation of a commission to ascertain the wishes of the local populations. The French, however, rejected the idea and insisted that the Sykes-Picot Agreement be carried out. The British suspected the French of wanting to establish a firm foothold in the Middle East and tried to change the terms of the agreement. An understanding was reached in September, 1919: Mosul would eventually be appended to Iraq rather than Syria, Palestine would come under British control, British troops would leave Syria, and the French would be compensated with a share of the Turkish Petroleum Company.

Syria and Lebanon

A son of Husein, Faisal, led the Arab revolt against the Ottomans and captured Damascus near the end of the war. He correctly foresaw France's intentions in Syria, but underestimated the extent to which Palestinian nationalism had flowered during the war. He was more concerned with the French than the Zionists. Consequently, he entered into negotiations with the Zionist leaders, seeking their aid in

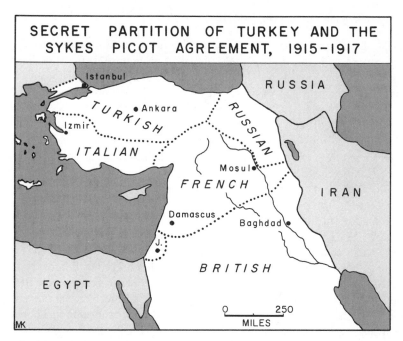

SECRET PARTITION OF TURKEY AND THE SYKES PICOT AGREEMENT, 1915–1917

Istanbul

Ankara

RUSSIA

TURKISH

RUSSIAN

Izmir

ITALIAN

Mosul

FRENCH

IRAN

Damascus

Baghdad

J.

BRITISH

EGYPT

0   250
MILES

Secret Partition of Turkey and the Sykes-Picot Agreement, 1915–1917. *Source*: Yahya Armajani, *Middle East Past and Present,* ©1970, p. 304. Reprinted by permission of Prentice-Hall, Inc., Englewood Cliffs, N.J.

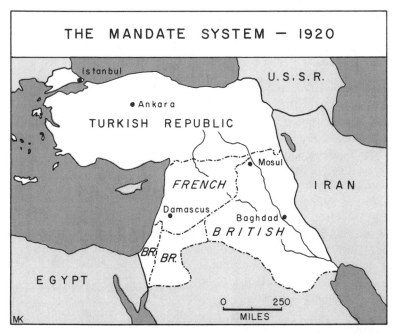

THE MANDATE SYSTEM — 1920

Istanbul

U.S.S.R.

Ankara

TURKISH REPUBLIC

Mosul

FRENCH

IRAN

Damascus

Baghdad

BRITISH

BR.   BR.

EGYPT

0   250
MILES

The Mandate System, 1920. *Source*: Yahya Armajani, *Middle East Past and Present,* ©1970, p. 304. Reprinted by permission of Prentice-Hall, Inc., Englewood Cliffs, N.J.

thwarting France; in return he accepted the legitimacy of Zionist aspirations. The French accord with the British placed Faisal in an impossible position. Since his agreement with the Zionists was conditional on the granting of Syrian independence, he repudiated the pact and was declared by the Arab Congress to be king of Syria and Palestine in March, 1920. The French protected their claim to Syria by seizing on Faisal's failure to reply to an ultimatum calling for the acceptance of the mandate; the French brought in troops from Lebanon and routed Faisal. Faisal had, in fact, sent a telegram of capitulation to the French, but it was apparently too late to stop the troops.

The Syrians of the interior were quite hostile to the French invasion; France responded with firm political and military action. To win over the Lebanese elite, France quadrupled the area of Lebanon. To fragment the anti-French nationalistic movement, Syria was split into separate autonomous administrative districts. Although Syrian administration was centralized after about a year, the French found that this cosmetic remedy did not solve their problems. The hostility of the Syrian population required France to maintain a military presence and suppress all political activity. Damascus was shelled on several occasions. Direct French rule was also imposed on Lebanon. Although there was considerable opposition in Lebanon, it did not rival that in Syria. However, the new, enlarged Lebanon now included areas populated by Muslim Arabs; the delicate balance of political, ethnic, and religious groups was upset, and tensions between the various indigenous groups occasionally spilled over into violence.

British and Free French forces invaded Lebanon and Syria in 1941 to wrest them away from Vichy France. When it appeared that the French would renege on their promises of independence at the end of the war, the British forced them to withdraw. Lebanon and Syria finally achieved political independence.

Iraq and Transjordan

The expulsion of Faisal from Syria in 1920 left the British in a particularly delicate position. The wartime promises made to Faisal's father, along with Faisal's widespread popular support, spelled increased instability and a loss of British influence. The British responded by engineering the election of Faisal as king of Iraq and by creating another area, Transjordan, where they installed Faisal's brother, Abdullah, as emir. The government of British India had supplied troops and administrators to Iraq during World War I. When the League of Nations gave Britain a mandate over Iraq instead of granting independence, widespread insurrection broke out. After a particularly bloody campaign to restore order, the British sought to install a friendly ruler and therefore selected Faisal in July, 1921. In 1922 Iraq was given a special status, and in 1930 it was granted nominal independence, with a continuing British military and administrative presence. The British, however, retained their preeminent position in Iraq for another quarter century.

Transjordan had been carved out of the new British mandate of Palestine. Abdullah had been made emir to mollify Husein and to keep him from invading Syria in revenge for his brother's defeat. By splitting the mandate, the British hoped to defuse Palestinian nationalism. In fact, British policy won the enmity of both

Arabs and Zionists who were seeking control of Palestine. Transjordan was an extremely poor and sparsely populated country and did not have a strong current of nationalism. It attained formal independence in 1946, but remained dependent on British and United States aid. It was, in short, a client state.

Generally, Britain's policy of indirect rule in Iraq and Transjordan better prepared those countries for independence than France's direct rule in Syria. This is not to imply that British policy was particularly far-sighted; although they were swayed by Wilsonian notions of self-determination, the British were weary of war and no longer wished to continue the heavy financial burden of direct rule. But by staying in the background, the British allowed the area's indigenous people to educate themselves for self-government and adapt to technological change. On the other hand, the French, ever fearful of increasing local power, kept their subjects politically and technologically ignorant.

A national consciousness—determined by the boundaries drawn by Europeans—began to form during the interwar years in Syria, Iraq, and Transjordan. The people who had for so long traveled between Baghdad, Damascus, and Amman with no sense of being in foreign cities were now beginning to observe the new international borders. However, passports were not the only things that kept Iraqis, Syrians, and Jordanians estranged from each other. Iraqis and Syrians had learned different European languages, worked with incompatible technologies (the electric system being a prime example), and started to perceive themselves as being of different nationalities.

EGYPT

The long-time (1883-1907) consul general of Egypt, Lord Cromer, brought financial order and economic progress to Egypt by establishing a highly effective administrative system and by major projects such as the first Aswan Dam. The nominal Egyptian rulers (and their even more nominal Ottoman rulers) were at the mercy of the British, but they had little reason to complain. Although the British controlled Egypt, they viewed their stay as temporary, brought order out of chaos, and prevented the nationalism of the urban intellectuals from gathering much steam. A 1906 incident in which British officers shot one villager and hung three others touched off deep nationalist and anti-British feelings. The British then began to make very limited concessions to nationalist demands for political representation and participation. These all but stopped when Egypt became a British protectorate in 1914.

Immediately after World War I, Saad Zaghlul, a nationalist and a respected administrator, asked the British for permission to circulate a petition for Egyptian independence. After they refused, he organized an independence movement. The British arrested and deported him in 1919. Riots followed, and after a time the British began to relent on some issues. Because of the weakness of the official "puppet" government and the considerable size of Zaghlul's following, the British decided to negotiate with him personally. But their concessions did not satisfy him or the other nationalists. After negotiations broke down, the British tried to maintain civil order by unilaterally declaring Egypt to be independent on February 28, 1922. The declaration contained, however, four "absolutely reserved" clauses in which the British retained control over areas they deemed vital to their interests: (1) the Sudan—and with it, the Nile River, (2) all foreigners and minorities in Egypt, (3) the communications system, and (4) Egyptian defense.

After returning from a second British-imposed exile, Zaghlul saw his Wafd party win a sweeping victory in September, 1923, in a parliament that had been recently declared by the king. Zaghlul was then asked to form a new government. Because the British refused to back down on any of their four conditions, he saw no point in organizing a government. More riots followed. The assassination of a key British official, Sir Lee Stack, prompted fierce British reprisals, and the nationalist movement declined. By the late 1920s, the movement was in disarray. In 1936, the Eyptian government signed a treaty with Britain based on the 1922 declaration of independence and the revision of the four clauses: The British high commissioner would leave, British troops would be restricted to the Suez Canal Zone, and the capitulations (regarding the special status of foreigners) would eventually end. The 1936 agreement was prompted by British and Egyptian fears arising from Mussolini's invasion of Ethiopia (1935), the death of King Fuad, the accession of King Farouk (a quiet and ambivalent nationalist sympathizer in those days), and the relatively quiescent state of the nationalist movement.

With the beginning of World War II, the British felt it necessary to reassert their control over Egypt. The country virtually became an Allied base for the duration of the war. Since many of the Egyptian political elite had pro-Axis leanings, the British intervened in Egyptian politics, especially in the selection of political leaders. The local Egyptian authorities were reluctant to take up arms against Britain's enemies: the British had humiliated the Egyptian nationalists whereas the Germans and Italians had not. As with the conclusion of World War I, Egyptian nationalism entered the post-World-War-II era with renewed vigor.

The Egyptian political struggles since 1882 had been three-sided and unevenly matched. Basically, the aspirants to political power, the nationalists, were strong enough not to be ignored, but weak enough to be manipulated between the British and the monarchy. The position of the king was delicate. He supported the nationalist cause to some degree to convince the British that the ruling elite would maintain civil order if power devolved to it after independence; on the other hand, he opposed the nationalist cause when it seemed to be getting strong enough to threaten the monarchy. For their part, the British discouraged nationalist causes that the king advocated and approved the causes when the king seemed to be getting too much power. The nationalists made only modest gains for several reasons: They advocated reform, not revolution; they were mostly members of the middle class; and various factions had been weakened by being played off against each other.

The first modern nationalist movement in Egypt had resulted in the 1882 British invasion. The nationalists had been jolted into action then by the financial collapse of the Egyptian government and the exploitative policies of Britain and France. Nationalists had gathered strength during the following decades, only to see their gains swept away by the British takeover during World War I. They again pressed their claims immediately after the war, gained some measure of self-rule, but then fell victims again to imperialist power. The trauma of World War II, another event that was basically a European affair, alerted the nationalists to the insufficiency of their past gains.

The Wafd Party and the Muslim Brotherhood

The nationalist groups in Egypt during the interwar period were of various persuasions, but they all saw the British as a common enemy. The two most important movements were the Wafd party and the Muslim Brotherhood. The popular Wafd party of Zaghlul was a secular reformist movement, one which basically accepted British ideas of representative government and, thereby, could accuse the British of perverting their own stated ideals. The Muslim Brotherhood, founded in 1928 by Hasan al-Bana, expressed its hatred of British domination by calling for a return to Islamic fundamentals, including the formation of an Islamic government. Estimates of its membership in the late 1930s range up to a million. The message of the Brotherhood was disarmingly clear: the wretched condition of the masses, the venal behavior of the elite, and the general degradation of their common heritage were due to the acceptance of Western ways. The solution to the situation was equally clear: get rid of the Westerners and their puppets and establish an order that would make the Koran the constitution of the country. Although the Wafd party had considerable influence with the middle-class voting population, the Brotherhood laid out a straightforward message that appealed to the masses. The Muslim Brotherhood's strident message was feared by the establishment. Because of this perceived threat, and because of occasional assassinations by zealots, it frequently had to operate in a clandestine way. An assassination attempt on Nasser in 1954 drove the group underground, and it was declared illegal. It remains a force although the current leadership of Egypt views it as a minor irritant.

The Muslim Brotherhood represented an early twentieth-century attempt to establish a new Islamic identity after two centuries of Western exploitation. The economy of Egypt was mangled, divisions among social classes widened, and secularism was on the rise. Many observers think that the Muslim Brotherhood is naïvely fighting a rear-guard action that it will ultimately lose. While these prognostications may yet prove true, it is now clear that the success of the Brotherhood in the 1930s helped similar political forces to coalesce in such far-flung countries as Libya, Iran, Pakistan, and Indonesia.

Egypt after World War II

After World War II, socialism gained widespread popularity in the Third World. Nationalists of all persuasions were quick to adopt current socialist slogans and formulate grandiose programs. Most socialist creeds were not based primarily on Marxism or any other intellectual system. Rather, they were more a reaction against the Western private enterprise system and commercial domination. Socialist programs called for an end to the gross income disparities in society. The misery of the masses was apparent enough, and the cause of their misery was attributed to the selfishness of the local elites, who were allies of the imperialists. As young intellectuals and technical specialists absorbed these ideas, nationalist movements began to gather momentum. Broad-based nationalist parties then attempted to draw in the masses, especially those in cities, who were more sophisticated than those in rural areas.

The situation in Egypt after World War II reflected these trends. When the British resisted the Egyptian government's demands for a troop withdrawal and a renegotiation of the 1936 treaty, popular sentiment erupted into major riots in Cairo. The situation was complicated by the desperate economic conditions and the failure of the Egyptian army to prevent the formation of the state of Israel, which many Egyptians regarded as another outpost of Western imperialism. On January 26, 1952, a month after forty-three Egyptian policemen had been killed in a pitched battle with British troops in Ismailia, rampaging masses burned many Western-owned buildings in Cairo. Six months later, on July 23, 1952, a group of young army officers, including Gamal Abdel Nasser and Anwar Sadat, and Muhammad Neguib, staged an almost bloodless coup and forced King Farouk to abdicate and leave Egypt three days later. The monarchy was abolished the following June.

SAUDI ARABIA

After capturing the Rashid stronghold of Riyadh in 1902, Ibn Saud began to consolidate his rule over the interior of the Arabian peninsula. He defeated the last Rashid forces in 1921. The British were divided as to what to do about this growing tribe of religious zealots. During World War I, it had looked as if Husein would not be able to control the important Hijaz region against the hostile Wahhabi forces of Ibn Saud. The British decided to back both Husein and Ibn Saud on the condition that British financial support would be withdrawn from whatever side first attacked the other. The strategy worked through the war years but crumbled after the last Rashid power had been destroyed. For it was then that Ibn Saud could turn his attention to the birthplace of Islam.

By 1924 Husein was in a particularly vulnerable position both at home because of poor administration and abroad because he unilaterally declared himself caliph after Atatürk had abolished the title in Turkey in March, 1924. Ibn Saud's forces struck and in short order forced Husein to abdicate in favor of his son Ali, and established a protectorate of sorts over the Hijaz. In 1926 Ibn Saud was proclaimed king of the Nejd, the central area of Arabia, and in 1932 of Saudi Arabia (incorporating the Hijaz). Thus a small band of Wahhabis, led by the Saud family, had spent the whole of the nineteenth century warring for temporary power in an "inhospitable and unimportant" area and had now achieved statehood. Given the region's chronic instability and poverty, one can forgive the British and others for their inability to see Ibn Saud's potential as a leader or the significance of the nation he created.

Saudi Arabian political stability was achieved through a combination of centralization and wise leadership. Ibn Saud extended the traditional system of Bedouin rule to the nation by demanding that all significant power flow through him, by carefully adjudicating complaints, and by ensuring that those who came under his rule were treated with magnanimity. As power was consolidated and the flow of petroleum started to transform life in Saudi Arabia, an essentially ad hoc system of government evolved. Although the line separating national from local power is still ambiguous, the council of ministers that was established in 1953 clarified the areas of responsibility and took over some of the powers of the king. The system has undergone continuous revision and adjustment since 1953, with the king and royal family steadily losing power.

The evolution of Saudi Arabia's administrative system, however interesting, pales in importance when compared with the history of its petroleum revenues. In the 1930s Ibn Saud used the first trickles of oil money to subsidize and calm tribes that were reluctant to stay within the nation and to strengthen the weak financial base of the kingdom. After a time, the trickle of oil revenues became a torrent. But the kingdom still had financial troubles because there was no system of accountability. By 1962 an alarmed council of ministers (and other powerful notables) had convinced the weak King Saud, son and successor to Ibn Saud who died in 1953, to submit the country's finances to modern budgetary procedures. By this time, the activities of some members of the royal family seemed to be based more on the visions of grandeur in *The Thousand and One Nights* than on the strict tenets of Wahhabi fundamentalism. Prince Faisal became king in 1964 when King Saud was forced from power by family pressures.

TURKEY AND IRAN

The two large non-Arab countries of the Middle East, Iran and Turkey, emerged from World War I in chaos. In each country reforming autocrats came to power—Mustafa Kemal (later named Kemal Atatürk) in Turkey and Reza Shah (later Reza Shah Pahlevi) in Iran. Each gathered power and brought order to their respective countries during the interwar period. Each instituted secular, nationalist, and developmental reforms. Each became aligned with the West, especially the United States, after World War II. Each, however, followed a distinctively different path: Turkey moved unsteadily and tentatively toward Western-style democracy, while Iran continued to be ruled by one family.

The policies of secularization—both substantive and symbolic—had definite political aims: to lessen the power of the religious establishment and create a new set of allegiances. In Turkey, the new allegiance was to be the nation and democratic institutions. In Iran, the shah became the locus of power and the central symbol of the nation.

Atatürk had a habit of ramming programs through the legislature and not tolerating any significant opposition, a habit that conflicted with his populist ideal of involving the masses in political life. He encouraged opposition movements, but suppressed them as they gained strength. Since his reforms often involved "radical" secularization, they were sure to be opposed and populist ideals temporarily shelved. Indeed, Atatürk considered the policies of his party—the Grand National Assembly—to be the only correct and permissible ones. However, Atatürk was far more than a simple autocrat. He had a considerable influence on the development of democracy in Turkey. He set up democratic institutions, broke the power of the old ruling elite, patched up Turkey's international relations, brought a sense of nationhood to the country, and laid the groundwork for positive economic gains. In short, he lived up to the name bestowed on him—Atatürk, "father of the Turks."

When Atatürk died in 1938, Ismet Inonu, a long-time ally, was the natural choice of the Grand National Assembly to be the second president of the republic. With the autocratic Atatürk gone, a pent-up desire for reform gushed forth. But the reformers had to bide their time as Inonu negotiated Turkey through the years of World War II, declaring war on Germany only in 1945, when it was quite clear that the threat of a German invasion was practically nil. As with World War I, Turkey emerged from the war in near economic collapse and under the threat of Soviet expansion southward. Under the Truman Doctrine of 1947 and other pacts, the United States gave Turkey (and Greece) significant military and economic aid in order to thwart perceived Soviet intentions. United States aid also put Turkey firmly in the Western camp.

The clamor for reform after a quarter century of rule by the same political party proved too great for Inonu to overcome. The 1950 elections resulted in a stunning upset, when the opposition party gained a legislative majority. The election marked a turning point in Turkish politics; a change of government had come about by popular vote. While the military had not intervened, it remained a formidable force in Turkish politics. Indeed, the internal financial troubles that had beset rapidly developing Turkey brought a military takeover in 1960. But the military leaders respected the role of political parties in Turkish life. Their stated goal, which they carried out within a year, was to return Turkey to civilian rule once a reasonable degree of social and economic order was established. The military staged another coup in 1971; again they promptly turned the reigns of power back to the civilians once order was reestablished. As if running in ten-year cycles, the military reluctantly took power once more in September, 1980.

Iran

The 1950 elections and the later military coups in Turkey contrast sharply with events in Iran. In 1951 the Iranian prime minister, Dr. Mohammed Mossadegh, a long-time nationalist, led an unsuccessful battle to nationalize the British-owned petroleum company. The Iranian legislature, the Majlis, was dominated largely by those interested in maintaining the status quo and had gained considerable political power in the previous decade. In 1940, the Allies had forced Reza Shah Pahlevi to abdicate because of his flirtation with Germany and his refusal to accept Allied demands to redivide Iran into British and Soviet spheres of influence. His young son Mohammed Reza Shah Pahlevi ascended to the Peacock Throne. During the 1940s the new Shah had his hands full simply maintaining the throne as both internal rivalries and Allied actions sheared power away from him and transferred it to the Majlis. Dr. Mossadegh then convinced the members of the Majlis that it was in the national interest and their personal self-interest to vote for nationalization.

Nationalization with due compensation was an established point of international law, but the Mossadegh-led Majlis met with British-led Western intransigence. The Western powers boycotted Iranian petroleum. World petroleum supplies were abundant enough to absorb the loss of Iranian production, especially since the region's other major producers did not support the Iranian nationalization and continued to sell their petroleum to the West. If they had cooperated, it is possible that Iran would have won the day and the course of Middle Eastern history would have changed. As it was, the economic toll of the boycott mounted and support from the Majlis dwindled; its members' nationalistic zeal fluctuated with the size of their purses. The Majlis's consequent rejection of Dr. Mossadegh's oil policy in the face of Western pressure reconciled it to the Shah, for whom a nationalist victory would have meant a loss of power. Dr. Mossadegh and his group of supporters became isolated. He could either capitulate or take his case to the streets. He chose the latter course and won a short-term victory; the outpouring of nationalization sentiment was strong enough to topple the throne. But in 1953, with the active support of the United States Central Intelligence Agency, the military intervened, arrested Mossadegh, and restored power to the Shah and the equally conservative Majlis. A revised agreement with the petroleum company was then drawn up; this new agreement changed the terms of the previous agreement but allowed for continued Western ownership. Those pressing for economic independence—the clergy, the communists, and a growing group of reformers—had lost the battle. Within a year Iran entered into a military pact with the United States and put itself firmly in the Western camp for the next quarter century. As Turkey struggled with a highly imperfect representative rule, Iran saw all its political and economic power become increasingly centered in the person of the Shah.

By the early 1960s, the Shah had promulgated the White Revolution, the goal of which was to hasten the industrialization of Iran and to better the lot of the peasants through a land reform program. It is no accident that the White Revolution shifted power away from the clergy and the restive urban technocrats and intellectuals. While it promoted economic growth, the White Revolution also promoted insecurity among the opposition and concentrated more power in the hands of the ruling elite. As the growing petroleum revenues enabled the Shah to transform the Iranian economy, they also made his continued tight control of all political processes increasingly problematic. The same social forces that had coalesced in the 1890 tobacco riots were again finding a common bond. There is some irony to the fact that the Shah's decisive support of the quadrupling of petroleum prices in 1973-74 accelerated this process. As the Shah immediately spent the riches that poured in, he began to lose control over the flow of events. The careful balancing of interests demanded by the informal Iranian political system degenerated into an indiscriminate bludgeoning of the opposition, as the SAVAK (the Iranian secret police) and its network of informants struggled against widespread resentment. The system was running amok.

FROM PALESTINE TO ISRAEL

By 1920 the forces that were to create the dilemma of Palestine for the remainder of the century were in place. The basic issue was, and remains, which group has the right to control the area.

The British were aware of the potential difficulties even before they were granted the mandate for Palestine. The Zionists clung to the idea of a national homeland as proclaimed in the Balfour Declaration. The Arabs demanded the same self-determination that had been promised to other contiguous Arab lands. Over the next twenty-five years, British responses to the situation clearly reflected the policy dilemma but did little to bring an acceptable resolution. They issued periodic White Papers that outlined the extremely low probability of a peacefully negotiated settlement, but formulated no coherent policy. The British momentarily cooled the passions of first one side and then the other without resolving the source of the conflict.

Nationalism had infected both the Arabs of Palestine and the Zionists by the end of World War I. Self-determination was the goal of each group. The British military administration and the civilian mandate government allowed Jewish immigration on a limited scale and made it easier for Jews to acquire property. Arabs and Jews were involved in several incidents in 1920, and in 1921 Arabs had made several significant attacks on Jewish settlements. The British promptly suspended immigration for a month until tempers subsided and then put the old policy back into force, temporarily acceding to violence and then continuing business as usual. They ignored the King-Crane Commission of 1919, which was organized by Woodrow Wilson, and British committee reports that indicated that there was little room for compromise.

Winston Churchill, then colonial secretary, stated in 1922 that the phrase "national home" in the Balfour Declaration did not mean that all of Palestine was to become a Zionist nation, but that a national home for the Zionists could be created in Palestine. The British also separated Transjordan, first created in 1921, from the Palestinian mandate, thereby shutting off Jewish settlements there. The Zionists viewed these policies as attempts to thwart their movement and abrogate the Balfour Declaration. Arab leaders saw the policy as working within the confines of the Balfour Declaration in that it simply redefined the specifics, and they therefore rejected the "clarifications." Indeed, for the next two decades, Arab policy was based on the premise of the illegitimacy of the Balfour Declaration. They therefore could not acknowledge Britain's repeated attempts to modify the declaration. Indeed, the Arabs rejected Britain's attempts to have Arabs and Jews sit on a joint consultative body in Palestine for the same reason; to sit in the same chamber would give legitimacy to the Zionists.

Although the Zionist community was composed of several competing factions, its government was solidly organized and well structured, and it could depend on British support for its major concerns. The Arabs of Palestine stood in stark contrast: while most politically aware Palestinian Arabs wanted self-determination, they had no effective political organization. Their rejection of the Arab-Zionist consultative bodies had its logic, but it was politically unwise because it deprived them of a forum in which to air their grievances.

The Arab Executive, a committee formed by the Third Arab Congress in December, 1920, was the most important Palestinian Arab organization during the first years of the 1920s. Since Syria had been occupied by the French earlier that year, the idea of Palestine becoming part of southern Syria had faded. The new Arab strategy was first to unify the Palestinians, second to protest British moves that facilitated Zionist settlement in Palestine, and third to prohibit the League of Nations from forming a mandate on terms unfavorable to the Arabs.

Although the Arab Executive managed to hold the various Palestinian Arab groups together for a couple of years, it split apart in 1923. In September of that year, the League of Nations finished drawing up the provisions of the mandate. Thus, one of the major forces for unity was lost. The Arab Executive was divided over what strategy to use. Should it lodge official protests and try to negotiate and persuade, or should it simply not cooperate at all? Some advocated not paying taxes, but landowners feared that this would lead to property confiscations. At the same time, some elite families revived their long-standing feuds. The Sixth Arab Congress (1923) was the last for the next five years. The Palestinian voice became muted.

Official negotiations ceased, and the Jewish and Arab communities became more isolated from one another. The Zionists prohibited Arabs from leasing or even working on land purchased by the Jewish National Fund. And Histadrut, the General Federation of Jewish Labor, was insisting that Jewish-owned establishments hire only Jews. Outside of Jerusalem and Haifa, where Arabs and Jews lived side-by-side, the two people lived and worked apart in an atmosphere of growing hostility.

Arab fears went beyond becoming a numerical minority in their own land. Most Zionists, after all, were Europeans, and however separated they had become from the mainstream of European society, they nevertheless were steeped in Western ways. In 1930, over 90 percent of all Jewish males in Palestine were literate as opposed to only 25 percent of all Arab males. About 75 percent of the Jews were urban residents, as opposed to 25 percent of the Arabs.

The relative calm that prevailed during the mid-1920s belied a growing sense of frustration and bitterness. The Jews comprised about 10 percent of the total population of Palestine in 1922 (the remainder consisted of 10 percent Christians and 80 percent Muslims). Their numbers grew at a moderate rate through immigration, except in 1925 when a relatively large number entered. Due to a harsh recession beginning in 1926, more Jews left Palestine in 1927 than entered. It seemed to the Arabs that the Zionist cause had lost its appeal, and that the Arabs would remain a firm majority. But 1927 proved to be an anomaly. By 1930 Jews comprised about 16 percent of the population. It was clear that Zionism was alive and vigorous.

The Seventh Arab Congress convened in 1928. Encouraged by the 1927 decline in Zionist immigration, the congress sought to present a united front to press Arab claims. The new Arab coalition sought legislative representation as a first step toward self-determination. But events were to severely weaken the coalition and lead to its dissolution in 1934. A few months after the meeting of the Seventh Congress, Zionists demonstrated at the Wailing Wall by raising the Zionist flag and singing the Zionist anthem. There were clashes with Arabs. By August of 1929, full-scale rioting broke out, resulting in 740 deaths (472 Jews and 268 Arabs). The cautious, elite-dominated Arab Executive was losing its grip on its base of power. Arab politics in the 1930s was fragmented at the top and radicalized at the bottom.

The British sent an investigating team to Palestine after the Permanent Mandate Commission of the League of Nations, in response to the 1929 riots, issued a report outlining Arab-Jewish tensions. The subsequent British White Paper recognized the seriousness of the situation and called for an immediate temporary end to immigration. Arab satisfaction from the position taken in the Passfield White Paper was short-lived. In England, the Zionist reaction was quick and vehement. An open letter from the British prime minister to Chaim Weizmann, the highly influential British Zionist, repudiated the latest immigration policy. This "Black Letter," as the Arabs referred to it, indicated to some Arab leaders that they could not hope to negotiate with Britain for independence. Britain was henceforth to be regarded as an enemy. An Arab boycott followed. Although they succeeded in having immigration reinstated, the Zionists were also troubled by British actions. While the British had acceded to Zionist pressures, it was quite clear that they had no clear commitment to the Zionists' ultimate goals. The British, then, were faced with hostility from both camps.

The rise of Nazi Germany in 1932 produced a steady stream of Jewish immigration to Palestine. The Jewish population of Palestine increased fourfold from 1933 to 1936; by 1936, Jews comprised over 27 percent of the total population. The Zionist resolve to accommodate Jews fleeing the horror of Nazi Germany aroused intense Arab bitterness. In April, 1936, terrorist violence broke out between the two communities. The Arab leadership, somewhat united by the crisis, called for a general strike. Within a month the strike became a civil war. The dispatch of 20,000 British troops and mass arrests halted the general strike and the civil war by the end of October.

Another British investigating commission arrived in Palestine in 1936. The British accepted the report of the commission and issued another White Paper calling for the partition of Palestine into Jewish and Arab sections with an international corridor extending from Jaffa to Jerusalem and beyond. The plan was rejected by both sides, and fighting broke out again in September, 1937. At one point the British had put several thousand Jews under arms to help quell Arab hostility. The arrangement broke down after the British hanged a convicted Jewish terrorist in June, 1938, setting Jewish terrorist groups off on a rampage of reprisals.

The adverse reaction to the 1936 White Paper advocating partition prompted the appointment of a commission to reconsider the exact boundaries. Although the report of the commission, which was published in 1938, contained three potential partition plans, it also pointed out that the notion of partition was impractical.

A conference in London followed in 1939. The participants worked for a peaceful resolution but they failed. The only interesting result was that the British government made the McMahon-Husein Correspondence public for the first time. After the conference, the British decided unilaterally that within ten years a united Palestine would receive a constitution that would guarantee Arab representation and protect Arab land rights. Jewish immigration was first to be reduced and then to cease after five years. Jews demonstrated their anger by burning and sacking government offices in Palestine and by launching terrorist attacks on the British.

Eight thousand Arabs and twenty-one thousand Jews from Palestine served in the British armed forces during World War II. Hostility to the British in Palestine, however, continued. The Jews were especially active because they considered the British policy to be a virtual death warrant for those fleeing the Holocaust. By 1946 the unofficial army of the Jewish Agency (to which the World Zionist Organization had changed its name in 1930), the Haganah, numbered 60,000. Various terrorist groups, most notably the Irgun (of which the later prime minister Menachem Begin was the leader) and the smaller Stern Gang, complemented this force. The Zionists had taken the initiative in attacking the Arabs and the British. The weaker but numerically dominant Arabs attacked the Jews and the British. The war-weary British attempted to quell the violence, which was now out of control. As more and more survivors of the Holocaust illegally entered Palestine, the British desperately grabbed for a solution. In 1946 an Anglo-American committee devised a variant of the partition proposal that again was rejected; a 1947 British proposal calling for a five-year British trusteeship met with a similar fate. The British were totally frustrated and angry over European and, especially, United States support of Zionism; the United States, however, had refused to allow mass Jewish immigration to its shores. The British washed their hands of the affair and turned the problem over to the fledgling United Nations.

A subsequent United Nations commission found what all previous commissions had noted: the demands of each side were understandable, inflexible, and irreconcilable. In November, 1947, the United Nations called for the partition of Palestine. The mandate was to end May 1, 1948, and the two states were to be established on July 1, 1948. The Arab states began to rally their forces in support of the now disorganized Palestinians, but it was too little too late. A Zionist offensive resulted in victories as the British pulled out. On May 14, 1948, David Ben-Gurion announced the formation of the state of Israel. The Zionists had Palestine, or at least a portion of it.

However, the formation of Israel did not give the Zionists complete security. The Arab population that had remained in Palestine, along with the sizable number who fled as the fighting became particularly vicious, viewed Israel as illegitimate, and the Zionists as a foreign power. Further, the Arab countries that had been defeated by the highly efficient Israeli army in the war following the declaration of independence suffered a deep humiliation. Although the Arab states surrounding Israel had a substantial numerical advantage, they were militarily weak. Their armies were ill-trained, badly equipped, and lacking in dynamic leadership.

According to the Arabs, Israel was just another outpost of Western hegemony. Various Arab leaders vowed that they would not rest until the state of Israel was destroyed. According to the Israelis, British vacillation, the Nazi Holocaust, and the refusal of the Western countries to accept large numbers of persecuted Jews proved Herzl's 1896 argument that only in their own sovereign state could Jews expect to be safe and secure. To the age-old Jewish dictum, "Next Year in Jerusalem," was added the cry, "Never Again."

There was no ground for accommodation on the issue of Palestinian rule. Both sides were desperate and bitter: the struggle had been waged for a third of a century, and almost every long-time resident knew someone who had been killed or attacked. The "Freedom Fighters" of one side were considered to be brutal "terrorists" by the other.

CONCLUSION

Most countries of the Middle East had achieved political independence by 1950. Few, however, had achieved self-determination. The Western powers had substantial economic and strategic interests in the area that they were determined to protect.

The new alignment of Western powers into Russian and American camps set the stage for renewed attempts to carve out spheres of influence. The American-led group sought to establish client relationships with the northern tier of nations— Turkey, Iraq, and Iran—in order to thwart Soviet aspirations. The United States also sought to protect Persian Gulf oil and the Suez Canal to the south. Since overt outside control of local political systems was quickly becoming a relic of the past, the great powers tried to maintain their influence by other means. They gave economic and technical assistance and military aid to muffle revolutionary impulses. The primary aim of the United States and the Western powers was to stop Soviet expansion, not to develop independent economies and military forces. To strengthen Middle Eastern countries against revolution the Western powers helped build a military and economic apparatus which was effective and resilient but still depended on Western support.

The postwar economic and military position of most Middle Eastern countries was extremely weak. The political elite of these countries generally wanted to avoid fundamental reforms. In this, they had much in common with the United States: they both sought political stability. The extent of military and economic dependency was the major point in question. However, the growing militant nationalism in the Middle East complicated the matter.

The need to achieve economic independence and strengthen the indigenous cultures began to be appreciated by those concerned with self-determination: political independence would not suffice. Those who saw economic dependence as the major impediment to self-determination found socialism particularly attractive. It was, after all, Western private enterprise that had transfigured and dominated the economies of the Middle East. A restructuring of the local economies to meet local needs was going to be necessary; but this would be almost impossible in a system dominated by foreigners and serving foreign markets. Furthermore, if the foreign private enterprise system controlled the course of local economic events, it also could be blamed for the continuing misery of the masses. (Private-enterprise systems have never been noted for economic justice—a concern for an equitable distribution of income. Socialism, on the other hand, is greatly concerned with income distribution.) Not all modernizers shared these thoughts nor were their ideas set out in a neatly framed system. Rather, the sentiments more often than not arose from a sense of dissatisfaction, a growing awareness that a fundamental reordering of society had to occur before full self-determination could be achieved, and that the restructuring could not take place as long as foreigners remained dominant.

Another source of dissatisfaction came to the surface during this period: it appeared that continued Western domination was stripping away the cultural fabric of Arab (and especially Islamic) society. Calls for an indigenous cultural renaissance had been made throughout the century, but the pulse of the movement, led by disaffected religious leaders, gained momentum in the postwar era. As with the secular modernizers, the clergy also called for an end to the current order. They sought a return to Islamic fundamentals rather than a culture heavily laden with Western values, whatever form of economic independence was achieved.

Middle Eastern political leaders thus faced a difficult choice. Accepting Western aid would enhance their economic and military strength and possibly mute some of the discontent caused by the "revolution of rising expectations." But this alliance would meet with resistance by those who perceived continued Western economic or cultural domination as a barrier to self-determination. The situation was complicated for several Arab countries because the American-led block supported Israel, a country which the Arabs generally thought of as a Western colonial settler state.

6

Modernization:
An Overview

Human social life today is changing with unprecedented speed. Certain trends set in motion a few short centuries ago have accelerated and spread until they have profoundly affected most of the world's societies. These trends are occurring on a variety of levels, from the technical and social to the philosophical. We often take these trends for granted as part of the natural course of human "progress," and rarely do we pause to question how they originated or how their various aspects relate to one another. Such questions are crucial, however, for an understanding of international relations today, especially between those nations that are more "developed" in terms of these trends and those that are less developed.

The purpose of this chapter is not to catalog the changes that have taken place in the Middle East but to discuss the phenomenon of modernization in the most general terms, to examine the social changes it typically brings, and to caution the reader as to some biases and preconceptions that might influence our view of the modernization process. While our specific examples will refer to the Middle East or to Islam, many of the generalizations about the modernization process would apply equally to other parts of the world. Subsequent chapters will provide more details about the modernization of the Middle East itself.

The term *modernization* is used by social scientists to refer to the complex of technical, social, political, economic, and attitudinal changes that they see emerging in the contemporary world. Sometimes modernization is defined very loosely and broadly, but for the purpose of the present discussion it is more useful to define it in a very specific way. Modernization, as we use the term, is the process of social change that results from the shift toward a technicalized society. This definition, of course, raises the question of what we mean by *technicalized society*. Technicalization has been defined as "a condition of calculative (and hence innovative) technical specialization, in which the several specialties are interdependent on a large enough scale to determine patterns of expectation in the key sectors of the society."[1] A technicalized society, then, is one in which the interplay of specialized technical considerations tends to take precedence over aesthetic, traditional, interpersonal, or other nontechnical considerations—in short, a society structured by the demands of specialized technical efficiency.[2] This is not to imply that pretechnicalistic societies had no interest in technical efficiency or that modern societies care for nothing else, but only that the unprecedented emphasis on specialized technical considerations has played a key role in recent social change. The ongoing processes of technicalization and modernization are bringing rapid change to all contemporary countries, from the poorest to the most affluent.

THE MODERNIZATION SYNDROME

Modernization includes an array of changes that typically accompany the spreading influence of technicalization. Some of these changes, including many economic and political ones, tend to occur repeatedly in different countries because they are causally related to the process of technicalization; others, such as style of clothing or taste in entertainment, are communicated as part of a growing international cosmopolitan culture. Some changes are predictable and others are not, and some may be fundamental to the modernization process while others are only incidental to it.

Perhaps the most fundamental elements in the modernization process are economic and technical in nature. The rise of technicalism in Europe was accompanied by certain changes that still seem inseparable from it, and central among these is the institutionalization of technical innovation. The ability to adopt efficient technical innovations was the key to success among the competing private business enterprises of seventeenth- and eighteenth-century Europe, and for that reason traditional European social forces that impeded free scientific inquiry gradually gave way to a cultural outlook that took for granted continuous inquiry and innovation. Such an outlook has had far-reaching consequences in noneconomic realms, but its effect on the techno-economic order has been most immediate. It has led to a rapid development of industrial production, the use of fossil fuels, complex machines, standardized mass production, a highly specialized division of labor and knowledge, and a substantial reinvestment of profits in the machinery of production (tools to make tools). This pattern of production has been accompanied by a growth of regional interdependence, so that even nonindustrialized regions tend to become part of a growing network for the exchange of raw materials and manufactured items. In this sense, economic modernization occurs to the extent that any region becomes integrated into the international economic order.

The economic effects of technicalization can be extremely beneficial to those in a position to take advantage of them. Technicalization can give human populations a substantial degree of power over the environment, and it can thereby serve the ends of *economic development*—the process by which a society increases the

[1]Marshall, G. S. Hodgson, *The Venture of Islam* (Chicago: University of Chicago Press, 1974), III:186.
[2]Ibid., pp. 181–96.

economic self-determination and material welfare of its people. At the same time, the economic effects of the spread of technicalization are not automatically beneficial. The power to affect the environment, for example, can be a boon to a society that can afford the luxury of good long-range planning, but may be a liability for those that cannot. Similarly, technicalization can provide the means for economic development, but it should be kept in mind that the economic powerlessness and spiraling poverty of some modernizing countries are also, in their own way, results of the spread of technicalization and the colonial domination associated with it.

In the economic realm, then, the modernization process entails the integration of each region into an increasingly interdependent network of producers and consumers, the whole of which is characterized by technical innovation, power over the physical environment, and increasing material affluence. It is difficult, however, to predict whether the terms of this integration will be favorable to the economic welfare or self-determination of particular countries; nothing in the modernization process necessarily ensures all nations a significant share in the fruits of the technicalized international economy.

Aside from its economic consequences, the technicalizing trend has many other direct and indirect social consequences. One of the most outstanding of these is the fostering of a greater awareness of cultural diversity, and with it the beginnings of a cosmopolitan world culture. This process of intercultural communication has been aided by Western penetration, by economic interdependence, by the spread of literacy, and by the development of improved modes of communication, all of which have helped to break down the relative geographical isolation of earlier times. Intercultural understanding has become an important issue for many of the world's people, and an increasing number see themselves, if not as "citizens" of the whole world, at least as actors in it.

Political institutions are deeply affected by the modernization process. A technicalized society needs a literate, informed, and competent populace; and such people can be a far more active political force than the urban and peasant masses of the older agrarian states. Improved communication makes it both possible and necessary for a government to enlist the support and participation of a larger sector of the populace. Besides the increase in mass participation, political modernization also emphasizes the specific, goal-oriented efficiency of political institutions at the expense of time-honored practices, hereditary social privilege, or personal affiliations such as kinship and clientship. One characteristic result of political modernization is the appearance of the political party, which in its various forms serves to legitimate political institutions and to mobilize public support for the goals and concepts that underly state policy. These changes may be welcome ones for many citizens in the modernizing nation; but in politics as well as in economics, the modernization process has consequences that may not be so welcome. One of these, to be discussed shortly, is the political domination of nonmodernized nations by modernized ones. Another is the domination of the populace by elites who are in league with the dominant foreign powers. While these facets of the modernization process may with some effort be avoided or overcome, their existence certainly needs to be acknowledged.

The attitude toward law indicates the changing social values associated with modernization. Although many of the aims of Sharia law were consonant with those of modern legal systems, the Sharia, like most premodern legal codes, was held in principle to be perfect and eternal. The function of the ulema was not to legislate the Sharia but to interpret it; the law itself was given by God and exemplified by Muhammad in its purest and most perfect form, and later generations could only extend it to new situations. The idea of a legislature as a body that meets regularly to change the laws is consistent with the modern notion of constant experiment and innovation aimed at improved efficiency toward specified ends, but it is blatantly inconsistent with the older idea that laws should be eternal.

On the sociological level, modernization changes typical attitudes toward status and achievement. Despite Sharia ideals to the contrary, much social power and recognition in premodern agrarian societies was accorded a person on the basis of kinship and descent. Modernization involves a shift toward specialized competence and achievement as the basis for social status and personal influence. Institutions also become more impersonal, and the special statuses or interrelationships of individuals become less relevant to the functioning of large-scale social institutions. (Many of these developments, however, have precedents in Islamic history and are very much in harmony with Islamic values.)

One of the more controversial issues in modernization involves the role of religion. Technicalization necessarily reduces the authority of religion, at least in some areas of life, for many of the demands of technical efficiency are bound to conflict with those of divine command. Historically, there appears to have been a general correspondence between secularization (the shift from religious to worldy thinking as a basis for decision-making) and modernization. The issue, however, is far from being a simple case of religion versus modernization. Religion may be de-emphasized in certain areas, such as government or business, while it enjoys a revival on a more personal level. Religious ideas can be reinterpreted in view of social changes. Religion often performs a vital service in mobilizing social and political commitment, and its benefits to modernizing countries may more than offset its occasional clashes with the technicalizing ethic. Furthermore, the recent revival of religion in some highly technicalized countries suggests that technical efficiency may not provide all the answers to human problems after all. In any case, it would be premature to predict a simple correlation in the Middle East between modernization and the overall secularization of society. The specific relation of Islam to modernization will be treated in more detail later in this chapter.

TRADITION AND RATIONAL CALCULATION

Many writers on modernization see the whole process as revolving around a single, fundamental change in outlook: the shift from tradition to reason as a guide for action. If "reason" refers to the calculation of immediate tangible benefits, it does become important in a technicalized society—often at the expense of religion or other traditional sources of authority. Arguing along these lines, some writers describe modernization in terms of a definitive attitudinal change. The modern person, they

say, has a flexible mind, is open to new and unfamiliar ways of thinking and be-
having, looks to the future and believes in the possibility of improvement, and
chooses among alternative courses of action by calculating costs and benefits.
The traditional person, on the other hand, is said to have a rigidly circumscribed
idea of his or her possibilities, to look to customary authority and established practice to justify action, and to be fearful of the new or unfamiliar. One widely read
study of modernization in the Middle East compares the "psychic mobility," imagi-
native flexibility, optimism, and "empathy" of the modernized person with the
supposedly unreflective, intolerant conservatism of the "traditional person." "Traditional" people become "modern" when their mental horizons are expanded
through exposure to new ideas ultimately originating in the West.[3] Many observers
have supported this view with general impressions and specific data. At the same
time, this conception of the modernization process has important limitations and
must be approached with caution.

First of all, not all "traditional" people have the same outlook. Studies have
repeatedly shown vast differences in the world views typical of small hunter-gatherer
bands, independent subsistence-farming villages, and state-organized agrarian societies. Even within the traditional Middle East, which is dominated by the latter type,
the nomadic herders, urban aristocrats, and rural peasantry are often worlds apart
in their attitudes. The image of the "traditional" person that one finds in much social science literature is based largely on peasants. Although peasants constitute the
bulk of the population in the traditional Middle East and many other parts of the
world, peasant life is a specific kind of traditional life that occurs under particular
conditions. Peasants are not merely farmers; they are a subordinate class in a highly
stratified society. They have typically lived under conditions of relative deprivation
even by the standards of their own society; their opportunities for political and
economic self-determination or betterment have been severely restricted by the
power structure of the traditional state; and they have generally been held in low
esteem by the urbanites and elites who controlled their lives. Generations of experience have taught them that outsiders care little for their welfare, that most changes
are likely to work to their disadvantage, and that the slightest upset may destroy
the narrow margin on which they survive. One does not need a theory of the traditional mind to see why they might be pessimistic about change. However, by
describing the peasant attitude apart from the conditions that give rise to it, and by
casting all traditional societies and classes in the peasant mold, we run the risk of
exaggerating the influence of rigid, fearful conservatism in traditional life.

The perspective of distance almost always makes other cultures look flat,
arbitrary, and deterministic compared with our own. Whether we are getting married or getting dressed in the morning, we see our own actions as guided by reason,
filled with subtle meaning, and tempered by personal freedom. The corresponding
behavior in another culture seems to us simple, stereotyped, and unreflective. "We"
put on neckties because we think, and "they" put on turbans because they do not—
or so it seems. Yet, close studies of traditional peoples, including peasants, have

[3] Daniel Lerner, *The Passing of Traditional Society* (New York: Free Press, 1958).

shown them to be more critically aware of circumstances and choices than is commonly assumed. Quite often, behavior that appears motivated by blind conservatism turns out instead to be based on a realistic assessment of the alternatives; thus many people are quite capable of grasping the significance of changing circumstances and able to adapt to them accordingly.

Although the Western observer frequently thinks that every exotic custom or idea has existed from time immemorial, a closer look at cultural history—especially that of the Middle East—reveals a continuous state of flux. The origin and spread of Islam is one good example of the speed and magnitude of change, even in basic beliefs, that can occur in a traditional society. While people everywhere are inclined to accept most of the beliefs and perspectives with which they were reared, they are everywhere capable of revising and criticizing these traditions when they no longer seem to fill their needs. We certainly do not intend to argue that there is no difference between traditional and modern world views, but rather that it is impossible to do justice to the differences by means of a simple dichotomy, and that our understanding of "traditional" behavior is not improved by viewing it as rigid, unreflective conservatism.

There is no denying that the modernization process does present people with a broader range of possibilities than they had previously known; it does often encourage people to break with tradition in favor of a rational calculation of benefits. On the other hand, some of the supposed differences between "traditional" and "modern" may be largely a matter of rhetorical style. For example, a political leader planning the invasion of a neighboring country may seek to justify it in a variety of ways: he may utilize a rationalistic rhetoric that stresses its benefits ("This invasion will bring peace, security, and good government to all concerned"); he may use a traditionalistic rhetoric that looks to the authority of the past ("These people have always been our subjects"); or he may use religious rhetoric ("God will look kindly on us for subduing the infidel"). All these styles of rhetoric have been used throughout history, but the rationalistic style is relatively fashionable in modernized societies. The use of such rhetoric does not in itself make one's actions particularly reasonable, any more than the use of a religious rhetoric means that one's actions are divinely guided, or a traditionalist rhetoric proves that a given practice is genuinely traditional. It is a mistake, then, to conclude simply from these differences in public rhetoric that one society's motives and actions are in fact more rational than another's.

THE DOMINANCE OF THE WEST

Even the most ardent Third World nationalist can scarcely deny that Western Europe played a central initial role in originating and spreading the social patterns that characterize modernization. But why the West? Many Westerners naïvely assume that the West has been in the forefront of cultural development for thousands of years, a view that is enhanced by grafting European history onto that of the Greeks while placing the Middle East in the vague category of "Oriental" or "Asian" cultures. By any objective standards, however, Western Europe could not be called a leader in world cultural development until very late in history. Even after the Renaissance, Europe was on no more than an equal footing with the older centers of civilization, and it was only in the eighteenth century that Europe decisively surpassed the Middle East in technology and commercial power.

The historical reasons for the technicalization of the West are difficult to unravel, but they may include some geographical and ecological components. In fact, some of the ecological conditions that retarded European civilization in earlier history may have aided its more recent rise. Among the most significant factors in the rise of technicalism in the West were the unprecedented importance of capital reinvestment and technological innovation, both of which were being built into the commercial institutions of eighteenth-century Europe. It is possible that entrepreneurial capitalism, which supported this competition for technical efficiency, was discouraged in the older civilizations where irrigation-based agriculture promoted the consolidation of a more centralized government control. In Europe, by contrast, an economy based on rainfall agriculture provided less of a basis for centralized control of the economy, and monarchs and central bureaucracies were less able to thwart and exploit would-be capitalists. The West's economic potential in the eighteenth century may have been bolstered by the fact that it, unlike the land-depleted Middle East, still had virgin countryside into which agricultural production could expand. Whatever the historical reasons for the priority of Europe in making the transition, the West's institutionalization of technical efficiency and technological innovation has done much to determine not only the character of the West itself but of the world order as well.

The West did not set out to conquer the world; rather, each European nation sought to extend its political and economic interests and to protect them not only from local threats but from other European powers. Whatever their nationality, Europeans invariably saw themselves as a superior people ruling and tutoring their inferiors, and were able to support this attitude with a technically efficient military force. Sometimes European domination took the form of direct occupation and political rule; but even when it did not, the pattern of domination remained similar. The European powers intervened as necessary to insure that local governments kept sufficient order to protect European interests, but not enough power to pose any challenge to European hegemony. Typically, the economic production of the dominated countries was structured to provide a limited range of raw materials most needed by the dominant power.

In some respects, European cultural domination was just as far-reaching as its political, military, and economic domination. Middle Easterners were classified along with the various Asian peoples as "Orientals," and it was widely held that such people were given to inscrutable peculiarities of thought, blind obedience to tradition, and insensitivity to suffering. The European colonial powers held slightly differing ideas of their mission to these peoples. The British, for example, saw themselves as bringing peace and international political order; they tended to preserve local institutions and to rule through them, rather than to install their own institutions among people who, they felt, could not be full partners in civilized life. The French, on the other hand, saw themselves as offering a superior culture, language, and tradition of civilization; and they did not hesitate to use direct rule to break down the "outmoded" institutions of the dominated countries. In all cases, however, the threat to the dignity of the dominated peoples was severe indeed, and its effects are still with us. Even Middle Eastern nationalism has sometimes been influenced by Western biases in subtle ways; for example, many Middle Easterners have tacitly accepted the classification of themselves as "Orientals," a category that has little meaning except as an expression of European ethnocentrism.

One of the lingering and pervasive effects of Western enthnocentrism is the tendency to confuse modernization with Westernization, and to hold up middle-class Europe and America as a universal model of modernity. It is intellectually and morally indefensible to assume that everything non-Western is necessarily backward, especially when much of Western culture comes from a pre-modern age in which Western civilization was less developed than that of the Middle and Far East. Yet it is often tempting, even for the non-Westerner, to equate modernization with Westernization. The political and economic dominance of the West during the past few centuries has made Westernization a companion of most other changes, so that Westerners and non-Westerners alike sometimes find them difficult to distinguish.

RESPONSES TO THE WEST

Unwelcome as the European penetration into the Middle East may have been, the region's political and religious leaders could not afford to ignore it. Not only did the West establish a growing political and economic influence with which local interests had to cope, but it also posed a direct cultural challenge. It was not merely a case of a dominant culture imposing its alien ideas; some of the West's achievements might actually be seen as enviable from a Middle Eastern Muslim standpoint. The Christian West had inherited the Muslim Middle East's old role as arbiter of the international order, and had promulgated new standards of legal and social conduct. Furthermore, Western ideology successfully carried on some of the ideals long upheld by Muslim law, such as curtailing the power of the traditional privileged classes, strengthening the nuclear family, protecting contractual relationships, and stressing individual social mobility and ethical responsibility. On a variety of levels, the Western presence required some kind of response.

One of the first responses attempted by the still-viable Middle Eastern powers was the forceful rejection of the West through a revival of political-military strength. Such efforts involved neither a return to the past nor a rejection of Western technology, but a calculated and selective use of innovation in an attempt to preserve political autonomy. The efforts of the Ottoman sultans in the late eighteenth century are typical in this respect: they brought in European advisors to help modernize the military, and sought at the same time to introduce organizational reforms in the government bureaucracy. Such programs, however, met with difficulties. Internal resistance to such reforms can be quite strong, especially among those with vested interests at stake. Furthermore, the European powers were ready to intervene—as they did with Muhammad Ali's similar modernization programs in Egypt—

whenever a threat to European interests was suspected. And finally, to the extent that such programs succeeded at all, it was hard to limit their effects to those initially desired; for example, military officers trained in Europe often introduced new ideas and aspirations that went far beyond the circumscribed intentions of the military modernizers. However salutory those changes might have been in the long run, their immediate effect was liable to be further social disruption and conflict.

When it became apparent that direct resistance to Western power was to no avail, leaders and influential classes in the Middle Eastern countries typically developed patterns of accommodation to the Western powers. They entered into arrangements—usually with a particular European nation—in which they tacitly recognized their own political and economic subordination but viewed themselves as "leaders" overseeing the "progress" of their backward countrymen. These arrangements, however, usually insured not only their own favored position in the distribution of power and wealth within their countries, but often did much to perpetuate the political and economic disadvantages of their countries in relation to the West. It was against these local leaders and classes, as much as against the West itself, that much of the later nationalist impulse was to be directed.

The inherent difficulties of both direct resistance and accommodation contributed to the numerous attempts by Middle Eastern peoples to reassert their demands for social and cultural self-determination. Generally speaking, they were trying to maintain their past cultural traditions while finding effective ways of coping with present situations. Strategies for accomplishing such goals range from nationalism to religious movements aimed at the revitalization of Islam. In some cases, the continuity with the past is a tenuous one: Egypt's Khedive Ismail (d. 1879) and Turkey's Kemal Atatürk (d. 1938) each asserted that their countries were properly part of Europe (and a historically important part at that), and accordingly proceeded with Westernization programs designed to "restore" their Europeanness. Atatürk's program included even the disestablishment of Islam as a state religion and the banning of traditional dress.

Turkey's program of self-assertion is a notable example of nationalism combined with secularization and Westernization. For many, however, the reassertion of cultural autonomy involved a more explicit continuity with traditional ideals and identities. Arabism, for example, began to take form in the nineteenth century among the Ottoman Empire's Arab subjects. At this time many Arabic-speaking people, including Egyptians whose ancestors had not necessarily identified themselves as Arabs, began to develop a sense of international Arab unity which looked to the Golden Age of the Abbasid caliphate for inspiration and attributed the decline of the Muslim world to Persian and Turkish influence. Islam itself provided another vehicle for the Middle Eastern cultural reassertion, subject of course to a broad range of interpretations. Some, like the puritanical Wahhabi sect in Arabia, sought to purge Islam of all impure "innovations," including even some accepted in Abbasid times. Islamic modernists, on the other hand, found Islam not only compatible with a liberal modern lifestyle but admirably suited to it. Among these were the Young Ottomans who during the 1860s developed the idea that Islam, properly understood, is an essentially progressive religion that embraces all the essential precepts of modern life, or at least all those worthy of admiration. According to such modernist thinkers, Islam ought to be purged not of innovation, but of the customary rigidity and conservatism that is so alien to its true nature.

In sum, a variety of responses to Western domination is possible, and most if not all of them can be called "modernization" programs in some sense. Egypt, as an example, has at one time or another considered a vast array of strategies. Its first modernizer, Muhammad Ali, attempted to technicalize the military in order to divert European penetration and extend his own power. Later leaders attempted various combinations of Westernization and accommodation. Meanwhile, popular sentiments were swayed by the appeal of differing, and sometimes conflicting, identities: should "modern" citizens of Egypt assert themselves first as Egyptians, or as Arabs, or as Muslims? If Muslim identity were to predominate, would it be of the liberal sort taught at the great mosque-university of Al-Azhar, or the conservative fundamentalism advocated by the militant Muslim Brotherhoods? In all this complexity, it is difficult indeed to label various programs and ideologies simply as "traditional" or "modern."

ISLAM AND MODERNIZATION

What sort of role may Islam be expected to play in the modernization of the Middle East, and how should we interpret recent signs of Islamic resurgence? For the many Westerners who include secularization and Westernization in their definition of modernization, the answer to these questions seems obvious: Islam can only be an obstacle to modernization, and one whose relevance will diminish as Middle Eastern nations progress toward modernity; any resurgence of Islam is merely a temporary and unrealistic retreat into the past. Such is the argument made by many observers over the past decades, but this view fails to come to terms with the increasing complexity and visibility of Islam as a political force. Many Muslims today are challenging the Western notion that Islam is inherently incompatible with modernization.

We have defined modernization as the set of social changes accompanying technicalization, and this definition deliberately leaves open the question of whether such changes necessarily bring a reduced role for religion. Is Islam compatible with the demands of technical efficiency and economic development? In many respects, the answer is "yes." Islam is a "this-worldly" religion insofar as it is deeply concerned with the historical process and the improvement of social conditions. It was developed in a mercantile setting and it shows no bias against commerce, profit-making, or material success. Indeed, it teaches respect for private property, supports a work ethic, and seems to draw connections between material success and eternal reward.

At the same time, there is reason to view Islam as incompatible with some economic practices developed in the West. For Muslims the economic order, like all aspects of social life, must be subordinated to the normative requirements of justice, godliness, and public interest. It is Muslim morality, and not the market or the confluence of various private interests, that Muslims believe should give the ultimate direction to society. For this reason the very idea of a technicalized society in the extreme sense, a society where all other values are subordinated to competitive technical efficiency, is unthinkable to Muslims. This is not to say that a Muslim society cannot advance indefinitely in its technical sophistication, but only that it must do so under the ultimate guidance of Muslim socioreligious ideals or it will cease to be a Muslim society in the historically accepted sense. Islam, while recognizing private property, reserves the "absolute" ownership of property for God alone, and insists that all human rights of property are contingent on the socially responsible application of those rights. Profiteering, exploitation, or hoarding are unacceptable economic behavior, and the Koran even forbids the taking of interest or the charging of rent on unimproved land. Such Islamic principles as these, along with the Koranic exhortation to share the wealth with the needy and the Prophet's general antagonism toward class privilege, are taken by some Muslims as evidence that Islam favors "socialism." We shall have more to say in later chapters about programs, parties, and leaders employing Muslim ideas and symbols in defense of "Muslim socialism." Many Muslims, however, believe that Islam is perfectly compatible with capitalism, provided the latter can be separated from the hedonism and social injustice which they see in the European and American systems. (To be sure, some compromises would be necessary in view of Sharia rules concerning such matters as interest, but it can be argued that every society makes compromises in equally important matters.) Most Muslims would agree that neither of the two extremes of laissez-faire capitalism or Marxist socialism is compatible with Muslim ideals. They would contend, however, that modernization does not necessarily depend on the strict adoption of either of these models, and some social scientists today are inclined to agree.

Many of the political ideals expressed in the Islamic tradition are remarkably close to those typically associated with modernization: the accountability of leaders to their constituency, for example, or the emphasis on individual rights as against ascribed statuses of class and kinship. It can be argued, furthermore, that some Middle Eastern political phenomena that do seem inimical to modernism, such as "patrimonial" leaders who use public funds to indulge their own lavish lifestyles, reflect pre-Islamic cultural traditions and not Islam as such. Yet in politics as in economics, we must recognize that Islam brings a unique background to the modernization process. Because Islam was always predicated on the unity of religion and state, the question of whether modernization requires a separation of religion and government is particularly pressing. Another related problem facing Muslim nations is that of democracy; while Islam is a populistic religion and many Muslim countries are democracies, the political and legal heritage of Islam is very different from the European bourgeois, secular, utilitarian intellectual heritage that allows Westerners to settle questions of public morality simply by taking a vote. While public opinion may guide politics and may even, for some Islamic modernists, influence the intepretation of the Sharia law, the Sharia itself cannot be legislated according to human convenience. And since the Sharia is socially relevant and takes precedence over any conflicting directives for the Muslim, democracy must have its limits.

The extraordinarily close tie between government and religion in Muslim tradition has given rise to a tendency for both incumbent governments and the forces of political opposition to legitimate themselves in Islamic terms. The claim to political power and legitimacy often depends on the ability to make a convincing case for one's own policies as "truly" Islamic and to discredit similar claims by one's political adversaries. Although this fact might make Middle Eastern politics appear overly preoccupied with theological contention, the questions that lie behind these disputes and the criteria by which they are resolved are as much political, sociological, and economic as theological. Islamic arguments are presented in favor of social change as well as social conservatism.

The ways in which political factions seek Islamic legitimation are as variable as the political entities themselves. For example, the Saudi royal family can point to its historical association with the conservative Wahhabi movement and the strict Wahhabi religious codes as evidence of Islamic purity, but it further strengthens its position by maintaining good relations with the ulema, consulting them on many decisions and innovations. By contrast, Egyptian rulers from Muhammad Ali to Sadat have taken steps to undermine or coopt the political power of the ulema and their legal and educational institutions. For many years, outside observers saw this political disenfranchisement of the ulema, along with the creation of a small Western-oriented elite, as evidence of Egypt's secularization. In fact, religion continued as a strong force in popular sentiment, and the rise of the militant Muslim Brotherhoods has put recent Egyptian political leaders on the defensive. Nasser and Sadat have each been careful to justify their foreign and domestic policies in Islamic terms even as they denounced the Muslim Brotherhoods and continued to advocate the separation of governmental and religious institutions. In Iran, the Pahlevi dynasty not only attempted to divorce the ulema from political power, but went a step further by emphasizing the pre-Islamic imperial heritage as a cornerstone of its legitimacy. Although there were many reasons for popular dissatisfaction with the Shah's government, the regime's failure to mobilize effectively the legitimizing power of Islam not only weakened its own power but placed a decisive weapon in the hands of the opposition and contributed to the "Islamic" character of the ensuing revolution.

All this suggests that to predict a simple correlation between modernizing changes and secularization, or to see the resurgence of Islam simply as a "backlash" against change, would be to overlook the importance of Islam as a vehicle for political mobilization. This is not to say that Islam is nothing but a tool of political ideology, for there are strong theological, ethical, and personal elements involved as well. The interaction of these factors can be seen in the recent phenomenon of the increasing popularity of veiling among women in certain parts of the Middle East including Egypt. Veiling in Egypt is somewhat surprising because Egyptian women in the past were relatively free of the custom, and all the more so because it is focused among college students and middle-class women, the same group that has made the most significant historical gains in "women's liberation" (*tahrir al-mara*). It has often been argued by Muslims that Islam does not require veiling but only a reasonable degree of modesty; a generation ago few middle-class and professional women saw any contradiction between modest "Western" dress and Islam. Thus the new "*Shari*" ("lawful") form of dress now being adopted by some women, which covers everything but the face and hands, must be explained in terms other than simply cultural or religious conservatism. One writer who has tried to account for the phenomenon points to a variety of causes. Such problems as Egypt's overpopulation and more than two decades of indecisive conflict with Israel have led many to believe that a rededication to Islam, and the accompanying renewal of Divine favor, are Egypt's only hope. This Muslim "fundamentalism" has affected some women both directly and indirectly through husbands and kinfolk; some men, it is said, have threatened to divorce wives who failed to don the new costume. There are, however, other reasons for the resurgence of veiling. In a time of increased need for extra income and the acute overcrowding of public places, the new costume allows women to take jobs outside the home and to function in public life without compromising their own modesty and their families' reputations. Some women have testified that the Shari dress has helped to resolve their own crises of personal identity, thus serving as a psychologically satisfying means of self-assertion. But perhaps most significantly, the Shari dress is for many women a symbol of protest against the perceived disintegration of society, against domination by the West, and against the pressure to follow questionable Westernizing and secularizing paths of development. It is at the same time an affirmation of collective self-determination and the validity of a cultural heritage. As John Alden Williams put it, "modernization is not being questioned; false models and false friends are being questioned."[4]

THE LIMITED EFFECTS OF ATTITUDE CHANGES

The modernization process carries with it certain changes in cultural outlook and psychological attitudes. Such changes are occurring in the Middle East as the result of increased communication, and most governments actively support many of these changes. Young people attend school, and even the illiterate elders in remote villages keep informed of national and international events by the ever-present transistor radio. In many places cultural attitudes are changing so fast as to create a gap between the old and the young, and the city and the village. Yet, if modernization is to allow Middle Easterners the same social, economic, and political liberties that the modernized Western nations enjoy, changes in cultural attitudes may not be enough. Although many theorists write as though attitudes are the prime movers of social change, not all of the problems of the Middle East (and comparable regions) will respond readily to changes in education, values, or cultural perspectives.

One of the central problems, both politically and economically, is population increase. With the sudden advent of new medical techniques, death rates declined dramatically in the Middle East, while birth rates remained essentially unchanged. The resulting population explosion is more than capable of offsetting the gains of even the most enlightened development programs. The population that cannot be

---

[4]John Alden Williams, "Veiling in Egypt as a Political/Social Phenomenon," in *Islam and Development*, John L. Esposito, ed. (Syracuse, N.Y.: Syracuse Univ. Press, 1980), p. 85.

absorbed by the rural economy migrates to the cities, where unemployment levels rise drastically. Unemployment in turn creates problems of its own. For decades Egypt, given an agricultural technology comparable to the West's, could have maintained or even raised its agricultural productivity with only a fraction of its actual agricultural work force. But such a technological solution would have created a larger social problem: what would become of the surplus unemployed rural population? On the other hand, the maintenence of a labor-intensive system of farming creates a primary incentive for a large family: peasants need children to work in the fields and increase the family's margin of economic security. Changing attitudes can only do so much. Egyptian peasants are aware of Egypt's population problem but still act on their more immediate self-interests, just as Westerners are aware of environmental pollution or energy shortages but shun corrective behavior in favor of the more immediate rewards of personal advantage or convenience.

If current trends are any indication, it seems that, culture change or no culture change, the gap between poor and affluent nations may continue to widen. Colonialism has done its part; it has created political and economic dependence in colonized nations without encouraging the development of diversified, locally viable economies or self-sufficient political institutions. But even with well-intentioned help from developed nations, some factors militate against development. It is all but impossible, for example, for beginning industries in developing nations to compete effectively with more established Western industries in international or even domestic markets. And, other things being equal, it tends to be more profitable to invest capital in regions already having high levels of investment—areas with well-developed systems of transportation, communication, and other amenities of commerce. Thus, capital may be least attracted to the areas that most need it. Even the development process itself may give rise to a new kind of "poverty," as traditional systems for providing such services as transportation and communication begin to disappear in the face of newer techniques, and those who cannot afford to use the new systems become more helpless than ever.

Similarly, political modernization may be thwarted by factors that attitudes alone cannot change. A modernized outlook cannot create political self-determination overnight in the wake of two centuries of colonial domination. Worse yet, the establishment of modern political institutions may be hindered by more powerful nations concerned mainly with maintaining their own economic interests and political security. In the face of such obstacles, modernizing attitudes may only increase a sense of desperation that can lead to seemingly "irrational" acts.

Changing cultural attitudes in the Middle East will most likely lead to heightened demands for equal dignity and affluence, and a growing commitment to the efforts needed to achieve it. Tragically, however, these demands and commitments may not be enough to prevent the widening of the gap between rich and poor, the powerful and the powerless. Should this be the case, political conflict within and between nations will increase.

7

The Drive
for Self-Determination

Most of the major nations of the Middle East achieved independence by 1950. However, for some, independence was neither permanent nor even meaningful. Super-power, regional, and internal struggles were still in the process of shaping, and being shaped by, government institutions in many countries. While the postwar decline of direct European political control was bound to change Middle Eastern political relationships, it was an open question whether those relationships and government institutions would be altered in a fundamental fashion. Amid this uncertainty came the growing recognition that attaining political independence was not the same as achieving self-determination. The latter was not likely to occur in a state if its economy was dependent on that of another, nor if the population looked to imperialist powers for cultural sustenance. Many false starts, policy reversals, and policy contradictions occurred. There was no readily available blueprint for action, no clearly defined and agreed upon analysis of the problems and solutions. All parties were feeling their way through a minefield of political dangers.

The three major sections in this chapter deal respectively with the impact of an ideology, the effects of a change in economic well-being, and the analysis of a particular arena of conflict. The first section deals with the role of Egypt generally, and Gamal Abdel Nasser particularly, with respect to self-determination and Arab unity. Although the complexity of internal and regional politics denies a neat encapsulization of events and trends, it is clear that the visions held by Nasser were widely shared, that there has been universal difficulty in affecting solutions, and that there has been widespread disagreement on what package of policies would best serve as a vehicle to meet the goal.

The general impact of increased petroleum prices forms the basis for the second section. The huge increases in petroleum prices have affected every nation in the area and have allowed, indeed forced, the petroleum-rich countries to quicken the pace of change. It is not immediately obvious to what extent the countries can direct these revenues into coherent and modernizing programs. We do know that the changes are likely to be massive.

The third, and longest section is given to an analysis of Israel and Israeli/Palestinian/Arab state tensions. The reader should not infer from the length of this section that these issues dominate the Middle Eastern landscape. It is quite clear that they are but one dimension of the larger scene and that most of the fundamental issues of conflict and accommodation would remain in force if the antagonists in this arena settled their differences. There are three major reasons why an extended discussion is in order. First, Israel has a unique place in the Middle East. The heritage of its people and the origins of its statehood differ in significant ways from the other nations of the region. Second, the Israeli/Palestinian/Arab state issues have had a high degree of international visibility which often has been translated into simplistic notions of "good guys and bad guys." While it is difficult not to get passionate when millions of lives hang in the balance, it would be foolhardy to ignore the complex reality and, thereby, throw reason to the wind. Third, this arena serves as an enduring example of the difficulties involved in conflict resolution.

THE NEW ARAB NATIONALISM

The 1952 Free Officers' coup in Egypt is a good example of a transition in the Middle East. The leaders of the coup represented a new force in Egypt particularly, and in the Middle East generally. Typically (but not exclusively) they were from non-elite families and had been among the first generation of their class that was allowed to rise in the ranks of the military. They viewed traditional regimes as preserving the status quo and maintaining the division between the haves and the have nots. Their revolution was premised on the belief that a continuation of the existing political order would consign the majority of the population to permanent impoverishment. They also thought that widespread political corruption and indifference to national needs was responsible for Egypt's humiliating defeat by the Israelis in 1948. It is clear that the Free Officers had no clear plan for their new postrevolutionary society; rather, they saw the new society rising like a phoenix from the ashes of the old regime.

Gamal Abdel Nasser emerged in 1954 as the leader of the Revolutionary Command Council (RCC), the name adopted by the Free Officers after taking power. Three years after the revolution he wrote of his disillusionment that a new social order based on equality and justice would evolve naturally. It became clear to him that the various groups competing to influence the reordering of Egypt generally were concerned with enhancing their own well-being without much regard for truly national concerns; he perceived them as attempting to change the actors in the political and economic hierarchy without changing the structure. He believed, therefore, that Egypt needed a transition phase between the old order and the new; he called this transition the "Guided Democracy," and the RCC was to be its guide. Nasser and his associates felt that individual competition had to be channeled if it was to result in positive change. In practice this meant that a just and democratic society could be attained only by temporarily limiting democratic action. With no clear definition of ultimate objectives and means, and given the day-to-day pressures of political life, Nasser and the RCC developed policy through experience and perceived necessity.

The Arab League was formed in 1945 in recognition of the power of collective action. The League did not provide much more than a forum for debate during the first decade of its existence, but events centering around Egypt during 1955–1956 highlighted the need for cooperative action and provided an impetus to engage in fresh efforts to attain it. The historic Bandung Conference of 1955 brought together for the first time a large group of Third World leaders who wished to develop a nonaligned status. They clearly expressed their desire to be free of United States and Soviet entanglements, the presumption being that the superpowers were unreliable allies who would manipulate Third World countries for their own interests. The superpowers generally discouraged notions of nonalignment and sought to exploit situations that would at least keep the nonaligned countries from being wooed by the other side. Nasser emerged from the conference as a leader of the movement. The United States was particularly alarmed by what it saw as Egypt's drift away from the Western bloc; it reasoned that if the Soviets vaulted the northern tier of U.S. allies—Turkey, Iraq, and Iran—its vital interests would be challenged.

The Suez Canal Crisis and the Israeli War (1956)

The United States decided to deny military assistance to Egypt on the grounds that such assistance would promote an arms race in the Middle East (irrespective of American arms sales to Israel). This decision provided the impetus for the decade-long Soviet ascendancy in Egypt. Nasser purchased arms from the Soviet bloc in 1954–1955 in return for promised future deliveries of Egyptian cotton. When the United States countered by withdrawing proposed financial assistance for the construction of the massive Aswan High Dam in 1956, Nasser nationalized the Suez Canal. Egypt and Britain had negotiated an agreement in 1954 which called for the end of British military presence in the canal but allowed Britain to use the military installations in time of crisis. Nasser's nationalization action thereby weakened Britain's position. Nationalization itself was not contrary to international law as long as just compensation was paid to the owners of the property. However, military actions took place before issues of compensation could be settled. About three months after the nationalization, Israel invaded and captured the Sinai Peninsula and the Gaza Strip, stopping short of the Suez Canal. Israel claimed it needed to disrupt Egyptian-based guerrilla raids into Israel, that Egypt's blockade of the Straits of Tiran severely compromised their vital interests, and that a three-day-old Egyptian-Jordanian-Syrian defense pact, accompanied by verbal declarations to destroy Israel, constituted an immediate threat to its security. A couple of days after the Israeli invasion, British and French forces attempted to capture the Suez Canal. Their objective failed, a cease-fire was quickly arranged through the United Nations, and all three invaders subsequently quit Egyptian territory. United Nations troops were placed in Gaza and at the head of the Gulf of Aqaba. The Soviet Union then offered to provide financial assistance for the High Dam at Aswan. The United States now had more reason than ever to believe that the Soviets were jumping the northern tier. However, Nasser's policy of nonalignment prevented Egypt from joining the Soviet camp.

Nasser emerged from the Suez crisis as an Arab hero, and Egypt's long history of modernization and leadership in the Arab world was reaffirmed. Along with the status accorded Nasser was a recognition that Arab unity could help meet major Arab goals, victory over Israel being high on the list. Nasser and the RCC had, of course, realized that it was worthwhile to cooperate with other "progressive" Arab states on some matters and with all Arab states against Israel, but Arab unity now began to assume a new meaning: instead of an end in itself, it came to be seen as a means to Arab victory in Palestine. Events in Syria were to provide Egypt with its first opportunity to exercise leadership under the banner of pan-Arabism.

Syria

In contrast to the relative ethnic and religious homogeneity of Egypt, Syrian society is characterized by considerable heterogeneity. Sunni Muslims form a majority of the population and are in an economically preferred position. However, minorities, particularly the **Druze** and the **Alawites**, dominate the senior ranks of the military partially due to the successful preindependence French policy of fragmenting power and the unwillingness of the Sunni elite to encourage their sons to enter the military as a career. Syria spent its first three years of independence, 1946–1949, under ineffective civilian rule; a coup in 1949 ushered in the first of many military governments.

In 1954 the Arab Socialist Resurrection Party, or **Baath**, gained considerable influence in the government, influence that it held through 1958 and that figured prominently in the 1958 drive to form a political union with Egypt. Baath ideology combines socialist thought with visions of past Arab unity. The Baathists argue that the unity of the Arab peoples will evolve naturally as the individual states move along a socialist path. Baathist influence in Syria in the 1950s, however, was far from being uncontested. From the right they faced the growing hostility of conservative elements who saw Baathist policies of income redistribution and nationalization as simple expropriation. On the left the relatively strong Communist party was seeking closer ties with the Soviet Union, a country which the Baathists considered to be imperialist. The threat of a communist takeover of Syria occurred at a time when the Baathists were suffering a loss of prestige and power; the Baathists felt compelled to act forcefully to lessen the chance of Syria falling under Soviet hegemony. Nasser's immense popularity as an anti-imperialist and his growing enchantment with broad socialist principles helped promote the union between Egypt and Syria. Such a union fit neatly into the Baathist ideology of Arab unity, while it offered the Baathists a hope of maintaining their own position in Syria.

The United Arab Republic

The United Arab Republic, UAR, was formed in 1958 following a relatively brief period of negotiation and a hasty working through of the mechanics of formal acceptance in each country. As opposed to Muhammad Ali's expansionist motives in the capture of Ottoman Syria in 1832, Nasser's aims were limited and were more a result of Syrian persuasion than any enthusiasm within Egypt. While the union undercut communist influence in Syria, Egypt's growing control of the Syrian bureaucracy and its sometimes heavy-handed implementation of previously legislated but largely ignored income-leveling policies, led to Syrian dissatisfaction with the union. Since the Baathists were the driving force behind the union, they suffered a corresponding loss of prestige. The experiment ended when the Syrian army forced the Egyptian high command to leave the country in September, 1961. Nasser accepted the decision rather than engage Syrian forces. A nonsocialist government was formed in Syria, but it was ousted from power in early 1962. A military Baathist group staged a coup in 1963; the Baathists had managed to regain a share of power.

The next round of power shifts resulted from a split within the Baathist party into a moderate faction led by people with political service in Syria, and a progressive faction led by younger men, generally army officers, who represented the minorities. Animosities between the two groups culminated in a 1966 coup in which Alawite officers played a prominent part. In 1970 another coup took place and the Alawite position became more firmly established under the leadership of General Hafez al-Assad. He headed the Syrian government through the 1970s, the longest continuous rule in Syria since independence.

Jordan, Iraq, and Lebanon

The formation of the United Arab Republic helped to trigger significant events in Jordan, Iraq, and Lebanon. Jordan and Iraq were still ruled under separate Hashemite kings who had been installed by the British after World War I. However, the monarch in each country, King Hussein in Jordan and King Faisal II in Iraq, was in considerable difficulty by the time the United Arab Republic was formed.

Jordan. Jordan was a client state of Britain. It depended on Britain for military assistance and subsidies to prop up its weak economy. The nationalists of Jordan saw British aid in particular and Western actions in general as part of a new imperialism. For example, they viewed Britain's 1954 Suez agreement with Egypt as a dangerous compromise since it allowed for reoccupation whenever British national interests were at stake. In 1955 Britain formed the Baghdad Pact with Turkey, Pakistan, Iraq, and Iran. Jordan was pressed by Britain to join, but nationalist reactions led to rioting in January, 1956. King Hussein, then twenty years old, responded to the crisis by expelling the British military command from the country, including General Glubb who had been in Jordan for twenty-five years. This popular move brought temporary respite to the monarch, but elections in October brought a pro-Nasserist and socialist majority to parliament. The British-French-Israeli invasion of Egypt a month later led the Jordanian government to sever ties with Britain, thereby ending the subsidy. Hussein began to receive financial support from the United States in 1957, but he faced considerable political opposition even though he had suspended the parliament. When Egypt and Syria formed the UAR, there was much local popular sentiment for Jordan to join. In order to counter this, and with advice from the United States, Jordan and Iraq hastily established an Arab Union. But in July, 1958, a revolution in Iraq ended Hashemite rule there and brought an end to the short-lived Arab Union. Hussein then was granted his request for two thousand British troops to be stationed in Jordan to help save the throne. Military and economic aid also was given by the United States to help the young king. Contrary to the expectations of most informed observers, the dynasty survived not only that scrape but also several other crises during the 1960s and 1970s.

Iraq. The July 1958 revolution in Iraq, led by General Abdul Karem Kassim, brought death to many of the country's traditional rulers, including King Faisal II and the veteran prime minister, Nuri al-Said. The coup was originally supported by an assortment of national and leftist groups. The alliance, however, began to unravel soon after the revolution. The Iraqi Baathists urged joining the UAR, but unlike the Syrian Baathists, those in Iraq were not sufficiently powerful to force the decision. Rather, Kassim played off the pan-Arab Baathists against the communists. The nationalist group, the National Democrats, gained early favor with Kassim but lost most of their influence within a year. A highly turbulent five years followed; the communists tended to gain in power as a group but individuals had to remain vigilant because of Kassim's frequent purges of top government leaders. Kassim himself was killed in a 1963 coup. General Abdel Salam Aref came to power. Aref had been an original member of the 1958 group that destroyed the monarchy and who himself had been purged in 1958. Aref brought Baathists into the government, but they were again purged within a year. When General Aref died in a helicopter accident in 1966, he was succeeded by his brother, Abdel Rahman Aref, the prime minister at the time, who held office until the 1968 coup, which brought General Ahmed Hassan al-Bakr to power. Again the Baathists returned to a position of prominence, but it was a Baathist party stripped of its pro-Nasserist fervor. By 1968 the pro-Nasserist and communist elements were widely distrusted in Iraq. Part of the strength of General Hassan al-Bakr's rule stemmed from the fact that many of his associates came from the same area in Iraq (indeed, many came from the same village). When illness caused him to resign in 1979, Saddam Husayn took power.

The difficulty of governing Iraq has been complicated by the pressure of communalism—the attempts of the various religious and ethnic communities to assert their power on the nation. Although Sunni Muslims are a minority, they have had a far greater hand in ruling the country than their numbers would indicate. The Shiite Muslims in the southeast form the largest bloc of citizens, about 50 percent, but they had been largely excluded from power. It was with some concern, then, that official Baghdad viewed revolutionary Iran's calls to the Iraqi Shiites to overthrow the government; their numbers are large and they had some basis for discontent. The other large minority, comprising nearly 20 percent of the population, is the Kurds. They are non-Arab Sunni Muslims with their own language and culture, and they have been extremely tenacious in their almost continuous struggle for autonomy against the governments where they are a sizable minority—Iraq, Turkey, and Iran.

Although the Treaty of Serves (1920) called for the establishment of an independent state, Kurdistan, this was not carried out. But Kurdish leaders still seek an independent Kurdistan and the governments of Iraq and Iran have had longstanding difficulties trying to assimilate them. The Kurds, while possessing numbers large enough to be a constant threat, about 8 million, are small enough in each country so that they have never had enough power to break away, and have been the pawns in regional politics. During the 1960s and early 1970s, the shah of Iran supported Iraqi Kurds in their battle against Baghdad. Kurds in post-revolutionary Iran have been aided by the Baghdad government. While these policies have allowed the Kurds an increased amount of cultural and political autonomy in each country, it has not led to a growing of the Kurdish independence movement since it is not in the interests of any country to have such a movement become too successful.

Lebanon. The rise of pan-Arab sentiments during the 1956–1958 period also had far-reaching consequences in Lebanon. The National Pact, an understanding rather than a formal document, went into effect in 1943 and guided Lebanese political life thereafter. The pact formally recognized the religious and cultural heterogeneity of Lebanon and divided the major governmental posts between the different groups who were to share power. It also stipulated that the Christians would not look to France for support, and that the other Arabs would abandon their hopes of affiliation with Syria. The formula for political rule was based on the results of the 1932 census which indicated that no single group constituted a majority of the population: of the three largest groups, the Christian Maronites comprised 29 percent, the Sunnis 21 percent, and Shiites 18.5 percent. Since the Muslim birth rate exceeded the Christian, it is probable that the Sunni-Shiite Muslim population gained majority status in the ensuing decades. However, because all parties doubted that a new pact could be worked out, the population figures of 1932 remained in force; no subsequent census was taken in Lebanon.

The government that came to power in 1943 lasted until 1952. In 1952 the president, Bishara al-Khoury, became isolated by a coalition of disaffected politicians of different religious affiliations. The government fell when the army refused to follow a presidential order to break up a protest demonstration. This change of government, called the Rosewater Revolution, brought Camille Chamoun to power. The coalition that brought the government down and elected Chamoun, the Social National Front, started to split into factions as soon as its source of unity, opposition to the former government, was removed.

The carefully managed balance of religious forces tended to support the status quo; any fundamental reordering of the system ran the risk of upsetting the balance in unpredictable ways. The Christian leadership had an added incentive to resist change, for Christians held more economic power than their non-Christian countrymen. But there also were forces calling for significant changes. For example, the Druze leader Kamal Jumblatt, while not a Muslim, supported a package of reforms aimed at liberalizing the political structure and equalizing the income distribution. The Muslim population saw Chamoun leaning toward France as pan-Arab sentiments swelled. When Chamoun did not take a forthright stand against the 1956 attack on Egypt, his image as a pro-European was reinforced. Discontent became more widespread and seemingly more dangerous for the Christian leadership as Muslims were swept into the pan-Arab movement.

By the time of his 1958 visit to Damascus in conjunction with the formation of the UAR, Nasser was more than a popular hero: to many people he symbolized the drive for Arab self-determination. Muslims from Lebanon flocked to Damascus to hear him speak. The event catalyzed Lebanese discontent. Many called for a new census to rid the country of its fictitious Christian majority; some suggested that Lebanon join Syria in the UAR. President Chamoun responded to this slow but inexorable wave of discontent by imposing piecemeal controls on political expression.

Lebanon was on the brink of civil war from May to October of 1958. A massive demonstration and general strike took place in May in response to overall conditions; it had been triggered by the assassination of a pan-Arab publicist. The pan-Arab Muslims were joined by a loosely organized group headed by the Druze leader Kamal Jumblatt and several prominent Christian leaders who saw Chamoun's policies leading to failure and, thus, a victory for the pan-Arab forces. In mid-July Hashemite rule in Iraq ended by revolution. As King Hussein of Jordan received British troops, President Chamoun called on the United States to send help under the Eisenhower Doctrine. Troops from the United States landed on the beaches of Lebanon before the end of the month. It is difficult to say what effect these troops had. Their presence probably cooled passions sufficiently to allow the Lebanese to forge a compromise out of an intractable situation. Although Chamoun was replaced by the end of July, fighting along communal lines continued on a sporadic basis. A cabinet which would endure was pieced together in October; it contained equal numbers of Muslims and Christians, thereby partially recognizing the changed demography. United States troops left Lebanon by the end of the year.

Although the Lebanese managed to avoid full-scale civil disorder until 1975, maintaining the fragile peace became increasingly difficult. First, calls for Arab unity and later for pan-Islamic unity were met with sympathy by a significant portion of the Arab population, thereby putting the system under direct attack. Second, the Western bias of the free market economy put Lebanon out of step with most other Arab nations and drew corresponding criticism. Third, there were periodic incidents with Israel. Lebanon managed to avoid conflict with Israel during the 1956, 1967, and 1973 wars without being completely ostracized by the Arab community of nations. But the border problems with Israel led to the civil war of 1975–1976, the entry of Syrian troops into Lebanon, and the deepening schism between the religious communities.

The Palestinians who were living in Lebanon did not pose a serious problem for the government until the mid-1960s. To be sure, having more than two hundred thousand Palestinians in loosely supervised camps administered by the United Nations caused much worry, especially since they had to be denied Lebanese citizenship in order to maintain the communal balance. But it was not until the rise in power and popularity of the Palestinian Liberation Organization (PLO) that the situation threatened to get out of hand. As Palestinian forces struck Israel, Lebanon suffered reprisal raids. The Lebanese government was in a difficult position. To suppress the PLO would anger the sizable and passionate anti-Israeli groups in the country and, most probably, lead to civil war. To allow the Palestinians to operate freely would result in further crippling reprisal raids.

By late 1969 an agreement between the Palestinian and Lebanese leadership was reached with the help of President Nasser. Essentially it gave the Palestinians the right to rule the refugee camps and to move freely through the country in return for a promise of cooperation with the Lebanese government. After King Hussein of Jordan defeated a PLO army in Jordan in September, 1970, the situation started to deteriorate; Lebanon became the only base from which the Palestinians could mount attacks on Israel. During the first few years of the 1970s, attacks on Israel increased. Israel responded with reprisal attacks.

Civil war broke out in April, 1975. A peace was hastily constructed, but it fell apart in August and fighting raged again. The army of Lebanon intervened during the first few months of 1976, but some units joined the forces favoring the Palestinian position. Things had irrevocably fallen apart.

It would be inaccurate to characterize the Lebanese civil war as divided strictly along communal lines. While communal divisions were certainly present, many Christian Arabs supported the Palestinian cause. In any case, the Palestinians and their allies gained the upper hand and threatened the largely Christian strongholds. Israel announced that it would decisively counter the present danger. When the Syrian army then sent forces to Lebanon to bring some order to the situation, Syrian President Assad was put in an extremely delicate position. The overriding immediate aim of Syrian policy was to defuse an explosive situation. The Palestinians and their supporters had to be held in check, but this meant that the Syrians would have to support the Christians. The irony was made complete by the open secret that the Christians were also supported by Israel.

The tragic conflict, which eventually claimed 60,000 lives, gradually subsided as the Syrians stabilized the Christian areas. A coalition of Arab nations originally led by Saudi Arabia hammered out an agreement with the parties and installed an Arab Deterrent Force in Lebanon. The force was predominantly Syrian; it consisted of about 22,000 Syrian troops and about 5,000 from the other participating nations. Lebanon limped through the remainder of the 1970s with a largely powerless government, the Syrian army controlling the countryside, a growing Christian army, a restive Palestinian population, the economy in shambles, and the future uncertain.

PETROLEUM AND THE PERSIAN GULF

During the 1970s the bulk of the world's petroleum exports passed through the Straits of Hormuz at the mouth of the Persian Gulf; strict economic considerations suggest that this situation will continue at least until the twenty-first century. Since the industrial power of the West and Japan is critically dependent on Persian Gulf petroleum exports, any threatened long-term disruption of petroleum supplies from the area would invite intervention from the great powers and thereby run the risk of starting a global conflict. Because the major petroleum-producing nations of the region—Iran, Iraq, and Saudi Arabia—may not be politically stable in the next decade, the fears of global conflict are well founded.

The Iranian Revolution

It is a somber irony that the Gulf's economic growth, which was made possible by the West's need for petroleum, is now a major cause of instability. For example, the checks and balances that the Shah of Iran employed to discourage any gathering of power outside of his control became ineffective with economic growth.

By the middle of the 1970s the modified traditional Persian system of creating insecurity among the potentially powerful had broken down. The Shah, especially through SAVAK, the large secret police organization, responded by applying more overtly repressive measures. It was as if the Shah had traded his rapier for a meataxe. Much has been written about the heavy-handed role of SAVAK—originally trained and supervised by the CIA of the United States—and how popular reactions against it helped to bring the downfall of the Pahlevi dynasty. However, it is also important to understand why those in power thought that these actions were necessary. As the old system of controls was breaking down under the weight of its own complexity, the Shah was faced with the choice of accepting a loss of power or redoubling his efforts to stamp out opposition. He chose the latter course and lost the gamble.

The apparent inability of the United States government to interpret the danger signals emanating from Iran during the Shah's decline was dramatically illustrated when President Carter toasted the Shah on New Year's Eve, 1977, with the remark that Iran was "an island of stability." The view from the palace, however, was not the same as the one from the streets of Teheran. By New Year's Eve of the following year, the United States government urged all of its citizens in Iran, some 40,000, to depart. The Shah left Iran for a "vacation" on January 16, 1979. He was to die in an Egyptian military hospital a year and a half later, never having returned.

The young, politically alienated urban technocrats joined the anti-government movement in a manner surprisingly similar to the 1890 tobacco riots. Again, it was the clergy who led the revolt. They had two deep sources of disagreement with the Shah. First, the policies of "modernization" introduced by the Shah were unabashedly secular in design. Second, some policies—land reform, for example—were designed partly to woo peasant support away from the religious authorities and over to the Shah. Ayatollah Ruhollah Khomeini had been in exile in Iraq from 1963 until 1978, when he was expelled as part of the Iraqi-Iranian attempts to patch up their contentious relations. Iraq also had its own reasons for wanting the powerful leader out of the country. Shiite Muslims comprise a majority of the Iraqi population and are concentrated in the southeast of Iraq. The Kurds, who are Sunni Muslims but not Arabs, account for about 20 percent of the population and live in the north. The Sunni Arabs of central Iraq have traditionally controlled the government and have generally been in an economically advantageous position. For obvious reasons, the government of Iraq preferred not to harbor someone of Khomeini's stature and ideology. The banishment of Ayatollah Khomeini from Iraq did not lessen his influence against the Shah. As the leaders of the tobacco riots used the telegraph to coordinate their actions, so Ayatollah Khomeini directed the Iranian revolution by telephone from Paris, until his return to Iran on February 1, 1979.

The streets of Teheran ran with blood during 1978 as demonstrations, many of them peaceful, were repeatedly met with brutal force. By December, 1978, it was apparent to most observers that the shah's time was limited.

The Iranian Revolutionary Government

Khomeini's return to Iran brought a massive outpouring of popular approval. The last government appointed by the Shah before he left Iran fell on February 11. Revolutionary Iran appointed a government headed by Mehdi Bazargan, but the civilian government was subject to the dictates of the Revolutionary Council headed by Ayatollah Khomeini and found it extremely difficult to conduct day-to-day business. Prime Minister Bazargan tendered his resignation several times before it was accepted by the Revolutionary Council on November 6. The Revolutionary Council ruled until the outlines of a new constitution could be drawn and a new president elected. Abolhassan Bani-Sadr was elected president in February, 1980, and the new parliament, the Majlis, was elected by May, 1980. The first Majlis of the new republic was dominated by the Islamic Republican Party—a group led by many of the country's most important religious leaders. The president, although closely aligned with this group when both were in opposition to the rule of the Shah, was generally considered to have a more secular orientation than the clergy.

While the transition from one form of government to another is always problematic, Iran faced a particularly difficult set of circumstances. First, it was attempting to establish an Islamic republic in a form apparently quite different from other governments adopting that label. A particularly difficult point involved the conflicts of authority between the president and the religious leaders. During the early days of Bani-Sadr's presidency, Ayatollah Khomeini directed the government to reverse its decisions on several occasions. It would have been difficult for the government even in the easiest of circumstances to decide on the limits of religious authority in matters not strictly religious, but the charismatic power of Khomeini was such that the issue was never in doubt: the government was forced to accede to his directives.

The crisis of authority deepened throughout the presidency of Mr. Bani-Sadr. In early June, 1981, Ayatollah Khomeini stripped the president of his role as commander of the armed forces. The Majlis then declared Bani-Sadr politically incompetent, clearing the way for Ayatollah Khomeini to dismiss him as president on June 22. The role of president was to be filled by a three person commission until a new president was elected. The three individuals, all members of the Islamic Republican Party, were the chief justice, the speaker of the Majlis, and the prime minister. Violence between the country's various political factions had been increasing in the months preceding the ouster of Bani-Sadr. The strife intensified during June, culminating in a June 28th attack in which a bomb was exploded in Islamic Republican Party headquarters in Teheran, killing 74 people, including the chief justice (Ayatollah Beheshti), several cabinet ministers and sub-ministers, 20 members of the Majlis, and other party leaders. The course of the Iranian revolution became highly problematic: Bani-Sadr was in hiding and being sought by the government, the political leadership was in disarray, and groups again were taking to the streets.

Although the particular twists and turns of events in post-revolutionary Iran have been impossible to predict, the revolution has followed a familiar pattern in that once the glue of common discontent toward the policies of the Shah was removed, the fundamental differences between the various groups surfaced. The enduring lessons are that successful revolutions are those which hold the various factions together once the old government has been removed, and that success or failure must be measured in terms of what has happened to the country some years after the seizure of political power.

The Iraqi-Iranian War

The new republic faced the nettlesome problem of dealing with the minorities in Iran. The Kurds of the north, a Sunni group, had begun to agitate for independence. The Iraqi government supported Iranian Kurds in their efforts, just as the Shah had supported Iraqi Kurds before a 1975 agreement with Baghdad. The government also faced challenges from the Buluchis of the southeast and the Azerbaijis of the northwest. For its part, Iranian radio was exhorting the Iraqi Shiites to overthrow their government. Other Persian Gulf countries with sizable Shiite populations—Bahrain, Oman, Qatar, and the United Arab Emirates—were understandably nervous. Even Saudi Arabia had cause for worry; its small Shiite population, located in the petroleum-rich northeast, was receiving the same message that was being sent to their Iraqi counterparts.

Iraq revoked its 1975 agreement with Iran which had ended Iranian support of the Kurds in Iraq in return for the settlement of a long-disputed border in the Persian Gulf area in Iran's favor. The agreement had set the border between the two countries along the Shatt al-Arab thalweg, Iraq's only route to the Gulf and thus the only route for petroleum exports from southern Iraq. Iraq apparently wanted to regain control of the waterway. The initial Iraqi assaults were verbal and attempted to foment trouble among the substantial Arab population in Iran's petroleum-rich Khuzistan area. Open warfare broke out on September 22, 1980. Iraq scored initial victories by taking some Iranian territory along the Shatt al-Arab and by damaging the important port and refinery city of Abadan. Iran responded by bombing Baghdad on several occasions and by making a considerable effort to hold Abadan. Intense fighting stopped after a couple of months but there was no formal resolution of the conflict through the time this was being written (July, 1981).

The U.S. Hostage Crisis

The security interests of the United States presented Iran with another problem. It was commonly believed that the U.S. Central Intelligence Agency had brought the Shah back to power in 1952. Would the United States attempt to do it again? The leaders of the revolution knew that they were in a stronger position than the 1952 nationalists, but they also knew that thousands of SAVAK and military personnel loyal to the Shah would take up arms at the bidding of the United States. Although the United States government tried to distance itself from the Shah, its messages to Iran were mixed and were received with skepticism. As a positive step, the United States announced on October 5, 1979, that it would resume the shipment of some military replacement parts to Iran. Most of Iran's immense arsenal of military hardware had come from the United States, and the United States had been supplying parts roughly on an "as needed" basis. Without an adequate supply of spare parts, Iranian military capability would be at a disadvantage. The promised parts, however, were not to be shipped because of events during the next month.

On October 22, 1979, the deposed Shah entered the United States to receive medical treatment for cancer. The United States government had been told repeatedly that the entry of the Shah into the United States would only inflame Iranian passions, increase suspicions against the United States, and endanger U.S. citizens still in Iran. On November 4 the United States Embassy in Teheran was occupied by individuals identified only as "students." About sixty U.S. embassy personnel were taken as hostages. In the following weeks many furious words were hurled about without much action. However, some points seemed clear: those holding the hostages were following the dictates of Ayatollah Khomeini, and the United States would refuse to meet Iranian demands to return the Shah to Iran.

The government of the United States worked to bring diplomatic sanctions against Iran in the United Nations; it also imposed economic sanctions of its own and encouraged its allies to do the same. It used intermediaries not generally thought of as being in its camp to try to negotiate the release of the hostages. These United States actions did little to cool Iranian hostility. However, it is questionable what difference a conciliatory tone would have made, for Iran was full of conflict and contradiction. In April, 1980, President Carter ordered military units to attempt a rescue of the hostages, but the mission was aborted when several problems made it impossible for the attack force to advance beyond a desert landing point south of Teheran. Given the apparent high odds against success, the fact that it was attempted at all indicates the president's overpowering need to end the crisis. As it was, the United States was forced to take a more patient stance. The hostages were released in January, 1981.

Saudi Arabia's Political Stability

On November 20, 1979, the day after "extremists," whose motivations were unclear to the outside world, took over the Grand Mosque in Mecca, the United States came under attack in widely scattered parts of the Islamic world. The attacks seem to have been sparked by a radio broadcast in which Khomeini implicated the United States in the Grand Mosque seizure. United States embassies were attacked in Calcutta, Dacca, Istanbul, Manila, Rawalpindi, and Lahore. The American embassy in Islamabad, Pakistan, was burnt down; two Americans were killed and several others narrowly escaped death after waiting hours for the local authorities to intervene.

Until the attack on the Grand Mosque, Saudi Arabia's political stability had been shaken only slightly. When King Faisal was murdered by a nephew in 1975, there was some speculation that it was a political act, but the assassin seems to have been mentally unstable. Faisal was succeeded in orderly fashion by King Khalid. Partially because of his weak health, he was to yield many major state responsibilities to Prince Fahd. Since Saudi Arabia's massive petroleum output and low population had allowed it to accumulate enormous financial reserves, the West was particularly fearful of political instability in Saudi Arabia; its petroleum was essential and it could severely disrupt world financial markets by moving its reserves from country to country. But the monarchy was politically cautious and conservative, and the Western countries viewed it as a moderate, "sensible" nation. Likewise, Saudi Arabia's adherence to strict Islamic ideals blunted criticisms of its monarchical form of government by most "progressive" Arab nations. Given this position and the desire to assume a greater leadership role in the Arab world, the Saudis developed a reputation as conciliators.

Saudi Arabia's public image of tranquility and stability, however, concealed as much as it revealed. Saudi society was undergoing massive and rapid change. Its per capita income was one of the highest in the world; it was one of the world's leading financial powers; and it had begun countless expensive construction projects. Only a few decades earlier, Central Arabia had been one of the poorest areas of the world. Social change has not yet occurred on as dramatic a scale as the change in income, however, the tens of thousands of Saudis presently studying in the United States and Britain are not likely to completely accept their country's traditional political culture or its Islamic austerities once they return. The seizure of the Grand Mosque in Mecca may have been an isolated event, but it is possible that such disturbances will begin to occur more regularly as the popular desire for more political participation increases.

South Yemen

The Peoples Democratic Republic of Yemen, generally called South Yemen, attained independence in 1967 when the British pulled out of Aden. In 1970, it became a Marxist state. As the only long-standing nonconservative government in the area, South Yemen has been involved in many political battles in the Arabian Peninsula. It has received aid from the Soviet Union, East Germany, and China. Although any state in this volatile region must be taken seriously, it is tempting to regard South Yemen as the neighborhood's bad boy. It has continually been in somebody else's backyard, but when dealt with sternly, has been dissuaded from doing much damage. However, this analogy does not illustrate its potential importance in the region (Ethiopia, Djibouti, and Somalia are all nearby across the Gulf of Aden) or its past involvement with rebels in Oman.

South Yemen gave aid to the rebels in the Dhofar province of Oman, hoping that they would convert the whole southern coast of the peninsula into a "progressive" force. Oman is a particularly strategic kingdom because of its position at the mouth of the Persian Gulf, by the Straits of Hormuz. The Dhofar rebels waged a war of attrition against the Sultan of Oman from 1964 to 1976. The sultan, however, received enough materiel and troops from Iran and Jordan, among others, to effectively crush the rebels in 1976.

ISRAEL

The Jews of Palestine were not able to bask in the glory of victory after the State of Israel was formed in 1948. For the last third of a century, their turbulent history has been dominated by war and the threat of war. Indeed, it was not until President Anwar Sadat of Egypt set foot on Israeli soil in November, 1977, that any Arab leader officially recognized that Israel was a permanent entity in the Middle East. Even then, President Sadat's act isolated him in the Arab world.

More than most nations of the world, much of Israel's daily life is directly, consciously, and openly affected by international events. It is no exaggeration to say that virtually every long-time citizen of Israel has known someone killed in war. The Israeli "siege mentality" has been born of experience and is firmly based in reality. Israel has been under siege since its inception. It has heard numerous calls for its destruction over the years, it has lost many of its sons and daughters in military action, and it has witnessed its enemies' tremendous growth in financial power and military capability. This is not to say that every Israeli agrees on how to resolve Israel's almost continual crisis. On the contrary, Israeli public opinion on most vital issues reflects the considerable heterogeneity of Israeli society.

The Political Setting

Israel's prime minister is the de facto head of government: the position of president is largely ceremonial. The prime minister is chosen from the members of parliament, the Knesset, and is instructed to put together a cabinet. Members of the Knesset are elected through countrywide proportional representation. The voters choose between "lists," each list representing a political party or coalition of parties. The 120 Knesset seats are divided between the lists according to the percentage of the national vote garnered; for example, a list gaining 10 percent of the vote receives twelve seats. Any single list must gain a minimum of 2 percent of the vote to be eligible for a seat. If the government is to function effectively, of course, it must maintain the support of a legislative majority on at least the key issues of the day. This point is essential for an understanding of Israeli politics; coalition politics has dominated the system because no single party has ever gained a clear legislative majority.

Although Israeli citizens have been presented with a wide range of lists in each general election, they generally select from three prominent groups: the labor-dominated left-center, the right-center, and the religious parties. The labor list formed the governments from 1949 through 1977. The right-center put together the ninth Knesset, which convened in 1977. The religious parties generally have gained between 10 and 20 percent of the vote and have been the group that the other two have turned to in order to form a legislative majority. Therefore, they have had an influence beyond their voting strength.

The labor list itself has been a coalition of several distinct parties that united for the purposes of the elections. Generally these parties have espoused a socialist ideal in domestic affairs. The most powerful labor group, the Mapai, held the loyalties of many Israelis through their control of the Histadrut, the widely pervasive labor organization. Since the Mapai drew its leadership primarily from the Histadrut, it has become identified by many as the group that in the past provided temporary relief to immigrants, helped them secure housing, and gave them employment. The other major labor groups were more strident in their socialism, more willing to subsume nationalist aspirations and identify with the working classes of all nationalities. The labor parties, formally called the Alignment since 1969, were able to garner a plurality of Knesset seats until 1977; they constructed their legislative majority by taking the religious parties into the fold.

The religious parties, as the name suggests, were concerned primarily with religious issues which they sought to introduce in the government—for example, the notion that Israeli Jews had the right to settle in all Biblical lands irrespective of existing political boundaries.

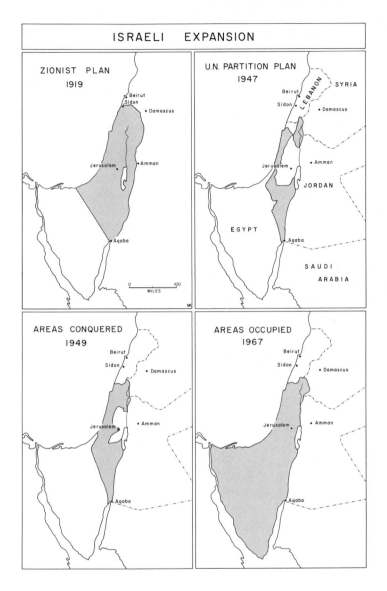

ISRAELI EXPANSION

ZIONIST PLAN
1919

Beirut
Sidon
• Damascus
Jerusalem • Amman
• Aqaba

0   100
MILES

U.N. PARTITION PLAN
1947

SYRIA
Beirut
Sidon • Damascus
LEBANON
Jerusalem • Amman
JORDAN
EGYPT
Aqaba
SAUDI
ARABIA

AREAS CONQUERED
1949

Beirut
Sidon • Damascus
Jerusalem • Amman
Aqaba

AREAS OCCUPIED
1967

Beirut
Sidon • Damascus
Jerusalem • Amman
Aqaba

Israeli Expansion. *Source*: Yahya Armajani, *Middle East Past and Present,* ©1970, p. 323. Reprinted by permission of Prentice-Hall, Inc., Englewood Cliffs, N.J.

The labor alliance started to lose power during the 1960s. There were several reasons for their decline, one ironically being their past success. Because they could not manage to win a majority of Knesset seats, and because the labor bloc itself was an amalgam of parties and viewpoints, they had to broaden their political position to accommodate more of the electorate. But in so doing, their political focus became blurred, and dissension within the party grew. A host of other factors contributed to their inability to gain a majority, including the changing profile of the voters (rural to urban, older to younger) and voter disillusionment with incumbents who had failed to ensure peace and security.

The performance of governments based on coalitions is always problematic. The labor bloc was large enough to prevent a quick succession of governments; but it had to depend on other parties and found it difficult to move away from the status quo. The status quo, however, meant insecure national borders and a large military budget.

Although there had been defections of important figures from Mapai during the 1960s, it was only after the 1973 war that the coalition began to face serious challenges to its premier position. The war resulted in heavy Israeli casualties, no military victory, and a psychological shock. In June, 1974, the government of Prime Minister Golda Meir was forced to step down in favor of another set of labor-bloc leaders headed by Itzhak Rabin. However, the new government also faced a rocky road. Israel was becoming more and more isolated internationally, the military budget grew larger and more burdensome, and the economy faced high rates of inflation. Since the Rabin government was forced to adopt the amorphous policies of its predecessors, it had difficulty in resolving the vital issues. Finally, in 1977, a series of financial scandals involving Rabin and some cabinet ministers eliminated the government's remaining strength.

The Democratic Movement for Change (DMC) then emerged as an important new coalition party. It was a single-issue party that advocated changing Israeli electoral laws to rid the Knesset of debilitating factionalism. The leadership of the DMC was drawn from a wide ideological spectrum, although much of the platform resembled that of the labor bloc. Their apparent aim was to gain enough seats in the Knesset to help form a majority in return for a promise of electoral reform. The results of the election dashed their hopes.

The Labor Alignment had its number of Knesset seats reduced from 51 in 1973 to 32 in 1977. Since the National Religious party, holding 12 seats in 1977, no longer desired to unite with the Labor Alignment, it proved impossible for the Alignment and the DMC (15 seats), along with other smaller parties, to form a majority in the Knesset. The big winner in the 1977 elections was the Likud party, which emerged with a plurality of 43 seats. After a month of negotiations, a government was formed in June, 1977, which aligned the Likud party with two religious parties (and later with the DMC, which reserved the right to disagree on questions including religion and occupied territories). Menachem Begin, the leader of Likud, became the new prime minister. The new government generally was considered conservative in domestic issues and aggressive in foreign policy: it advocated a selective dismantling of socialist policies in favor of private enterprise, and the settlement of Israelis on land occupied since the 1967 war. Indeed, Prime Minister Begin referred to the occupied areas as being "liberated." As the new government became established, it remained unclear whether the basic shift away from labor bloc positions would continue. Analyses of the 1977 election indicate that Israelis voted against the Labor Alignment rather than for the Likud coalition. Israel continues to hammer out its policies through coalition politics.

The Likud coalition had fallen apart by 1981. An inflation rate greater than 100 percent led the Minister of Education to declare that a substantial boost in teacher salaries was needed if he was to remain in the coalition. The Minister of Finance replied that a substantial increase in teacher salaries would add fuel to the inflationary fire and that he would quit the coalition if it was granted. Intense negotiation failed to resolve the differences and preparations for elections to the tenth Knesset were made. The particularly acrimonious nature of the campaign indicated quite clearly that the political leaders sensed that the Likud surge first experienced in 1977 was not a fluke and that no single party held the loyalties of most Israelis. The results of the June 30, 1981 election gave Labor and Likud 49 seats each. The smaller parties generally lost seats but gained in bargaining power since both Labor and Likud eagerly sought their favor in hope of forming the needed 61 seat majority. Israel, therefore, continued to be governed by a fragile coalition.

Social Setting

The coming to power of a nonlabor government in 1977 was in many ways the political expression of the social change that had been occurring since 1948. The composition of the Israeli population in 1950 was markedly different from what it was two years earlier. Estimates (open to some question) made by the United Nations team that drew up the 1947 partition plan showed a total population of 1.8 million, two-thirds being Arabs. By the end of 1949, the Arab population had fallen to about 160,000 and represented one-eighth of the total; the Jewish population had roughly doubled to 1.2 million. The Arabs became a minority. Jewish immigration continued to be heavy through 1952. Thereafter, natural rates of increase and immigration contributed equally to the population growth. By 1980 the population of Israel was 4 million, 85 percent of which was Jewish.

Israeli society is a complex amalgam which nevertheless invites categorization and, thereby, oversimplification. Perhaps it is easiest to begin with a three-way ethnic breakdown: European Jews, Oriental Jews, and Arabs. The European (**Ashkenazi**) group also includes Jews who immigrated to Israel from North and South America, and South Africa; but the major distinguishing factor is the common parental or cultural lineage with European Jewry. The great majority of Jews who came to Palestine during the five preindependence waves of immigration were from Europe; the first four primarily from Russia and Eastern Europe; the fifth wave included a considerable number of German Jews fleeing the Holocaust. The leaders who emerged from the first four waves set the ideological tone for the young state, a blend of socialism and Zionism that emphasized the virtues of working the soil. The fifth wave came to Palestine largely out of desperation. These people faced death in Nazi Germany and had been denied adequate refuge in the Allied countries. Their motivation was survival, and not necessarily the socialist-Zionist pioneering spirit that had guided former immigrants. Although their impact on Israeli society should not be overemphasized, many of these immigrants were urban, middle class, skilled, and more closely in touch with Western European culture than those from Eastern Europe and Russia. Their numbers were large and their votes had to be courted. Nevertheless, immigrants of the first four waves headed every government save one—that of Rabin, a Sabra (native-born Israeli). The postindependence wave of Eastern European immigration was largely over by 1952.

In the first few years following independence, many Jews from Asia and Africa immigrated as Arab governments acted in increasingly unfriendly ways and as local populations sometimes vented their anger at Israel toward these people, who by and large had nothing to do with Israel. During the first twenty-five years of independence, Israel absorbed three-quarters of a million of these immigrants, the largest group, 255,000, coming from Morocco. The effect on the social structure of Israel has been profound. Jews of African-Asian origin, called imprecisely either Sephardic or Oriental Jews, came to Israel to escape hostility and did not share the Western values and orientations of the Ashkenazi Jews. Their shared Jewishness was all that bonded them with their fellow Israelis. Although there are notable exceptions, the Oriental Jews of Israel generally have a substantially lower than average per capita income, have had less education, hold less significant government posts, have less desirable housing, and are viewed in a somewhat disparaging light by many of their fellow citizens. They are the soft underbelly of the Jewish population of Israel. The most notable exceptions to these generalizations are the **Sephardic** Jews who were long-time residents of Palestine. The Sephardic Jews of Palestine were totally conversant with local Arab culture and had an articulated social structure in place well before the Zionist movement started. This small Sephardic elite tended to view all Jewish immigrants with some disdain.

Although many Sephardic Jews found government posts under the British mandate, neither they nor the Oriental Jews of more recent arrival shared fully in Israeli political life after independence. Their numbers swelled during the first decade of statehood until they became the Jewish majority by the 1970s, and the Ashkenazi-controlled major political parties had to woo their votes. The scene was complicated by the rise in numbers of another identifiable Jewish group, one that cut across Ashkenazi and Oriental distinctions: Sabras, or native-born Israelis. Although generally associated with their parents' group and marrying within that group, Sabras started to form another social force and comprised over half the Jews in Israel by 1977, most of them of European parentage.

If the Oriental Jews are the underside of Israeli Jewish society, many Arabs are in the position of belonging to a different culture while being citizens of Israel. The flight of Arabs out of Palestine from 1947 to 1949 was motivated largely by a concern for personal safety, the same concern that brought many Jews to Palestine. Since the fighting in Palestine in 1947–48 was largely between Jewish and local Arab forces, it is not surprising that various Jewish groups actively sought to rid the fragile state of the hostile Arab population. The most famous—or infamous—terrorist act of this early period was the massacre in the village of Deir Yasin where 250 Arab men, women, and children were killed. While the political leaders of Israel officially opposed the act, they did not proceed in a forceful manner to end terrorism by the armed bands that cooperated with the military.

Arab migration from (and within) Israel destroyed any semblance of order and coherence in the remaining Arab population. The two sources of leadership, the urban professional elite and the traditional leaders of villages, generally had fled. Of the major cities of Israel only Nazareth maintained a large Arab population; only a few thousand remained in the other urban centers. A wide-open and often bitter competition for power took place in many rural areas. There was no center around which the Palestinian Arabs could rally. They were further divided along religious lines: 70 percent were Muslim, 21 percent Christian, and 9 percent Druze and other religions. In the immediate postwar years, Palestinian Arabs had no political leadership and suffered extreme economic deprivation.

Neither Zionist theory nor past political policy gave the leaders of the new state a clear formula on how to deal with an Arab minority in a Zionist state. Indeed, some Israelis hoped for a time that the problem would solve itself—that the flight of the Arabs would continue until none were left. In any case, the fledgling state had other pressing problems to deal with in order to survive. The economy was in chaos, the machinery of government was incomplete, and thousands of indigent, relatively unskilled immigrants were flowing in. The ad hoc policy toward Palestinian Arabs was mainly concerned with the maintenance of state security.

The geographical concentration of the Arab population made administration somewhat simple. A few months after Israel was formed, the army units which had occupied Arab-populated areas were formally charged with administering them. Since most of the Palestinian Arabs lived in areas that were Arab under the U.N. partition plan, a military administration was logical in that Israel was an occupying force. However, the Military Administration was to continue until 1966, well after annexation of these areas. Regardless of its other policy measures, the emplacement of what essentially was an army of occupation defined the basic attitude of the state toward these "part-citizens." However, even within the Military Administration the principles of administrative action were not clearly spelled out; security remained the only articulated goal.

Security would be enhanced if the Arab population were fragmented geographically and politically, if their economic power were limited but not desperately low, and if their emerging leadership were placed in a dependent situation and coopted. Many of the Israeli government's policies can be connected to one or more of these aims. For instance, land use and land rights policies have consistently had the effect of stripping land away from the Arab population, especially in those areas the government has deemed necessary to place under full Jewish control. Travel restrictions made it difficult for Arabs to establish political unity; and other policies established tight control over the Arab labor force. Occasionally the policies of the Military Administration resulted in spectacular displays of violence. In October, 1956, for example, forty-nine residents of the Arab village of Kfar Kassim, were killed for disobeying a curfew order of which they were unaware. The growing tensions surrounding the 1956 war and the need for absolute control led to the tragedy. That the responsible officers were given relatively light sentences confirmed the Arab view of the Israeli government's attitude toward them.

By the mid-1970s, the Arabs in Israel began to demonstrate a sense of nationalism, but it is not clear if they will attempt to win the rights of first-class Israeli citizens or seek a separate existence. Their power has remained weak, and their association and identification with the active Palestinian organizations operating out of Israel has been distant. They have remained dependent.

Israel and the Border States

Following the May 14, 1948, declaration of statehood, Israel immediately went to war against Egypt, Iraq, Lebanon, Syria, and Transjordan. The initial round of fighting lasted for a month and was followed by a month-long truce administered by the United Nations. Ten more days of fighting was followed by a second truce. Sporadic fighting and truce arrangements occurred throughout 1948. Finally the British government declared that it would act on the 1936 treaty with Egypt that allowed British troops to enter Egypt to protect vital British interests. This announcement, and pressure from the United States government on Israel, helped bring about a series of bilateral armistice agreements between Israel and its neighbors.

The war and the armistice agreements increased Israeli territory by more than 30 percent beyond what was allowed for in the partition plan. The Israeli army, although outnumbered substantially, mounted a series of crisp and well-coordinated attacks on the various Arab armies. However, the Israeli success was due at least as much to the ineptitude of the Arab armies and the lack of coordination between them. While various Arab leaders charged that Israel won because of Western support, several Arab nationalist spokesmen expressed their dissatisfaction with the kind of leadership that resulted in such humiliation. Terrorist activities ripped through Egypt in the latter part of 1948 and throughout 1949; the Egyptian prime minister was assassinated. The winds of discontent in Egypt continued to blow until the Free Officers' revolution in 1952. Three coups occurred in Syria during 1949–50; none of the leaders, however, engaged the public's imagination. King Abdullah of Jordan was assassinated in July, 1951. The shame of the 1948 defeat resulted in more Arab reprisals against their own governments than against Israel. Their anger was well placed, but it would take another quarter century before Arab armies could match Israeli forces.

The task of creating and maintaining stability in newly created states generally has proved to be a formidable task. Israeli leaders had their job complicated by continued hostile relations with Arab states and by Israel's special population and economic problems. The flood of Jews coming from Europe after the close of World War II and from Arab countries during the late 1940s and early 1950s put the new state under tremendous strain. Israel, after all, was to be the homeland for all Jews. Indeed, the Israeli declaration of independence implied, and subsequent legislation (the Law of Return) granted, this right. Therefore, all immigrants had to be accepted. On the other hand, the economic and social system was put under an enormous burden, so enormous that many feared Israel would collapse. In 1952 the Jewish Agency, the organizers and financiers of most of this immigration, in an attempt to ease the crisis, introduced certain financial criteria for immigration. However, the new criteria for immigration did not solve other pressing problems, including that many immigrants did not adhere to the Zionist-socialist ideology on which the early settlers had founded Israeli society, and that the flight of Arab farmers and the cessation of agricultural trade with Arab states caused a food shortage that assumed crisis proportions.

Many immigrants had to be settled on the land, but most were not ideologically suited to life on a *kibbutz* (a form of collective farm developed by earlier settlers), nor in the cooperative agricultural villages, the *moshava*. The government placed many immigrants in farming villages under the supervision of instructors who gave technical information, executive direction, and ideological guidance. Ideally the villages were to be located behind the border settlements and evolve into autonomous cooperatives. This process was carried out by fits and starts, with some successes and failures.

The first several years of statehood, then, were difficult. However, the population, food, shelter, and state security problems were adequately solved by the mid-1950s. A considerable amount of ingenuity and hard work had been required, but the job was eased considerably by a large amount of foreign aid flowing into the country that made it possible for Israel to cope with the situation. Immediately after independence the ratio of the value of imports to exports was about 15 percent—that is, for every dollar spent on imports only fifteen cents was earned from exports. The ratio climbed to 60 percent in the 1970s, but the absolute value of the gap increased. The gap between international spending and earning was covered by international remittances—gifts and loans from governments and individuals. About 15 billion dollars was received during the new nation's first twenty-five years. Twenty-five percent came from Jewish Fund collections, 25 percent from German reparation and restitution payments, 9 percent from bond sales, 13 percent from direct, unilateral transfers (generally from individual to individual), 13 percent from U.S. government loans and gifts, 7 percent from direct private investment, and 8 percent from various short and medium term loans. Much of Israel's economic growth was due to these sources.

The 1956 Arab-Israeli War

As Israel steadied its economy and settled its immigrants, the Arab nations limited their anti-Israeli activity to the issuing of bellicose statements. They generally did not have firm control over their own internal political situations. However, Nasser's success in nationalizing the Suez Canal aroused Israeli fears of Arab unity. A few years earlier, Israel had initiated its policy of severe military reprisals against any government from whose territory attacks on Israel were launched. The policy was designed to discourage further attacks by making the punishment exceed the original transgression. Although Israel was censured by the United Nations on several occasions, it held firm to its policy. Israel and the West were deeply concerned with the pan-Arab sentiment which was growing under Nasser's leadership and Egypt's drift toward the Soviet bloc. Israel was also concerned with the increasing number of raids from Egyptian territory, and Egypt's refusal to allow Israeli ships through the Suez Canal and especially the Straits of Tiran. Israel invaded Egypt on October 30, 1956. Within four days, Israel was in control of the Sinai and the Gaza Strip. One day after the start of the Israeli invasion, the British and

French announced a joint expedition to seize the Suez Canal, an action that the United States opposed. When the fighting ended a few days later, the British and French held Port Said at the northern terminus of the canal. An eventual settlement called for the removal of the invading forces from Egyptian soil and the stationing of United Nations troops along the Egyptian-Israeli borders (primarily the Gaza Strip and the important Straits of Tiran, through which Israeli shipping could reach the port of Aqaba and thereby avoid the Suez Canal).

The Arabs henceforth considered Nasser a hero. He had turned back Israel, France, and Britain, and had earlier rebuffed U.S. attempts to limit Egyptian military strength. Israel had scored an impressive military victory but found itself in a more delicate position than before as Nasser's influence and the pan-Arab movement gathered momentum. During the decade following the 1956 war, Nasser remained the undisputed leader of the Arab world, although he had to share some of his prestige with Ahmed Ben Bella after the success of the Algerian revolution. He was also concerned with the situation in Yemen, and had had to send 70,000 troops to support the republicans against the Saudi-backed royalists.

The 1967 Arab-Israeli War

From 1956 to 1966 Israeli-Arab tensions remained just below the boiling point as a host of large and small issues—including important disputes over water rights in the Jordan River, changing relative military strength, and shifting Arab alliances—threatened to fan the conflict again.

For two years the Syrian government had permitted Al-Fatah, the military arm of the fledgling Palestinian Liberation Organization (PLO) to use Syria as a base for raids into Israel. In May, 1967, various Arab leaders became convinced that Israel was about to launch a massive reprisal attack against Syria. As a visible display of Egypt's willingness to go to war, Nasser had Egyptian troops march through Cairo on their way to the Suez Canal. This action sounded a battle cry in the Arab world, which then called on Nasser to crush Israel. Since his popularity had begun to wane, Nasser needed to be firm and decisive if he was to remain the leader of the Arab world. Confrontation politics are always dangerous, but especially so when each side has developed a "worst case" scenario. On May 19, 1967, Egypt requested that United Nations troops be withdrawn from Egyptian territory. The United Natons complied promptly—too promptly to suit many observers. On May 24, Nasser announced that the Straits of Tiran were closed to Israeli ships. The die was cast. The Six-Day War started in the morning of June 5; the Israeli air force destroyed most of the Egyptian air force while it was still on the ground. Quickly and efficiently Israel pressed the advantage it secured by air; within a week it had taken the Sinai and Gaza from Egypt, Jordanian territory west of the Jordan River, and the strategic Golan Heights from Syria. In contrast to the postwar agreements of 1956, Israeli troops continued to occupy territory in which well over a million Arabs lived. The war was another crushing humiliation for the Arabs, and Nasser offered his resignation.

Israel gained a clear military victory and established three buffer areas it

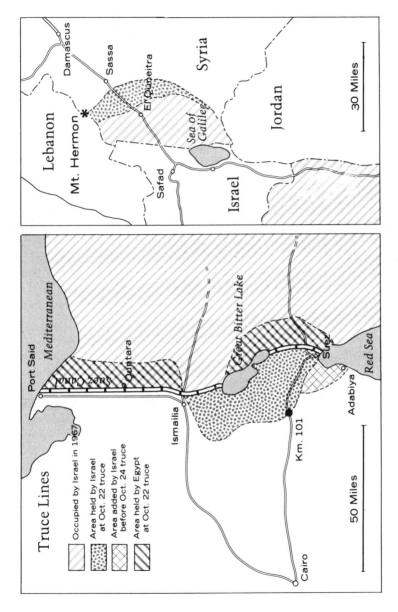

Truce Lines

Occupied by Israel in 1967

Area held by Israel at Oct. 22 truce

Area added by Israel before Oct. 24 truce

Area held by Egypt at Oct. 22 truce

Port Said

Mediterranean

Suez Canal

Qantara

Ismailia

Great Bitter Lake

Km. 101

Suez

Adabiya

Red Sea

Cairo

50 Miles

Lebanon

Mt. Hermon

Damascus

Sassa

El Quneitra

Syria

Safad

Sea of Galilee

Israel

Jordan

30 Miles

1967 Truce Lines. *Source:* William R. Polk, *The Arab World.* Cambridge, Mass.: Harvard University Press, 1980, p. 353.

considered vital to its security. But it also had to control well over a million additional Arabs at a time when the Palestinian movement was gathering steam. Israel's occupation of Arab territories put it in a difficult position in the United Nations. The Security Council of the United Nations responded by adopting Resolution 242, which required, among other things, Israel to withdraw its forces from occupied territory.

THE PALESTINIANS

The Palestinian diaspora that resulted from the Israeli victory was largely to Arab countries. In 1950 about 900,000 Palestinian refugees were in camps operated by the United Nations in Lebanon, Jordan, Syria, and the Gaza Strip. The plight of these people was deplorable. The United Nations relief effort was minimal; the food ration was limited to 1,600 calories a day, and housing often consisted of scraps of material loosely thrown together to form primitive shelters. No national Palestinian leadership had arisen before the establishment of Israel, and refugees grouped together on a traditional village basis. Throughout the 1950s the outside world heard little about the refugee camps, except for occasional news shorts showing their humiliating and stultifying living conditions. The rest of the world seemed to wish the Palestinians away; the Palestinians were unable to generate any coherent response to their plight. On the few occasions when they protested their conditions, they were suppressed by the host Arab governments, the most notable early example being Egypt's actions in the Gaza Strip in the 1950s.

Organized resistance eventually did develop, beginning with the formation of Al-Fatah in the late 1950s, and the creation of the Palestinian Liberation Organization in 1964 through an initiative of the Arab League. It was apparent to the various national leaders that the festering discontent in the refugee camps was being used to form effective paramilitary units dedicated to the overthrow of Israel. These groups took heart in the success of the Algerians in thwarting the best efforts of France through a combination of tight organization, urban guerrilla terrorist activity, and tenacity. Palestinians began to think that they too could bring a Western power to its knees. However, there were significant differences between the two situations, one being that the bulk of the Palestinians and the heart of the resistance movement were outside Israel. Israel's reprisals against any nation from which anti-Israeli actions originated, coupled with its military superiority, deterred the Arab League. The League thus decided to control the Palestinian activists. It thought that the PLO could serve as a Palestinian umbrella organization and at the same time be subject to the League's control. Al-Fatah, under the leadership of Yasir Arafat, however, remained active.

With the end of the 1967 war, Palestinian fortunes began to rise. For most of the 1960s Palestinian leaders had disagreed with Nasser's dictum, "Unity Is the Road to Palestine," preferring instead "Palestine Is the Road to Unity." The outcome of the 1967 war made it clear to them that their hopes for nationhood would be dashed if they followed Nasser's proposition. The Palestinians believed that only they could and would act to defeat Israel. Therefore, they ignored Arab pleas for unity. The various "front line" nations, those bordering Israel, however, faced the prospect of having independent armies in their territories, armies bent on destroying an enemy that the nations themselves were not prepared to attack. The PLO could no longer be expected to control the different Palestinian groups or obey the wishes of the Arab League. Each country therefore gave tacit support to a particular Palestinian organization, supported its growth, and tried to control its activity. Well over a dozen sizable groups and a bewildering array of splinter groups formed between 1967 and 1969. In 1969 Yasir Arafat of Al-Fatah became the head of the PLO. Apparently the thinking in Arab capitals was that Arafat's successful organization would be controlled more easily if he were given a new mantle of authority.

King Hussein of Jordan tended to view the Palestinians as potential citizens of Jordan rather than aspirants to a separate nation. Since the PLO had between thirty and fifty thousand troops in Jordan by 1970—forces better described as a conventional army than as guerrilla fighters—and since the fractious liberation movement was demanding more and more autonomy in Jordan, the king could either sit back and watch his country being dismantled or take decisive action. "Black September" is the name the Palestinian movement gave his response; in September, 1970, Hussein ordered regular Jordanian troops against the PLO. Thousands of Palestinians were killed, and Palestinian power in Jordan was broken. The only remaining sanctuary close to the Palestinian homeland, Lebanon, absorbed large numbers of refugees and found itself traveling down a dangerous road. The Palestinians were in decline, but they remained a force to reckon with.

The PLO was not significantly involved in the 1973 Arab-Israeli war except for promoting strikes in the occupied West Bank. In November, 1973, the Arab heads of state declared the PLO the sole legitimate representative of the Palestinian people. To Arab leaders, the move made sense for several reasons. Jordan's King Hussein had been discredited as a representative of Palestinian interests due to the events of Black September; it was necessary to include the PLO in any peace negotiations; and the PLO now seemed to be more flexible than before on many issues. In November, 1974, Yasir Arafat addressed the United Nations and saw that body pass resolutions declaring the right of Palestinians to seek independence, and granting the PLO permanent observer status in the United Nations. The PLO had attained international legitimacy. But it was not recognized by Israel and, therefore, could not enter into direct negotiations. Nor was it accorded more independence of movement by the Arab nations. Its fortunes took a turn for the worse during 1975 when Lebanon fell into civil disorder. The PLO had been hinting that it could accept the continued existence of Israel if Palestinians were granted an independent status on West Bank territory. Israel indicated that it could accept a Palestinian "entity" on the West Bank only as long as that entity was formally part of Jordan and as long as Israel was allowed to maintain defense forces in the area. While these positions were far apart, they at least allowed the participants room to negotiate and continue the slow process of finding a mutually acceptable solution. But the moderating forces in the PLO lost ground to the "rejectionists"—those who saw the elimination of Israel as the only possible foundation for a Palestinian state. Since the PLO could not control rejectionist activities during the collapse of Lebanon, its claim to preeminence was compromised. When the Lebanese situation finally calmed down, the rejectionists suffered a decline and the PLO gained prestige.

THE 1973 ARAB-ISRAELI WAR

The end of the 1967 Arab-Israeli war did not bring peace. Israel continued to hold the occupied territories and build settlements on them. It faced a line of hostile Arab states, especially Egypt, and was burdened with an enormous defense budget.

By 1973 Egypt's President Anwar Sadat had had three years of experience in office. He had ceased to be viewed as a weak, sometimes comical, figure and had begun to assert his own brand of leadership. The 1967 war had been devastating to the Egyptian military and economy. Since the economy had already been extremely weak, partially due to the abrupt and untimely way in which Nasser nationalized many industries in the early 1960s and the high population growth rate, the capacity of the average Egyptian to endure hardship was being severely strained. The Soviet Union was reluctant to give President Sadat the military aid he needed, probably because of the possibility of upsetting the movement toward detente with the United States. In July, 1972, President Sadat ordered the immediate departure of the 40,000 Soviet military personnel and their dependents from Egypt. The oil-rich Arab states already were supplying Egypt with considerable aid and, in any case, could not be expected to deliver military hardware. If Egypt would have allowed the status quo to continue, the minimal demands of the military would have worsened the already dangerous economic situation. The government of Israel, seeing Egypt's plight, then set down more stringent conditions for peace, obviously hoping that President Sadat would accede. But acceptance of the Israeli position would have endangered Egypt's aid from the oil-rich states and possibly triggered a coup. President Sadat then embarked on a fruitless international diplomatic offensive as a last step short of war. Because he saw no other way out of the stalemate, Sadat and President Assad of Syria then planned a joint attack on Israel for October 6, 1973. The war, called the Ramadan, or Yom Kippur war, was launched on time. Carefully trained Egyptian forces managed to penetrate Israel's defenses for the objective of seizing a strip of the Sinai east of the canal. However, Israeli forces crossed the canal at another point and isolated the Egyptian army. A cease-fire, sponsored by the United Nations with the encouragement of the great powers, took effect on October 24. It took until the following May for terms to be worked out on the Syrian-Israeli front.

The Israeli army had again proved capable of meeting the Arab threat. It had recovered from the initial forays of the Egyptian army and mounted its own offensive; it also beat back Syrian attempts to regain the Golan Heights. But the results of this conflict were different from the earlier wars on at least a couple of counts. First, the cost of the effort in terms of money and men was staggering. It was obvious that neither side could afford many more such ventures. Second, the Egyptian army performed as a tough, skilled unit. Although it did not in any sense win the military battle, it was obvious to many that a limited Egyptian victory was well within the realm of possibility.

It seems that President Sadat's gamble in initiating the war had paid off. The Egyptians had mounted a successful limited strike and invited the great powers to help Egypt find a way to break the stalemate with Israel. It was a high-risk strategy, one which came dangerously close to initiating direct military involvement by the United States and the Soviet Union. But the stalemate was broken as the U.S. secretary of state, Henry Kissinger, took the lead in promoting a new settlement. In the months after the war, Dr. Kissinger and a number of other interested parties flew repeatedly from one capital to another in what was called "shuttle diplomacy." After a time, terms of peace were established between Egypt and Israel. President Sadat had put much stock in efforts of the United States to bring the needed settlement. The Syrians, still engaged in combat against the Israelis and unable to win back any territory, were understandably upset by Egypt's separate agreement with Israel. Sadat's actions were considered to be a form of appeasement, and Sadat became isolated in the Arab world. Syria's President Assad assumed the leadership of the front line states. Nevertheless, President Sadat continued his efforts to bring a lasting peace to Egypt. His most spectacular move was to go before the Israeli Knesset in November, 1977. Although the major issues between Egypt and Israel were not resolved by this dramatic initiative, it did set the stage for further talks, the most important being the Camp David talks between Prime Minister Begin, President Sadat, and President Carter. Egypt and Israel continued their sometimes fractious negotiations through the remainder of the 1970s, resulting in a gradual Israeli withdrawal from the Sinai and a partial normalization of relations between Egypt and Israel.

Egypt's partial accommodation with Israel continued to alienate it from Syria and its supporters, and the Palestinians. It was charged that Egypt forgot the Palestinians in a selfish and shortsighted attempt to gain temporary security. Sadat's dismantling of Nasser's socialist economy was seen as further evidence of his Western bias. Syria, the new claimant to Arab leadership in the struggle against Israel, was caught in an ironic swirl of events. As noted earlier, Syria had found it necessary to invade Lebanon to control Palestinian activities and avoid Israeli reprisal attacks. As the 1970s ended, Christian separatist forces controlled a sizable strip of southern Lebanon, with the help of Israeli materiel and military aid. Syria effectively controlled the rest of Lebanon (not including parts of Beirut and some mountainous areas), including the Palestinians.

The Israeli settlement of occupied territories, a long-standing source of hostility, continued apace throughout the decade. As with so much else in Israel, the settlement policy assumed a military importance: the settlements were placed along border areas near Arab towns and crossroads, especially in the West Bank, to increase security. The movement culminated, at least in a symbolic sense, in 1980 legislation declaring undivided Jerusalem to be the capital of Israel. The Arab world trembled with rage, called for a jihad, but took little action. Indeed, the Israelis seemed not to notice the broad international condemnation that poured forth on this issue. Israel had survived its first third of a century; it entered its second third increasingly isolated from the world community, with a questionable military superiority, and with domestic economic instability.

CONCLUSION

The nations of the industrialized world have had many decades to develop their forms of government, economic structures, and cultural perspectives. Most countries of the Middle East have not had time to gently sift and winnow such weighty ideas. Rather, they have been thrown headlong into the race for modernity and are still in the process of defining their identity. We can expect to see many changes in the Middle East in the last years of this century although we can identify only the broad contours.

Many of the important issues during the past thirty years in the Middle East are connected to the drive for self-determination. Although most of the countries had gained formal political independence by 1950, they still faced the task of charting an independent economic course and settling on a coherent cultural identity. Their job was complicated by the acceleration of worldwide technological and organizational revolutions which acted to make the world more interdependent. Greater world interdependence meant that one nation's policy changes could easily conflict with the interests of other nations, and that they would have to make a greater number of decisions between mutually beneficial and harmful interdependencies. Statements of many Third World leaders reflect the dilemma; they generally have been quick to point to the difficulties, but have not been able to arrive at affirmative policies. However, some guides to the future are identifiable from the decisions of the past.

First, neither the Soviet Union nor the United States can feel sure of having this or that bloc of Middle Eastern nations in its camp. The nations of the Middle East are now able to act more independently. It also seems likely that the various regional relationships will continue to be fluid. For example, Libya during the 1970s sought political union at times with Egypt and the Sudan, but has had hostile relations with these nations at other times. It also strongly backed the "progressive" government of Iraq during some periods and strongly opposed it at others. The relationship of the Palestinians with Arab nations and Israel are another ready example. The changing alliances and relationships reflect that the actors are still in the process of searching for fundamental common interests which will transcend transitory conflicts.

We also know that the Middle East's dominance of world petroleum markets will continue to have a major effect on regional and global politics. For example, the 1980-1981 war between Iran and Iraq brought statements of neutrality from Western governments along with warnings that the West would not tolerate an expansion of the war that might close the Straits of Hormuz. Such superpower pressures on the Middle East are certain to continue. Furthermore, the financial strength of the petroleum-rich countries will continue to alter regional relationships between have and have-not nations. Conflicting interests will also continue to surface between the have nations; for example, Iran, which has few petroleum reserves can be expected to have an attitude toward petroleum pricing different from Saudi Arabia, which has large reserves.

Perhaps of greatest ultimate importance, Middle Eastern societies will continue to change at a rapid pace. Modernization has stimulated a search for a new sense of identity which is bound to take different directions across countries and through time. The most arresting manifestation of this search has been the resurgence of Islam as a regional, national, and personal symbol of identity. It is difficult to know whether this resurgence will act as a vehicle through which social tensions will be played out, will serve as a causal agent itself, or create its own dynamic. In any case, the Islamic resurgence promises to be a significant political force.

8

The Economic Setting

The Middle East presents a remarkably wide spectrum of economic circumstances. It includes some of the richest and poorest nations in the world and some of the most fertile and barren land. Some of these nations have been cosmopolitan for a millennium or more, while others only recently peeked beyond their boundaries. Some mix religion and politics in a strict puritanical system, and others advocate secular socialism. The Middle East's unusual diversity of conditions generally is not appreciated. This chapter and those that follow will elaborate on the diversity of circumstances, as well as the areas of commonality and the various conflicts that surface in the context of this pluralism.

Some cautions should be mentioned at the outset. As has been noted in the first half of this book, nations are complex and most short statements about them tend to be incomplete. Many works—from Baedekers to sophisticated technical analyses—deal with the economic conditions of the individual countries under study. Our approach will be to deal with central themes of conflict and resolution rather than geographic or national entities. The student also should realize that the precision implied by statistics is often illusory. Indeed, some of the available statistics purporting to describe the Middle East are in gross error due either to faulty measurement or bias. Numbers have political uses, of course. The government of Lebanon, one of the most advanced countries in the area, has consistently lacked data on the measurable economic and social characteristics of its Muslim and Christian populations. The always precarious balance between the two groups could have been thrown into disarray through political action premised on such information.

Since Israel was given extended coverage in Chapter 7, the authors have decided to omit it from a full-blown analysis in this chapter. Data on Israel, however, is included in several of the tables in this chapter. The economy of Israel has many problems common to the various Arab states, but it differs considerably in other respects. As contrasted to its Arab neighbors, its labor force is more highly educated and from a different cultural setting, its agriculture is more capital intensive, its industry contributes a greater percentage to national income, and it has received greater amounts of international aid. Common problems include significant migration, the need for careful water management, and the need for a large and expensive military sector. The reader should be aware that the exclusion of Israel from this chapter results more from considerations relating to the organization of this book rather than from a notion that the economy of Israel is fundamentally different.

Table 8-1 indicates the per capita income levels of various Middle Eastern economies for selected years. Although these figures are not exact, they are sufficiently reliable to provide a general idea of the level of economic activity. All the countries listed have experienced some increase in per capita income, although there have been tremendous variations. In the early 1960s, Israel was clearly the leader (excepting Kuwait), having a level of per capita Gross Domestic Product ($939 U.S. in 1960) about double that of Lebanon and four to seven times that of the other adjoining countries. By 1980 the situation had changed dramatically: the measured lead of Israel increased over its oil-poor neighbors, but suffered substantially relative to the petroleum-exporting states.

Table 8-1   PER CAPITA GROSS DOMESTIC PRODUCT FOR SELECTED YEARS
(Current U.S. dollars)

Country	Year	Per Capita GDP	Country	Year	Per Capita GDP
Algeria	1960	246	Lebanon	1960	481
	1976	954		1970	603
	1977	1,102		1975	1,131
Bahrain	1970	1,111	Libya	1960	143
	1977	6,129		1975	5,395
Egypt	1960	129		1977	7,422
	1976	392	Oman	1970	388
	1977	485		1975	2,781
Iran	1960	204		1976	3,034
	1976	1,999	Qatar	1970	388
	1977	n.a.		1975	11,800
Iraq	1960	245	Saudi Arabia	1960	282
	1975	1,222		1976	6,155
	1977	1,620	South Yemen	1970	116
Israel	1960	939		1976	213
	1975	3,942	Syria	1963	210
	1977	4,079		1976	777
Jordan	1960	168		1977	839
	1976	434	Turkey	1960	196
	1977	697		1976	1,022
Kuwait	1963	4,877		1977	1,134
	1975	11,307	Yemen	1960	51
	1977	n.a.		1974	172
				1975	170

SOURCE: *Yearbook of National Accounts Statistics, 1979*, Volume II (New York: United Nations, 1980), pp 3–9. Copyright, United Nations (1980). Reproduced by permission.

Per capita income figures do not show what each citizen has available to spend; they indicate how much of national income each individual would have if the income were evenly distributed. The enormous gulf between the rich and the poor found in some of the states is thus ignored, as are military expenditures. The fact that Egypt has devoted about 30 percent of its GNP to military needs while Kuwait has spent a much smaller percentage, means that the measured gap between the two countries is much larger than indicated. The growth record, whether viewed from the simplicity of Table 8-1 or from a more sophisticated framework, was reasonably satisfactory during the 1960s if one ignores Egypt and impoverished Yemen and South Yemen. Petroleum price increases in the 1970s assured some countries of phenomenal growth and put the countries without oil under ever-greater strain, especially those countries that had established an industrial base and needed oil.

Table 8-2, showing the origin of Gross Domestic Product, gives a different schematic view of most of the economies under study. The petroleum-exporting countries that were latecomers in the industrialization process—Libya, Oman, and Saudi Arabia (plus the United Arab Emirates, which is not listed)—have become ever-more dependent on petroleum. Those that had developed an industrial base by 1960—Iran, Iraq, and Kuwait—had about the same percentage of GDP originating from the industrial sector in the mid-1970s as a decade earlier, indicating a substantial growth in the industrial base during the period (since petroleum prices started their steep increase around 1970).

Table 8-2   ORIGIN OF GROSS DOMESTIC PRODUCT

Country	Year	GDP (local currency)	1	2-4	3	5	6	7	8-9
Egypt	1960	1,459.3	28	20	n.a.	3	10	7	25
	1974	3,956.0	31	21	n.a.	3	9	4	24
	1977	7,341.0	24	23	22	4	11	7	20
Iran	1960	332.4	27	26	10	4	8	9	19
	1975	3,651.5	9	47	11	8	5	4	25
	1976	4,689.2	9	48	10	9	5	3	25
Iraq	1960	601.4	16	45	9	4	5	7	17
	1973	1,664.1	14	45	9	3	7	5	21
	1975	4,022.4	7	63	6	2	5	4	17
Israel	1960	4,577.0	9	18	18	7	8	6	28
	1975	83,708.9	5	21	n.a.	9	n.a.	n.a.	16
	1977	153,999.9	7	29	n.a.	8	11	9	46
Jordan	1960	98.3	15	8	6	5	21	11	32
	1973	268.5	12	12	9	6	18	7	34
	1977	477.6	9	16	11	6	14	9	30
Kuwait	1966	854.0	0	66	4	4	9	3	17
	1973	2,111.0	0	74	4	1	5	3	16
	1975	3,279.0	0	77	5	1	6	3	13
Lebanon	1964	3,200.0	12	15	n.a.	6	32	8	27
	1972	6,365.0	10	16	n.a.	5	32	8	31
	1975	7,251.0	10	16	n.a.	5	32	8	31

TABLE 8-2 ORIGIN OF GROSS DOMESTIC PRODUCT (*Cont.*)

Country	Year	GDP (local currency)	Percentage Distribution*						
			1	2-4	3	5	6	7	8-9
Libya	1962	172.4	9	28	5	6	8	5	34
	1973	2,193.2	3	52	2	12	6	6	19
	1977	5,731.5	2	58	3	11	5	5	n.a.
Oman	1970	104.7	16	69	0	8	2	1	5
	1974	568.5	3	69	0	10	5	2	11
	1976	827.0	3	65	0	10	6	3	11
Saudi Arabia	1962	8,673.0	10	55	8	2	6	5	20
	1975	135,047.8	1	83	5	4	3	3	7
	1976	200,751.8	1	69	4	13	4	4	9
South Yemen	1969	56.6	20	26	25	1	11	5	,36
	1974	77.9	n.a.	n.a.	n.a.	n.a.	n.a.	n.a.	n.a.
Syria	1963	3,980.0	30	16	15	3	19	8	24
	1975	20,198.0	18	23	12	6	24	7	23
	1977	25,993.0	20	19	7	7	25	5	24
Turkey	1960	47.0	38	17	15	5	9	7	19
	1975	515.0	26	22	19	5	13	9	21
	1976	659.0	27	21	18	5	13	8	21
Yemen	1969	2,214.6	72	2	1	3	13	2	7
	1973	3,709.7	61	3	2	4	15	2	11
United States	1975	1,513.8	3	28	23	4	18	6	39
	1977	1,878.8	3	29	24	5	18	6	37
Japan	1974	135,344.4	5	37	35	7	18	7	31
	1976	167,266.2	5	32	30	8	16	7	30

*1=Agriculture
2=Mining and quarrying
3=Manufacturing
4=Electricity, gas, and water
5=Construction
6=Wholesale and retail trade
7=Transport and communication
8-9=Other

SOURCE: *Yearbook of National Accounts Statistics, 1979* (New York: United Nations, selected years). Copyright, United Nations. Reproduced by permission.

THE ECONOMIC RECORD

Two overriding phenomena have shaped the economic record of the Middle East during the past thirty years—war, or the threat of war, and the success of the Organization of Petroleum Exporting Countries (OPEC).

Arab-Israeli hostilities dominate the area. Israel and the countries bordering it have consumed a substantial chunk of their resources for military strength in the past three decades, resources that could have been directed toward economic growth. These hostilities have had deleterious effects beyond the pure waste of committing resources to nonproductive uses; the occasional outbreaks of war and the constant possibility of war disrupt plans and projects, discourage investment, and divert attention from nonmilitary objectives. The disruptive effects are greater in the less-developed countries than in their richer counterparts, for the less-developed economies are far more fragile than the developed ones. A poor country is poor, in part, because it does not have the physical infrastructure—networks of communication, transportation, education, and electrical power—the right variety and amounts of economic resources, and the social and political complements that are necessary for sustained growth. These countries experience significant setbacks when they have to absorb outside shocks to their economies. This is exactly what happens when the local military machine is obliged to garner resources that otherwise could be used to build a stronger national economic foundation.

In assessing the post-World-War-II record of the various countries, one must account for these dislocations. Egypt, for example, has engaged in four wars with Israel and a not inconsequential war in Yemen, along with several confrontations with Libya. In the best of circumstances the task of creating an economy capable of sustained growth is difficult; the need to be in an almost constant state of military readiness has greatly compounded the problem. Jordan has had to contend with a tremendous influx of Palestinians, Syria has been engaged with Israel, the delicate balance in Lebanon has unraveled, and so on. Israel, of course, has felt particularly beleaguered, being constantly under threat, although massive international aid for many years buffered the problem. Given these conditions, the countries under study have experienced more growth than one would expect. But the prospects for sustained rapid growth were dim until 1974.

One of the most remarkable transfers of wealth the world has ever seen was ushered center stage by the success of OPEC. The members of OPEC roughly quadrupled the price of petroleum between October, 1973, and January, 1974. By 1980 Saudi Arabia, the leader, had accumulated more financial reserves than most other countries of the world. The other petroleum producers in the area, most notably Iraq and Iran, also had spectacular increases in revenue. The result of this recent accumulation of financial power is being felt, in greater or lesser degree, throughout the world. The petroleum-producing countries now have the financial wherewithal to promote economic development; their allies have benefited through various direct and indirect measures, and their enemies have suffered. Much of the Middle East has been changed forever because of OPEC actions; and because of this, the world has also changed.

ORGANIZATION OF ECONOMIC ACTIVITY

The three major economic goals of most countries are growth, stability, and an equitable distribution of income. There is much debate as to which of these is the most important and how the goals are best pursued once a reasonable consensus is reached on the "correct" mix. Indeed, governments and universities resound with arguments that champion a range of solutions from private enterprise to socialism. The issues have importance beyond scholarly debate; the choices are real and the stakes are high.

Several countries are proponents of "Arab Socialism," while others have monarchies that directly control much of the "private" enterprise of any note. Others have taken a more eclectic stance. Arab Socialism is propounded by Libya, Iraq, Syria, South Yemen, and Algeria. But there seems to be little consensus among them as to what the ideology of Arab Socialism is and what its effects have been. The lack of a clearly defined and consistent ideology is due to several factors, including disagreements across national boundaries, and espousals of an idea without any particular plan of action. What is clear is that the socialist governments came to power with a definite desire to provide greater economic growth, stability, and a more equitable distribution of income and wealth. In order to meet these goals, the leaders initiated land reforms, froze prices, and nationalized major industries. But these measures are better described as nationalistic than socialistic, especially when they are designed to lessen foreign influences in the economy.

It is probable that some of these countries have professed socialism because it is a convenient way for their political leaders to eliminate business opposition, or to strike an appropriate international posture; and it is possible that their professed ideals will fade as circumstances warrant. In 1973, three years after the death of Gamal Abdel Nasser, clearly the leading proponent of Arab Socialism in the region, Anwar Sadat declared an Egyptian "open-door policy" to foreign investment. A little more than a decade earlier Nasser had severely restricted not only foreign business operations but also private domestic investment. Nasser's relationship to the business class probably had something to do with his decisions. The abrupt change in Egyptian policy may have been based on Sadat's desire to curry favor with the late conservative King Faisal (d. 1975) of Saudi Arabia. Ideologies may shift dramatically with the political climate.

Iraq, considered a radical state, reacted strongly against the post-Nasser economic drift in Egypt. A few months after the open-door policy was announced in Egypt, and after the 1973 Arab-Israeli war, Iraq proposed that the Western supporters of Israel should be punished through a boycott of petroleum sales. By adopting this policy they proved their radical mettle to the world at large. Of course, the world at large may not have known that Iraq was selling its petroleum to the U.S.S.R., which in turn sold petroleum to Western Europe. Without impugning Iraq's motives, it is fair to say that Iraq was able to maintain its international reputation as a "hardline" state without having to suffer significant revenue losses from decreased petroleum sales.

The same kinds of observations can be made about those countries that profess to follow private enterprise as an operating principle. In a few countries, most significant ventures initiated by the private sector are tied directly to the government either through formal public participation or through the intervention of well-placed individuals in the government. The deposed Iranian royal family, for example, gained ownership shares in many significant industrial ventures in that country. The royal family participated both because it desired wealth and because it perceived a need to exert control over industrialists and the growing industrial sector. In many cases this kind of intervention has had a profound effect on the functioning of the marketplace. Competitive private enterprise markets in the Western world are largely impersonal and exclude all considerations except for those of price and performance. The highly personalized industrial ventures in Iran under the shah or in Saudi Arabia, for example, should not be expected to yield the same results. It is difficult to know what to call such systems: perhaps etatism will suffice. In any case, they are not private enterprise systems as generally thought of in the West.

Although the ideological stance of the various nations may be important, we must look beyond surface pronouncements and deeds. The remaining sections of this chapter will analyze how different circumstances lead to different policy measures, and why the same policy measures may lead to different results. Issues of ideology and its transformation into action by national leaders will be the subject of the following chapter.

LAND

Table 8-3 gives the geographical areas of the various Middle Eastern countries. Saudi Arabia is the twelfth largest country in the world; Iran ranks fifteenth, being about one-half the size of India; Sudan and Algeria are the two largest countries in Africa. In comparison, Kuwait, Bahrain, Qatar, Israel and Lebanon are very small indeed.

A great percentage of the land in the Middle East is either not arable or only marginally so. With a few minor exceptions, all of the arable land in Egypt runs along the Nile; that of Libya is contained in a narrow band of land along the Medi-

Table 8-3 COUNTRY SIZE AND POPULATION DENSITY

Country	Surface Area (km^2)	Population Density
Algeria	2,381,741	8
Bahrain	622	429
Egypt	1,001,449	39
Iran	1,648,000	21
Iraq	434,924	27
Israel	20,770	167
Jordan	97,740	23
Kuwait	17,818	63
Lebanon	10,400	294
Libya	1,759,540	2
Oman	212,457	4
Qatar	11,000	9
Saudi Arabia	2,149,690	4
South Yemen	332,968	5
Sudan	2,505,813	7
Syria	185,180	42
Turkey	780,576	54
U.A.E.	83,600	3
Yemen	195,000	35

SOURCE: *Statistical Yearbook, 1978* (New York: United Nations, 1979), pp. 68–74.

terranean. The Arabian peninsula has significant arable land only in parts of Oman, Yemen, and the Hijaz region of Saudi Arabia. Much of the Iranian steppe and the even more mountainous terrain of Turkey is unsuitable for high-yield agriculture. The vast deserts of the Middle East often have been compared to a sea; while they have an unrelenting, harsh, and beautiful power, they have also made it very difficult to establish adequate communication networks among the peoples of the Middle East. These formidable deserts are both barriers and vast havens. However, their power to promote insularity has eroded considerably in the twentieth century. The finances necessary to overcome the power of the deserts—to cross them with roads, build airports, purchase transportation systems, dam rivers, and build radio transmitters—were generated in some countries by colonial administrations and in others by nationalist modernizing forces, by means of taxes and oil revenues. Whatever the source, the deserts are slowly being changed. They will, however, continue to present severe constraints on life in the Middle East.

Water is the scarcest resource in the Middle East. Egypt has the Nile. The Tigris and Euphrates both start in mountainous Turkey and wind through Iraq, the Euphrates also cutting across Syria. There are only a few significant rivers in the area. The most fertile areas of the Middle East lie in the valleys of these great rivers and the Levant. Other agricultural areas generally must depend on rainfall.

The Nile River is the lifeline of Egypt. At Aswan, the width of productive land is only a few hundred meters on each bank of the river. The productive valley widens as one travels north, fanning out into the great Delta north of Cairo. For thousands of years the annual flooding, occurring with great regularity, provided a natural replenishment of necessary soil nutrients, as well as drainage. The Delta long was viewed as the breadbasket of the region and later as the source of cotton for English textile mills. Harnessing the great power of the Nile would give farmers a dependable source of water year round, increase the yields from a single planting, enhance the region's ability to double crop, and meet the nation's demand for electricity. The building of the massive Aswan Dam and the filling of Lake Nasser behind it was hailed, therefore, as a project that would alter the face of Egypt. The financing, however, was beyond the government's ability. In the mid-1950s the United States negotiated with Egypt to provide financing and technical assistance to the then young government headed by Gamal Abdel Nasser. The Egyptian government was groping for a positive course; it was trying to end the corrupt and inefficient rule of the royal family that was overthrown in 1952. As part of the move toward a nonaligned status, and because it needed to be ready for war with Israel, the Egyptian government shopped in the world arms market for military goods. Rebuffed by the United States, it signed an arms agreement with Czechoslovakia in 1955. This prompted the United States to withdraw its support for the Aswan Dam project and implicitly invited Soviet sponsorship and a consequent ascendancy of Soviet influence in Egypt. Consonant with its history, Egypt thus became a focal point for world politics. This time, however, Egyptian nationalism provided a check on the benefits to be gained by world powers.

The building of the Aswan Dam necessitated a massive movement of people from villages located where Lake Nasser would form. The Nubian villagers, well out of the mainstream of modernizing influences and culturally more akin to the citizens of Khartoum to the south than Cairo, were uprooted in a wholesale fashion and relocated in parts of existing towns or in newly formed villages. Since the rhythm of the river was the heartbeat of the local culture and economy, the relocation amounted to radical surgery. These people were thus forced to rely on the central government much more than previously. They had to abide by new rules, as compensation was calculated, rents and land rights were established, and new social order was set in place.

The dam had different consequences for the fellahin to the north because the river level was now constant. The water table began to rise, and as it did so, the soil became saturated with salt. By the mid-1970s, the centuries-old high productivity of certain parts of the Delta had decreased dramatically. The decrease was especially marked in cotton production; cotton is particularly sensitive to the level of salinity in the soil. Keeping the Delta region productive by lowering the water table required two basic strategies: control over water use and improved drainage. Each of these efforts required the government to impose regulations and spend considerable sums of money. The government had to control the operation tightly because individual economic incentives worked against actions that corrected the problem. Ironically, the increased availability of water has led to tighter water controls.

While the government controls the amount of water flowing into many irrigated areas, it cannot easily control how it is shared, a difficulty that has caused hostility between neighboring farmers. The allocation of water for individual farm use has been complicated by the modernizing effect of machine-driven pumps, and by the land reforms that have significantly reduced average farm acreage and thereby increased the number of farm units to be controlled. The provision of adequate drainage presents similar difficulties. Substantial capital expenditures are needed for drainage, but an individual landholder will not significantly improve productivity acting alone. Likewise, if all of the farmer's neighbors spend their precious capital for adequate drainage, the lone party who resists will still share in the benefits as the water table recedes. The government, therefore, must finance and control drainage in a systematic fashion.

The boon to agricultural productivity, which was the *raison d'être* of the Aswan Dam, is now seen to be offset by important negative side effects that have strained the scarce financial and administrative resources of the government. Many of these side effects were anticipated before the building of the dam. However, the need to feed a quickly growing population and provide adequate electricity was thought to be more important.

Both the Tigris and Euphrates rivers originate in the Armenian highlands of Turkey, are fed by melting snow, and flow into the Persian Gulf. But the rivers are dissimilar in some important ways and present different kinds of opportunities and problems. The Euphrates cuts across Syria and Iraq on its journey. It has only a few major tributaries and, therefore, is rather slow moving and has a regular flow. The Tigris passes directly from Turkey into Iraq and has many tributaries. It is liable to heavy flooding, having a swift current and carrying a large volume of water. Irrigation from the Tigris is complicated by the timing of the floods and the irregular level of the river. Flooding usually occurs in the spring, in about the middle of the growing season for most crops (except rice and barley). The land cannot simply be inundated as it is in Egypt. A system of catchment areas must be employed so the water can be released at the appropriate times. And here too, provision has to be made for adequate drainage to prevent excess soil salinity.

These problems were faced a thousand years ago by the Abbasid caliphate which exploited the fact that the Euphrates, a western neighbor of the Tigris around Baghdad, has a higher elevation than the Tigris. A canal system was built between the two rivers that allowed for catchment, irrigation, and drainage. Regular maintenance was required, as the Euphrates carried a substantial amount of silt. If the Tigris flooded, a considerable additional effort was needed to clear the irrigation system. Relatively large and continuous infusions of capital were necessary to keep the system running. Since the irrigated lands were owned by many different parties, and the benefits of maintenance and repair were spread unevenly among them, the absence of a well-defined and enforced set of rules discouraged private investment in the canal system. An effective and stable government was needed to maintain agricultural productivity on the irrigated lands. Once the Abbasids passed their zenith, the system fell into decay for a millennium. Although some progress in developing and maintaining irrigation systems has been made since World War II, the general political instability and limited financial and administrative resources of the governments of both Iraq and Syria continued to result in low levels of productivity.

This situation contrasts markedly with that of Egypt. Government actions maintaining adequate drainage certainly have affected agricultural productivity in Egypt, but short-term neglect did not lead to a total failure of the system—at least not until the Aswan Dam was built.

The difficulties of raising agricultural productivity in Iraq through irrigation have been exacerbated in recent years by the construction of the Euphrates Dam in Syria. Quite obviously, Iraq has some reason to fear that Syrian use of Euphrates water could affect Iraqi irrigation and, hence, productivity. The Syrians, on the other hand, see the dam easing their agricultural problems by bringing a regular and sufficient flow of water to a relatively large area.

As opposed to Egypt and Iraq, Syria has had to depend heavily on rainfall to raise crops. A statistical quirk illustrates the extent to which Syria's agricultural output is dependent on rainfall; the quirk is that a measured decrease in nationwide yields per hectare generally indicates an upward movement of total agricultural yield. The explanation is quite straightforward. Much of the agricultural land in Syria is only marginally productive and depends on above-average amounts of rainfall to realize any output. If the rain fails to materialize, yields fall to zero and the land is not counted as being under cultivation. In good years some production is forthcoming, but it is generally below the average yields from the less marginal land. Hence measured productivity per hectare falls as total production increases.

LAND DISTRIBUTION

Agricultural land distribution and ownership patterns are generally considered to affect productivity. Obviously, they are also indices of economic justice and power. All of the countries in this survey have seen significant changes in the pattern of land ownership in the twentieth century. There have been formal agrarian reform programs in six of the countries—Egypt, Iran, Iraq, Syria, Libya, and South Yemen. There have been no reform programs in Jordan, Lebanon, or Saudi Arabia. Land ownership and use patterns have changed considerably in Israel, but it is best to consider Israel apart since the circumstances of these changes have been unique.

Various land ownership patterns have developed in the Middle East, but three types are most common: The first kind is **mulk**, or private ownership. The second is **miri sirf**, land owned by the state, generally with very strong usufruct (right of use without ownership) rights granted to the tenant. In practice, this is often little different than mulk. The third is **waqf**, a uniquely Islamic institution. One type of waqf allows for title to the land to be given to some officially recognized religious or social institution, sometimes with the condition that the family and heirs of the donor are to receive some share of the proceeds from the land either until the family line no longer exists or for some specified period of time. Another form is strictly private.

Turkey

Turkey and Iran, the two large non-Arab Muslim countries in the area, have had very different experiences in land redistribution and agricultural development. Turkey put itself on the path of modernization with the thoroughgoing Westernizing revolution of Kemal Atatürk. Years of Ottoman neglect of agriculture, except as a tax base, were quickly reversed. At least three distinct periods stand out in Turkish agricultural history since the formation of the republic in 1923. First, during the years of Atatürk (1923–38), the oppressive tax structure was reformed and a host of infrastructure projects were developed. The second era began after the close of World War II. The government engaged in a considerable effort to improve storage and marketing facilities as well as to introduce mechanization. Up to 1960, agricultural output expanded tremendously. Wheat production nearly doubled between 1948 and 1953, allowing Turkey to become a net exporter of this grain for a short time.

A great deal of this expansion came about by extending the area under cultivation as opposed to increasing the yields per hectare. This resulted in two deleterious effects that slowed the agricultural growth rate from 1960 to 1980, the third phase. Because most of the new lands were marginal, they lost whatever productivity they had during each period of drought since there is relatively little irrigation in Turkey. Second, the methods used to expand the area under cultivation resulted in a loss of soil fertility and a greater run-off of water.

Egypt

The 1952 revolution in Egypt ushered in a substantial program of land reform and redistribution that proceeded by fits and starts for the next two decades. In

1952 about 1.2 percent of the largest holdings encompassed 45 percent of the agricultural land. In contrast, the smallest 72 percent of the holdings accounted for 13 percent of the land, an average of about one *feddan* (1.06 acres) per holding. Because of population pressures and a lack of alternative employment, the rental rates charged by the mostly absentee owners of the large estates were very high. The first lands to be expropriated were those of the royal family. These lands, plus the waqf lands in their possession, accounted for 5.5 percent of the total agricultural land. Land reforms also lowered the maximum feddans which an individual could hold from 200 in 1952, to 100 in 1961, and finally to 50 in 1969. At first, the larger landowning families simply split their holdings among various family members and thereby avoided being severely affected. The law, however, was gradually tightened, and by 1970 the government had redistributed 18.6 percent of all agricultural land.

The Egyptian process of land redistribution also involved regulations controlling rental rates (not greater than seven times the annual land tax), the establishment of cooperatives, the provision of easy credit, a special scheme for orchards, and an attempt to lessen the number of holdings that were split among different parcels of land.

Syria

The process of land reform followed the same general pattern in Syria. However, due to the extreme variability in land productivity, the redistribution was based on estimated incomes to be derived from the land; therefore, larger parcels were given to those on land low in productivity. As with many countries, the redistribution effort proved far more difficult than the promulgation of laws restricting maximum size. In Syria as in Egypt the class of large landholders was more tenacious than anticipated. The reforms quickened in pace only as the political power base of this group diminished.

Libya and Iraq

In Libya and Iraq the large landholders were rather suddenly shut out of the political decision-making process, although the situation in each country was somewhat different. Libyan agricultural land holdings were of two polar types: a small number of large estates located in relatively good and well-irrigated land, mostly owned by Italian nationals, and vast stretches of marginal land, mostly (about one-third in 1960) owned on a tribal basis. The 1969 overthrow of the monarchy led to the expropriation of the Italian farms in 1970. The Libyan agricultural reform methods fit both the ideology of the socialist government and the agricultural situation. A mere redistribution of the poor lands would not accomplish much, if any, gain in productivity. Likewise, the average yields of the large productive farms probably could not have been retained if the farms were split up. These large units, therefore, were transformed into state farms. The redistribution of marginal lands was tied to an ambitious scheme to invest some of the country's considerable oil revenues in order to raise agricultural productivity; wells, roads, and marketing facilities were included in this effort. Attempts also have been made to strongly discourage, if not eliminate, absentee ownership of arable land.

In Iraq, local sheikhs—generally better described as political dignitaries rather than religious leaders—were transformed into landholders in the twentieth century largely because the British attempted to transform the communal tribal ownership patterns into those of private ownership. The 1958 revolution left the sheikhs without a political power base, and the carving up of their holdings was assured. State lands, the *miri sirf*, also provided a base for redistribution. But the state of Iraqi agriculture and the country's political instability led to highly uneven results for this potentially highly productive nation.

The agricultural land of Iraq is dependent on irrigation to support even reasonable levels of productivity; declines in agricultural productivity occur when the central authority neglects its responsibilities in this area. The neglect, although abating somewhat in the twentieth century, did little to help the redistributive measures designed to enhance productivity. The political instability from 1958 to 1968, and modest financial resources, discouraged progress. The Iraqi government was also distracted by the continual problem of the Kurds to the north, a problem which took on the characteristics of a full-scale civil war.

Iran. Large-scale land reform started in Iran in 1962, and without the impetus of a revolution. The Shah redistributed some royal lands in the 1950s, but the White Revolution promulgated in January, 1963, promised for the first time a set of sweeping changes throughout the economy, including substantial land reform (the revolution was called "White" because it was to be peaceful). Before the redistribution, absentee landlords controlled much of the fertile lands in Iran; the peasants generally had no tenancy rights. The landowners often owned huge tracts of land that encompassed many villages. To minimize evasion of the law, redistribution was stated in terms of villages rather than area. Legislation in 1965 closed some loopholes in the law, transferred waqf land administration to the central government, and presented the landholders not affected by the 1962 legislation with five basic choices: (1) lease the land, (2) sell the land, (3) divide the land between themselves and the peasants on the basis of old sharecropping agreements, (4) form a cooperative with the peasants, or (5) purchase peasant rights to the land and continue farming. This wide range of choices clearly reflected the triangle of tensions then present between landlords, peasants, and the Shah. The Shah needed to reduce the landowners' power, or at least give the appearance of doing so, but it was so great that an attempt at outright expropriation seemed inadvisable.

The results of this land reform can be analyzed fairly accurately by examining what happened in a particular village.[1] Before redistribution, about half the land in this village was in (public) waqf status, the other half being owned by a single individual. The peasants farming the waqf lands secured tenancy rights through the government. The landlord chose to split his property in half (the basis of the old sharecropping agreement), keeping, as might be expected, the most fertile land under his control. The peasants who worked this land, therefore, were excluded from redistribution policies. Other similar results followed: The largest and most fertile parcels

[1]Craig, D. "The Impact of Land Reform on an Iranian Village," *Middle East Journal*, XXXII (Spring, 1978), 141–54.

lying outside the new domain of the landlord were worked by the family and friends of the village headman who up till then had been the manager of the lands. On gaining property rights, almost half of these village elite rented their land to the headman and became absentee landlords themselves. Also, the custom of drawing lots every three to five years to ensure that particular peasants would not be permanently consigned to the least fertile land ended, of course, when title was assigned. This meant that some of the landed peasants were put in a permanently disadvantageous position.

It is very difficult to assess the effects of these events on agricultural productivity. However, the peasants became increasingly stratified socially and economically, a new class of absentee landlords developed, and the *de facto* changes in power relationships with the central bureaucracy were different than stated. Quite obviously, some of the goals of the program were achieved—many peasants gained ownership or secured tenancy rights to the land. But in a country plagued with low productivity in the best of times, the new sets of problems generated from the reforms did much to blunt the overall positive effect.

Most countries of the world would prefer to be self-sufficient in agricultural production. Indeed, most have made considerable efforts to achieve this goal; and most have failed. The countries of the Middle East are no exception. Although all of the Middle Eastern countries are unlikely to meet the goal of self-sufficiency in the foreseeable future, the region could make considerable strides in this direction by the end of the century.

Total output can be increased in two general ways: an increase in the yield per unit of existing agricultural land, and an increase in the number of units cultivated. The post-World-War-II record of the countries under consideration is mixed. Yields for the important foodstuffs grown in Egypt (wheat, rice, and barley) have increased substantially and compare favorably on a worldwide basis. This has been accomplished through labor-intensive cultivation and without much aid from the high technology of Western (and some Israeli) agriculture. The record of Iraq, although not as good as that of Egypt, shows the same general trend. These are the two countries that have access to long stretches of major rivers. The record of the remaining countries, except for Israel, is mixed. Both Syria and Iran have shown increases in the yields of some crops and decreases in others. The yields of wheat, for example, have decreased in Syria because marginal land has been brought under cultivation. Such poor yields, however, are not necessarily due to the chemical composition of the soil. Water is the scarce resource; its availability could markedly change the situation. Underground water deposits found in the last two decades in Jordan, Libya, and Syria, for example, could call forth relatively high yields per unit if they could be brought into the production process at a reasonable cost. The Euphrates Dam in Syria could do the same. Another potential bright spot is that, except for Israel, the gains thus far have been made without heavy capital expenditures or a relatively heavy reliance on fertilizers or pesticides by individual farmers.

The performance of the agricultural sector of Middle Eastern nations, while falling short of the area's needs, has been reasonably good. It is difficult to project these trends into the future because the ecological balance is particularly sensitive in the Middle East; the productivity gains have not resulted primarily from a whole-sale transfer of Western technology, nor have they simply appeared as manna from heaven. The successful innovations have been those that have considered the partic-ular needs of the area. Whether or not more of these successful innovations will occur is a highly problematic and important question. It is problematic because of our inability to identify the forces that lead to sustained innovation and growth. It is important because of the area's very high rate of population growth.

POPULATION

Although the population of the Middle East has been increasing for at least a cen-tury, the post-World-War-II growth rate acceleration is of particular interest. It is one of the ironies of history that local, national, and international efforts to pro-long life have led, albeit indirectly, to more suffering. Increasing the population base without increasing the food supply results in less food per person. The average annual rates of population increase have ranged between 2 and 3 percent in the last couple of decades; at these rates, the population will double about every quarter century (see Table 8-4).

Table 8-4   POPULATION OF MIDDLE EASTERN COUNTRIES

Country	1978 Population, Midyear (millions)
Algeria	18.5
Bahrain	0.35
Djibouti	0.1
Egypt	39.6
Iran	35.2
Iraq	12.3
Israel	3.7
Jordan	3.0
Kuwait	1.2
Lebanon	3.0
Libya	1.74
Mauritania	1.5
Morocco	18.9
Oman	0.8
Qatar	0.2
Saudi Arabia	7.9
Somalia	3.4
South Yemen	1.9
Sudan	17.4
Syria	8.0
Tunisia	6.1
Turkey	43.2
U.A.E.	0.7
Yemen	5.6

SOURCE: *Demographic Yearbook, 1978* (New York: United Nations, 1979), Table 1.

The population increases of a few countries have come about through massive movements of people rather than natural increases in the indigenous population. The exodus of Palestinians from Israel into Jordan and the Gaza Strip has markedly altered conditions in each area. Indeed, the event has dominated much of what has happened in Jordan since independence. At independence Jordan was an extremely poor country and had few natural resources. The flood of Palestinians into Jordan following the formation of the state of Israel more than trebled the population. Already impoverished, Jordan faced seemingly insurmountable problems since the majority of the refugees were destitute. The addition of the West Bank to Jordanian territory added 7 percent to the total land area and 30 percent to the total of arable land, but these benefits did not come close to compensating for the massive influx of humanity.

During the 1950s almost all expert opinion was pessimistic on the ability of the Jordanian economy to function in a reasonably coherent and growth-inducing fashion. Throughout that period Jordan received a substantial amount of international aid. Although Jordan remained a very poor country, during the 1960s, signs of positive movement started to appear. Many Palestinian refugees were highly skilled and experienced in commerce and industry. This imported skilled labor, along with considerable Jordanian efforts to improve education, especially at the postsecondary level, began to increase the country's productivity.

The 1967 Israeli occupation of the West Bank and the success of OPEC since 1973 have complicated Jordan's problems. The occupation, of course, meant that a good portion of Jordan's cultivated land was lost and that a new wave of refugees entered the country, thus putting an even greater strain on the system. Nevertheless there was one benefit to Jordan from having such a relatively large body of skilled workers; many found employment in neighboring countries and remitted part of their earnings. Thus, the country received a relatively large infusion of foreign exchange earnings.

The mobilization of PLO forces in Jordan and the consequent pressure that these forces put on Israel, coupled with the Israeli policy of retaliation, led to King Hussein's decision to have Jordanian troops do battle against the armed Palestinians in September, 1970. This brought home in stark and tragic relief the fact that many of the residents of Jordan held other national allegiances. The East Bank, an area showing progress amidst the abject poverty of the refugee camps, was not fully under the control of the Jordanian government.

The success of OPEC signaled another difficulty for Jordan. The rapid expansion of the OPEC countries created thousands of high-paying jobs for skilled workers. By 1978 Jordan was facing a shortage of skilled workers—greater than one quarter of its labor force worked abroad. Its major asset, human capital, was depleted to the point that skilled positions within Jordan were understaffed. The rough balance gained by "exporting" its skilled labor supply had turned sharply against Jordan.

The small population, oil-producing countries are the major importers of skilled labor. They include Saudi Arabia, Bahrain, Kuwait, Libya, Qatar, and the United Arab Emirates. Egypt, Syria, and Jordan are the major suppliers. Indigenous entrants to the labor force are often absorbed in government service as a matter of

Table 8-5 CAPITAL-RICH STATES: EMPLOYMENT BY NATIONALITY, 1975

Country	Percentage Nationals	Percentage Non-Nationals	Total Employment
Saudi Arabia	57.0	43.0	1,799,900
Libya	57.5	42.5	781,600
Kuwait	30.6	69.4	299,800
United Arab Emirates	15.2	84.8	296,500
Oman	66.0	34.0	207,700
Bahrain	60.4	39.6	75,800
Qatar	18.9	81.1	66,200
Total	51.3	48.7	3,527,600

SOURCE: J. S. Birks and C. A. Sinclair. *International Migration and Development in the Arab Region* (Geneva: International Labor Organization, 1980), Table 8, p. 132.

policy rather than need. Although this policy tends to keep measured unemployment lower than otherwise and serves to pacify potentially disgruntled members of the work force, it also results in a considerable amount of disguised unemployment since the measured productivity of these workers is often nil. Apparently notions of economic efficiency have taken a back seat to political and social issues.

The small population, oil-producing countries present a rather dramatic picture of the extent of labor migration in the Middle East. Taken as a group, in 1975 the labor-importing countries had about 30 percent of their population and 50 percent of their workforce composed of migrants. In some countries the percentages are higher. Expatriates make up over one-half of the total population and about 70 percent of the labor force in Kuwait, for example. This, of course, significantly influences the government's domestic policies. It also has a substantial impact on the foreign affairs of Kuwait, since about one-quarter of the expatriates (one in every five workers in Kuwait) are classified as coming from Jordan, a high percentage of them being Palestinians. The government of Kuwait has found itself in a rather delicate position whenever Arab states have had to stand up and be counted on Palestinian issues. The generally conservative Kuwaiti government has had to guard against a reaction from the Palestinian expatriates if it takes the wrong stance.

Table 8-5 indicates the extent to which some of the countries under discussion depend on foreign labor to fill their needs. These figures should be treated with a good deal of caution because many are merely rough guesses; and, even if some are accurate, they do not distinguish between the type of labor and the duration of stay. The estimates of the number of Yemenis in Saudi Arabia are an example of the provisional nature of these statistics. Official estimates indicate that about half (200,000) of the foreign labor pool (400,000) in Saudi Arabia in 1970 was from Yemen. But some observers believe that there may be twice as many workers from Yemen as officially counted.[2]

Labor migration in the Arab areas has been substantial for many years. However, the increase in industrial activity in the oil-rich states during the 1970s sub-

[2] A. Farrag, "Migration Between Arab Countries," in *Manpower and Employment in Arab Countries* (Geneva: I.L.O., 1976), p. 92.

Table 8-6   COUNTRIES OF ORIGIN OF MIGRANT WORKERS, 1975

Country	Workforce	Percentage Abroad
Jordan (East Bank)	532,800	28.1
Oman	137,000	28.0
Yemen	1,425,900	20.3
Syria	1,838,900	3.8
Egypt	12,522,200	3.2
Sudan	3,700,000	1.2
Total	20,156,800	4.9

SOURCE: J. S. Birks and C. A. Sinclair. *International Migration and Development in the Arab Region* (Geneva: International Labor Organization, 1980), Table 11, p. 136.

stantially increased the demand for, and sources of, migrant labor. Relative political stability and substantial economic growth in Iraq, for example, led many Iraqi workers in foreign countries to return home. The most dramatic change, however, was the increase in the number of Asians—mainly Indians and Pakistanis, but including substantial numbers of Koreans—working in the Persian Gulf states. There are several complementary reasons why the increased demand for labor was not met by Arabs. First, the major suppliers already had substantial percentages of their workforce abroad (see Table 8-6). Second, skilled and semi-skilled workers were in particularly short supply in the supplier nations. Third, the Asian labor market was well-organized, Asian labor was relatively cheap, and the labor force was sometimes tied to construction projects awarded to Asian firms. By 1975, Asians accounted for 20.3 percent (349,900) of the migrant labor forces in the labor-importing Arab countries. They formed 46.7 percent of foreign labor in the United Arab Emirates, 16.8 percent in Oman, and 10.9 percent in Saudi Arabia.[3] It is likely that this trend will continue for several decades.

The lack of a complete and accurate breakdown of the type of foreign labor in some countries, obviously, makes the job of the planner difficult; and, as stated above, it also complicates political life. Without a recognition of the dependence on imported labor, the student of the Middle East may be at a loss to explain some chosen policies.

Egypt provides a classic and sad case of an overpopulated country. Its population increased from 22 million in 1953 to 40 million in 1980. Virtually all of the jump is attributable to natural increases. Since almost all of the arable land in Egypt is along the Nile River and Delta, this narrow strip is one of the most densely populated areas in the world. Because the amount of arable land, although increasing somewhat through irrigation, is close to being constant, there has been ever-increasing pressure on the land to produce more. But the additional labor could do little to add to production since the methods employed already were highly labor intensive. This combination of population increases and a constant amount of land to be worked is close to fitting the Malthusian dilemma of population increases resulting

[3] J. S. Birks and C. A. Sinclair. *International Migration and Development in the Arab Region* (Geneva: International Labor Organization, 1980), Table 9, p. 133.

in permanent subsistence living. Egypt has avoided taking the dreary course predicted by Malthus through the application of modest technological advances, a reorganization of landholding patterns, greater availability of water from the Aswan Dam, and the shifting of crops from cotton to food. Egypt still has to import food however. The race between productivity and population has been a close one. A substantial number of the unemployed rural population has moved to the cities for some economic relief.

Cairo holds about 20 percent of the population of Egypt. Although some of the increase in the past three decades, from 2 million in 1950 to 10 million in 1980, can be attributed to flight from the war-torn cities of the Suez Canal area, most of it has been due to people leaving the farms. Once in the cities, the rural people have not been assimilated easily or quickly. Indeed, they often form pockets of essentially rural culture and lifestyles which are surprisingly resistant to change.

It is quite clear that the movement of people from rural to urban settings upsets traditional patterns, but it is not clear whether or not these changes are to be considered modernizing or dysfunctional. Generally the rural migrants do not have skills useful in the urban environment. Further, there is considerable worldwide evidence that at least for the first several years in an urban setting the individual is apt to be alienated from the urban society and has considerable difficulty in adapting to the regimen of factory life if he is lucky enough to land a job in the first place. Tardiness, absenteeism, and quit-rates generally are quite high. The factory, it seems, is a particularly difficult place to adjust to. At the same time, evidence (from areas other than the Middle East) has indicated that the factory is the single most effective source from which to accumulate that set of attitudes which are considered "modern." A rapid increase in the population of major cities also can lead to the breakdown of city services. Transportation becomes a nightmare as thousands of vehicles are jammed into what is essentially a pre-twentieth-century road network; electrical supply capability is strained; the telephone system becomes virtually unworkable.

There are, then, different sources and consequences of population problems— the overarching problem being one of resource imbalances. First, the dramatic decline in infant mortality (and increased life expectancy) through the widespread application of public health measures substantially increased the population base of all the major countries in the Middle East since World War II. Second, there have been significant movements of people across national boundaries. Third, there has been a relative shift of the population to urban areas. These changes are related in an integral fashion to political and social problems as well as to economic phenomena. One of the most important economic considerations relates to unemployment.

Most countries profess full employment as a primary goal. A brief account of a government's problems in attempting to meet this goal may give the reader a sense of how serious the situation is. The first job is to figure out what percentage of the population is to be counted as part of the labor force. As is true of many other less-developed countries with high rates of population growth, the countries of the Middle East have a great many people who are generally considered to be out of the labor force. This means that those who work have to produce a greater surplus than would otherwise be the case. The calculation of these "dependency ratios" gives the government a first glimpse of the magnitude of the problem it faces; but these are slippery statistics, ones that need immense revision and more information if they are to be useful in formulating policy. For example, defining members of the labor force involves questions concerning the role of women and the minimum acceptable age of entry into the labor force, issues that are not easily resolved. Then there is the question of the skill characteristics of the labor pool relative to present and future skill requirements.

Since government actions, fiscal and otherwise, have pronounced effects on the flow of labor to urban areas, one must also consider how those flows will change when particular policy measures are being considered. For instance, will an attempt to improve urban conditions merely lead to an increased flow into the cities and thus thwart the original effort and disrupt agricultural planning?

Most observers would agree that there are significant labor problems in the agricultural sector of most less-developed countries. Typically, however, one does not find much open unemployment in agriculture; rather the problem is one of underemployment. *Underemployment* has a technical definition in economics, but it can be generally described as a situation where at least some of the labor force is not working to full capacity. The usual implication is that these "surplus" workers could be freed from agricultural work with little or no decrease in output. But this conclusion is not necessarily the correct one and is, in any case, too simplistic. For instance, there is a tremendous seasonal fluctuation in the demand for labor in most of the Middle East. Labor must be available on a standby basis to perform essential tasks. Another qualification is that the labor force in agriculture is not homogeneous; custom dictates that some tasks are to be performed by men and others by women and children. Since the family household (extended or nuclear) is the basis of most small farms in the Middle East, it becomes difficult to sort out the work patterns of the various types of labor. Generally, it seems that the cycle of seasonal work for men, although substantial, is less pronounced than that for women and children.

Equity considerations and efficiency also may clash when rural land use and labor deployment policies are being considered. It seems that large plots require less seasonal labor than small plots. Although the reasons for this tend to be specific to the area under study, generally we can assume that the cultivator of the larger plot has greater access to capital inputs (e.g., chemical fertilizers, pesticides, tractors). A policy of creating larger plots, therefore, would free underemployed labor and make it available for other productive uses. But there are several conflicts involved in this approach; a move toward larger plots is not easily accomplished. Considerations of equity have led a large number of countries to legislate land reform programs, which in turn have resulted in smaller average holdings. If seasonal laborers could be released from the land, one must then determine where they would be employed. Industrial growth on a substantial scale is needed to absorb this labor, and that growth has not been forthcoming in most of the countries under consideration. Also, since women and children are most apt to be seasonal workers, it presumably would be they who would be freed for alternative employment. Obviously, there would be considerable resistance to any such move.

Another problem in evaluating the labor force is that urban unemployment is open and obvious as contrasted to that in the agricultural sector. Therefore, the planner may begin with a bias and develop plans which commit more resources to urban areas than are warranted by strict economic criteria. This tendency is buttressed both because of the politically volatile nature of the urban population and because most notions of modernity, both naïve and sophisticated, are linked to industrialization and industry is linked to urban areas.

INDUSTRY

Because of OPEC's success, industry in the Middle East has grown dramatically. There are several prerequisites for large-scale, sustained industrial growth. Communication systems, power, transportation, and education are needed if a modern industrial structure is to emerge and prosper. The history of all of the industrialized countries of the world indicates that this process takes a long time, that it generally proceeds by fits and starts, and that "economic miracles" have their roots in earlier centuries, not decades. Because of OPEC, several oil-rich economies are being transformed at an unprecedentedly fast rate.

Until the spectacular increase in the price of petroleum, Egypt, Turkey, and Iran were the focus of most speculation about the course of industrialization in the Middle East. They have large populations, thus providing the potential for domestic markets, as well as a longer history of significant industrial activity than the other countries of the region. Industrialization in Egypt received its first substantial impetus under Muhammad Ali in the 1820s. This ambitious attempt ground to a halt after a couple of decades and was largely moribund until the 1920s when Egypt received a measure of independence. Industrialization in Egypt moved slowly for the next thirty years; it finally began to receive close attention in the 1950s under Nasser. The 1960s in Egypt saw the large-scale nationalization (and weak industrial performance) of major industries; during the post-Nasser period there was a selective encouragement of private enterprise, but with little apparent economic gain.

Iran began to industrialize more than a century later than Egypt. The years between World War II and 1960 were spent laying a foundation of sorts upon which industrialization could occur. Fueled by petroleum revenues, the process has accelerated since then. By the middle of the 1970s, per capita income in Iran was about five times that of Egypt, up from less than double in 1960. In any discussion of the future of industrialization in the two countries, most observers favored Iran. Petroleum sales provided the money to purchase capital goods and to quickly train a "modern" labor force. (In 1978 one out of every nine foreign students studying in the U.S. was Iranian.) However, the Iranian revolution and the war with Iraq seriously disrupted economic activity in Iran and made the predictions of sustained industrial growth questionable.

Lebanon and Kuwait provide another set of contrasts. Lebanon has a long history of commercial and industrial development. Its relatively mature economy, its geographic position, and its tradition as the financial hub of the Middle East allowed some impressive industrial growth during the 1960s and the first half of the 1970s. Since most of the industrial establishments are centered in and around Beirut, however, the devastation of that city in 1976 halted Lebanon's industrial activity in the second half of the decade.

Kuwait, long an earner of substantial amounts of foreign exchange through petroleum sales, has attempted lately to diversify its industry and not rely exclusively on petroleum-related production. But this will be difficult to do without a wider regional market.

Saudi Arabia and Libya are recent entrants in the race to industrialize. Even though petroleum production in Saudi Arabia started a quarter century earlier than in Libya, it was only during the 1970s that a concerted effort to industrialize began. Iraq, the other major petroleum producer in the area, also can be expected to be transformed substantially. Indeed, Iraq seems to have the most favorable balance of resources of all of the countries surveyed.

PETROLEUM

Oil has been called black gold—and for good reason. Petroleum has been the focus of many a country's national and international affairs during this century. European control of Middle Eastern petroleum at the onset of World War I later prompted Britain's Lord Curzon to remark that ". . . the Allies floated to victory on a wave of oil." About a half a century later, some were predicting that the rise in petroleum prices would create a new Arab Golden Age. Whether this occurs or not, petroleum is certainly the dominant economic influence in the Middle East; it has been responsible for one of the most rapid transfers of wealth in world history—a true revolution.

Table 8-7 highlights this revolution. It indicates the international reserve positions of selected countries in selected years.[4] International reserves are, roughly speaking, what a country has in the bank—its claims on the resources of other nations. Saudi Arabia, for example, earns U.S. dollars, German marks, and Japanese yen from petroleum sales. A small percentage of its revenues is put in gold, the remainder in bank accounts and financial instruments in various world financial centers. To the extent that Saudi Arabia holds U.S. dollars, it has a claim on U.S. production—that is, it has the dollars to purchase the goods and services of the U.S. In 1953 the United States had about 46 percent of the free world's total reserves and the Middle Eastern countries had about 1 percent. By 1973 the situation had changed markedly: the United States had about 9.8 percent of the total, about the same as all Middle Eastern countries together. By 1980 the United States' share had

[4]The table denominates reserves in terms of Standard Drawing Rights, SDRs, a measure used by international financial organizations, especially the International Monetary Fund. SDRs represent a weighted value of selected currencies.

Table 8-7   TOTAL RESERVES: WORLD AND SELECTED COUNTRIES
(millions of SDR)

Year End	World	U.S.	U.K.	Germany	Japan	Saudi Arabia	Iran	Iraq	Venezuela
1955	51,154	23,458	2,670	1,773	892	—	185	—	484
1958	57,280	22,540	3,068	5,879	1,033	73	254	—	1,062
1963	66,476	16,843	3,148	7,651	2,058	514	242	—	745
1968	77,749	15,710	2,422	9,948	2,906	662	291	—	922
1973	152,263	11,919	5,368	27,497	10,151	3,214	1,025	1,287	1,999
1974	180,171	13,115	5,667	26,461	11,042	11,667	6,847	2,673	5,320
1977	262,237	15,965	17,335	32,713	19,149	24,725	10,098	5,759	6,762
1979	302,381	15,149	15,709	43,224	15,667	14,791	11,681	n.a.	5,931

SOURCE: *International Financial Statistics* (Washington, D.C.: International Monetary Fund, selected years).

fallen to about 5 percent while that of the Middle East had risen to 19.4 percent, Saudi Arabia alone accounting for 9.4 percent of the world's total.

The half century preceding World War I was a time of rapid change in the Middle East. The Ottoman Empire was in disarray and decaying despite sporadic bursts of energy and direction. Turkey and Egypt accumulated very heavy public debts; one-third of Turkey's government expenditures and one-half of Egypt's were applied to debt servicing. Turkey was declared bankrupt in 1875 and Egypt in 1876. European interests in the area were becoming more pervasive and were setting the stage for twentieth-century events.

By the turn of the century, most major investments in the Middle East were European in origin and ownership. European domination, of course, did not begin with these investments. The course of growing Western influence began well before Napoleon occupied Egypt in 1798, as commerce between the two areas grew. European investments in dams, canals, railroads, and electrical systems built up gradually as the Middle East became more secure. But the surge of nationalism in the Middle East around the beginning of the twentieth century forced Europeans to relinquish direct control of some of their investments.

In the two centuries preceding the opening of the Suez Canal, Britain gained control of the Persian Gulf through a series of military maneuvers and treaties with local shiekhs. The route from India through the Persian Gulf, up through Basra and Baghdad, and then to Mediterranean ports provided a vital communications link for the empire until the opening of the Suez Canal. The area was again central to British interests in the 1890s because Britain wished to thwart German influences and because of the discovery of substantial amounts of petroleum in Iran.

After securing control of the Suez Canal, the British had been content to control commerce on the Persian Gulf and not travel inland; but the discovery of a large petroleum field in Iran in 1907 changed their intentions. The industrial revolution, although first fueled by coal, was becoming increasingly dependent on oil and other petroleum products. Petroleum products also were becoming increasingly valuable for military uses. Therefore, large consumers sought a steady and dependable supply. In 1900 the United States and Russia produced 90 percent of the world's petroleum. When the Iranian field east of Abadan was discovered, the British moved to assure their control over the area. Although the British had concessions for Iranian petroleum as early as 1872 (and then in 1889 and 1901), the rights were not considered particularly valuable. In 1908 the Anglo/Persian Oil Company (later changed to Anglo/Iranian) was founded. As tensions in Europe heightened, British needs for a dependable source of petroleum increased, partially because the British navy was converting its fleet from coal to oil; the British government became more anxious. In May, 1914, about one week before European hostilities broke into open conflict, the British government acquired a 50 percent interest in the venture.

The finds in Iran stimulated exploration for oil in southern Iraq. The results of negotiations completed in 1912 allowed for the formation of the Turkish Petroleum Company (TPC). The TPC was reorganized in 1914 and again in 1920, when German interests were removed and France and the United States moved in. The participation of United States firms was accomplished through vigorous diplomatic activity. In 1920, there was widespread fear of an impending oil shortage in the United States. Indeed, the U.S. government even considered direct government participation instead of relying on private enterprise, but decided against it.

The agreement that formed the TPC, later renamed the Iraqi Petroleum Company (IPC), contained a proviso that limited the seeking of concessions to the area within the Ottoman Empire which was shown by a red line drawn on a map. The Red Line agreement stated that the individual companies in the IPC would not act in a fashion that would upset the balance of company power within the red line. They were not to operate any other fields in the area and thereby gain relative power.

Although British interests had the only concessions in Arabia, there was no production until 1934. In 1930, Standard Oil of California (SoCal) had gained an option from a British syndicate for Bahrain. Petroleum was found in 1932, and exports started to flow two years later. In 1933 SoCal gained the concession for the al-Hasa province of Saudi Arabia. Petroleum was found a few years later. In 1934 Gulf Oil and British Petroleum (BP) entered Kuwait.

The entry of United States firms into Saudi Arabia and the subsequent development of the huge oil fields found there threatened the dominance of the IPC, especially after SoCal joined with Texaco in 1936 to form the Arabian-American Oil Company (ARAMCO) in order to take advantage of the Far Eastern marketing network of Texaco.

The fear of a petroleum shortage immediately after World War I sparked a flurry of exploration during the next two decades. World supply had increased markedly by 1930 through various major fields coming into production, most notably in the Far East, Middle East, Venezuela, and the United States. With the increased world supply more oil firms entered the market; the "majors" maneuvered futilely to retain control of the world petroleum market.

Petroleum was in abundant supply during the worldwide depression of the 1930s. As the machines were turned off due to the depression, so was the demand for petroleum products: the fears of an oil shortage turned into fears of a large and continuing glut. The sustained depression, especially in the United States, caused changes in the industrial structure. Weak firms, especially those that were not vertically integrated, generally failed.

By the beginning of World War II, it was apparent that Middle Eastern petroleum would be vital to the world oil market. The United States, although supplying much of the petroleum products needed by the Allies during World War II, feared that its postwar position would be weak. Again there was talk of the need for direct government participation and for protecting the United States position in the Middle East. Saudi Arabia provided the United States with a major foothold in the Middle East. In efforts to keep the support of the Saudis, lend-lease agreements were put into force whereby the British actually extended the aid since Saudi Arabia was not eligible. It should be remembered that Saudi Arabia was still a very poor country and received only modest revenues from the petroleum industry. The Saudis needed aid. Largely because the United States feared that the British would use their influence as intermediaries to curry Saudi favor, Saudi Arabia was made eligible for direct lend-lease aid in 1944. But there was another problem; the Saudi government wanted to increase production in order to increase its revenue. The U.S. government wanted to assure an adequate supply, but ARAMCO did not have the financial resources necessary to substantially expand Saudi production. The U.S. government first planned to buy directly into ARAMCO and then to build a pipeline to the Mediterranean in return for preferential prices and guaranteed strategic reserves. Both plans failed to come to fruition, and the U.S. government finally (1948) arranged with the financially stronger Standard Oil of New Jersey (later named Exxon) and Mobil, both IPC members, to buy into ARAMCO (30 percent and 10 percent respectively). The entry of these IPC members signaled the end of the Red Line agreement.

By 1948 seven Western companies controlled Middle Eastern oil: four were based in the U.S.—Standard Oil of New Jersey, Mobil, SoCal, and Texaco; one was British—British Petroleum; and one was a joint British-Dutch venture—Royal Dutch/Shell.

The selling price of any product, of course, is determined by the interaction of supply and demand. Although the record of the petroleum industry after World War II is too complex to be forced into a couple of equations, it is nevertheless instructive to highlight these two basic forces. The tremendous worldwide economic expansion which occurred in the decades following World War II increased the demand for petroleum products considerably. In addition, the Western nations and Japan were building energy-intensive societies and shifting ever-greater percentages of their energy sources from coal to oil. The combination of these forces meant that the demand for petroleum was doubling every six and one-half years.

The steady price of petroleum throughout the 1950s and most of the 1960s indicates that the supply of petroleum was increasing at about the same pace as the demand. The character of the industry, however, was changing in substantial ways. New independent firms were entering the oil industry, and the producing countries themselves began to feel new strength. The entry of more firms into the industry meant, quite simply, that the seven firms which controlled Middle Eastern petroleum production were slowly losing their influence in the market. Governments demanding greater revenues from petroleum exploitation were thus in a better position to bargain. For example, because of its very heavy reliance on Libyan production Occidental Oil was more likely to respect Libyan demands for increased monies than if it had widely diversified holdings. In contrast, the Iranian attempts at nationalization of the petroleum producers in 1951 failed in large part because of the relatively plentiful and more diversified world supply. The Middle East also was becoming more important with respect to production and proven reserves. During the 1960s it became clear to close observers of the scene that there had been a fundamental change in the market: a greater percentage of world supply originated in the Middle East, petroleum supplies started to lag behind demand in the latter part of the decade, and an upward pressure on prices began to be felt.

The Organization of Petroleum Exporting Countries (OPEC) did not have any significant power in the first decade of its existence (1960-1970). The organization of the industry and the plentiful and diversified supply of oil blunted its efforts to raise prices substantially. The situation had changed markedly, however, by 1970. During that year the postrevolutionary government of Libya started negotiations for substantially increased payments from the petroleum companies. Algeria and Iran had gained better concessions in 1969. Although these actions represented a breakthrough for the producing countries, they were also viewed as special cases. Revolutionary Libya, strongly backed by "radical" Algeria and Iraq, called for much greater revenue increases than previously sought and threatened outright expropriation if its demands were not met. Libya succeeded for various reasons. World supply-and-demand conditions, which were aggravated by the 1967 closure of the Suez Canal, caused prices to rise; the Occidental Oil Company was vulnerable because almost all of the petroleum for its European operations came from Libya; the companies operating in the Middle East were unable to form a common front; the home governments of the oil companies could not bring any unified pressure to bear on the producing countries; and OPEC was presenting a relatively united front. Prices were increased further after President Nixon's August, 1971, announcement of a proposed devaluation of the U.S. dollar (which meant that the dollar earnings of the petroleum-exporting countries would lose purchasing power). They also rose because of a continuing decline in U.S. petroleum production, worldwide inflation, and unabated increases in petroleum demand. Upward pressure on prices and calls for increased participation, partial ownership, and outright expropriation continued through 1973.

Intense negotiations between OPEC and the oil companies through the first ten months of 1973 resulted in substantially higher posted prices. These increases came without direct reference to the Arab-Israeli situation. Members of OPEC, Arab and non-Arab, were simply exploiting worldwide market conditions; they were seeking to get as much revenue as possible before their precious natural resource was depleted. The decline in the value of the U.S. dollar was eroding the purchasing power of petro-dollar earnings, giving more reason to increase prices.

The 1973 Arab/Israeli war provided the catalyst which permitted the Arab members to make OPEC a more or less full-fledged cartel and to roughly quadruple petroleum prices in less than a year. Any such dramatic OPEC action needed the support of the largest producing nation, Saudi Arabia. The late King Faisal needed to be convinced that this bold and dangerous move was the proper policy: Saudi conservatism and substantial Saudi ties to the U.S. dictated against a precipitous break with past policy. However, Western, and particularly United States, support for Israel during and immediately after the 1973 war convinced the Saudi leadership that a dramatic increase in the price of petroleum and a selective boycott by the Arab members of OPEC was necessary to change Western policy.

The boycott was lifted in March, 1974. The higher prices remained in effect. The industrial world struggled through the next couple of years attempting to adjust to the change. Of particular importance were the massive balance of payments problems that resulted from the price increase and the related—but not necessarily causally determined—inflation that continued to plague them. A simple example will clarify what was happening. Assume that the United States was producing the same number of goods each year. Now suppose that the price of imported oil increased and the United States continued to import the same number of barrels. More dollars were flowing out of the United States, and less were being spent by U.S. consumers on U.S. goods. Now suppose that the exporting country spent all of those earned dollars on U.S. goods. With the same total amount of money being spent on the same total amount of goods, the straightforward result is that the oil producer had more goods and the United States had less. The only way out of this situation was to eliminate spending on imports by conserving energy and developing internal sources.

The U.S. government, however, failed to respond with a clearly defined program. Attempts to develop comprehensive energy programs floundered throughout the decade. Instead, individual actors, aided by a pliant government, attempted to recoup their losses by spending more. In terms of our simple scenario, they pumped more money into the system. More money chasing the same amount of goods results in inflation. And inflation meant that members of OPEC could purchase less with each "petro-dollar" earned. OPEC, therefore, raised prices in order to recoup its position. The 1970s inflation in the United States was not caused primarily by OPEC actions; rather, continued U.S. inflation virtually guaranteed further rounds of OPEC price increases. Since the United States remained the most powerful economy in the industrialized world, it transmitted these problems to other countries.

Although the situation was far more complicated than the foregoing description suggests—especially important were the complications that arose from the exporting countries not spending all of the petrodollars they earned—it represents the nub of the issue. The members of OPEC had control of a large enough percentage of world petroleum supplies to call the tune. They had become a full-fledged cartel that controlled the supply in the supply-demand equations. Most petroleum companies clearly understood these shifting power relationships by the late 1960s. At least one went so far as to launch an advertising campaign calling for a more sympathetic view of the Arab cause. Others sent similar messages to official Washington. They knew that they were engaged in a rear-guard action and were attempting to forestall the inevitable. The U.S. public had another point of view. Most people saw the situation as resulting from a U.S. government blunder or from oil company actions. Conspiracy theories abounded. It was as if the public could not quite believe that a group of Third World countries could have the power to foment such disorder and then "get away with it." Indeed, it was the first time that a group of Third World countries had secured such a position.

The Third World countries that had begun to industrialize but had no oil could not fully share in the jubilation. Instead, they suffered. They were not economically strong enough to adopt the Western attitude of considering the price increases to be an unfortunate irritant that caused problems but nevertheless could be lived with. The major Arab members of OPEC responded to the plight of the poorer countries by stepping up their aid programs. The Western nations had surrendered their grip on the political systems of the Third World during the preceding years of the century. Was the success of OPEC the first major victory of a future economic trend?

None of the foregoing should suggest that the OPEC members all agree on the extent of the price increases. The position of any individual country depends on its particular economic needs. The countries aiming for very high prices generally have economies that can absorb all of the goods their petrodollars can buy; they have reasonably solid industrial bases, large populations, and low petroleum reserves. Iran and Iraq are the Middle Eastern members of OPEC that most readily fit this pattern. The price moderates, led by Saudi Arabia, generally are countries that have large petroleum reserves, small populations, and far less-developed economies. They do not have the ability (or the desire) to spend all of their petroleum earnings to strengthen their economies.

The powerful industrialized countries of the world are dependent on OPEC supplies. Being dependent, these countries have had to reorder their policies toward the Middle East, especially their attitudes and actions toward Arab-Israeli hostilities. Petroleum became a political tool of the first order after 1973; alliances had to be altered and new approaches to conflict resolution developed.

9

Political Elites

The study of political and social elites has been extraordinarily rewarding to social scientists. Among the reasons for this is the fact that most complex societies have well-defined elites. These elites are prominent; they are easily identified and studied. Elites are intimately involved in the processes that produce and resolve group conflict over the allocation of resources; they exist in all of the arenas of conflict, whether they be local, regional, national, or international; and elites prompt or resist or reflect changes in the social, economic, and political processes.

In all but the most simple societies, certain people perform political functions; they make the binding decisions of the society. These people, the elite, can be distinguished from those who do not exercise substantial power, the public or the masses. In other words, at one level or another, and with varying degrees of effectiveness, an elite is comprised of those people who decide "who gets what, when, and how." And since those decisions are going to both satisfy and disappoint members of that society, especially since allocations take place in an environment of relative scarcity, the activities of the elite both resolve and generate conflicts. For example, a decision to transfer land from traditional landowners to their previous tenant farmers will satisfy the demands of the tenant farmers but will motivate the landlords to seek some form of compensation for their losses. Thus, the elite in its action creates new demands on the system as it attempts to reconcile existing conflicts.

Members of an elite tend to represent the interests of the group of society from which they spring. A member of an elite whose ancestors were small farmers can be expected to represent the interests of those with similar backgrounds, *to a predictable degree*; and an elite member whose ancestors were landless peasants would be expected to represent a substantially different point of view, especially on those problems that directly involve the conflicting interests of landholders and tenant farmers.

If members of the elite represent their own groups of origin with some predictability, then the composition of the elite can reveal much about the state of politics in a given society. For example, the overrepresentation of one segment of society in the elite would imply that disproportionate shares of that society's produce were going to that group. And on the other hand, the absence of a potentially important elite group—the educated professional class, for example—would imply that the group was being disproportionately penalized by the actions of government. Thus, the composition of the elite is of great importance to the society attempting to modernize; for a modern society attempts to involve most or all of its citizenry in the pursuit of a new social and political consensus. Consensus is *not* built by excluding large or important groups from the political process or the elite. Thus, the general representativeness of the elite is an important indicator for anyone attempting to understand the political process in a given country or region.

The analysis of the elite in a transitional society—and most of the systems under study here are in a transitional state between the traditional and the modern—will generally reveal an elite of changing composition. In particular, we should be alert to changes in the elite that indicate an expansion of the elements of society participating in political decisions and to evidence that indicates traditional opposition to that change. It is axiomatic that established elites will oppose such changes, since those changes involve a dilution of the elites' past influence. Conflict is implicit between those elements of the elite proposing and supporting modernization and those elements of the elite opposing such changes. In most of the countries of the Middle East, this process expresses itself in terms of religious elite opposition to the modernizing efforts of the bureaucracy, professional classes, and the military. Since World War II and the nominal political independence of the nations of the area, this conflict has occurred between the traditional religious elite of the Middle East—the ulema—and the government, usually dominated by the military bureaucracy.

Although we have discussed the peculiarities of the ulema in earlier chapters, it is important to recall some of its primary characteristics, particularly since it complicates our analysis. First and foremost, the ulema is unusually diffuse; it has no clear hierarchy, or rules of membership, or formal organization. Existing independent of the political order, it has nonetheless historically penetrated and influenced that order, reflecting the pervasiveness of Islam in general. The ulema is consequently difficult to pin down in sociographic terms. But there is no denying its existence and no denying its desire to maintain its authority deriving from sacred or religious sources. And it is the ulema's maintenance of sacred sources of authority and knowledge that brings it into conflict with the focus of modernization. For modernization, as it developed in the West, recognized the authority of man, not God. Thus, the ulema as the front-line bastion against secular authority, often finds itself in fundamental opposition to the secular values of Western-style modernizers. As we shall see, this opposition takes various forms in the political systems of the Middle East. Historically, the ulema has sought to influence and advise government rather than serve formally as officers of the state. They have further preferred to exercise moral vetoes over unacceptable policy. There are indications that this policy may be changing in Iran, Saudi Arabia, Libya, and the Gulf states; but basically the political power of the ulema has been negative—oppositional power rather than the power of positive influence or accommodation.

By contrast, the modernizing forces in the Middle East can be described as the opposite of the political style of the ulema. The forces generally supporting modernization in the Middle East are the governmental entities that gained political power in the aftermath of independence. Although nominal political power at that time was held by hereditary monarchs (such as Farouk in Egypt and the Hashemite monarchs of Jordan and Iraq) more actual political power was held by the bureaucrats and military officer corps of those governments. And as the political pressures of independence grew, the actual formal political power of these elites grew, ultimately displacing the hereditary traditional authorities in many countries such as Egypt, Iraq, and Libya. In other countries, such as Saudi Arabia, Iran, and the U.A.E., a system of shared powers between the traditional and the bureaucratic-military elites developed.

It is not surprising that the modernizing elements in the political elites of the Middle East should so often come from the bureaucratic-military cadres, for the preceding colonial regimes tried to create a capable, modernized bureaucracy *without* an attendant modernized, independent political structure. Thus, at independence, those elements which had been most exposed to the logic and philosophy of secular modernity were the bureaucrats and the military.

Consequently, we expect to find the elite structures of these Middle Eastern political systems in a state of flux reflecting the low level of consensus in the society as a whole. The historical traditional order preceding the transitional stage to modernization was characterized by relatively high levels of consensus and elite congruence, and presumably the emergent modern order will be as well. Just as predictably, the intermediate transitional state will reflect the growing conflict over the objectives and basis of sociopolitical organization.

During those periods in a country's history when elite consensus and integration predominate, the leadership of the country can be indifferent or undistinguished without great cost, for the widespread agreement upon processes, institutions, goals, and the like will provide adequate direction to even the most unimaginative regimes. But when elite conflict and competition are evident, and consensus absent, the resources, imagination, and capability of the individual head of state becomes of great consequence. Since the Middle East finds itself in just such a transitional bind, we will spend some time in the next chapter analyzing the emergent styles of political leadership in the region. We will attempt to show the political and social consequences of varying political leadership styles, including styles that we shall call traditional, modern-bureaucratic, and charismatic.

TRADITIONAL, TRANSITIONAL, AND MODERNIZING ELITES

Figure 9-1, 9-2, and 9-3 present models of the elite structures of traditional, transitional, and modern Middle Eastern societies. Before discussing each of these elite categories, a few remarks on the diagrams themselves are in order.

In these models, we distinguish between three levels, or *strata*, of society: the elite, represented by the smallest group of circles in the center of each diagram; the ruling class, or those groups from whom the elite is regularly recruited; and the mass publics, those members of society with considerably fewer resources and influence, who make up the majority of the society. The broken lines surrounding the ruling class vary in the three diagrams; they are intended to indicate the ease with which movement from the mass public to the ruling class can occur. If there is real opportunity for persons of demonstrated merit or capability to move from the mass public to the ruling class, we describe the society as having open, or permeable, boundaries; and if there is little possibility of an individual moving from one class to another, we label the society closed, or impermeable. The quality of permeability is of great importance to a society's ability to adjust to the changing demands of modernization.

Another feature of our model reflects the degree of cohesion, or consensus, in the elite. In this model, the closer the elite elements are, the higher the degree of consensus among them. You will notice that two of the identified elite models have relatively high degrees of association, while the transitional model indicates a high degree of bifurcation and internal conflict. Finally, while these models describe national elites, they can also apply to regional and local elites as well. All countries in this area are, in effect, mosaics of elite structures.

THE TRADITIONAL ELITES

In many respects, we have already discussed the traditional elite structure in the preceding chapters dealing with classic Islamic social organization and the early stages of modernization. We need, however, to put that knowledge into the context of elite competition in the contemporary world. A short review of the main components of each elite is appropriate here, however, and we shall begin with the center of the traditional elite, the monarch (caliph, sultan, bey, or sheikh) and his immediate subordinates (traditionally, the diwan).

In most classic Islamic states, the ruler perpetuated his control largely on the basis of the elite's acceptance of his traditional right to rule. Particularly in Sunni political systems, a very high priority was placed on the maintenance of the established rule, with many theorists claiming that even tyrants should be obeyed until the very structure of the Islamic community itself was threatened. Shiite communities are less disposed to accept established authority, but even in these communities, established authority had high credibility. In most traditional Islamic states, the head of state ruled on the basis of a widespread belief that such rule was correct and, moreover, divinely determined.

The bureaucratic apparatus that supported the monarch, however, was subject to greater vagaries. The *diwan*, drawn primarily from privileged families in the nobility and ruling class, were much more subject to being removed from office, not uncommonly at the caprice of the hereditary monarch. In some traditional systems, notably the Turkish Janissary corps and the Egyptian Mameluks, rulers and high ministers might come from slave origins, devoid of family connections. Such arrangements were designed to minimize family or clan-related court intrigues, but often succeeded only in substituting one form of intrigue for another.

The diwan, and their aides and staffs, administered the kingdom; they col-

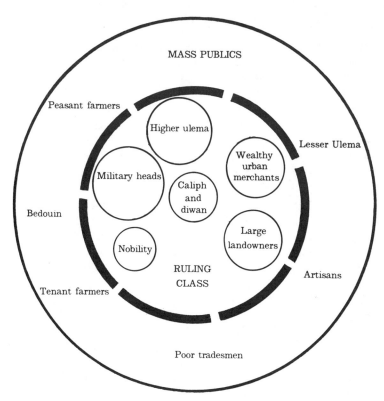

FIGURE 9-1. The Traditional Elite

Elite Characteristics:
—Low permeability
—High elite consensus
—Small ruling class

Nations in Traditional Classification:

North Yemen   Qatar
Oman   United Arab Emirates

lected the taxes and maintained the appropriate records. The record keepers, the **katib**, provided the source from which many of the ministers of the diwan were recruited and exerted much influence on the matters of court. The caliph, diwan, and katib, combined with the caliph's favorites, constituted the bulk of the court in a traditional Islamic state.

Also of the elite, but not so regularly or intimately a part of courtly life, were the wealthy merchants of the capital city, large landowners, military officers, and the higher ulema. All of these elements played a restraining role on government: practically, in the merchants' and landowners' reaction to taxation; and morally, in the higher ulema's criticisms of policy. The ulema, in particular, limited the role of government by deciding what questions should be resolved by the caliphate, and what questions were in the exclusive domain of the Islamic community, essentially the greater and lesser ulema. The relationship between caliphate and ulema was periodically rocky, and many a traditional authority defied the moral sanction of the ulema, formally and informally, successfully and unsuccessfully.

Many of the conflicts between caliph and higher ulema in Sunni states centered on religious opposition to efforts at "modernization" or changes in the social and political structure of the state. One major exception to this pattern has been the continually strained relationship between the monarchy and the Shiite higher ulema in Iran. In this case, the Shiite mistrust of political authority (see Chapter 3) has resulted in the higher ulema espousing a strong form of constitutionalism as a basis for government. In this restrictive sense, the Iranian ulema has been among the forces striving for a more "modern" political system, fomenting conflict with the authoritarian aspirations of the Iranian shahs. This conflict has persisted down to the present day in Iran. However, in other areas of life such as the liberalization of women's roles or secular education, the Iranian ulema's position is nearly indistinguishable from that of the Sunni ulema.

The military hierarchy has also been a persistent element in the ruling class and the elite of the Islamic state and of traditional political authority. There is no Islamic tradition separating military authority from political, social, or religious authority. Moreover, military life has traditionally been a means of social access and upward mobility. Particularly in linking outlying bedouin military forces with the urban caliphate and elite, the military played an important role in the integration of the traditional elite. And as we shall see, the military is an important force in both the transitional and modernizing elites.

Generally, the traditional elite has a very low permeability—that is, the ruling class is very stable and outsiders move into it only with great difficulty. With the exception of the ulema (particularly the lesser ulema) and the military to some degree, social mobility was largely unknown in the traditional elite. Elite circulation was historically confined to the established ruling class and resulted in considerable unresolved tension. Indeed, many of the theorists of Islamic society, including the well-known Ibn Khaldun, attributed the decline and fall of the caliphates to the increasing restiveness of the mass publics (peasants and bedouins), and the inability of the ruling class and elite to respond to them. The very cohesiveness of the traditional elite, its homogeneity and small size, contributed to its ultimate demise.

The weakness of the traditional state becomes most obvious when conflicts arise. In the traditional Middle East, political control, as a rule, declined proportionately to the distance from the political center. With the ruling class and elite centered primarily in the capital city, it was but a matter of time until the periphery suffered from neglect or exploitation. Common causes of provincial unrest came from such factors as deteriorating irrigation systems, increasingly exploitive taxes, or failure of the government to protect farmers and merchants from banditry and other forms of predation. As opportunists perceived the possibilities deriving from these growing demands, the power of the central authority would dwindle to a point of crisis. If the traditional authority was lucky or aggressive, the threats might be laid to rest. If not, new elites and political structures, often drawn from restive elements within the ruling class and not from the mass publics, would be constituted and the whole process begun again.

In the late nineteenth and early twentieth centuries, these traditional Middle Eastern political systems—notably the Ottomans and their client states—came under heavy pressure from the national systems of Europe. The traditional political elites found themselves hard-pressed to respond adequately to superior European political, military, and economic power. As the threats became real dangers and Europeans finally took control, some traditional elites adopted a new, modern world view. These modernist claims, and the horrified traditionalist response to them, are the primary features of the next elite system, the transitional.

However, some countries resisted the pressures of modernization. They include Qatar, the United Arab Emirates (which are difficult to generalize about), Yemen, and Oman. Many of these countries are more anomalies or curiosities than substantial nations. Fujaira, for instance, one of the states of the United Arab Emirates, has a total estimated population of around 26,500 and is still ruled by a traditionally supported sheikh. The oil resources of these countries raises their importance far above what their level of development would call for.

Many of these nations could more properly be labeled "imminently pre-transitional," since they have been unable to resist the pressures of rising revenues and regional politics. Also, there is a pronounced unevenness of development within the group; Abu Dhabi, for instance, shows many signs of rapid transformation to a transitional form of elite structure, while Fujaira still lingers on the periphery of the Middle Ages. An anecdote here may clarify this point.

In the mid 1960s, American oil companies aggressively began to seek development rights to the princely sheikdoms of the Persian Gulf. A prominent American businessman related the following experiences, both taking place in the same week. The week began with the negotiations with the ruling family of Abu Dhabi; the negotiations were highly informative but uneventful. The negotiators were housed in fairly modern facilities and entertained in a conventional manner. Modern bureaucrats attended the delegates during all of these exchanges, which were civil and unremarkable.

Several days later, the same team opened negotiations in another sheikdom. Here, the entire atmosphere was permeated with the ambience and style of a social system centuries earlier. The negotiations culminated with a royal banquet, held in the traditional quarters of the sheikh, constructed largely of mud-brick and furnished primarily with oriental carpets. The entire assemblage squatted on the floor for dinner. During dinner, each guest was attended by a Nubian slave, who retrieved the indicated dishes from the communal bowls spread about the table. Entertainment was provided by a professional glutton who, among other things, consumed more than six roast chickens and drank a whole case of Coca-Cola. The entertainment seemed remarkable only to those Westerners present and unfamiliar with the traditional lifestyle of the Middle East.

Such regimes would appear to be particularly vulnerable to change. Their ownership of, or proximity to, substantial petroleum reserves will make them increasingly subject to external and internal pressures for change. Most of these systems will in the near future become transitional political systems.

THE TRANSITIONAL ELITES

The consequence of elite disagreement over the basic forms and derivations of authority produces a type of structure called *transitional*. The term is most often used to denote the stage between the disruption of traditional authority and the triumph of technical modernization; however, it might just as easily occur prior to an aggressive reassertion of traditional leadership, although this is unusual. It does seem to apply to the turmoil afflicting contemporary Iran and the rise of conservative Islamic political parties.

The transitional elite (see Figure 9-2) has a dotted line separating the elite and ruling class into two polarized and contending groups. Although the specific composition of the elite can vary from country to country, certain groups or elements are likely to have a prominent role. For instance, wealthy landowners who owe their prosperity to the support of the traditional leadership still participate in political decisions. The military, often the first group to be systematically exposed to the influence of secular modernity by reason of their education, can be usually counted upon to support modernizing programs. The bureaucracy, trained in the science of modern administration by a prior colonial administration, will also tend to support modernizing change. Those elements of the traditional elite with hereditary power

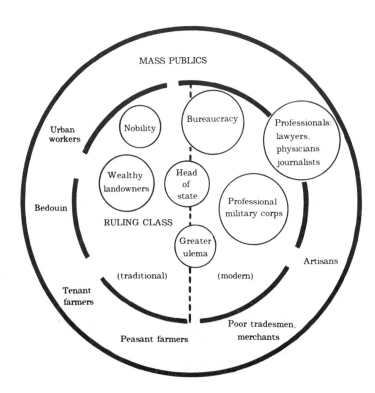

FIGURE 9-2. Transitional Elite

Elite Characteristics:
—Regular permeability
—Low elite consensus, internal elite conflict
—Growing ruling class, presence of
   "new" groups in ruling class

Nations in Transitional Classification:

Bahrain	Libya
Iran	Saudi Arabia
Jordan	South Yemen
Kuwait	

can be counted on to cling to that power, by and large. And most of the greater and lesser ulema can also be counted upon to take sides in the issues at hand, although their decisions can frustrate both traditional and modernizing elements in the elite.

The transitional elite is generally composed of and represents more social groups than the traditional elite, in spite of the transitional elite's disagreement over the means and ends of political, social, and economic life. Internal conflict in the elite can produce irregular policy, wavering between the demands and desires of a fragmented society. This may often lead to frustrating inconsistencies that produce growing dissatisfaction from both traditional and modernizing elements. Thus, transitional societies are subject to growing internal pressures that demand resolution. Not uncommonly, these pressures build up to political violence—assassinations, demonstrations, and the like. On a more positive note, such behavior short of violence bespeaks a broader level of political participation and is one of the early signs that the pressures of change are building. The transitional society and its elite—as disorganized and chaotic as they sometimes seem—carry the seeds of a new social order based on greater participation and wider social consensus.

One major reason for the prominence of the transitional elites is that two major oil producers in the area—Iran and Saudi Arabia—are both in a state of transition. When combined with their transitional associates—Libya and Kuwait—we have accounted for the bulk of crude oil production in the Middle East as well as its reserves. And as befitting a group of nations with such fundamental importance to the rest of the world, the group is characterized by substantial variation in political style.

The transitional elites in the Middle East have provided the arenas for some of the most important political changes in the entire region. The fall of the Shah of Iran in 1979 is, of course, the most dramatic of these changes and in some respects the most important. But the style of politics and elite organization in Libya, Kuwait, and Saudi Arabia have been equally as important and deserve some mention here.

The fall of the Shah can be directly related to the strains placed on his political authority by a failure to accommodate new groups in the political elite and by a parallel failure to maintain the support of the more traditional groups in Iran. For example, the newly emergent professional middle class was largely uninfluential in the Shah's autocracy. Since this group holds a near-monopoly of modern technology and skill, it can be ignored only at the ruler's peril. Ironically, the ambitious technical modernization program of the Shah simultaneously enhanced the size and potential power of the middle class at the same time as it alienated them. Thus, disaffected professionals found it advantageous to join with the forces of the traditional Muslim leadership against the Shah. The opposition of the Shiite ulema, again ironically, was based on the disruptive and secularizing influence of the Shah's modernization program. The combination of traditional and modern opposition was too much for the Shah's primarily military base of support, and he was forced to leave the country. The results of the change—particularly the attempt to establish an Islamic republic—are still uncertain.

By distinct contrast, the elite changes taking place in Saudi Arabia have been occurring more *within* the ruling family and its coalitions. As princes and retainers of the monarchy have received substantial educations in the elite institutions of the

West—Oxford, Cambridge, M.I.T., Harvard, and the Sorbonne, for example—they have become increasingly aware of the need to adapt to the pressures and advantages of modern social organization. Indeed, the organization of OPEC has been often attributed directly to just such influences. As of this writing, the Saudi elite appears to be attempting to modernize the economic and technical facets of Saudi society without making corresponding changes in the political and social facets. This is a very difficult maneuver, for as the experience in Iran suggests, the educated and professional classes begin to desire power and influence. Ordinarily, analysts would be inclined to predict failure in this effort and disagree only on the timing of the ouster of the monarch and his ruling family. But the extraordinary wealth of Saudi Arabia, combined with its relatively small indigenous population, may allow for unusual and unanticipated developments. It is clear at this point, however, that the Saudi system has gone from traditional to transitional elite politics in a fairly short period of time, largely within the framework of the hugely extended royal family. The abdication of King Saud in favor of his more progressive brother, Faisal, and the publicly emerging differences of opinion between the royal princes under King Khalid provide evidence of both the changes and the relatively short time frame within which they occurred. The rivalry in the royal family has come down recently to competition between two branches: the Sudairi, led by Crown Prince Fahd and Sheikh Yamani, the minister of petroleum, includes many of the technically trained and sophisticated bureaucrats; and the Jilwa, led by Prince Abdullah, head of the National Guard, which is the branch traditionally concerned with the cultivation of the tribal loyalties that have supported Saudi rule. This in itself indicates more flexibility in the system than is generally the case in monarchical-transitional regimes. Certainly the impact of these changes will be momentous.

Developments in Kuwait suggest a variation on Saudi themes. In Kuwait, a much smaller monarchy, political power is increasingly demanded and received by immigrant populations—particularly the Palestinians—that have dominated the professions and the middle class. This sharing of power could reduce potential political conflict rather dramatically and probably holds the seeds of constitutional monarchy or some other form of modern elite structure in the foreseeable future. Once again, the enormous petroleum income complicates our analysis; but at this time, the emerging political elite of Kuwait appears to be fairly stable and capable of managing the transition to a modern regime with minimal disruption and violence. Kuwait's strong opposition to Israel is a consequence of recent elite changes.

The prevailing situation in Libya is in stark contrast to that in Iran and Saudi Arabia. In fact, there are few regimes as misunderstood and disliked in the Western world as the regime of Col. Muammar Qadaffi in Libya. In Libya, the change from traditional to transitional status came with the elimination of the monarchy in 1969. In its place has developed a unique blend of Muslim puritanism and radical Arab nationalism, personified by Qadaffi, a charismatic leader. The Libyan regime is run largely by its military bureaucracy, but with some unusual and irregular contributions from a small professional elite and an equally small traditional ulema. Libya, one of the major oil exporters of the region, is particularly uneven in its development, even for the Middle East. Thus, changes within the transitional elite structure of the country can be anticipated, although constrained by the erratic influence of Col. Qadaffi. Qadaffi's attempts to replace regular bureaucratic organization with democratic people's delegations have confused the situation in Libya substantially. Elite consequences are sure to follow from these innovations, but their character and direction are uncertain. The major capability of the Libyan elite at this time seems to be for destabilizing and confusing the international system. Libya's forceful support of radical and terrorist groups, including the Palestinians, brings substantial potential to these movements. It is not surprising that the apparently opposing regimes of Libya (Qadaffi) and Iran (Khomeini) can agree on the subject of Palestinian rights, and the impact of this fact holds great imlications for the political future of Israel, Egypt, and Jordan in particular.

The Jordanian political system has no substantial economic resources. In fact, Jordan's major economic asset had been the West Bank of the Jordan River, now an occupied territory of Israel. Jordan is apparently one of the least viable of the nations of the Middle East, and its continued survival is due to substantial foreign aid. What modern, middle-class elements it does have are largely foreign, and largely Palestinian at that—a fact leading to the bloody confrontation between Palestinian guerrillas and the Royal Jordanian Army in 1970–71. This confrontation, important for both the Palestinian and Jordanian elites, was caused by a growing recognition of both parties that political power was slipping increasingly into the hands of the Palestinian dominated bureaucracy. Relying primarily on the bedouin dominated Arab Legion, King Hussein managed to expel the most militant of the Palestinians at that time, who fled to southern Lebanon and elsewhere.

A solution to the Arab-Israeli conflict would most likely undermine the current Jordanian elite. Whether any future Palestinian nation on the West Bank is independent or linked closely to Jordan, it will cause a substantial shift in Jordan's internal political balance. If the West Bank is formally returned to Jordan, large numbers of better-educated Palestinians unsympathetic to the established regime will tip the political balance away from the traditional elements currently supporting the king. If the West Bank is given nominal or real independence, Jordan will permanently lose its only substantial economic base, as well as much of the rationale for the foreign aid it receives from the West and from the states opposing Israel. The largely military-bedouin elite presided over by King Hussein will most likely not survive such changes. And, as in such cases, one can only guess what the emerging government will be like.

Events in South Yemen (People's Democratic Republic of Yemen) clearly suggest that the country is in an early stage of transitional elite control. The only radical, leftist state on the Arabian peninsula, South Yemen is dominated by a single revolutionary party, the National Liberation Front. This party appears to contain mutually hostile pro-Soviet and pro-Chinese factions. The government is very closely linked to the most violent of the Palestinian opposition groups, providing aid and training facilities for guerrillas and saboteurs. South Yemen has also continued a hostile relationship with the Republic of Yemen, its more conservative neighbor to the north, and Oman to the east, where it has supported a war of national liberation. It has received direct military aid from Cuba, a nation with presumably few vital interests in the area. It should be quite clear that in this instance Cuba is playing the role of surrogate for the Soviet Union.

The significance of contemporary politics in South Yemen is most likely its potential to destabilize other small states on the Arabian peninsula. Certainly, the impact of the Yemeni revolution outside the city of Aden is minimal. Thus, the elite is for the most part narrowly drawn and not particularly representative. It does, however, reflect a growing appreciation of the benefits of industrial and military development, a factor that marks it clearly as a transitional regime.

All of the transitional regimes of the Middle East are important to the region and to the larger world community. As indicated earlier in this chapter, these regimes are all in an incipient state of change. They thus constitute much of the kindling for the Middle Eastern tinder box—and the general direction of their change will have profound implications all over the world.

THE MODERN ELITES

In contrast to the transitional elites, the modern elite is one whose day has come. The traditional elite has been either excluded from rule completely or had its influence substantially reduced. Emergent groups who represent larger sections of the population now hold sway. These new groups find themselves in the heady but unaccustomed position of being able to exercise real political power. The political experimentation following the power consolidations of the modern elite may cause instability in policy at first, but eventually an equilibrium should be reached in which the decisions of the new elite will begin to have discernible effects on the society.

Figure 9-3 illustrates the composition of the modern elite. The central figures in the elite will generally be the head of state and his government ministers. It is likely, but not necessarily certain, that the head of state will have reached that position through a career in the bureaucracy or the military. A more unusual approach may be through the emergent party system, or even through the professional modern elites such as medicine, law, or related fields. Even less probable but still possible is advancement from the mass public, since the modern elite is characterized by greater permeability. The established officer corps and nonpolitical middle- and upper-level civil servants complete this rough outline of the modern elite. The ulema and the wealthy landowners still may be present, however. They continue to occupy positions of privilege in a modern society, but they have lost much or all of their political influence.

Several things distinguish modern elites from traditional and transitional elites. One of the greatest differences lies in the modern elites' world view or philosophy. In contrast to the traditional and transitional elites, modern elites are much more likely to see the world as a place that can be radically changed by political, social, and economic policy. In other words, they see the social and political order as a consequence of man's activity and policy, rather than as the result of divine order or some asserted tradition. This point of view often, but not always, associates itself with a secular belief system—that is, a belief system centered on human rather than divine values. For this reason, the modern elite often finds itself in fundamental conflict with religious or sacred values. Some modernizing leaders—such as the former shah of Iran or Prime Minister Bhutto of Pakistan—have found religious opposi-

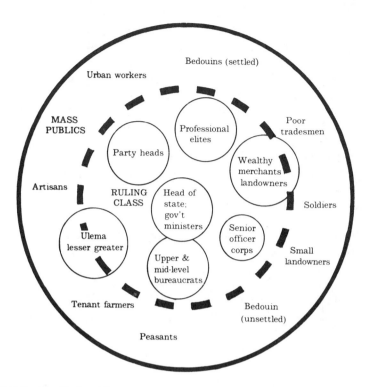

FIGURE 9-3. The Modern Elite

Elite Characteristics:

—High permeability

—High elite consensus

Nations in Modern Classification:

Egypt   Lebanon (until 1974)

Iraq   Syria

Israel   Turkey

tion to their rule to be fierce and ultimately successful. Other modern Arab leaders—for example, Qadaffi of Libya—claim that a modern viewpoint can be supported by traditional Muslim authority and law. The ulema itself may be split over this problem, some inveighing against any semblance of human-centered values or policy and others adopting a more flexible viewpoint.

One of the most prominent features of contemporary Muslim politics is the growing interest in the possibility of establishing modern Islamic republics, states capable of both "modern" control over environment and policy without relinquishing the claims of Islam over social life generally. Only Pakistan and Iran so far have established Islamic republics. Their future is uncertain but the experiment is attracting widespread attention throughout the Muslim world. Their success or failure will have large consequences for other Muslim states, whether traditional, transitional, or modern.

The triumph of a modern elite does not in any way eliminate group conflict, or for that matter even minimize it. To the contrary, the composition of the modern elite includes more groups in the political process than do the traditional or transitional political systems. Moreover, the intensity of conflict may increase as well, particularly as more and more elements in society make stronger and stronger claims on social services and goods. For example, traditional and transitional societies generally have low levels of public literacy. As modern societies increase literacy, they also increase the social and political awareness of groups of their particular situations vis-à-vis other groups in the society; thus the social good—literacy—carries with it the premise of higher political consciousness and hence more and greater political participation. The result is an increase in the scope of conflict and subsequent greater attention to conflict resolution. Issues and publics that are simply not relevant to the traditional regime are suddenly and irreversibly part and parcel of a geometrically expanding political process. Both mischief and progress attend this change.

International conflict can also be related to these elite systems. The secular-modern regimes of Egypt, Syria, and Iraq have often found themselves individually in conflict with the transitional regimes of the Sudan and Pahlevi Iran, or the traditional regimes of Saudi Arabia (under Saud and Faisal) and Kuwait. Their various beliefs are often seen as mutually exclusive and irreconcilable.

Our contemporary focus on the Arab-Israeli conflict in the Middle East often blinds us to the equally valid differences existing within the Arab and Muslim world. These differences are likely to play larger and larger roles in the immediate future, particularly as different elites make claims on the political loyalties and sensibilities of citizens in other countries. This level of conflict is difficult to resolve without resorting to widespread violence—violence that is all too capable of spilling over into other arenas of international conflict. The 1980–81 war between Iraq and Iran is a good recent example.

Modern elite systems—Egypt, Turkey, Syria, Iraq, Lebanon, and Israel—while sharing the characteristics of a more open structure—are clearly a heterogenous group of nations that have substantially different histories and cultures. The specific compositions of their elites are also different, although they tend to share similar outlooks on modernization.

Turkey

Under the Ottoman sultans, Turkey was the model of a traditional elite. It was the first Middle Eastern nation to throw off the mantle of the traditional past and embrace European modernization, perhaps because it alone straddles Europe and Asia. Although many political and economic changes occurred in Turkey under the sultanate, Turkey emerged as a modern political system with the remarkable innovations of Mustafa Kemal Atatürk, who proclaimed a new, secular republic in 1923. Atatürk, supported by his political party, the Republican People's Party, mounted a strong and sustained attack on the traditional order. Reforms ranged from the general to the specific, but the major thrust was the secularization of political power, a corresponding reduction of the power of the Muslim hierarchy, and the virtual elimination of the institutions of traditional rule. Atatürk aimed at no less than the total transformation of Turkey from a weak, illiterate, agricultural nation to an industrial nation with all the attendant skills and attitudes that this implies. The very idea of a political party, even a single-party system, implied levels of public political participation undreamed of in the preceding regime.

From these revolutionary beginnings, Turkey has moved toward a complex, industrial, participatory system. The rudimentary forms of truly competitive political parties now exist in Turkey, although periods of military rule have occurred in 1960, 1971, and 1980-81.

The Turkish political elite have made some progress toward their goals. The vision of Atatürk has yet to jell in the economic sector, and some traditional elements—particularly Muslim conservative groups—have put considerable strain on the country's political institutions. And yet progress has been made; Turkey's politics are remarkably participant in comparison to those of the transitional countries, and freer than most other modern countries in the Middle East—no mean achievement for any country in this part of the world.

Future elite conflict is likely to revolve around the demands of Muslim conservatives for some degree of restoration of the faith, the stresses of U.S.-Soviet competition in the area, and the always touchy relations with Greece over Cyprus. As noted earlier, the achievement of a modern elite structure does *not* signify an end to internal political conflict, but rather signals a change of arena and scope of conflict. In this regard, Turkey has shown itself capable of adjusting to some serious political conflicts in recent history; and the future promises more and tougher challenges. The permeability and representativeness of the Turkish elite should be a considerable asset in meeting these tests.

Egypt

Unlike Turkey, Egypt had long been a victim of direct imperialist control and continued to be until comparatively recent times. The Egyptian revolution occurred in 1952 with the revolt of the Free Officers. This revolt, which expelled the corrupt and ineffective monarchy of King Farouk, brought to power in Egypt a junta of young army officers, most of them trained abroad. This group of officers was subsequently to demonstrate extraordinary cohesiveness, bringing a revolution of considerable scope to a faltering Egypt. Initially led by Gen. M. Neguib, the group was ultimately headed by Col. Gamal Abdel Nasser, one of the most remarkable leaders to grace the political landscape of the Middle East.

Under Nasser attempts were made to create a party of national revolution. Several formulas were tried, and in 1962 the efforts jelled in the formation of the Arab Socialist Union. The union was conceived of as a party of national integration and ideology, bringing the masses into political contact and cooperation with the central regime. Under Nasser, the party took on some distinct characteristics that were to have profound effects both in Egypt and in the Middle East generally.

Nasser, a charismatic leader of the first order, tapped or created a reservoir of sentiment that is now called *Arab nationalism*. Essentially arguing that the Arab people were split unnecessarily and unwisely into a number of competing camps and nations, Nasser made an emotional appeal for a new Arab unity, one that would reclaim a prominent world role. Nasser's vision inspired many movements across the Middle East that were often viewed with suspicion outside of Egypt. Cynical observers were to see in Nasser's calls for Arab unity the distinct possibility of Egyptian political dominance. Others were disturbed by the coincidence of Nasser's Arab unity with his concept of Arab socialism and mass political participation. Nasser's forthright opposition to the traditional elites of Egypt did not endear him to the beleaguered traditional and transitional elites of other Middle Eastern countries.

Nasser had a particular vision of Arab socialism. This combination of politics and economics should not be viewed as socialism in any European or Marxist sense; rather, it was more a socialism of secular Islam. Its practical expression came in terms of the nationalization of basic industries, the expulsion of foreign ownership, and the construction of hospitals, mosques, and schools in as many Egyptian villages as possible. There was no sophisticated understanding of socialist economics in Nasser's formula. There was, instead, a concern for the common man expressed in terms of his daily needs and concerns—concerns like food, a place of worship, employment, and national ethnic pride.

The implementation of Nasser's socialism had benign political effects: mass public participation in the Arab Socialist Union, a very real improvement in Egypt's international prestige, and the integration of the professional and political classes with the military bureaucracy. But it nearly created an economic disaster: high inflation, low industrial productivity, high unemployment. But as critical as we may justifiably be of Nasser's economic policies, we cannot deny his beneficial influence on Egyptian and Arab politics. His symbolic value to the emergence of an appropriate twentieth-century Arab identity is enormous.

Nasser's death and the consolidation of control under Anwar Sadat brought many substantial changes to Egypt and its elite. Under Sadat, the scope of the elite broadened as government policy became more tolerant of people and institutions in the private sector. In the late 1970s, Sadat launched an ambitious program to create a parallel private economic structure; and he attempted to create competition between left, right, and center parties in the Arab Socialist Union. These efforts have broadened the representativeness of the elite, although their effects are still too new to evaluate completely.

Sadat's rather bold changes of Nasser's political vision have not come cheaply or without opposition. Attempts in 1978 to raise the artificially low price of bread met with widespread and angry public demonstrations, forcing the government to back down in its attempt. Nasser is still a potent symbol in the hearts and minds of the Egyptian peasantry and bureaucracy, and one is more likely to encounter his picture in a peasant home than that of Anwar Sadat. It is clear that much of the thrust of the Egyptian revolution under Nasser survives; and it is also clear that Sadat is making a mark on that revolution himself, as the Egyptian treaty with Israel (1979), the dramatic break with the U.S.S.R., and the wooing of Western industry to the Nile have demonstrated.

Sadat's government, however, has come under increasing domestic pressure from groups dissatisfied with these changes. Palestinian organizations have placed a price on his head, as has Libya's volatile Col. Qadaffi. The Muslim Brotherhood, violently repressed by Nasser in the early days of the revolution, shows signs of resurgence; it has been encouraged by the Islamic revolutions in Libya, Iran, and Pakistan. And Arab nationalists, unhappy with Sadat's unilateral peace with Israel, are beginning to oppose Sadat's rule.

As we have seen, Egypt is under enormous pressure from problems of ideology, population, and war. The elite structure of Egypt has apparently broadened and expanded in recent years; it is now an asset in the confrontation of those issues and threats. The ultimate political asset—a population politically aware and capable of mobilization against a common foe—may be Nasser's final legacy to his successor, Sadat.

Syria

Syria shares many characteristics with Lebanon and the people of Palestine. One of the most economically viable of the Middle Eastern countries, Syria has considerable arable land and a relatively well-educated population. Syria has for many years exported its professional and commercial expertise, an indicator of her relatively developed and sophisticated elites. Syria's borders were the result of arbitrary decisions by the victorious European allies; it is also one of the front-line states in the Arab-Israeli conflict. Like Egypt and Lebanon, Syria has carried much of the financial and personal burden of the confrontation.

Syrian politics have been dominated since the early 1950s by a combination of party ideology (the Baath party) and military opportunism. Currently, Syria is run by a military-bureaucratic elite whose power is periodically confirmed by national elections. Most influential positions, including the president, are currently held by Alawite Muslims, a small and obscure sect. There is substantial resentment in the Sunni and Shiite communities over this inequity. Those individuals who have experiences both in the military and the Baath party are most likely to compete successfully for office.

Although the Baath party, in both Syria and Iraq, has a substantial ideology of nationalism and moderate socialism, its contemporary importance is best seen when compared with Nasser's Arab Socialism. As we mentioned earlier, Nasser's motives were not viewed sympathetically by many established political authorities. The Baath ideology, stressing similar goals but with importantly different symbols, became a bulwark against the Egyptian-dominated movement for Arab unity.

Syria has gained a measure of political stability under Baathist military rule, a stability that stands in marked contrast to the highly unstable early days of its independence, when the coups d'etat were literally too numerous to count reliably. A modicum of economic growth has been achieved, and internationally Syria has achieved a far greater influence in the Arab bloc than her size and power would indicate.

The Syrian political elite has become progressively more representative in the past decade, as national elections and the promulgations of a more-or-less democratic constitution demonstrate. Syria is one of the most socially progressive of the

Middle Eastern nations—the status of women, for instance, is traditionally higher in Syria than in the rest of the Middle East. Syria is one of the potentially bright spots in the area, in spite of its very minimal petroleum reserves.

Iraq

Iraq, being both Baathist in ideology and a geographic neighbor of Syria, might be expected to share many of Syria's political characteristics. This, however, is not so. The Iraqi form of Baathism has been consistently more radical, and political conflict in Iraq has been resolved at a much higher level of violence. Since the overthrow of the monarchy in 1958, Iraq has been ruled by a series of political juntas. Most elite conflict has taken place in the military, most often in the form of bloody coups. There is also the continuing problem with the Kurdish minority in the northern mountains of Iraq. Fiercely independent and stubborn, the Kurds have fought an "on and off" war of national independence since Iraq gained its independence, a war often costly to Iraq in terms of lives and political stability.

This problem with the Kurdish minority is not, of course, restricted in any way to the Iraq. The Kurds, the largest and most militant stateless minority in the Middle East, occupy the contiguous territory of Iraq, Iran, and Turkey. All these countries have pursued policies at one time or another ranging from neglect to open hostility and even genocide. The Kurds currently find themselves treated as a "nongroup" in Turkey, are under military pressure to conform to the Islamic revolution in Iran, and have been subjected to a brutal resettlement strategy in Iraq, designed to move them away from the oil-fields in the north and into the deserts of the south. They are the group least likely to benefit from government policy or economic development. Their plight is increasingly desperate and any viable solution seems distant.

The Iraqi regime has been implacably opposed to Israel and quick to blame Western diplomacy for the continued vitality of Israel. Consequently, the Iraqi elite has sought closer ties with the Soviet Union and Eastern Europe, and markets a considerable percentage of its great crude oil production in those areas. Although Iraq is by no means a satellite of Soviet foreign policy, the Iraqi elite maintains closer ties with the Eastern bloc than does nearly any other Middle Eastern state; there are, however, recent signs that this policy is beginning to change.

As a result of this international orientation, many members of the Iraqi political elite have been educated in Soviet schools. The coalition between the Baath and the Iraqi Communist parties in a "national front" further alienated the Iraqi elite from her neighbors, particularly Syria. This strained relationship was demonstrated in the Iraqi-Iranian war of 1980–81, in which Syria openly sided with Iran.

For whatever reasons, Iraqi development has not been as impressive as the development of other oil-rich nations, nor as politically impressive as the recent changes in Syria and Egypt. The inability of the elite to develop participatory links with the public may account for some of this, and there are signs that the Iraqi elite itself perceives this as a problem. In the late 1970s, the Iraqi government eased some of the restrictions on foreign education, a policy that may lead to a broader-based elite with more members of the professional middle class than has hitherto been the case. This would help the subsequent development of the Iraqi political process by allowing for conflict resolution in a broader and more humane manner.

Lebanon

Until the spillover of the Arab-Israeli conflict literally tore it asunder, Lebanon was the most cosmopolitan country in the Middle East. Beirut, a city of charm and energy, was a center of commerce and finance; it had attracted a highly skilled and mobile international population. Blessed with considerable national resources, including a well-educated and ambitious population, Lebanon seemed to have a very bright future.

The Israeli invasion of Lebanon in 1978, primarily to eliminate Palestinian terrorist bases, put an effective end to the dream of the Lebanese. But in point of fact, the dream was fragile long before. Lebanon, another of those countries based on a series of unwise and shallow judgments made in Europe, was composed of at least three highly differentiated ethnic groups—Christians, Muslims, and Druze. Never integrated into a national political or economic unit, these groups lived in proximity but not intimacy. The National Pact or charter of Lebanon, promulgated at a time when the Muslim and Christian populations were nearly equal, parceled out political offices to particular ethnic groups. For example, the president was required to be a Maronite Christian while the prime minister had to be a Sunni Muslim. These and other offices were apportioned on the basis of the supposed relative balance of religious-ethnic groups at the time of the National Pact. National censuses were forbidden for fear of upsetting the delicate balance between the groups.

The fiction of stable, counterbalancing religious groups served Lebanon well until it was forced, seemingly against its will, into the mainstream of the Arab-Israeli confrontation. Since the invasion of Lebanon by Israeli units in 1973, Lebanon has been plagued by a civil war that has been aided and abetted by foreign intrigue. Links between Israel and right-wing Christian groups have been documented, for example; and Syrian troops occupy most of Lebanon at this time ostensibly for peace-keeping purposes. Lebanon is currently in a state of civil war. Had her political system been based on a truly integrative national political elite, she might have avoided this painful fate. But most clearly, her current difficulties reflect the complex interplay of historical forces, national and international elite conflict, and the smoldering potential of ethnic conflict.

Israel

In some respects, the Israeli elite is the most modern of the Middle Eastern elites; and in other respects, it is among the most traditional. It is modern in that its members are highly educated and largely of European origin. The Israeli elite has mastered the technological skills and values necessary for a modern society. For those who qualify for elite status—primarily on the basis of religious preference, technical competence, and social origin—the established political process is participatory and representative.

There are, however, large and important groups effectively disenfranchised in the Israeli system. First and most obvious are the Arabs who number in the hundreds of thousands and who live in both the traditional area of Israel and the various occupied territories of Gaza, the Golan Heights, Sinai, and the West Bank. From the government point of view, the Arabs constitute a serious security problem and as a consequence they are subject to a wide range of political, economic and social controls.

Disenfranchisement is not the fate only of the Arabs, however. Intra-Israeli conflict has been well-documented in recent decades, with the result that certain Jewish groups have very little access to the ruling class. Tensions have developed between the politically dominant European Jews (Ashkenazi) and the more recently arrived and less modern oriental Jews (Sephardim) from Asia and Africa. Moreover, there are growing separations between recent immigrants from both the Ashkenazi and Sephardic communities and the second-generation descendants of the founders, the Sabras. Growing levels of inflation have exacerbated these tensions. Finally, there are those in Israel who promote radical solutions to the Arab and oriental immigrant problem—solutions ranging from forced emigration to violence. Some of these groups, through dramatic and precipitate actions, have made moderation of the larger Arab-Israeli dispute very difficult.

Future Israeli elite development will be directly linked in one way or another to the state of the larger Arab-Israeli conflict. It is also clear that the Israeli nation has had to pay an extremely high social and economic price in this conflict. One of the most salubrious consequences of an Arab-Israeli peace would be a lessening of tension in the Israeli elite and probable improvements in its permeability and representativeness.

CONCLUSION

It is clear that political, social, and economic pressures in the Middle East ultimately affect the elite structure of politics. The Middle East is unusual in having a wide variety of elites—traditional, transitional, and modern. It is also clear that changes in the composition of an elite can ultimately cause profound changes in the policies and world view of a political system. Unfortunately, these effects are not specifically predictable.

On the other hand, we can safely predict that these changes will produce new strains and demands upon the political system, and that these strains and demands will create new and often unexpected conflicts both domestic and international. We can thus with some confidence predict a continuation of the unsettled nature of contemporary Middle Eastern politics. And without doubt, we can predict that Islam, in its various forms, will be intimately involved in that process. These factors, combined with the commonplace but accurate observation that the world is growing smaller, suggest that the political implications of these changes in elite structure will influence all our hopes and lives.

10

Political Leadership
in the Contemporary
Middle East

Having discussed the ruling elites in the Middle East, we shall now focus on those individuals in the highest political offices: monarchs, generals, and presidents, etc. While effective leadership is important to the world's affluent and powerful societies, it is even more important to the disadvantaged and recently independent countries that are confronting serious internal and external challenges. Countries in which the institutions of government are new, fragile, or discredited have a far greater need for effective leadership than those with long histories of political order and stability.

There are three basic styles of political leadership: traditional, modern bureaucratic, and charismatic.[1] We shall examine a leader representative of each style and show how his career exemplifies that style's essential nature. We shall then examine other contemporary Middle Eastern leaders and see how their styles of rule fit the pattern. Finally, we shall briefly examine how these leadership styles affect domestic and international politics.

The three basic leaderships styles are necessarily broad and general, and do not account for fine differences nor do they accurately predict the political consequences of any one kind of leadership; they are only rough guides. To illustrate the three types, we shall focus on three prominent figures in twentieth-century Egyptian politics: King Farouk (traditional), Gamal Abdel Nasser (charismatic), and Anwar Sadat (modern bureaucratic).

TRADITIONAL LEADERSHIP

Traditional leaders base their claim to leadership on the assertion that they are the clear and logical successors to a line of leaders that stretches back in time and that is legitimized by practice. They are leaders because of historical forces, and they

---

[1]This leadership typology originated with Max Weber, the great German sociologist. Our use of it, however, differs substantially from his. See Gerth, Hans, and Mills, C. Wright, eds., *From Max Weber* (New York, 1964).

claim the right and obligation to continue. They often imply that their leadership is necessary to maintain the social order on the right course. Traditional political orders, while conservative, are not rigid or unyielding to change; but they may be slow to implement a schedule of changes or react to changing conditions. They expect change to occur over relatively extended periods of time. As Almond and Powell observe, there is a definite promise of performance implied in the assertion of the right to rule:

> . . . most traditional societies have some long-range performance expectations built into their norms of legitimacy; if crops fail, enemies invade, or floods destroy, then the emperor may lose the "mandate of heaven," as in Imperial China; or the chiefs their authority; or the feudal lords, their claim to the loyalty of their serfs.[2]

The traditional leader depends on the force of tradition, or his interpretation of it, to establish his legitimacy as a ruler. *Legitimacy* refers to the public perception of the ruler's right to his position of leadership, and is not restricted to traditional leaders alone. The willingness of the populace to accept a particular leadership structure as right and defensible legitimizes the political process as it exists. But it is no substitute for effective policy nor can it protect an ineffective ruler forever.

Some examples of traditional legitimization may clarify the problem. There is a logic to the use of tradition as a legitimizing symbol. The Shah of Iran, for instance, often publicly argued that the Persian cultural tradition demanded monarchical leadership, that the Iranian political practice for thousands of years found its most effective and satisfying expression in a monarch. As monarch, Mohammed Reza Pahlevi was therefore performing an important service for the Iranian people.

The rulers of Egypt made similar arguments, although with a difference. The frustrations that beset Napoleon when he attempted to institute self-government in Egypt were based at least partially on a long-standing belief that Egyptians somehow lacked the requisite skills for self-rule. The Mameluks and the family of Muhammad Ali worked to perpetuate this opinion. And while these opinions helped legitimize their respective rules, they were not in any way sufficient to prevent their ultimate destruction.

That tradition may legitimize but not stifle change is also well-demonstrated in Saudi Arabia. There is no gainsaying the importance of tradition in legitimizing the Saudi leadership. But tradition has not been a logical reason for continuing a weak leader in office. The transition from King Saud to King Faisal, based on decisions within the royal family itself, suggests that this traditional elite was responsive to contemporary difficulties. Tradition was mobilized to legitimize the change and the new leadership.

The right or legitimacy of traditional leaders is often bound up in the intersection of political and religious tradition: the king or sultan may also be the de-

---

[2]Gabriel Almond and Bingham Powell, *Comparative Politics* (Boston: Little Brown, 1978), pp. 31–32.

fender of the faith, for example; or the sheikh may be patron of the ulema as in the relationship of the Egyptian monarchy with the mosque university of Al Azhar. These roles and symbols, given great weight by their persistence over time, are the most important factors in legitimizing the traditional regimes.

In the absence of competing claims, traditional leaders may find the invocation of ancient roles and symbols adequate to protect their base of power. Given the twentieth-century phenomenon of competing claims from charismatic or modern bureaucratic aspirants to office, traditional leaders have often been forced to attempt limited reforms within the recognized tradition. And so, traditional leaders have attempted to modernize their political, social, and economic systems without sacrificing their right to rule. The Tanzimat reforms in Ottoman Turkey can be interpreted in this light, as can the White Revolution of the Shah of Iran. In both cases, the traditional leader attempted to come to terms with modern technology and administrative procedures without relinquishing his monopoly of political power. It is instructive that both efforts ultimately failed.

King Farouk of Egypt

Many characteristics of traditional political leaders are exhibited in the experience of King Farouk of Egypt, the last Egyptian monarch. Farouk's rule (1936-1952) embraced a period of time that saw a fundamental redrawing of the international political order, including the rise of Soviet and American power, the concomitant decline of European—especially British—influence in the Middle East, the emergence of mass political parties, and the political reassertion of Islam and Islamic groups. Farouk's response to these changes demonstrates both the essence of traditional leadership as well as its fundamental defects.

Born in 1920 into the royal lineage founded by the great Egyptian leader Muhammad Ali, Farouk was raised in a strong tradition of royal absolutism. The line of Muhammad Ali treated the whole of Egypt as its personal possession. King Farouk proved himself to be no stranger to this tradition.

The royal family, like most of the ruling houses of Egypt for the past three thousand years, was not of Egyptian extraction. In the case of Farouk's family, the line was founded by an Albanian adventurer, Muhammad Ali, with very tenuous ties of loyalty to the Ottoman Empire. Enormously successful at realizing the political, social, and economic potential of nineteenth-century Egypt, Muhammad Ali was frustrated by European, especially English, intervention. A large, extended family buttressed by extensive retainers and officials saw Egypt as a private fief run for its own benefit. With few ties to the Egyptian masses, the royal family routinely assumed its right to absolute rule and consistently opposed the extension of political rights or influence to native Egyptians.

Farouk himself was educated and socialized in a conservative atmosphere; he was exposed to periodically rabid Anglophobia and persistently pro-Italian sympathies. Farouk's tutors included the most notable ulema of Al-Azhar University, who instilled in him a serious appreciation of his role as protector of the faith. King Fuad's death at a time of European influence placed Farouk on the throne at age

16, still in his minority. A regency council was formed to advise and educate him in his responsibilities as ruler of Egypt.

Farouk's father, King Fuad, saw the emergence of the first legitimate mass political party in Egypt, the Wafd. Much of Fuad's political labors in later life were devoted to frustrating Wafd aspirations to power, a program continued by the young king. The combination of mass political activity and growing nationalism had a disquieting effect on the royal house. By complex political maneuvers, Fuad and Farouk attempted to exclude the Wafd from power. Thus, they both demonstrated one of the chief characteristics of traditional political leadership: a great reluctance to *share* political power with anyone, particularly with mass or nationalist groups. This is not to imply that Farouk was bereft of policy or ambition—indeed, there is evidence to the contrary. The point is that these ambitions never included a broadening of the base of political power.

Farouk demonstrated his traditional orientation to political power in other ways. His fascination with ceremony, pomp, and circumstance reflect the concern of the traditional leader for rituals and rite that confirm the assertion and maintenance of traditional authority. Decked out in rich uniforms for every occasion, Farouk's movements around his kingdom were spectacles in themselves: elegant livery, scores of retainers and entertainers, international celebrities and sumptuous banquets in luxurious palaces or country estates. Grandeur was not only a perquisite of office, it was an obligation; and Farouk became increasingly enthusiastic about it.

In a similar vein, the royal house under Farouk became internationally noted for its hedonism. Drunkenness, particularly offensive to the emerging Muslim Brotherhood, sexual abandon (often reported graphically in the international press) and disturbingly regular accusations of official corruption involving minor members of the royal family, were commonplace. Farouk's appreciation for attractive women became an international symbol of Egyptian royal decadence, set in the most luxurious spas of Mediterranean Europe.

There was a curious tension between Farouk's hedonism and his public attitude toward Islam. One could not call him personally pious, particularly in view of his devotion to Koranically prohibited pleasures: wine, women, and pornography. On the other hand, Farouk took his role as "defender of the faith" seriously; he made substantial contributions to the maintenance of Al Azhar and welcomed a number of political exiles to Cairo. He also subsidized programs designed to maintain Egyptian prestige in the larger community of Muslim nations, which lacked any focus of authority since the abolition of the caliphate. These practices solidified his relationship to the higher ulema at the same time that his hedonism was coming under growing criticism by fundamentalist Muslim groups.

Despite these irritants to the prestige of the royal house, Farouk's rule and government enjoyed a legitimacy that demonstrates the strength of traditional leadership. Most analysts of the period assert that Farouk's government far outlasted its effectiveness. Aside from noting the population's predisposition to accept the traditional, there is little in the last ten years of Farouk's rule to suggest that his political, social, or economic *performance* commanded popular support for the government.

The final blow to Farouk's rule in Egypt resulted from a combination of domestic and international forces. Farouk's pro-Italian sympathies quickly ran afoul of international events in World War II, resolving in favor of his British enemies. In addition, the public was becoming dissatisfied with his opposition to the Wafd party, and the increasingly militant fundamentalist Muslim Brotherhood was disillusioned by his personal licentiousness. Riots in Cairo involving the Wafd, extremist groups, the Muslim Brotherhood, and students became commonplace. The final blow came with the miserable performance of the Egyptian military in the war against Israel in 1948, although the full implications of the war were not to become clear to the public until the revolution of July 23, 1952. Charges of corruption and ineptitude gained widespread circulation and validity. The war became a focus of resentment against the low level to which Arab prestige had sunk. Farouk became increasingly unable to manipulate the forces of Egyptian politics, and instability and drift became the governmental norms.

Farouk's fall and abdication was a result of actions by the military, not the political forces that opposed him for so long. His final attempts to abrogate the Anglo-Egyptian treaty in 1951 produced a series of ugly confrontations between Egyptian and British forces, which in turn set off a series of antigovernment and antiforeign riots in the urban centers of Egypt. The army's inability to handle these incidents further inflamed the king's opponents, and British efforts to reinforce their garrisons added even more fuel to the fire. Finally, on July 23, 1952, a group of military officers known as the "Committee of Free Officers" overthrew the government and established the Revolutionary Command Council under the titular leadership of General Naguib. On July 26, the council requested the formal abdication of King Farouk. Farouk complied, abdicating in favor of his son, and promptly departed for Italy. Farouk never recovered his influence in Egypt. His abdication itself demonstrated his inability to come to terms with the emerging political order.

> Towards the middle of the afternoon, it was announced in a broadcast from Cairo that "some very important news would be given at six o'clock." Everybody understood and prepared to listen.
> All round the Ras El Tin palace and along the coast road to Alexandria an enormous crowd had gathered, tense with expectation and with mixed feelings of anguish and joy. Then came the prodigious sight: the royal exit in the rays of the setting sun, on to the sea which a hundred and fifty years earlier had brought, to the Egyptian shore, the Albanian soldier of fortune, Mohammed Ali, the great-great-grandfather of the sovereign who was now taking his leave.
> At ten minutes to six . . . Faruk, in his splendid white uniform of *Admiral of the Fleet*, came slowly down the palace steps towards the sea. He was followed by Queen Narriman, carrying the new king, six months old. . . . While the royal flag was being fetched from the palace, a cruiser in the bay fired a twenty-one-gun salute.

General Naguib went aboard. . . . Faruk appeared to be touched, behind the screen of his dark glasses. "Take care of my army," he said. "It is now in good hands, sire," Naguib replied. The answer did not please Faruk, who said in a hard voice, "What you have done to me, I was getting ready to have done to you." Then, turning on his heel, he took leave of the conquerors.[3]

Farouk's final years became a mishmash of sybaritic excess in the most expensive and exclusive resorts of Europe. Throwing himself with abandon into the gambling tables, the dining tables, and the arms of many an attractive companion, Farouk ended his life as a corpulent playboy dedicated to things of the flesh and the moment—a sad ending in many respects, far removed from the promise of leadership in the sixteen-year-old youth who ascended the throne in 1936.

King Farouk, of course, is hardly the best example to use of a traditional ruler. He was weak and was unable to rise effectively to the challenges of his times. Indeed, he helps to maintain the myth of decadent Middle Eastern rulers. Compared to the historical importance of the Shah of Iran or Ibn Saud of Saudi Arabia, Farouk is something of a footnote to contemporary history.

However, King Farouk's example is important for several reasons. First, the crises of leadership that have afflicted the decolonializing world have *often* involved the reluctant departure of ineffective traditional leaders. To focus on strong leaders would distort our analysis. Second, the myth of decadence is not a myth. Absolute rulers, traditional and otherwise, have not shown themselves to be disinterested in pleasure or pomp or luxury. Indeed, much of the basis for their legitimacy comes from just such a claim to the perquisites of royalty. Finally, the influence of weak and ineffective leaders on world history is arguably as important as the impact of the few "great men" of our times.

We will return to the subject of traditional leadership at the end of this chapter. The crisis of confidence in traditional leadership, which undermined King Farouk just as it undermined many other Middle Eastern leaders in this century, leads to three possible alternatives:

1. Traditional political governance from a different political ruler, an apparently unlikely and short-term phenomenon.
2. Leadership based on the claims of the modern bureaucratic managers in the society, such as the military or a nascent political party.
3. Charismatic leaders who offer their transcendent leadership as a substitute for the claims of tradition or bureaucratic efficiency.

In the period after the fall of the Egyptian monarch, the third alternative materialized in the form of Gamal Abdel Nasser, a young officer in the movement that called for Farouk's abdication. Definitely a charismatic leader, Nasser was to have an important effect on Egypt and the Middle East.

[3] Jeanne and Simonne Lacouture, *Egypt in Transition* (New York: Criterion Books, 1958), pp. 156–59.

CHARISMATIC LEADERSHIP

As defined by Max Weber, a charismatic leader possesses particular characteristics that set him apart from normal leaders. A charismatic leader is, in a word, unique. He possesses personal characteristics that are suited to a peculiarly intense leadership style; and he is capable of creating or participating in an intense, reciprocal psychological exchange with his followers. His actions and proposals are legitimized by reference to some transcendent source, either religious, historical, natural, or mystical. Recent world leaders recognized as charismatic include Adolph Hitler, Charles De Gaulle, Tito, Sukarno, and Gamal Abdel Nasser.

Our definition and description of charismatic leadership is complicated by two factors. First, charismatic leadership is often erroneously equated with other leadership characteristics such as personal beauty, rhetorical skill, popularity, and the like. Thus, the use of the term in general circulation may distract us from the necessary distinguishing characteristics of the charismatic leader. Secondly, charismatic leadership appears to be idiosyncratic to the culture in which it occurs; thus the characteristics of a charismatic leader in Egypt would differ from those of a charismatic leader in, say, France or England. The chemistry of the relationship between leader and followers changes according to the particulars of the culture and historical circumstance. Despite these difficulties, the phenomenon of charismatic leadership is real and is important in any analysis of Middle Eastern politics. Charismatic leaders have had, and continue to have, enormous impact on the politics of the region. The Sudanese Mahdi, Gamal Abdel Nasser, the Ayatollah Ruhollah Khomeini, and Col. Muammar Qadaffi—all have had, or have, the potential to alter dramatically the course of political events.

In spite of the idiosyncratic qualities of charisma, there are some general observations we can make about the phenomenon. First, charismatic leadership almost always appears during a social or political crisis—particularly a crisis in which the prevailing institutions of government have been discredited or destroyed. Examples might include the ruinous inflation in Germany that preceded the rise of Hitler or the legislative-executive deadlocks that preceded De Gaulle's second entrance into French politics. Theoretically, the public in these situations is predisposed to seek a heroic leader to provide a substitute for discredited authority.

Another expectation is that the charismatic leader will promulgate substantial and convincing images of a new order, perhaps ordained in heaven, that will raise the community to new levels of activity and accomplishment, or in another variant, restore the community to its rightful place in the world. In giving substance to the visionary demands of a disillusioned populace, the charismatic leader provides them psychological sustenance and heightened self-esteem.

Yet another characteristic of charismatic leaders is their resonant rhetorical gift—resonant in the sense that they can raise sympathetic responses from the followers. This rhetorical gift may vary dramatically in style. Compare, for instance, the dramatic histrionics of Adolph Hitler with the icy, Olympian quality of De Gaulle's pronouncements. Whatever the style, the successful charismatic leader has the ability to move a nation by the power of his rhetoric. Indeed, in many cases the rhetoric may be more politically important than the substance of the policies articulated.

Finally, the charismatic leader leads by example. Once again, this quality seems idiosyncratic to culture. The simple, introspective life of a Gandhi can be contrasted with the cheerful hedonism of Sukarno in Indonesia or Marcos in the Philippines. But in each case, the leader in his personal life sets a standard of personal behavior that strikes the populace as desirable and ennobling.

These characteristics provide the public with personal knowledge of the leader. He fills a place in the collective psychology of the nation. The leader in turn gains a larger-than-life perspective on himself, thriving and growing on the demands and support of the followers. Thus, a powerful, reciprocal psychological exchange is established, which ultimately allows a single personality to substitute for a complex of institutions.

As powerful as this reciprocal dynamic can be, there is a critical defect in charismatic leadership. That defect is the mortality of the leader himself, upon whom the whole social transaction is based. Charismatic leaders, like ordinary mortals, die, and the transition from a charismatic leader to his successor is fraught with hazard. Charismatic leaders do not appear on demand. Thus, one cannot count on replacing one charismatic leader with another. Usually, charismatic leadership must give way to either traditional rule or modern-bureaucratic leadership—so nature and the human condition dictate. Let us now turn to the charismatic leadership of Gamal Abdel Nasser.

Gamal Abdel Nasser

Nasser presents an interesting counterpoint to King Farouk. Born in Alexandria in 1918 into the family of a low-level civil servant, Nasser was ethnically Egyptian, as opposed to the Albanian origins of Farouk. Educated in the new modern schools of the time Nasser entered the Egyptian military academy in 1936. Farouk's first military job was as chief of state at age 16. Where Farouk was elegant and pampered, Nasser was simple and ascetic.

Nasser's physical and personal qualities have inspired many writers to attempt to capture the factors that contributed to his commanding presence. The following passages by Jeanne and Simonne Lacouture are representative:

> What first impresses you is his massive, thick-set build, the dazzlingly white smile in his dark face. He is tall, tough, African. As he comes toward you on the steps of his small villa on the outskirts of the city, or strides across his huge office at the Presidency, he has the emphatic gait of some Covent Garden porter or some heavy, feline creature, while he stretches his brawny hand out with the wide gesture of a reaper, completely sure of himself. His eyes have an Asiatic slant and almost close as he laughs. His voice is metallic, brassy, full, the kind of voice that would be useful on maneuvres in the open country....
>   The impression of strength remains when he relaxes. He has an air of youthfulness, together with a certain timidity. He is gray at the temples but

his hard face, that reminds you of a ploughshare, sometimes takes on an adolescent look.[4]

Nasser, in short, was heady tonic to a people accustomed to foreign rule and previously convinced that government was not an Egyptian aptitude. His personal presence, reflecting both real and potential power, combined with an electrifying rhetorical style, spoke directly to the powerlessness of the mass. Nasser, it seems, became the personal embodiment of the aspirations of the people. He in turn grew in response to their fervent commitment.

Nasser entered politics indirectly. His biographies indicate an early dissatisfaction with foreign rule and political corruption, but he originally intended to reform the Egyptian military. Nasser and his associates did not come to power in the revolution of July 23, 1952, with any plan for political rule. Instead, it appears that political power and responsibility was thrust upon the officers as they began to recognize the inability of Farouk and the Wafd to work cooperatively for reform.

Ideologically, Nasser's early political views can be summarized by the formula "Fight Against Imperialism, Monarchy, and Feudalism." Only later, as he matured in the office of president, did Nasser's political views develop. These views demonstrated the cosmological quality of Nasser's leadership. Particularly in his promotion of Arab socialism and pan-Arabism, Nasser demonstrated the charismatic leader's claim to some cosmological source of authority. In making regular symbolic reference in his speeches and writings to the greatness of the Arab past, the Egyptian past, and to Islam and the Umma, Nasser not only provided a cultural and historical identity to the Egyptian people, but he legitimized contemporary policy in non-Western terms. In many respects, this can be labeled a triumph of form over substance, for Nasser never specified the policy implications of his ideology consistently. Nevertheless, for the fragmented and uncertain Egyptian community of the 1950s and 1960s, the Nasser prescription was just what was needed.

Nasser's relationship to Islam reveals his lack of ideological precision. Although he recognized a direct relationship between Islam and Egypt's past and present, and although he appeared to be personally pious and upright, Nasser was nevertheless a secular political leader. Early on in the revolution the Free Officers came into conflict with traditional Islamic forces—the ulema, which was in league with the monarchy and was opposed to the revolution, and the Moslem Brotherhood, which did not recognize any distinction between politics and religion. In steering a course between these forces, Nasser and the Free Officers opted for a view that derived inspiration from Islam and its writings, but simultaneously honored the principle of separation of church and state. This separation was anathema to the leadership of the Brotherhood, and a nasty confrontation was inevitable.

Nasser's socialism was ambiguous and imprecise. Essentially a philosophy of equitable distribution, Nasser's socialism has been rightly criticized for economic

[4]Jeanne and Simonne Lacouture, *Egypt in Transition* (New York: Criterion Books, 1958), p. 453.

naïveté and a devotion to publicly managed projects of dubious value. While these projects were politically palatable, their contribution to a coherent economic policy was negligible. The steel complex at Helwan is a case in point. The claims of this grandiose project could not be justified by even the most optimistic economic projections. The project was to supply most of Egypt's need for steel, employ large numbers of Egyptian workers, and ultimately to contribute to the balance of payments through export. Of these goals, only the employment of more and more Egyptians was accomplished.

Similarly, the revolution's effort to guarantee jobs to every college graduate created a swollen bureaucracy that operated on the principle of disguised unemployment. This policy often resulted in several people sharing a job that could be handled more effectively by one employee. Intolerable inefficiencies were thus built into state enterprises and made administration very difficult. Once again, the political gain outstripped the economic realities.

The differences between Nasser and Farouk are quite sharp. There is one point, however, in which their leadership styles converge. The personal presence and lifestyle of each leader supported his claim to political authority. Of course, their lifestyles differed dramatically. Farouk's love of pomp and ceremony contrasts sharply with Nasser's modest private life. Each to a great degree personally demonstrated in his private life the basis of his claim to power.

Finally, both leaders' careers came to abrupt ends. Farouk abdicated to a life of leisure one jump ahead of the executioner; Nasser died unexpectedly of a heart attack in 1970. Neither of them left office under "normal" circumstances—i.e., as the result of regular or normal political processes. Of the two leaders, Nasser clearly left the greater impression on Egyptian politics. As Bruce Borthwick points out, in spite of the difficulties besetting the regime, "Nasser had . . . received the 'gift of grace' that endows charismatic leaders. He and the Egyptian people were one; his actions and his voice were theirs. They would not let him resign in June, 1967, and when he died suddenly on September 28, 1970, the masses poured out their emotions for him in a frenzy of grief."[5] To this day, portraits of Nasser occupy the place of honor in the simple homes of the Egyptian peasantry. The imprint of Farouk is a historical curiosity, and no more.

The ultimate consequences of Nasser's charismatic leadership are manifold. First and foremost, through his charismatic claim on political power, Nasser gave Egypt a focus of legitimate power. In a time when the existing institutions of power were discredited (such as the monarchy, nobility, and political parties), his exercise of charismatic power filled what would have been a dangerous vacuum. Moreover, the cosmological qualities of Nasser's leadership, such as his commitment to the Islamic Umma, Arab culture, and the Egyptian nation, provided a potent national identity for the Egyptian masses. His powerful rhetoric and commanding presence provided real evidence that his claims and goals were viable and realizable, if difficult to achieve.

[5] Bruce Borthwick, *Comparative Politics of the Middle East: An Introduction* (Englewood Cliffs, N.J.: Prentice-Hall, Inc., 1980), p. 182.

However, Nasser's rule had its negative aspects. His economic policies were at best naïve. His international adventures, as in the case of his military intervention in Yemen, often strained Egyptian capabilities beyond their limit. And his persistent confrontations with Israel committed vast proportions of the Egyptian economy to wartime production. Finally, his flirtation with international communism (domestic communists were suppressed and jailed) could have generated yet another wave of foreign intervention in the Middle East.

All in all, however, Nasser's leadership was of great benefit to Egypt. Ultimately the force of his leadership spilled over to the new institutions that implemented the revolution and prepared the way for modern-bureaucratic politics. Thus, Egypt moved from a political process dependent on a single, fragile personality, to a political system characterized more by institutional stability and strength.

MODERN BUREAUCRATIC LEADERSHIP

Modern bureaucratic leadership is predicated on the promise of adequate short-term performance in government. Claiming technical and organizational superiority over the older, traditional means of governance, modern bureaucratic leaders promise to transform society through the application of management skills. In short, these leaders believe that contemporary problems can be solved, that man can purposively change his physical and social environment if only given the chance and the right organization; and that these changes can lead to several possible social, economic, and political outcomes.

Although all modern bureaucratic leaders base their right to rule on their ability to perform and solve problems, some rule within publicly accountable systems (democratic) and others within authoritarian systems. Publicly accountable modern bureaucratic leaders recognize the right of the public to evaluate periodically their performance and decide whether to retain them in office; authoritarian, or Kemalist, modern bureaucratic leaders reject the regular review of their right to rule, arguing instead that no one has the ability to judge their leadership or its performance.[6] Authoritarian leaders often conceive of their political rule as a period of political trust and tutelage during which society learns and practices the skills and procedures that will lead to genuine publicly accountable politics. In most cases, authoritarian modern bureaucratic regimes are military in nature; publicly accountable regimes have usually emerged from a political party background. In the emerging countries, where modernization was first achieved among the military, it is not surprising that Kemalist regimes predominate.

ANWAR SADAT

The immediate successor to Nasser in Egypt was another member of the original Free Officers, Anwar S. el-Sadat. Original predictions suggested a relatively short tenure in office for Sadat, seeing him presiding over a period of transition during

---

[6]*Kemalist* refers to the modernizing authoritarian rule of Kemal Atatürk in Turkey. Atatürk's regime instituted widespread reforms in Turkey that were aimed ultimately at the creation of a democratic process.

which more capable leaders would contest for the mantle of power. (Similar predictions had been made for the institutions of governance that had developed during Nasser's rule, particularly the Arab Socialist Union and the People's Assembly.) Both Sadat and those institutions have proved much more durable than anticipated. By 1981, the Sadat regime had been in office for over ten years and had made a number of substantial changes in political emphasis and direction. Far from a caretaker or transitional leader, Sadat proved himself to be a legitimate and strong leader in his own right.

Sadat's personal history is not unlike that of Nasser. Like Nasser, Sadat was born into a peasant family and benefited from a liberalization in education policy. Like Nasser, Sadat entered the Egyptian military academy during the time when the regime was trying to develop an Egyptian officer corps. And like Nasser, Sadat participated in the Free Officer movement that lead to the coup of 1952. It is surprising, then, that there should be so few similarities in the leadership styles and political views of these two men.

Anwar Sadat is not a charismatic leader. His claims to the loyalty of the government and the public are based on his performance. He hoped for a low-keyed, coherent managed solution to Egypt's problems of the 1970s. Indeed, to compare Sadat's political thought to Nasser's is to compare the thought of a technician to that of a dreamer. Moreover, Sadat's rhetorical style bears little or no similarity to Nasser's impassioned, moving speeches.

Sadat's personal style contrasts sharply with those of Nasser and Farouk. Comfortable in Western dress, Sadat often appears in a conventional Western suit and tie, as opposed to Nasser's simple tunics and Farouk's elaborate uniforms. Sadat lives in an impressive villa although it hardly compares with Farouk's palaces. Mrs. Sadat wears the latest Paris fashions and moves in the highest international social circles. Sadat is comfortable with modern political leaders around the world. He cultivates an image of international sophistication in dress, language, and personal manner.

Nothing underscores the difference between Sadat and Nasser more than their respective treatment in the American press. Where Nasser was often presented in uncomplimentary terms with thinly veiled suggestions that he was a communist or radical, Sadat has been presented as a leader of quiet authority and dignity. As regular guests on American talk and interview shows in the 1970s, Mr. and Mrs. Sadat personally raised Egypt's national image by their humane, warm, and comfortable styles. Such democratic sophistication would not have occurred to a Farouk, nor have been tolerated by the ideologically mercurial Nasser. Sadat is definitely a different kind of political animal.

Sadat has reversed Nasser's economic policies, particularly those toward private industry. Sadat has openly sought foreign private investment in Egypt, strengthened ties with the United States and Western Europe, and pursued a political solution to the Israeli question and Palestinian demands. Domestically, he has permitted new political parties to develop, although they are carefully controlled. He has subtly tried, and failed, to demythologize Nasser.

Sadat believes that his reforms have relieved much of Egypt's economic and military burdens, and to some degree he has been proven correct. Most of the Sinai has been recovered, and commercially exploitable oil resources are expanding dramatically. The West has given military and technological support, but foreign investors have been reluctant to enter the mixed Egyptian economy. Ultimately the failure of the Egyptian-Israeli peace talks over the question of Palestinian autonomy has given ammunition to his enemies in and out of Egypt. As a result, Sadat has retrenched on many of his recent political reforms, the secret police have become more active, and a number of political opponents have been placed under house arrest.

Some of Sadat's reforms have met with widespread resistance. In 1977 he attempted to raise the price of bread, which had been subsidized at artificially low prices since the revolution; there were riots in Cairo in which mobs burned luxury hotels and nightclubs catering to foreigners and chanted "Sadat-Bey, Sadat-Bey."[7] Foreign corporations attempting to enter the Egyptian economy report that in spite of sympathy at high government levels, mid-level and low-level bureaucrats do not share this enthusiasm and make life miserable for Western business managers.

In governing Egypt, Sadat has certain advantages that were not available to either Nasser or Farouk. He has a tested set of bureaucratic and technocratic institutions upon which he can rely for counsel and for implementation of policy. These institutions are less efficient than many of their counterparts outside Egypt, but they are a distinct improvement over the administrative vacuum that attended Egyptian political crises earlier in the century.

The problems besetting Egypt are nonetheless very real; its population growth is nearly out of control, its economy is stagnating, and radical and conservative Arabs oppose Sadat's moderate line. Sadat must contend with Muslim fundamentalists, "socialists" who are unhappy with his encouragement of the private sector, military elements who are sympathetic to Soviet foreign policy, communists, anti-Israeli hard-liners, and those who would again take up pan-Arabism. Sadat, like any other leader, is likely to be frustrated in his attempts to find definitive solutions to these pervasive problems. The quality of leadership, during Sadat's term and after, will continue to be of critical importance to Egypt's future. (See page 206.)

CONSEQUENCES OF LEADERSHIP STYLES

The contemporary Middle East presents a melange of leadership styles. Traditional and modern bureaucratic leaders predominate numerically (see Table 10-1), but charismatic leaders like Ayatollah Khomeini and Col. Qadaffi have a disproportionate amount of influence. Many of the international strains and tensions in the Middle East are partially a result of divergences between leadership styles.

Traditional leaders make up the largest group in the Middle East. True to

---

[7]*Bey*, the traditional title given to Ottoman officials, is not a compliment in revolutionary Egypt.

Table 10-1 CONTEMPORARY LEADERSHIP STYLES
IN THE MIDDLE EAST

Traditional	Modern Bureaucratic	Charismatic
Bahrain	Egypt under Sadat (K)*	Egypt under Nasser
Egypt under Farouk	Iraq (K)	Iran under Khomeini
Iran under Mohammed Reza Pahlevi	Israel (for Jewish citizens)	Libya under Qadaffi
Jordan	Israel (occupied territories) (K)	
Kuwait	Lebanon before 1973	
Oman	South Yemen	
Qatar	Syria (K)	
Saudi Arabia	Turkey	
United Arab Emirates		
Yemen		

*K = Kemalist Modern Bureaucratic

form, these leaders oppose modernization or modernize in only strictly technological ways; they all resist any substantial sharing of powers. The enormous oil revenues of Saudi Arabia, Oman, the U.A.E., and Kuwait permit them to manage their economies and give them some political breathing time. For those traditional leaders in poor countries—Hussein of Jordan, for example—the maneuvering time is considerably reduced. In the case of Jordan and Yemen, foreign subsidies have been crucial in maintaining the existing political authority, a compromise with independence distasteful to all leaders.

Serious challenges to existing authority have emerged in all of the countries under traditional leadership. The fall of the Shah of Iran is a likely harbinger of things to come. The Yemen Arab Republic is already in a state of civil and international conflict. In Kuwait an increasingly restive Palestinian middle class has become more and more influential. In Bahrain Shiite minorities and highly trained middle-class groups yearn for political influence. In Jordan domestic and international tensions have nearly toppled King Hussein a number of times. In Saudi Arabia, the precarious health of King Khalid complicates a delicate political situation, increasingly complex since the Great Mosque at Mecca was seized in 1980; and divisions within and without the royal family almost ensure political conflict over a successor and the emerging form of government. Oman, increasingly a factor in the international politics of the Persian gulf, is bordered by a Marxist revolutionary state to the West, conservative Arab states to the North, and an unpredictable Iran across the straits. In short, the traditional states of the Middle East, rich and poor alike, appear to be fragile and potentially volatile. Intelligence estimates in 1979–1980 predicted at least three unstable governments on the Persian Gulf, excluding Iran. Most of these traditional polities are fighting a rear-guard action. The inevitable transition to modern bureaucratic or charismatic rule will be quite hazardous to these countries and to those nations dependent on their petroleum exports.

MODERN BUREAUCRATIC STATES

The second largest group of political systems in the Middle East is governed by some kind of modern bureaucratic leadership. Four of these states—Egypt, Iraq, South Yemen, and Syria—are ruled by Kemalist regimes. The military or civilian leaders in Syria and Iraq profess adherence to Baathist ideology, although the two countries are ruled in quite different ways. While Sadat believes in the public accountability of leaders, he has not yet abandoned his tutelary role or entrusted substantial political authority to the parties or legislature. The Arab Socialist Union and the National Assembly, while influential, are still subject to his veto. With the possible exception of Syria, where considerable resentment festers because of the domination of the Alawite regime of President Assad, none of these regimes seems likely to face successful internal challenges soon.

The government of Iraq is undergoing change. Although it has been plagued for some time by feuding within the ruling Baathist military group, and although it is the most pro-Soviet of the Middle Eastern states, Iraq appears to be emerging as a stable and competent political regime. Encouraged by its growing petroleum revenues, in the mid-1970s Iraq embarked on an ambitious program of economic and social investment. Simultaneously, the leadership's anti-Western posture softened, and growing numbers of Iraqi students enrolled in European and American universities, particularly in management and technology programs. Recent events suggest a growing disenchantment with communist influence in the Iraqi army, a disenchantment that has led to a number of executions and imprisonments and explorations with non-Soviet European governments regarding trade and technology. The fact that Iraq's stable regime has sought a more genuinely moderate, nonaligned foreign policy is one of the few encouraging political developments in the contemporary Middle East, although these tendencies were strained by the June, 1981 raid by Israel on Iraq's nuclear reactor.

Of the two non-Kemalist modern bureaucratic regimes, one country, Turkey, has a recent history of relatively free and open review of leadership. Only occasionally has the military felt it necessary to intervene and suspend the political processes, and then only to back off after a period. The current situation in Turkey, pitting the left against an emergent and revitalized Muslim conservative coalition, has placed very serious strains on the government, strains serious enough to tempt the army back into exercising direct military power. Prior experience suggests that the military rule established in 1980 will be of relatively short duration.

Lebanon, currently under a state of civil war and occupied by Syrian, U.N., and, occasionally, Israeli forces, all of whom share power with private Christian, Palestinian, and independent armies, is proof of just how bad things can get when domestic and international forces combine to challenge or undermine existing political authority. The pre-1976 government of Lebanon, predicated on the fiction of relatively equal and stable Muslim, Christian, and Druze populations, functioned in an effective and publicly accountable way. It was, in many respects, something of a showplace for democracy in difficult circumstances. The enormous contrast then and now suggests that when all pretense of political civility disappears, the potential for political and social disorganization is great. No effective leadership of any variety is likely to emerge until the international forces withdraw from Lebanon, and the balance of terror between the internal forces resolves conclusively in some way.

The leadership situation in Israel deserves discussion. The categorization of the regime as certainly modern bureaucratic, but uncertainly democratic or Kemalist, depends on whether one is talking about Israeli citizens within the normal confines of Israel (pre-1967 boundaries) or about the administered Arab populations of the West Bank, Gaza Strip, and Golan Heights. The problem would not be so great were the populations involved not so large. We must distinguish, then, between the democratically responsible leadership of conventional Israel and the authoritarian leadership of the occupied territories.

Israel has proven many times over its ability to change leadership within the structure of public accountability. Prime Minister Menachem Begin represents a conservative religious coalition, the Likud party, which came to power in May, 1977, and broke the dominance of the Labour party, which had been in power since 1948. Begin's responses to Arab demands and terrorist raids have been much harsher than his predecessor's; in addition he has encouraged Israeli settlements in the West Bank. (We shall deal with this policy in greater detail in the next chapter.) However, the formal inclusion of the West Bank and Gaza Strips into the state of Israel is sufficient to classify Begin's regime as Kemalist authoritarian, since it is unlikely to extend full political rights to the Arab populations.

Begin's leadership is certainly conventional in its base of authority. Although Begin was personally involved in the founding of Israel, in no way can he be considered a charismatic leader. His leadership is predicated on the public approval of his performance in office.

Begin's leadership is endangered by the poor state of his health. He has been hospitalized during his stay in office several times for heart problems. Since most of the international negotiations on the Arab-Israeli conflict have been conducted personally by Begin, Sadat, and President Carter, Begin's periodic absences do not bode well for the future.

Over the next decade, Israel faces a variety of difficult problems, of which the Palestinian question is only one. Growing inflation, conflict between segments of the Jewish population, the cost of defense, and immigration will test Israeli leadership severely over the decade of the 1980s. The leadership that succeeds Begin's hard line will have its work cut out for it.

CHARISMATIC RULE

Two Middle Eastern countries, Iran and Libya, were under charismatic rulers in 1980. Both rulers can be described as irregular, unpredictable, and dramatic; but their governments and ideologies are inherently different.

Ayatollah Ruhollah Khomeini

Ascetic and gaunt, Ayatollah Ruhollah Khomeini appears to confirm the trite Western stereotypes of Muslim fanaticism. This predisposition to judge harshly was exacerbated by the outrage generated by the Iranian militants' seizure of U.S. diplomats and embassy employees in November, 1979. Thus, it is hard to find a publicly sanctioned, dispassionate description and analysis of Khomeini and his beliefs.

Khomeini is clearly a charismatic leader. He believes that his ultimate authority is derived from Allah, an indisputably cosmological referent. His speech is laced with hyperbole and Jeremiads against the West, the Shah, the devil, and all corruption and debasement. His followers respond with strong outpourings of emotion. His branch of Islam, Iranian Shiism, is mystical and chiliastic. He wishes to use the Shiite tenets of Islam as the basis of a new, revolutionary economic, social, and political organization.

Khomeini's opposition to the Shah's regime and to Western influence in Iran is partly based on his personal history. Khomeini's father was allegedly murdered by a landlord closely allied with Shah Mohammed Reza Pahlevi. Raised as an orphan, Khomeini was passed from relative to relative largely out of charitable obligation. His training, exclusively in traditional religious schools and subjects, was exactly opposite to the modern education promoted by the Pahlevis. As an adult, Khomeini was often in trouble with the regime which restricted his movements and preaching and finally exiled him. His promotion to the rank of ayatollah was prompted, it is claimed, by other Muslim clergymen's attempts to protect him from the Shah's courts and certain imprisonment or execution. Long periods of exile awaited the Ayatollah, during which his son was murdered, allegedly by SAVAK. Thus, Ayatollah Khomeini has had a long history of personal and religious opposition to the Pahlevi regime.

Khomeini's political behavior bewildered most Western correspondents. Two Shiite traditions may explain some of it. First, the Shiite community has long practiced the right of **taqiyyah**, or dissimulation. If the defense of the faith requires it, the faithful may say or do anything that would allow them to pursue the true way. Thus, public consistency is irrelevant in this view: what counts is the ultimate service to God's will. Khomeini felt free to exploit the American hostages, a condition prohibited by conventional Islamic doctrine, since doing so would advance the larger interests of Allah and the Umma.

The second tradition is the low status of political officials in Shiite Islam. Ayatollah Khomeini avoided the regular, continual exercise of political power. Khomeini apparently wished instead to correct or direct politicians by exercising a moral veto when they deviated from the divine will. Khomeini's exercise of power was thus irregular and intermittent, a fact of life that confounded and confused the Western observer.

One also needs to understand something of the political and religious history of Iran. The doctrine of taqiyyah, for example, developed in response to the persecution of the Shiite faithful by established Iranian political authority. Dissimulation, when necessary, advances the interests of the good community. It is not a simple or universal justification for lying. The Ayatollah's symbolically rich speech similarly derives from the long Persian tradition of complex, poetic language. Much of it is impossible to translate accurately into English. An example of the difficulty is the *heech* controversy of 1979.

Heech is an Iranian word of some subtlety. It can mean "nothing" in both a literal and/or an ironic sense. Upon returning to Iran from exile in Iraq and France, Khomeini was asked by Western newsmen how it felt to return to Iran after all those years in exile. Khomeini expressed his contempt for such a superficial question with the observation, "*Heech*." The newsmen interpreted his response to mean that he had no feelings, emotional or otherwise, about his return and concluded that he was coldly self-controlled. Khomeini intended to convey his disgust at being asked such an obvious and superficial question. Unfortunately, Khomeini's efforts were rewarded with misunderstanding. Khomeini's behavior and justifications remain valid for Iran and largely misunderstood in the larger world arenas.

Khomeini's charismatic power is not restricted to Iran; it also operates among Shiite minorities along the Persian Gulf and in Jordan, Syria, Iraq, and Lebanon. In addition, many fundamentalist Muslim groups recognize Khomeini's impact and wish to emulate his success without adopting the Shiite disciplines. These groups are potentially destabilizing forces in much of the Middle East. Finally, Khomeini's rabid anti-Western attitude taps a venerable tradition of opposition that dates back to the maturation of European imperial power in the area. As a successful leader, attempting the radical dewesternization of Iran based on the tenets of Islam, Khomeini was a living example of the political potential of Islamic revival.

Col. Muammar Qadaffi

No less an enigma to the West is Col. Muammar Qadaffi, the unofficial head of state of Libya, a country with few people and considerable oil wealth, located next to Egypt on the Mediterranean coast of Africa. Qadaffi has held power since the Revolutionary Command Council removed King Idris from power in 1969. Since that time Qadaffi has consolidated and expanded his political power. His position is currently secure as head of the military group ruling Libya.

Qadaffi's power is also indisputably charismatic, although it differs substantially from Khomeini's power. Qadaffi is a radical, modernizing charismatic leader who has based his policy on unique, innovative interpretations of the Koran. Personally pious and reputedly ascetic, Qadaffi rejected the authority of the hadith and sunnah, preferring instead his own reading of the Koran as the sole authority. His personal philosophy is detailed in the Green Book, the handbook of the Libyan revolution. Qadaffi thus finds himself in opposition to the conservative ulema, whereas Khomeini's power derives from it. Although both men are anti-Western and anti-imperialistic, Qadaffi is enthralled by Western technology and science.

Qadaffi and Khomeini also differ markedly in physical appearance. Khomeini appears dour, dark, and sober, with downcast eyes, and dresses in the traditional garb of the mullah; Qadaffi is quick to flash a bright, toothy smile, dresses in flattering quasimilitary tunics. Where Khomeini's rhetoric is apocalyptic, Qadaffi's is more persuasive and personal.

Like Khomeini and Nasser, Qadaffi aspires to leadership in the larger Muslim community. Qadaffi has openly espoused the causes of numerous revolutionary and terrorist groups around the world, and offered hospitality to their leaders. Qadaffi's influence has spread to the Philippines, where Libya has supported the Moro National Liberation Front. It has also spread to Uganda, and to Egypt and the Sudan, where Libya has been openly hostile toward the modern bureaucratic regimes of Sadat and Numeiri. In 1981, Libya intervened in the civil war in Chad, ostensibly to aid the Muslim groups in their consolidation of power. The government in Chad backed away from a proposed formal union, however, and the extent of Libyan control or influence there is problematical. One of the staunchest of anti-Israeli Muslim leaders, Qadaffi has provided aid, comfort, and a base for operations to diverse groups in the Palestinian nationalist coalition. These causes, and his personal claim to a universally valid view of Muslim revolutionary government, have not been well received in the conservative or secular governments of the Middle East. The disappearance of Imam Musa'Sadr in Libya in 1977 increased Qadaffi's distance from the Shiite community, including that of Ayatollah Khomeini. And increasingly prominent Libyan assassination squads targeted against Qadaffi's political opposition in exile in England and Italy have further blackened Libya's international image. Libya, moreover, has tilted decidedly toward the U.S.S.R. in its foreign policy, although there seems to be little Soviet influence in Libyan domestic policy.

Since 1977, Qadaffi has kept Libya on a revolutionary course. Based on his philosophy as expressed in the Green Book, Qadaffi has embarked on a course of radical democratization in the context of the original Islamic revelation. Detractors are quick to point out that Qadaffi may in fact be confusing his own role with that of the prophet. Nevertheless, Qadaffi seems quite intent on forming a system of "People's Power" committees, unions, and boards. Ultimately these peoples' committees are intended to replace the RCC, although the RCC and Qadaffi still appear to be in complete control of the Libyan political process. Qadaffi, however, is making a serious effort, and Muslim fundamentalists throughout the Middle East find his experiment in revolutionary Islam interesting and compelling.

CONCLUSIONS

The contemporary Middle East presents a mosaic of leadership styles with definite implications for conflict and conflict accommodation. The traditional Muslim leaders of the Middle East are conservative. Fighting a rear-guard action against increasing demands for a larger share of political power, traditional leaders are coming under increasing domestic and international political pressure. Although traditional leaders of rich or potentially rich states may be able to buy time politically, in the long run, their right to power will be undermined by the social effects of such wealth. The lucky leaders will be exiled; the unlucky ones will be hounded like the Shah or assassinated like Abdullah in Iraq.

Most traditional regimes will be replaced by modernizing bureaucratic regimes, either democratic or authoritarian in nature. These regimes will try to mobilize mass political sentiment, but keep it under strict control. Technological and economic progress are more likely under these regimes, but they are not guaranteed. They will come increasingly under the pressure of fundamentalist Islamic groups seeking to establish Islamic republics, that derive their form and mandate from the Koran and Islamic tradition. This assault on the secular aspects of the modern bureaucratic regime may lead to instability and internal conflict, with predictable negative consequences for the systems. Modern bureaucratic leaders like Sadat of Egypt, Assad of Syria, and Saddam Hussein of Iraq, basing their claim to power on demonstrated policy results, will find themselves more and more challenged by credible alternative concepts of the public good and public order. These concepts, arising from a mixture of religious, political, and foreign influences, will produce potent claims for future performance, finding root in increasingly sophisticated political publics.

It is impossible to predict when charismatic leaders will appear or what the consequences of their regimes will be. They are capable of creating emotional political storms that float over the fragile boundaries of nation-states. Nasser, Khomeini, and Qadaffi, all of whom enjoy or enjoyed substantial support outside their native countries, challenge the authority of both traditional monarchs and modern bureaucratic leaders. Their potential for destabilization and mischief and political good are great. Currently Ayatollah Khomeini's sermons reportedly enjoy a wide circulation in the fertile crescent. Col. Qadaffi has attempted to oust Sadat from Egypt and Nemeiry from the Sudan in order to extend his leadership into new areas. A nominal Libyan union with Syria has been discussed. It does not take a political soothsayer to predict the probable consequences of charismatic rule in, say, Saudi Arabia with its petroleum wealth or in Egypt with its large population and critical position in the Arab-Israeli conflict. And finally, on a much more abstract level, we must recognize the potential for charismatic leadership in the Muslim Umma, a leadership capable of transcending familiar national entities. Such leadership would have worldwide influence. Islamic tradition is certainly predisposed in this direction.

Anwar Sadat was assassinated on October 6, 1981 while viewing a military parade. The composition and motive of the assassins were initially unclear. Many of the president's enemies laid claim to the act. Significantly, the government was able to manage the transition of power smoothly, an indication that progress had been made in the institutionalization of power. Sadat's successor was vice-president Hosni Mubarak. Public reaction to Sadat's death was restrained and calm, contrasting with the near-hysteria following Nasser's death. These observations were made in the immediate aftermath of the assassination. The real test of Egyptian political institutions will come in the long run.

11

International Relations in the Contemporary Middle East

The international system has many features not found in national political orders. The most important of these features is the lack of a legitimate sovereign power, or even of some entity with a viable claim to the exercise of sovereign power. In comparison to the average national system, the international system is nearly anarchic—political power is at once broadly diffused among its actors and yet enormously concentrated among a few. Furthermore, international power is transitory and difficult to assess comparatively.

The actors that comprise the international order have a power base that can be broken down into three areas: *economic power*, or the power to produce or acquire material goods; *political power*, or the power to coerce or influence their own populations or the populations of other states; and *military power*, the ability to gain goals through the direct application of organized coercive force. These capabilities are not distributed evenly among the actors in the international system. Saudi Arabia, for instance, possesses enormous economic power based on its extensive oil reserves, but has a population insufficient in size and technical sophistication to maintain a truly international military capability. Egypt, by contrast, has a large population sufficiently skilled to maintain a large military machine, but lacks the economic base to develop it without foreign aid. The relative international power of Saudi Arabia and Egypt, then, must be calculated on different bases, quantitative and qualitative. This enormously complicates the calculations involved in international politics, particularly since one actor's analysis of the capability of another is a most basic determinant of its foreign policy.

The relationships between international actors embrace a wide field of human activity. International relations occur at many levels and in many functional arenas. For example, no state can isolate itself from international trade, for to do so it would have to greatly reduce its economic activity. Thus, any nation finds it necessary and desirable to allow the movements of goods and services into its territory as varying amounts of goods and services flow out. Most states, then, are involved in some level of international economic exchange that requires cooperation with both friendly and potentially unfriendly powers. It is instructive to note that at the nadir of Iranian-American relations, Iranian oil was still being imported by the U.S. at the rate of some 80,000 barrels per day—a fact as politically unpalatable to President Carter as to Ayatollah Khomeini. International relations, then, possess a logic to some degree independent of the best wishes or intentions of their actors— or to put it another way, international politics and economics make strange bedfellows.

Actors in the international system pursue a combination of specific and general goals that can be lumped together under the term *national interest*. The national interest presumably directs the foreign policy of a nation, at least at the strategic level. For instance, the national interest of the Soviet Union has long required a safe, warm-water port, while the contemporary U.S. national interest requires regular delivery of petroleum from its Middle East sources. Needless to say, these two national interest goals have a potential for conflict in the area of the Persian Gulf.

The problem in analyzing international relations strictly from the national interest viewpoint can be summarized briefly. First, nations may in fact not clearly perceive their true national interests: American involvement in Viet Nam in the 1960s is a case in point. Second, power, the base of implementation of national interest, is an enormously complex entity. Miscalculations of one's own power, or the reputed power of another actor, can inject a quality of uncertainty into international relations. An example is Nasser's miscalculation of Israeli responses to his mobilization in 1967. Finally, international relations are only rarely dyadic—i.e., involving only two nations. Although for analytic purposes we often discuss foreign policy in dyadic terms, most international exchanges involve the interests of secondary and tertiary actors. These complex intersections of national interests—both primary and secondary, immediate and long-term—create the Gordian knots of the international process. All too often the solution to these problems is war, with its attendant human miseries and material losses.

STRUCTURE OF THE CONTEMPORARY INTERNATIONAL ORDER

None of the preceding should be interpreted as denying order or process in international relations. The Middle East, in particular, has seen the rise and fall of many separate international systems. The Middle East has witnessed the development of an international theocratic movement during the early days of Islamic expansion, in which the world was seen as a contrast between the *Dar al Islam* (world of peace) and the *Dar al Harb* (world of war); centralized bureaucratic empires based successively in Damascus, Baghdad, and Cairo; loose relationships between competing centers of power, as peripheral kingdoms arose in the Maghreb, Spain, Europe, Central Asia, Persia, and India; the consolidation of power in the decentralized millet system of the Ottoman Empire; the intrusion of European imperial power, predicated on a classic balance of power in Europe; and finally after World War II, the bipolar conflict between the U.S. and the U.S.S.R. In the 1980s, yet another international order presents itself, with concomitant challenges and changes in the international environment.

The origins of the contemporary international order can be found in the deterioration of the system that emerged just after World War II and prevailed until the early 1970s. This first order, the bipolar international system, was produced by an unusual concentration of military and economic power in two rival political systems, the United States and the Soviet Union. Perceiving each other as threats to their own national interest as well as to the larger political order, the alliances surrounding these two superpowers grew rigid and confrontational. The term, Cold War, which applied to the early period following World War II, suggests a confrontation between the two blocs just short of overt military hostilities. During this time, the two superpowers enjoyed a nuclear monopoly and rapidly growing economies. Stymied in their confrontation in Europe, they turned to the nations of the Third World—Africa, Asia, Latin America, and the Middle East—for potential alliance partners in their crusade against international communism or international capitalism.

From the point of view of international actors in the Middle East, this transition was frustrating. Neither the United States nor the Soviet Union had well-established bases in the area. European power, while on the wane and definitely inferior to that of either superpower, was nonetheless still something to contend with. Finally, the polarized ideological claims of capitalism and communism did not find fertile intellectual soil in the Middle East.

Regional factors also injected themselves into the emerging international order. Primary among them was the creation of Israel in 1948 and its subsequent protection by the United States. This issue, transcending such questions as Arab unity, water resources, economic growth and development, or Islamic resurgence, provided the mechanism for the entrance of bipolar politics in the area. The unevenness of American policy toward the Arab states, combined with its unwillingness to hedge on the question of Israeli security, provided the Soviet Union with an entrée, particularly to Egypt, Syria, and Iraq, the major powers confronting the Israeli state. But in spite of great Egyptian, Syrian, and Iraqi dependence on Eastern bloc sources for weapons and expertise, the U.S.S.R. was unable to capitalize on its advantages domestically in these countries. The United States, for its part, confused the desire for independence in these countries with a drift toward communism and reacted hostilely to Soviet gains there. Thus, the bipolar alliance system did not extend completely into the Middle East, and both Soviet and American policy goals were frustrated.

The 1960s saw the gradual erosion of the "eyeball-to-eyeball" confrontation between Soviet and American global power. The age of detente ushered in a period in which Soviet and American ability to control their alliances and dictate policy declined. The emergence of competing centers of economic and political power—Japan, Western Europe, and China—ultimately produced an international system in which the great powers of the U.S. and the U.S.S.R. were reduced by the growing economic powers of their allies and by the loss of their nuclear monopoly. The resulting international system, maturing in the early 1980s, can best be described as an emerging set of relatively independent power centers orbiting loosely and often erratically around the U.S. and the Soviet Union. Moreover, additional sources of international power appeared to be maturing, based on the growing economic and political systems of Asia, Africa, the Middle East, and Latin America. These centers of power were more and more inclined to define national interest in their own terms. All of this contributed to the complexity and potential instability of the international order.

Let us now examine the implications of this change for the international system that is the Middle East. Our method will be to move from macroanalysis, to regional analysis, and finally to a consideration of dyadic relations involving the foreign policies of Egypt, Saudi Arabia, Iran, and Israel.

In each of these sections, we will discuss three phases of international relations in the Middle East. Phase I, 1945-1948, embraces the immediate postwar period; Phase II, 1948-1974, includes the period of transition from tight bipolar confrontation to loose bipolar competition; Phase III covers the period from the 1973 Arab-Israeli war and Arab oil embargo to the present.

THE GREAT POWER SYSTEM
AND THE MIDDLE EAST

In the relatively short span of thirty years, actors in the Middle East have gone from a system in which their policies were largely reactive to the policy goals of the U.S. and U.S.S.R., through a period in which international power appeared to disperse toward other industrial states of the temperate zones, to an international system in which many Middle Eastern nations can realistically view themselves as capable of originating international exchange, politically and economically, if not militarily. Some Middle Eastern actors—most notably Saudi Arabia, Egypt, and Iran—see themselves as major actors in the international arena. Decisions reached in Riyadh, Cairo, and Teheran now have repercussions in Moscow, Washington, and Tokyo.

The current system contains a number of international power centers that have substantially altered the relative influence of the U.S. and the U.S.S.R. This is not to say that the power and national interests of these two megapowers are unimportant. To the contrary, their pursuit of their national interests is in many ways more important and more dangerous given the greater number of probable actors. The primary effects of policy shifts may be predictable, but the secondary and tertiary effects, involving other actors indirectly, are rarely predictable and controllable. For example, as the U.S. reduced its dependence on Iranian oil imports in the late 1970s (a primary policy decision), Japan and other U.S. allies simultaneously increased their imports of Iranian crude (a secondary effect), which in effect increased their vulnerability to pressure from Soviet intervention in the Persian Gulf.

Of the two great superpowers, the United States held the most enviable position of power in the Middle East. European (specifically British and French) power in the area was generally replaced by American power. The United States was historically removed from the abuses of colonial policy in the area, and many Arab leaders looked with affection toward the U.S. Thus, the period after World War II saw an extension and expansion of U.S. power in the Middle East, oriented toward an alliance system aimed at frustrating Soviet moves, particularly in Turkey and Iran.

Table 11-1 simplifies the foreign policy objectives of the great powers in the Middle East from the end of World War II to the early 1980s. The table suggests some sharp changes in policy over that relatively brief period of time.

U.S. FOREIGN POLICY

Phase I

United States policy toward the Middle East was not coherent or logical during Phase I. Indeed, after World War II, the United States' concern for the Middle East grew as it recognized that its allies (Britain, France) were unable to play their traditional roles.

The United States also feared that the Soviet Union, the other principal winner in World War II, would attempt to exploit the political uncertainties in Greece, Turkey, and Iran. This concern led to the Truman Doctrine, a statement of real opposition to Soviet imperialism in the area, and which committed the U.S. to direct military and economic support for the threatened areas.

As in other areas of the world, the United States found itself moving into unfamiliar political seas in order to fill what was generally recognized as an incipient power vacuum. The exploitation and importation of crude petroleum was clearly of a secondary nature in its foreign policy priorities. Critically, moreover, the U.S., in honoring its commitments to the governments and policies of its allies, set itself squarely in the camp of Middle Eastern conservatism. This early commitment, as we will see, ultimately played havoc with U.S. credibility and prestige in the area.

Phase II

During Phase II, United States policy and presence in the Middle East has been inextricably linked with the Israeli question. Truman's hurried recognition of Israel, combined with U.S. influence in the United Nations, placed the U.S. squarely in the role of protector of the Israeli state. This, coupled with intractable Arab opposition to Israel, provided the Soviet Union with its first major successes in Middle Eastern policy. From 1958 to 1975, the U.S.S.R. was able to exploit the situation resulting from U.S. support for Israel by supplying arms and advisers to Egypt, Syria, and Iraq. Thus, the United States attempted to maintain a preeminent power position while the Soviet Union attempted to exploit potential weaknesses in the U.S. posture. It may be a tribute to the diplomacy of Middle Eastern nations that neither power managed to envelop the area with its alliance systems or to systematically dictate policy in the area.

This period in international relations saw a determined American effort to extend the tight bipolar alliance system into the Middle East and to link NATO in

Table 11-1 FOREIGN POLICY PRIORITIES IN THE MIDDLE EAST, 1945–1980

Phase	U.S.A.	Soviet	European (England, France)
I (1945–48)	1. Extension of influence.	1. Extension of influence into Mediterranean, Turkey, and Iran.	1. Reestablishment of prewar influence.
	2. Exploitation and protection of promising petroleum production in Saudi Arabia and Iran.	2. Frustration of U.S. power and prestige in M.E.	2. Exploitation and protection of petroleum production and trade relations in M.E.
		3. Support of Isreal.	3. Support of Israeli migration to Palestine.
II (1948–74)	1. Support and protection of Israel.	1. Extension of military influence into M.E. via anti-Israeli governments in Syria, Egypt, and Iraq.	1. Maintenance and expansion of petroleum production and trade relations.
	2. Maintenance of influence and prestige against Soviet invasion; Baghdad Pact.	2. Frustration of U.S. power and prestige in M.E.	2. Maintenance of prestige and influence in M.E.
	3. Exploitation and protection of petroleum production in Saudi Arabia, Iran, and U.A.E.		3. Support of Israel.
III (1974–present)	1. Exploitation and protection of petroleum production in Saudi Arabia and U.A.E.	1. Maintenance of influence in Syria and Iraq.	1. Maintenance and expansion of petroleum production and trade relations.
	2. Support and protection of Israel.	2. Frustration of U.S. power and prestige in M.E.; support of national liberation movements in Yemen and Oman, PLO Al-Fatah.	2. Frustrate U.S.–U.S.S.R. efforts in M E.
	3. Maintenance of influence and prestige.	3. Stabilize political situation on borders with Afghanistan and Iran.	
		4. Access to M.E. petroleum and warm-water ports.	

Europe with the SEATO alliance in Asia. The Baghdad Pact (1955) represented the greatest success of the U.S. in this regard. It was seen in the U.S. as a logical response to Soviet aggression; many Middle East leaders, however, saw themselves in danger of being pulled headlong into the ideological confrontation between the U.S. and U.S.S.R. Nasser succeeded in popularizing the concept of nonalignment in the area; and the pact, lacking full support by the signatories after Iraq's withdrawal in 1958, was replaced by direct aid to Iran. Full support of the Shah was implemented by means of a bilateral mutual assistance treaty in 1959.

During this period, Middle Eastern petroleum production was a relatively low order of priority for the U.S. American oil fields until the early 1970s were more than capable of supplying most domestic petroleum needs. Thus, the maintenance of its influence, the protection of Israel, and the frustration of Soviet ambitions provided the motivation for U.S. policy. Until the late 1960s, the U.S. was able to accomplish all of its objectives simultaneously. The emergence of the Palestinian independence organizations, however, coupled with growing international recognition of their rights and legitimacy, made the support of Israel very costly to U.S. influence and prestige. The Soviet Union capitalized on this situation by breaking relations with Israel and providing arms and aid to Egypt, Syria, and Iraq. U.S. decision makers assumed the worst, that Soviet aid meant Soviet control; and a period of very tense, even hostile, relations between the U.S. and these nations ensued. In short, during Phase II, the U.S. was able to consolidate its alliance positions with the "northern tier" states—Turkey, Iran, and Pakistan—while its relations with the core states of Syria, Egypt, and Iraq deteriorated. Strains even appeared between the U.S. and its client states Jordan and Saudi Arabia, at once pro-American and increasingly anti-Israeli. The maintenance of any alliance in which conflicting goals are present is extraordinarily difficult. The U.S. was called upon many times to put out "brush fires" in the area. The attempted nationalization of Iranian oil in 1953, the Suez Crisis of 1956, and the crisis in Lebanon in 1958 are examples. Ultimately, these foreign policy objectives were to become more clearly and forcefully contradictory. Particularly clear by 1974 was the incompatibility of maintaining and expanding the Middle East's petroleum flow to the West and the unyielding support of Israeli policy.

Interventions in Iran. During this early Phase II diplomacy, the U.S. was forced to intervene directly in the Middle East. The first of these interventions was prompted by developments in Iran from 1951 to 1953, a period in which Iranian politics were dominated by the leadership of Premier Mohammed Mossadegh. Mossadegh effectively challenged the Anglo-Iranian oil agreements and moved to nationalize the company's holdings. Simultaneously Mossadegh virtually isolated the young Shah from political power, taking control of the army and moving to abolish the representative assembly, all with strong support from the Iranian public. American and British interests responded with a carefully orchestrated policy of intrigue that ultimately brought Mossadegh's downfall and the return of the Shah. The Shah's power, based on his increasingly effective control of the military, waxed from that period on. The petroleum production of Iran was finally organized on a consortium basis in which American and European corporations shared the profits on a fifty-fifty basis with the Iranian National Oil Company. From this time onward, and particularly during the White Revolution, the Shah enjoyed generous support from the U.S., who perceived Iran as playing a "policeman's role" in the important Persian Gulf. Resentment over U.S. support for the Shah became an important factor in Iranian politics after the successful revolution of 1979. The U.S. labored unsuccessfully to escape the consequences of its support for that repressive regime.

The Suez War. The second major U.S. involvement in the Middle East also had long-term consequences for U.S. interests in the area. From 1948 onward, Egypt and Israel were periodically at some level of armed hostility, ranging from small guerrilla raids to larger punitive expeditions. Egypt sought American arms, the better to engage the superior capabilities of the Israeli armed forces. The successful Israeli raid on the Gaza Strip in February, 1955, led Col. Nasser to request arms sales from the U.S. and Great Britain. These requests were emphatically rejected.

Rebuffed by the Americans and the British, Nasser turned to the Eastern bloc for relief, concluding a barter deal (cotton for arms) with Czechoslovakia. U.S. reactions were abrupt, resulting in the July, 1956, cancellation of U.S. support for the construction of the High Dam at Aswan. The connection between this refusal and Nasser's independent pursuit of Soviet arms through Czechoslovakia was clearly made by the U.S. Moreover, in backing out of its commitment to the dam, the U.S. threatened the very heart of Nasser's development plan for Egypt. Relations between Egypt and the U.S. deteriorated rapidly from this point.

Nasser reacted to this great-power action by nationalizing the Suez Canal Company in July, 1956. The canal, of great importance to Europe as a trade route and defense link, had heretofore been operated by a corporation dominated by Britain and France. Their immediate response was to oppose the nationalization, freeze Egyptian funds in their respective banks, and seek a U.N. solution to the problem. U.S. interest in the proceedings was indirect until Nasser made it clear that Israeli shipping would continue to be denied access to the canal. Britain and France became increasingly restive about the failure of the U.N. to condemn Egypt. This frustration was to lead ultimately to the Suez War of 1956.

The events of the Suez War suggest collusion between Israel, France, and Great Britain. The war began with Israeli occupation of Gaza and penetration and control of the Sinai, up to the canal. France and Britain demanded that the belligerents (Egypt and Israel) withdraw to positions ten miles on either side of the canal. Egypt's rejection of this ultimatum prompted the invasion of the canal zone by British and French paratroops and the occupation of Port Said.

After a period of intense collective and unilateral diplomacy by the United States, United Nations troops (UNEF) were placed between the belligerents, and they were exhorted to withdraw from the territory. In point of fact, the U.S. placed heavy pressure on its allies, particularly Israel, to withdraw. French and British troops quit the area by December, 1956. Finally, in March of 1957, an agreement was reached for Israeli withdrawal from the Sinai.

The resolution of the Suez War found the U.S. opposing the actions of its strongest allies, Israel, France, and Great Britain. This pro-Arab action led to considerable strains in the Western alliance but did little to persuade Nasser that U.S. policy was ultimately benevolent.

The Lebanon Crisis of 1958. The third U.S. intervention in Middle Eastern affairs was generated by the Lebanon crisis of 1958, an intervention that saw the movement of U.S. marines into Beirut on July 15. The details of the Lebanese political situation that produced the American intervention were complex, involuted, and confusing. The Lebanese political situation was becoming increasingly unstable, and the delicate balance between Muslim, Christian, and Druze interests was deteriorating. This deterioration had attracted the attention of Egypt, which was directly intervening in the struggle on behalf of the Muslim groups there. The successful revolution in Iraq, on July 14, heightened the feeling of tension. At the request for aid by President Chamoun, the U.S. Sixth Fleet moved 3,600 marines into Beirut to stabilize the situation. This tactic, combined with intense behind-the-scenes negotiations, brought some order into the Lebanese conflict and helped to forestall a civil war. The action was successful, and the Lebanese regime survived until the civil war in 1975 and the Israeli-Syrian interventions from 1976 onward. Nonetheless, this event revealed the willingness of the U.S. to intervene *directly* in Middle Eastern affairs if it felt its national interest was at stake—a right it steadfastly denied to its allies and adversaries alike.

Phase III

The United States is currently in Phase III of its Middle East policy—a phase in which its commitments to Israel are being modified by its need for regular supplies of Middle East petroleum. The seven-month Arab oil embargo of 1973–1974 was initiated in direct retaliation for U.S. support for Israel in the war of October, 1973. This war, first initiated by a surprise attack by Egyptian forces, was ultimately concluded by means of intervention via the U.N. As a result, the United States, by shipping arms to Israel, first prevented the collapse of the Israeli military, and then, through its diplomatic activity in the United Nations, it rescued Egypt from probable defeat.

Since the October war, the United States' attempts to play both sides of the Arab-Israeli conflict have been unsuccessful in rescuing its prestige in the area. Indeed, U.S. policy seems to have alienated both sides in the conflict. Israeli complaints about U.S. waffling on aid have become more frequent in the 1980s, culminating in the public invective of Prime Minister Menachem Begin. Arab rejectionist states have not been satisfied or mollified by U.S. support for Egypt or increasing U.S. arms sales to Egypt and Saudi Arabia. More and more, the U.S. is being pressured to consider the Arab view in the Arab-Israeli conflict. The diplomacy of the Carter administration, in particular the Camp David Accords, which led to bilateral negotiations between Egypt and Israel, was most probably the United States' only realistic option.

The Camp David agreements have resulted in the cessation of diplomatic hostilities, the return of most Sinai territory to Egypt, and the opening of genuine diplomatic and trade relations between the two countries. The negotiations, however, have not gone beyond the most basic questions regarding Palestinian autonomy on the West Bank and Gaza. The problem of Jerusalem, claimed by Israel as her historic capital, and an important religious site for Christianity and Islam, also proves to be difficult. However, since Egypt has borne the brunt of military confrontations with Israel, an outbreak of war is unlikely.

The embryonic foreign policy of the Reagan administration does not hold the promise of substantial change in U.S.-Middle East policy. Early administration decisions to accede to Saudi requests for longer range and more sophisticated fighter/bombers were balanced by promises to increase military aid to Israel. As in the preceding administration's foreign policy, neither side is ecstatic about the U.S. effort to play both sides. Another example of the likely continuity between the Carter and Reagan foreign policies is to be found in the Reagan administration's acceptance of the agreements with Iran negotiated over the U.S. hostages, although the negotiations were distasteful in theory to the new administration.

Reagan administration efforts to organize an anti-Soviet alliance in the Middle East were gently rebuffed in the early months of 1981. Administration concern for Saudi security prompted its approval of the sale of sophisticated radar planes (AWACS), to Saudi Arabia, a decision that produced considerable pro-Israeli objections in the U.S. Congress. And finally, the June, 1981 Israeli air raid on the Iraqi nuclear facility near Baghdad prompted the administration to suspend shipment of four F-16's to Israel, which also strained relations. It is instructive that the U.N. resolution condemning the Israeli raid and calling for compensation was a joint product of American and Iraqi diplomats at the U.N. Such a collaboration would have been unthinkable a decade earlier. All of these examples underscore the difficulty of maintaining traditional U.S. policy priorities in the decade of the 80s.

SOVIET FOREIGN POLICY

Initially, Soviet foreign policy toward the Middle East was opportunistic and reactive. It was opportunistic in that the Soviet Union attempted to exploit the postwar difficulties of Greece, Turkey, and Iran in its historic attempt to secure a year-round warm-water port. It was reactive in that it attempted to exploit the consequences of U.S. policy in the Arab-Israeli conflict.

In Phase I of its Middle Eastern policy, the Soviet Union attempted a combination of subversion and guerrilla intervention in the northern tier nations. Soviet diplomatic pressure on Turkey was intense, particularly as regarded its navigation rights in the Bosporus Straits and the redefinition of the Thracian border in favor of Bulgaria. This, combined with more direct military adventures in Iran, prompted President Truman to declare the Truman Doctrine and unilaterally commit the U.S. to the defense of these states. Soviet ambitions in these areas were frustrated, and Soviet policy in the Middle East became more reactive to U.S. policy.

In Phase II, the Soviet Union seemed primarily interested in exploiting the difficulties raised by the U.S. commitment to Israel. Thus, in order to find a way to move her growing military capability into the Mediterranean, the Soviet Union began courting the most rabidly anti-Israeli states. Her first major opportunity came in Egypt, hard on the heels of the Israeli raid on Gaza, the French-British-Israeli attack on the Suez Canal, and the U.S. cancellation of support for the Aswan Dam. The Soviet Union abandoned its initial support for Israel, moved into the arms race in a major way, and ultimately committed itself to the construction of the High Dam. Soviet arms aid was supplemented by a vigorous economic aid and trade policy that succeeded after 1958 in orienting the trade relations of Egypt, Syria, Yemen, and Iraq toward the Eastern bloc. Extensive cultural programs were also implemented, many involving extensive educational opportunities for Arabs in Eastern Europe and the U.S.S.R. These programs, combined with its support of nonalignment movements worldwide, succeeded in raising Soviet prestige and influence at the expense of the U.S. The Soviet Union was able to turn some of these gains into tangible results. It was given military facilities in Egypt, most notably an extensive naval base at Alexandria, and communication and airfield facilities at Luxor. At one point, Soviet technical and military experts in Egypt numbered close to 20,000. Similar gains were scored in Syria and Iraq, although not on such a grand scale. Its support for the front-line states against Israel and later for the Palestinian guerrilla movements, some of which received technical aid and support from Soviet allies, also contributed to the heightening Soviet prestige in the area.

Most of the Soviet Union's overt political gains during Phase II were nonetheless intangible. Soviet attempts to influence directly the governments of Nasser and Sadat in Egypt were frustrated. The Egyptians seemed adept at taking gifts from the Russian bear while simultaneously avoiding its hug. To a lesser degree, similar events transpired in Syria and Iraq, where allegedly communist-inspired coups were detected and crushed, accompanied by army and university purges. When Sadat ordered the Soviets out of Egypt in 1972, American influence and prestige enjoyed something of a recovery. Even Syria and Iraq, in recent years, have slowly reoriented themselves toward a more positive, but wary, relationship with the U.S.

Phase III of Soviet foreign policy roughly paralleled U.S. policy shifts. The Soviet Union has aggressively supported wars of national liberation in the area. Frustrated in its attempts to consolidate its advantages in the fertile crescent, the Soviet Union turned to overt military aid and surrogate (Cuban) intervention, most notably in Yemen and Ethiopia, where it has become involved in the Eritrean dispute. The Soviet invasion of Afghanistan in 1979–1980 raised warning signs all over the Middle East, particularly among those states formally committed to Islamic rule. The Soviet occupation of Afghanistan lowered its prestige and influence in the region, and heightened Middle Eastern awareness of its poor treatment of Soviet Muslim groups.

From a geopolitical perspective, the turmoil on the Persian Gulf presents the Soviet Union with some risky opportunities. Intervention in Iran could conceivably produce both a warm-water port and increased access to foreign petroleum. A successful venture in Oman could place the Soviet Union in a position of influence at the very opening to the Persian Gulf. And success in the northern tier, bordering as it does on the Soviet Union itself, could be exploited militarily and politically. On the other hand, the United States' response to such success is hard to envision. The movement of Iran into the Soviet orbit, for example, could upset the international balance to such a degree that the U.S. would resort to military action. The Soviet Union has avoided such a direct confrontation with its nuclear adversary since the Cuban Missile Crisis of 1962. For the time being, it is likely that the Soviet Union will seek to benefit from the instability of the northern tier without moving into the area.

There is a substantial irony to this state of affairs. Many Middle Eastern intellectuals have long believed that the U.S. and the U.S.S.R. are basically identical; they are both interested only in maintaining and extending their political and military power. For these two adversaries, accustomed to seeing each other in absolute, polarized terms, such a conclusion must seem outrageously inaccurate. Nonetheless, in the 1980s, this judgment is prevalent among the diplomats of Asia, Africa, and the Middle East.

BRITAIN AND FRANCE

As indicated earlier in this chapter, the postwar international scene saw a substantial reduction of British and French power. Both nations emerged from World War II victorious but exhausted. Even with the direct help of the U.S., these two countries were hard pressed to reassert their authority over their former colonies. Both reluctantly began a series of retrenchments.

Of the two, Britain's withdrawal from strategic power was the more graceful, the less disruptive. While the French opposed two divisive and difficult wars of national liberation in Viet Nam and in Algeria, the British planted supposedly independent, pro-British regimes in their former colonies. When things got out of hand, as they did in Iran in 1952–1953, Britain participated in intrigues designed to bring a friendly face to the throne—in this case the return of the Shah from exile.

Both countries, as Chapter 5 indicated, attempted to use World War I and World War II diplomacy to extend and develop their influence in the Middle East. Pursuing a course of naked self-interest, the British and the French promised, at one time or another, everything to everybody. In the end, the Middle Eastern state system, a pastiche of kings, emirs, presidents, and sheikhs, presiding over geographical entities drawn by committees in Europe, emerged. In this emergence, the power of the British and the French paled in comparison to that of the United States and the U.S.S.R. Thus, they contented themselves with attempting to perpetuate their cultural and economic influence in the area under American military protection. Israel received enormous support in return for taking in the great numbers of displaced European Jews. Extensive oil resources were being developed in Iraq, Iran, Kuwait, and in Saudi Arabia.

In Phase II the British and French turned their attention primarily to trade relations. The abortive Suez War in 1956 effectively ended what predisposition they had for an overt military role in the area. After that time the orientation of the European powers became essentially commercial and focused on the exploitation of the increasingly important petroleum reserves. During this time, it also became evident that support of Israel had become secondary to other objectives. French and British arms were sold indiscriminantly in the Middle East, to the anguish of both the U.S. and Israel. These sales demonstrated the growing inability of the U.S. to control its alliances.

In Phase III of their Middle Eastern policy, the U.S. allies have grown even less dependent on American initiatives and policy direction. Britain, France, and West Germany have, since 1974, sold increasingly sophisticated weapons and technology to assorted Middle Eastern governments. Even nuclear technology, over specific, energetic U.S. opposition, has been made available to such Middle Eastern governments as Iraq, Egypt, Libya, and Iran. All of these countries—except Libya—have the combination of financial, physical, and intellectual resources necessary for the construction of nuclear devices. This, combined with the probable nuclear arsenal in Israel, raises the spectre of nuclear confrontation in some unspecified future. This recognition certainly prompted the 1981 Israeli air raid on the Osirak Reactor near Baghdad, a raid launched irrespective of anticipated diplomatic fallout. Iraq's president Saddam Hussein subsequently called for aid from "peace-loving" nations to aid in the development of Arab-controlled nuclear weapons, for the specific purpose of countering Israeli nuclear devices.

During this period, the governments of Europe have become even more dependent on Middle Eastern petroleum. France, Germany, Italy, Belgium, and Holland must import most of their petroleum from the Middle East. They hastily separated themselves from the embargoed U.S. By 1980, all of the major governments of Western Europe scrambled for privileged status in trade relations in the area, exchanging technology for precious petroleum.

European relations with Israel have generally paralleled world opinion. Israel has found most European countries hostile toward its policies on Palestine and Jerusalem. In the U.N., they have joined the majority on Israeli aggression and imperialism and have been vocal in their insistence that Israel accept Resolution 242 (1967), which calls for a return to the prewar boundaries.

Western Europe, during Phase III, began to act as though it was but one of a number of centers of world power. In 1980 and 1981, the European Common Market called for new peace talks in the Middle East that would exclude the Soviet Union and the United States. As the contemporary international system matures, we can expect to see more independent European and Japanese policy initiatives. One can only hope for a peaceful resolution of these disputes. The stakes, for all the players, are extraordinarily high.

CHINA AND JAPAN

The foreign policies of China and Japan toward the Middle East have become important in the last decade. During Phase I, both China and Japan deferred completely to the policy dictates of the U.S.S.R. and the U.S. Toward the 1960s, during Phase II, both countries turned their attention toward the Middle East, but not in the intense or manipulative way of the megapowers or the European powers. China has historically supported Arab movements toward nonalignment and occasionally offered minimal support to wars of national liberation in Southern Arabia. Its interest in frustrating the growth of Soviet power has led China to supply military replacement parts to Egypt after the Soviet Union cut them off. Japan, during this period, became a progressively larger consumer of Middle Eastern oil, upon which she is near totally reliant to fuel her industry. Japan has thus placed a high premium on innocuous, positive diplomatic relations in the area.

In Phase III, China has become more directly active in her attempts to frustrate Soviet gains in the area. Overt Chinese support for anti-Soviet elements in Afghanistan has been instrumental in keeping the U.S.S.R. engaged in repressive actions there. The Chinese have also opposed Soviet interest in the horn of Africa. China appears to be interested in a worldwide alliance designed to frustrate Soviet "hegemonism." The coordination of U.S.-Chinese policy in this regard has been minimal and of little importance to the contemporary Middle East, save for Afghanistan and Pakistan. As indicated earlier, Japan has seen her dependence on Middle Eastern (particularly Iranian) oil grow to critical proportions. Japan thus has had her latitude of action severely restricted and has resorted to a low profile in her international policy in the area.

In summation, all great-power actors have recently found the Middle East a difficult area in which to implement policy. Changes in the very structure of the international system have frustrated Soviet and American policy initiatives in the area. The growth of economic power centers outside the bipolar axis have increased the number of players in the game. And Middle Eastern leaders have shown themselves to be surprisingly adept practitioners of classic diplomacy.

REGIONAL RELATIONS

The Middle East is an area seemingly designed for intensive regional activity. As noted elsewhere in this text, the region's nations have many physical similarities: aridity, uneven population distributions, oil reserves, communications, and transport centers. Moreover, they share many ethnic and cultural similarities: large blocs of contiguous Arabs, Turks, and Persians, the predominance of the Arabic language, and the pervasive influence of Islam. Thus, there are many physical, ethnic and cultural bridges across the national boundaries of the state system. Accordingly, there have been many attempts—public and private—to exploit these similarities.

The oldest of the regional associations in the Middle East is the Arab League. Founded in Cairo in 1945, the league initially was comprised of Egypt, Iraq, Saudi Arabia, Syria, Transjordan, Lebanon, and Yemen. Although there were serious internal divisions within the league from the outset, it accomplished some positive action. Critical histories of the league invariably stress its early difficulties in coordinating the war against Israel in 1948. In this war the mutual suspicions between the Hashimites, Saudis, and Egyptians severely split the Arab forces. In the Phase II period, the league was successful primarily in nonpolitical areas—for example, in social and economic cooperation. It has never been able to resolve the fractious politics of its Arab constituency and has survived by avoiding those difficult problems for the most part. More effective efforts at Arab unity have been pursued from the base of national power, as in Nasser's pan-Arab movement, the Baath party, and

OAPEC. In Phase III, the league has been little more than a ceremonial sounding board for diverse Arab interests.

During Phase II, there were two notable attempts to achieve Arab political unity. The first was the pan-Arab movement launched by Nasser in 1958, the second was the formation of the Baath party, which was based on the philosophy of Michel Aflaq and found its most receptive constituency in Syria and Iraq. These two movements have often been at odds, each accusing the other of advancing the national interests of its founders.

Nasser's pan-Arab objectives were couched largely in terms of national union. Based on a loosely articulated ideal of Arab unity and cooperation, Nasser's movement was considerably more pragmatic than the ideological basis of the Baath movement. Where the Baath depended on loyal cadres to spread its ideology and raise it to power, Nasser pursued the constitutional union of Egypt with a variety of potential partners. At one time or another, Egypt has been unified with (or has proposed unification with): Syria, Iraq, Yemen, Libya, and the Sudan.

Nasser's pan-Arab strategy produced some tangible results. The 1958 union of Egypt and Syria, the United Arab Republic, survived until 1961, when the federation succumbed to a Syrian army coup. Some critics argue that the failure of the union was prompted by Nasser's efforts in 1959–1960 to effect a truly economic, political, and military union—one that would to some degree extinguish remaining Syrian political identity. Others argue that Syrian nationalism simply proved too potent an obstacle for union. Nasser's attempts at federation with Yemen (1958) were much looser and much less ambitious. Union with Iraq in the 1960s was frustrated by a military coup and the subsequent entrenchment of Baathist regimes in both Syria and Iraq. In spite of these frustrations and failures, Nasser maintained his commitment to Arab unity via political union. Most countries of the Middle East counted among their populations groups strongly supportive of Nasser's dream. These groups were in the main not strong enough to implement his vision of unity, although they were strong enough to continually worry their governments. These governments continued throughout Nasser's presidency to suspect his motives, question his actions, and frustrate his international ventures.

Baathism is at once a political party and a political philosophy. It is one of the very few indigenous political party movements in the Middle East. Based on the work and writings of Michel Aflaq and Salal al-Din al-Bitar, it was founded in 1953 and is committed to the ultimate goal of Arab unity through nationalism, socialism, and pan-Arabism. The Baath (Resurrection) party specifically aims to recover past Arab greatness. Baathism found its normal constituency among the intellectuals and military of Syria, Lebanon, Jordan, and Iraq. Since 1963, it has successfully maintained itself in power in Syria and in Iraq. It should be noted that in Syria, Baathist support came largely from the civilian sector; in Iraq, Baathist power resided mainly in the military, many of whom had earlier supported union with Nasser's Egypt.

The Baathist regimes in Syria and Iraq have been in the forefront of the assault on Israel. Between 1965 and 1975, Iraq openly supported Palestinian separatist and terrorist organizations. Iraqi troops were moved into position during the

1967 and 1973 wars with Israel, although they were for the most part noncombatant.

Syrian foreign policy during Phase II moved closer and closer to the Soviet Union, particularly after dissolution of the union with Egypt. Relations with Israel and the U.S. were frigid, cool with the traditional Middle Eastern states (Saudi Arabia, Iran), and increasingly friendly with Libya and Algeria. Substantial economic and cultural ties with the Soviet Union and the Eastern bloc were maintained.

The Baathist regimes of Syria and Iraq have often been at loggerheads, in spite of their ostensible commitment to Arab unity. Both countries have relatively long and potent histories of nationalist feeling, and it is possible that these factors have been determinant in their foreign policy. Thus, they have only given lip service to regional unity movements.

A digression on the role of Islam in the regional politics of the area is necessary here. During Phase II, Nasser's pan-Arabism, Baathist ideology, and the traditional systems of the day all stressed the importance of Islam as a common source of tradition and identity. In nearly all of the participating states, however, Islam was conceived of in politically secular terms. It was fashionable to recognize the existence of Muslim society (a society composed primarily of Muslims) as a desirable reality, while simultaneously rejecting the idea of an Islamic state (a state based on the Koran and Islamic tradition). While there were exceptions to this professed secularism—the Muslim Brotherhood, mainly, and a number of Sufi orders—there were no serious challenges to the political orthodoxy of the day. Arab socialism in particular depended on Islamic sources for inspiration, but few economists were willing to suggest that modern economies could be based on the principles contained in the Koran, the hadith, or their subsequent commentaries and codifications.

PALESTINIAN INTERNATIONAL ACTION

Any discussion of political terrorism, regardless of how dispassionate or neutral, will inevitably raise emotional objections from those who initiate it or suffer from it. In these objections, the motives of either side in the equation of terror are reduced to the most simple and limited perspective. "Terrorists are simply bloodthirsty animals," say the objects of terrorist attacks. "No, we are freedom fighters attempting to overthrow a pitiless, merciless, repressive regime," respond the terrorists, "and we must fight these monsters to the death with whatever means are at our disposal." Thus, in the final analysis, one man's terrorist is another man's freedom fighter. This fact, coupled with the widespread use of terror and political violence in our modern world, makes analysis difficult.

And yet, there are dispassionate and insightful observations that one may make about terrorists and their objectives, counter-terrorists and theirs. Above all, terrorists seek the creation of a psychological mood. Terror works best in the glare of intense publicity and coverage by the mass media. This coverage can transform a small-scale and apparently random act into a gnawing sense of anxiety in the target population. We know of no government overthrown simply by the cumulation of terrorist acts. Thus, terror tactics, although morally reprehensible, can best be perceived as a sort of harassment or irritant, an activity that can claim the attention of government but rarely topple it. Reprisals against terrorists can, ironically, result in losses to the afflicted government, especially if the reprisal is not cleanly and clearly focused against the terrorists themselves. Thus, government attempts in Northern Ireland to suppress terrorism have generally created a fund of ill-will among those nonterrorists who are nonetheless disadvantaged or hurt by the policies. Policies of restraint are generally the most profitable in the long run, while policies of overreaction may in fact lead to substantial changes in the climate of world public opinion.

All of this has direct applicability to the situation in the Middle East, particularly as regards the Arab-Israeli conflict. Only the most studiously isolated individual is not aware of the wide-scale use of terror by the Palestinian groups seeking confrontation with Israel. And Israel, particularly under the guidance of Prime Minister Begin, has made no secret of its intention to repay terrorist activity in kind, following the biblical injunction of "an eye for an eye, a tooth for a tooth." Combined with the contemporary cry of "Never again," the government of Israel has invoked powerful symbols in its decision to utilize a counter-terror strategy in its dealing with the Palestinian Arabs.

What follows in the next few pages is an attempt to place this pattern of terror and reactive terror into the flow of contemporary international relations. It is not an attempt to draw moral lessons from either side's utilization of terror or violence, but simply to identify the consequences of those actions. Moreover, our effort here is not to catalogue those activities, but rather to emphasize those events that had the most symbolic importance in defining and redefining adversary roles in the conflict.

Totally frustrated in their efforts to obtain relief before 1967, Palestinians began to express their frustrations by violent means. Lacking a national base or homeland, the Palestinian movements were genuinely regional, moving from country to country as the patience and tempers of their hosts wore thin. Of the many formed, the two major organizations were the Palestine Liberation Organization (PLO) and the Harakat al-Tahrir al-Falastini (Al-Fatah). Both of these organizations have, between 1965 and 1975, accomplished a most dramatic change of status. From the image of bumbling PLO bureaucrats or of rag-tag, terrorist revolutionaries (Al-Fatah) furtively slinking across the Middle East landscape, they have become accepted internationally as the government in exile of the Palestinian nation and have been welcomed in many of the capitals of the world and the U.N. This transformation was not accomplished without difficulty and pain. Dispersed across the Middle East, substantial groups of Palestinians inhabited dehumanizing refugee camps in Lebanon, Syria, Jordan, and the West Bank. Others, more fortunate, occupied expatriate positions in the economies of nearly all the nations of the Middle East; they have become a valued resource, given the high level of education they attained before the creation of Israel. Leaders of this fractured community could with good reason suggest that the Arab states had little interest in solving the Palestinian question, since to do so would reduce the pressure on Israel. Thus, it was not until the 1967 Arab-Israeli war that the Palestinian organizations found the tide of events moving, although sluggishly, in their direction.

Ironically, it was the Arab losses and Israeli victory in 1967 that gave the PLO and Al-Fatah the needed impetus. The movement of Israel into the West Bank created a new flood of dispossessed Palestinians, many of whom found the claims of the PLO and Al-Fatah attractive. Simultaneously, the defeat of the Arab armies undermined the prestige of the Arab states and their leaders, creating something of a power vacuum, at least where the confrontation with Israel was concerned. At any rate, the two Palestinian organizations suddenly found themselves in positions of preeminence in the Palestinian diaspora.

Al-Fatah, under the leadership of Yasir Arafat, became the most successful group in terms of violent operations against Israel. Operating initially out of bases in Jordan, Al-Fatah launched a number of attacks against Israel, attacks which ultimately produced an Israeli raid on a Jordanian staging area. The Israeli raid, although successful, encountered stiff Palestinian resistance, and was perceived by many young Arabs as an effective action, bringing increased attention and more volunteers to the organization. Between 1968 and 1970, Al-Fatah and other smaller Palestinian groups engaged in increasingly violent guerrilla and terrorist activities, culminating in the hijacking of a number of jets—a Swissair DC-8, a TWA 707, a Pan American 747, and a BOAC VC 10. These audacious actions captured the attention of the international mass media, inevitably bringing the Palestinian organizations into public prominence. With this public prominence came discussion of Palestinian grievances. Ultimately, the PLO was granted observer status in the General Assembly by the United Nations.

Nineteen seventy marks a watershed year for the Palestinian movements. Black September, the expulsion of the Palestinian guerrillas from Jordan, proved to be a serious setback to the movement. Moving to Lebanon, from 1970 to 1972, groups of Palestinians accelerated their military and terrorist activities, leading the Lebanese government to repressive measures. Palestinian units began to operate openly in Southern Lebanon.

Phase III Palestinian activity has benefited from a growing world recognition of the fact that Jewish relief had resulted in Palestinian injustice. It has also benefited from growing financial support from OPEC Arab members including Kuwait, Saudi Arabia, the U.A.E., and Khomeini's Iran; from the United States' growing inability to ignore Arab wishes in regard to the Palestinian question; and finally, and not insignificantly, from what is peacelike as Israeli tendencies to overreact to terrorist raids on its territory. The West Bank settlement policies of the Begin administration, in particular, convinced many governments of Israeli intransigence toward negotiated Palestinian autonomy on the West Bank.

OPEC AND ISLAM

Regional Arab relations in Phase III have been dominated by two emergent trends: first, the effect of OPEC petroleum pricing on the incomes of Saudi Arabia, Iran, Libya, Kuwait, Iraq, and the U.A.E.; second, the emergence of Islamic fundamentalism as a potent force in Arab politics. These two trends were in fact intertwined.

With the exception of Iraq, the major petroleum-producing countries in this region are also religious conservatives: Saudi Arabia is dominated by the severe Wahhabi school of Islam; Iran is governed by fundamentalist Shiite revolutionaries led by the ulema; Kuwait and the U.A.E. are ruled by traditional leaders who rely on the support of the ulema; and Libya is currently dominated by a unique Islamic fundamentalism developed by Muammar el-Qadaffi. These countries have utilized their substantial oil revenues to support religious goals. Kuwait and Saudi Arabia have tied loans and investments to specific Islamic reforms in Egypt and the Sudan. Iran and Libya have supported a variety of anti-Israeli, anti-Western movements across the Middle East, both Sunni and Shiite. Fundamentalist movements have gained ground in Syria, Lebanon, Iraq, and Egypt, all working toward the establishment of an Islamic state, a government based specifically and exclusively on the precepts of Islam. The Muslim Brotherhood, long proscribed since its conflict with Nasser in Egypt early in the revolution, found new bases of support in Egypt and the fertile crescent. These movements, fragmented across many lines, posed a singular threat to the prevailing secularism of the international order of Phase II.

Coordination of policy and collection action have tended to proliferate in the area in recent years. The success of OPEC, and of its Arab subgroup OAPEC, has led to a number of international development projects funded out of the growing revenues of the petroleum-rich states. These projects have at the minimum a semblance of collective control. Joint economic ventures between OAPEC members, such as the huge dry-dock facility in Bahrain, are also examples of collective action. The successful pursuit of Palestinian rights in the United Nations has been mentioned earlier, and recently Arab members have coordinated the freezing of deposits for World Bank projects seen as hostile to the Palestinian cause.

Islam itself has prompted a large number of international conferences and organizations, as a growing Islamic international community searches for ways to implement Islamic principles in banking, commerce, and social and political organization. A group of forty-two Islamic nations met together in 1980 to consider and protest the Soviet action in Afghanistan, and a small number of them actually broke off relations with the U.S.S.R. as a result. A similar meeting was held in Taif, Saudi Arabia, early in 1981. This meeting affirmed the earlier position taken on Afghanistan and additionally took a very dim view of the Iran/Iraq War, which was perceived as damaging to the Umma. The conference has been persistent in its efforts to mediate the Iran-Iraq conflict. These evidences of an Islamic revival provide some of the logic and impetus to the growing multilateral entities in the Middle East. We will consider the future implications of this trend in the concluding chapter.

Finally, nuclear politics appear to be taking on a regional flavor. The Israeli nuclear arsenal has long been recognized as a major factor in any final Middle Eastern confrontation, although the specifics of those nuclear weapons are carefully guarded secrets. Arab responses to the Israeli nuclear armament have included regional support for the development of nuclear weapons, often described as the "Islamic bomb." Documented reports of cooperation between Iran, Pakistan, and Libya are current. The Israeli preemptive strike against Iraq's nuclear reactor was thus set against a backdrop of a changing nuclear world. Complicating matters is the fact that nuclear technology is no longer the dark secret that it once was: the technology is now available for purchase and many Middle Eastern states have sufficient financial resources to do so. All of this suggests an enormously more complicated international system, one capable of taking the world to the edge of nuclear catastrophe. If these trends work out as it appears they may, we will have to abandon our cliché about the "tinderbox" Middle East and replace it with more apocalyptic imagery.

THE FOREIGN POLICIES OF EGYPT, SAUDI ARABIA, IRAN, AND ISRAEL

In this section, we will discuss the respective foreign policies of Egypt, Saudi Arabia, Iran, and Israel. Collectively or independently, these nations have been responsible for most of the international initiatives and exchanges in the region.

Egyptian Foreign Policy

In the postwar Middle East, Egyptian foreign policy concerned itself with the following major issues: opposition to colonialism-imperialism, opposition to Israel, Arab unity, and, after the revolution, opposition to conservative Arab regimes.

For some 2,000 years Egypt had been the prime example of a colonized state. In that long span of time, rarely had the Egyptians been ruled by anything faintly resembling an Egyptian ruling class. The rejection received by Napoleon when he proposed self-rule to the Egyptian ulema was characteristic of the relationship between Egypt and her rulers: Egyptians could not imagine organizing and supervising their own affairs. All of this was to end after World War II, when Egypt struggled to free itself of European domination. Farouk's foreign policy consisted of attempts to play one set of European powers (England and France) off against another (Germany and Italy). Since the Egyptian revolution and the rise of Nasser, however, the concept of anti-imperialism took on greater depth and meaning, until it meant to many the complete removal of foreign influence from Egypt. This rejection of foreign influence, moreover, was an issue with domestic origins and consequences—an issue to which the Egyptian masses would respond wholeheartedly. Opposition to imperialism-colonialism became as important to domestic policy as it did to foreign policy.

Nationalism and anti-imperialism are very often delicately intertwined, producing a complex fabric of action and reaction. The question is in some final sense unresolvable: does an anti-imperialistic movement create nationalism, or is anti-imperialism itself created by emergent nationalistic feeling? The resolution of this question must await further study. At this point, and especially in the case of Egypt, we must note the existence of a symbiotic relationship between the two forces—a relationship that has enormously complicated Egypt's pursuit of a consistent foreign policy.

Although Egypt was nominally independent of direct foreign control before Nasser's rise to power, many colonial problems needed resolution. These problems dominated Egyptian foreign policy in early Phase II. Among them were the relationship between Egypt and the Sudan, both former British dependencies (political union was one of the early ideological demands of the revolutionary movement); British rights to control and defend the Suez Canal; and a pattern of mutual defense agreements negotiated before and during World War II. The range of possible solutions was limited because these issues evoked powerful emotions in the Egyptian public, particularly in Cairo, where *any* agreement with a foreign power would be seen as suspect. The great powers insisted that these problems were but a subset of the larger bipolar confrontation of East and West.

The question of the Sudan's relationship to Egypt was solved peacefully, but not in a way that was consistent with Egypt's initial objectives. A series of elections led the Sudan to ultimately opt for independence rather than union. The other problems were more complicated and led to international tensions. The sensitive problem of Egypt's relations with the West and the problem of its security goals, conflicting as they did with Egypt's difficulties with Israel, resulted in the Suez crisis and the frustrations over the Aswan Dam detailed earlier in this chapter.

The Suez crisis and the Aswan Dam controversy confirmed Nasser's belief that relations with the Western alliance were going to be uneven. The United States' and Europe's response to Egypt's negotiations for Eastern bloc arms was hostile and proved that promised economic and technical aid had clearly visible political strings. Accordingly, Nasser moved more and more to a posture of nonalignment and began to play an important role in that world movement.

Egypt took a leadership role at the first major nonalignment conference in Bandung, Indonesia (April, 1955). Spurred on by his distaste for the Baghdad Pact and the extension of the bipolar conflict into the Middle East, Nasser subsequently hosted many of the major meetings of the nonaligned powers and forcefully argued for nonaligned foreign policy in the region. Nasser attempted to coordinate his nonaligned foreign policy with such neutralist leaders as Nehru of India, Tito of Yugoslavia, and Sukarno of Indonesia. He attacked the Eisenhower Doctrine of 1957, and continued his unrelenting opposition to European imperialism.

In the 1960s, Egypt's opposition to Western imperialism and to Israel necessitated closer military relations with the Soviet Union, upon whom it was now solely dependent for arms. This, combined with the growing number of Soviet technicians assigned to the Aswan Dam project, confirmed many Western judgments that Egypt, along with Syria and Iraq, had slipped irretrievably into the orbit of the Eastern bloc. These reactions were premature and underestimated Nasser's ability to take aid and maintain his own independence of action. The Soviet Union, for its part, was never able to consolidate its gains in Egypt and in 1972 departed on Sadat's orders.

Egypt's relationship with Israel has been paradoxical; Egypt has lost every military encounter with Israel but has won much more in the peace settlements. Israel's obviously superior military forces defeated Egyptian armies in 1948, 1956, 1967, and 1973; Israel also intervened with small tactical units in neighboring Arab nations at will during the same period. Each victory became more expensive to Israel and Egypt alike, requiring extensive and speedy military rearmament. Egyptian losses in these encounters far outstripped the losses of her allies, leading to the widespread observation that other Arab states were willing to fight the Israelis "to the last Egyptian."

Despite these consistent military losses, Egyptian prestige in the Arab world was enhanced by these defeats. World public opinion turned gradually in a pro-Egyptian direction, and Israeli interests in the U.N. began to wane. In both Egypt and the wider world, the struggle against imperialism and colonialism came increasingly to be seen as continuous with the struggle against Israel.

The political results of the 1967 Arab-Israeli war illustrate Nasser's gift at turning liabilities into assets. The war itself began as a result of Nasser's miscalculation. Increasingly irritated by the presence of UNEF forces on Egypt's territory but not on Israel's, Nasser ordered the removal of the U.N. barrier troops. Shortly thereafter, he announced his intention to blockade Israeli shipping at the Straits of Tiran. Since Nasser was at the time involved in a costly and frustrating venture in Yemen, it is doubtful that he expected the Israeli attack that occurred on June 5, 1967. At the end of the brief war the Israeli army occupied all of the Sinai, had taken the Golan Heights from Syria, destroyed most of the Iraqi air force on the ground, and occupied Jerusalem and the West Bank of the Jordan River, which was part and parcel of Jordan. These losses were traumatic to Nasser and the Arab states. U.N. intervention once again brought a cease-fire and an end to the fighting. On June 9, Nasser submitted his resignation as president, citing his failure in the war. The Cairo masses refused the resignation with an outpouring of support, prompting Nasser to rescind his resignation and resume his leadership role. What in military terms could be described as a rout, became a reaffirmation of Nasser's leadership position in Egypt.

United Nations involvement did not stop with the cease-fire. Most important was the passage of U.N. Resolution 242 on November 22, 1967. This resolution called for the removal of Israeli armed forces from all the territories gained in the 1967 war, and called upon all the nations of the region to recognize each other's rights to "live in peace within secure and recognized boundaries free from threats or acts of force." This resolution was greeted with mixed emotions by Egypt and her allies. While they approved of the return of the conquered territory, they were not pleased with the second point of the resolution, which would permanently recognize Israel's right to exist in peace. Events in the 1970s found the Arab states anxious to accept the resolution and Israel reluctant to surrender the territory. In the final analysis, support of Resolution 242 became a key item in the Arab propaganda conflict with Israel. The support of the resolution was an important factor in the shift of world opinion toward the Arab and Palestinian cause.

Egypt's venture in Yemen was also frustrating. The Egyptian army was largely removed from Yemen on an emergency basis to shore up defenses after the 1967 war. From 1962 to 1967, the Egyptians had intervened substantially in the Yemeni civil war on the side of the republican forces. During this period Egyptian troop strength rose to around 80,000 in Yemen. They were opposed by Saudi Arabia, who provided logistical and communication support to the ousted Imam, and by tribesmen in the Yemeni hill country. As with the 1967 war, there was no clear solution to this conflict in sight. The expenditure of many lives and dollars resulted in a coalition government, with the royalists and the republicans sharing power. The Egyptian goal, the establishment of a pan-Arab revolutionary regime, was frustrated. The Saudi goal of rescuing a traditional system from revolutionary pressure was also frustrated. The conflict between the modernizing pan-Arabs led by Nasser and the conservative traditional leaders led by Saudi Arabia was not resolved: Saudi and Egyptian relations reached a low point.

From the 1967 war until his death in 1970, Nasser pursued a political solution to the Arab-Israeli conflict. This political strategy necessitated regional cooperation, both formal and informal. Egypt's encouragement of the PLO and Al-Fatah during this period is an example of its informal diplomacy. At the time of his death, Nasser was presiding over a pan-Arab conference in Cairo designed to resolve the Black September conflict between the Palestinian Fedayeen and the Jordanian army. This exemplified his formal diplomacy in the post-1967 period.

Egyptian relations with Libya, its Western neighbor, were relatively uneventful prior to the emergence in 1969 of Col. Muammar Qadaffi as the Libyan ruler. A charismatic leader, Qadaffi possessed a sense of mission and saw himself as Nasser's heir-apparent as head of the pan-Arab movement. The tension between the leadership styles of Sadat and Qadaffi soon became quite apparent, although Sadat acquiesced in a proposed Egyptian-Libyan union in 1972–1973. Sadat's reluctance was probably based equally on his misgivings about the great differences between the two countries demographically and economically and his appraisal of Qadaffi's erratic and radicalizing leadership. The union never got off the ground, but it brought the two leaders into open confrontation. By 1974, the Egyptians claimed they had discovered a Libyan plot against Sadat's government. Since that time, relations between the two states have been cold, occasionally erupting into overt conflict. Libya's support of terrorist movements and her leadership role in the anti-Israeli rejectionist bloc have set her at formal diplomatic odds with Egypt. Libya has taken the severest stand against Sadat for his bilateral negotiations with the Israelis and has reputedly placed a price on his head. As the promise of the Camp David Accords dimmed, Libya's pressure on the Egyptian leader took on more international weight. Egypt thus found itself, in Phase III, increasingly estranged from the Arab states that she once sought to lead. Egyptian diplomatic efforts during the 1980 Iran-Iraq war were largely ignored in the Arab states, confirming Egyptian isolation. For its part, Iraq accepted limited Egyptian military aid during 1981.

Egyptian Foreign Policy under Sadat. The foreign policy of Anwar Sadat constituted a dramatic shift in emphasis from that of Nasser. Under Nasser, Egypt had pursued a policy of Arab unity through revolutionary action and development. Sadat sought friendly relations with all Arab states, regardless of their revolutionary status. The hostility that previously marked Egyptian relations with Saudi Arabia and Jordan, for instance, declined markedly. Sadat put great emphasis on the political resolution of the Israeli question, building on Nasser's belated conversion to this policy. Sadat's personal gifts allowed a public-relations offensive to be launched in the West, particularly in the U.S., where he showed himself to be very adept at talk shows and news interviews.

Soviet influence also declined under Sadat's leadership. Soviet involvement in the attempted coup against Sadat in 1971, and its hesitance to supply sophisticated new weaponry to the Egyptian army, eventually resulted in its abrupt expulsion from the country in July, 1972. Since that time, U.S. influence and arms have gradually replaced the Soviet presence.

Sadat's commitment to a political solution to the Arab-Israeli conflict did not prevent him from initiating the war of October 6, 1973, the Ramadan, or Yom Kippur, War. Sadat's attack on the Israeli Bar-Lev line met with short-term success but incurred heavy armaments costs to both sides; Egypt and Israel called for immediate arms deliveries. The U.S. responded with airlifts to Israel, which the Israeli army was quick to exploit. The Israeli army was able shortly afterward to reverse the Egyptian gains and reestablish their positions along part of Suez Canal. The Egyptian Third Army was effectively surrounded when the Israelis crossed the canal.

At this point, the Arab states proclaimed an oil embargo against the U.S. and its Western allies. This embargo caused the U.S. to exercise its influence more evenly; as a result, the Israeli army did not follow up on its advantages in the Sinai, and the Egyptian Third Army was extricated from the cul-de-sac into which it had been thrown. Subsequent "shuttle diplomacy" conducted largely by U.S. Secretary of State Henry Kissinger resulted in a cease-fire and the initiation of many rounds of diplomacy between the U.S., Israel, and Egypt. Once again, having lost the war, Egypt may be said to have won the peace.

These diplomatic exchanges, referred to collectively as Sinai I and Sinai II, resulted in the following: the withdrawal of Israeli forces back to the Mitla and Gidi Passes; the monitoring of the neutral zone between the passes and the canal by U.S. electronic surveillance; recovery by Egypt of the oil fields in the Western Sinai; and reopening of the Suez Canal with its attendant revenues. But most of all, the U.S. had been drawn into the Arab-Israeli confrontation in a more balanced manner. From this time on, Sadat sought closer relations with the U.S. and attempted to use these relations to bring increased diplomatic pressure to bear on Israel. Thus the stage was set for Egyptian foreign policy in Phase III.

Sadat's postwar diplomatic offensive reached its zenith in his dramatic November, 1977, address to the Israeli Knesset. The visit of an Arab head of state to Israel was an enormous symbolic and substantive act. His speech effectively broke the diplomatic deadlock that had emerged in early 1977. From this point on, Egypt engaged in bilateral negotiations with Israel, a fact bitterly opposed by the Arab rejectionists—Syria, Iraq, Libya, South Yemen, Algeria, and the PLO. These negotiations unfortunately produced little or no tangible results. They did, however, prepare the way for the remarkable events associated with the Camp David Accords, reached in September, 1978.

The Camp David Accords have been described as a triumph of personal diplomacy for President Carter. During eleven days of face-to-face negotiation at Camp

David, Maryland, Carter convinced Sadat and Begin to agree to a set of accords that would create a "framework for peace" in the Arab-Israeli conflict. The accords can be divided into two sections. The first accord dealt with the bilateral relations between Egypt and Israel. It involved the return, by stages, of Egyptian territory in the Sinai, and the normalization of relations, including the eventual exchange of ambassadors. By 1980 large numbers of Israelis were touring in Egypt, at least one Jewish temple was reopened in Cairo, and reports of the opening of Kosher restaurants circulated in the Western press. To protect Egypt from the potential criticism of the rejectionist states, however, the first accord was linked in principle to a second accord dealing with the West Bank and the Gaza Strip. The second accord directly addressed the problem of the occupied territories and the future of the Palestinian people. The Palestinians, in the loosely worded agreement, were to be granted "autonomy" on the West Bank, although the implications of this term were not spelled out.

The negotiations that followed between Egypt and Israel proceeded fairly smoothly where the disengagement of their forces and the return of Sinai territory were concerned. Simultaneous negotiations on the second accord immediately began to stall on the question of the West Bank. Ultimately, while the first part of the accords was fully implemented, resulting in a near normalization of relations between Israel and Egypt, no discernible progress was made on the subject of Palestinian autonomy. In fact, shortly after the Camp David Accords were announced, the Begin government began to increase the number of Jewish settlements on the West Bank; and late in 1980, it announced that henceforth Jerusalem would become the indivisible capital of Israel by action of the Knesset. Apparently, Israel's leaders did not share Egypt's concepts of autonomy.

Predictably, Egypt came under intense Arab criticism for backsliding on the confrontation with Israel. Even the more conservative states of Saudi Arabia and Kuwait joined in the condemnation of Egypt. Radical groups announced the formation of assassination teams aimed at Sadat. Egypt, for its part, gained economically and socially in the bilateral agreement with Israel, but at the cost of its leadership position in the Arab world. Israel gained a secure border that was guaranteed by her most dependable international ally, the United States. The Palestinians, as usual, lost another chance for self-determination and independence.

As Egypt came more into confrontation with her Arab neighbors, she became more dependent on American aid and comfort. Cooperation between the two nations occurred in the economic, political, and military areas. Nasser's cherished nonalignment policy became a casualty of Sadat's pragmatism.

Saudi Foreign Policy

Saudi Arabia is the one Arab country that immediately after World War II could point to a long-standing relationship with the United States. This relationship began in the 1930s as American oil companies began to appreciate and exploit the enormous petroleum reserves of this recently consolidated kingdom. In fact, the earliest relationships between Saudi Arabia and the West were exclusively the product of the oil companies' initiatives. King Ibn Saud, in desperate financial straits in 1933, required a loan of £30,000 in gold sovereigns, as part of the original oil concession agreements. This loan, put up not by the U.S. government but rather by the participating oil companies, came at a critical time for the king, allowing him to maintain the loyalties of key elements in his new tribal coalition. The American government was at this time disinterested in the affairs of this remote region. The loan apparently produced enormous good will toward the oil companies in particular and toward the United States in general. In the future, in spite of cordial relations with Britain and concerted efforts by the Germans and Japanese just before World War II, Ibn Saud expressed his preference for America. He was to pursue this preference during World War II, in spite of his experts' counsel to the contrary and in spite of lost potential oil revenues from sales to the Axis powers. His loyalty proved to be an enormous asset to the United States during the war and immediately thereafter.

The emerging relationship between the U.S. and Saudi Arabia just after World War II can be fairly characterized as "special," a term connoting an unusual mutality of interests and policy between the two states. U.S. interests in Saudi oil were also complemented by its interest in maintaining and expanding its air base at Dharan, a base that linked Western interests in India with the Mediterranean, as part of the larger Western attempt to contain possible Soviet expansion. U.S. payments to Saudi Arabia, both governmental and corporate, began to rise annually. The new-found wealth prompted the initiation of a number of ambitious development projects from 1947 on, which in turn necessitated the movement of a large number of American technicians and advisors to the kingdom. The development projects, which ran the gamut from communications, transportation, and electrification to public health and public education, significantly raised Saudi prestige in the Middle East. Ibn Saud's ministers entered into the international relations of the region fully. From this time, Saudi Arabia was to be one of the major actors in the Middle Eastern international order.

One of King Ibn Saud's first international ventures in the postwar period concerned the future of the Palestinians. Relying on his special relationship with President Roosevelt, King Ibn Saud sought and received assurances that no decisions affecting the future of the Palestinians and Jerusalem would be made without consideration of Arab wishes. Ibn Saud's public espousal of the Palestinian cause heightened his prestige among the Arab states. It also made for his first major disappointment in U.S. policy, as President Truman virtually ignored Roosevelt's promise of consultation in his hasty recognition of Israel in 1948.

Saudi Arabian prestige and power were clearly on the rise at the time of King Ibn Saud's death in 1953. He was succeeded in power by his son Saud Ibn Abdul-Aziz. Simultaneously, the new king's younger brother Faisal was named Crown Prince. The new King Saud was a far less effective monarch than his father.

King Saud, from 1953 onward, changed the basic thrust of Saudi foreign policy. Where his father had pursued a policy of close alignment with the U.S., Saud moved into a closer alliance with revolutionary Egypt, accepting the principles of nonalignment put forward by Nasser. Simultaneously, Saudi Arabia opposed the Hashemite Kingdoms of Jordan and Iraq. The Hashemite family, long influential in the tribal politics of the Arabian peninsula, had been among the final obstacles to Ibn Saud's consolidation of his kingdom. Fear of possible Hashemite reprisals from bases in Jordan and Iraq motivated much of Saudi international policy. Ibn Saud protected himself against potential Hashemite intrigue by allying himself with England, the major international guarantor of the Hashemite house. King Saud approached this problem by formally adopting in 1955 the Egyptian revolutionary policy toward Jordan and Iraq. This policy essentially involved a continuing attempt to isolate diplomatically the two countries and to support actively antimonarchical movements there. However, although Egypt and Saudi Arabia had common interests, including opposition to Israel, it was becoming increasingl' clear to the Saudi elite that Saudi Arabian interests would ultimately conflict wit Egypt's.

Growing dissatisfaction over King Saud's conduct of policy, domestic and foreign, led to efforts within the royal family to limit his power and to enhance the power of Crown Prince Faisal, acting as prime minister. These efforts bore fruit in 1958. The emergence of Faisal as the primary decision maker signaled what was to become an important shift in the foreign policy posture of Saudi Arabia.

Under Faisal's influence, King Saud became increasingly cool toward Cairo and increasingly cordial toward Iraq and Jordan. Encouraged by the U.S., which feared growing Soviet influence in the area, Saudi Arabia ceased its attempted destabilization of Jordan and Iraq. This is the same period in which the Eisenhower Doctrine was pronounced, offering and guaranteeing necessary aid to any Middle Eastern State suffering foreign aggression. King Saud endorsed this declaration after a state visit to the United States. Any pretext of nonalignment or neutrality was demolished.

Crown Prince Faisal proved to be an effective leader. His domestic reforms quickly restored fiscal stability to the kingdom. His foreign policy was more nonaligned and neutral, a foreign policy informed more by Saudi self-interest than international alliance politics. Substantial domestic policy gains were scored, all of which contributed to a recovery of Saudi prestige in the Middle East. Relations with Cairo became formal and correct, but not warm. Soon, the two countries would enter into protracted hostilities in Yemen.

Faisal's initial period of rule was challenged by dissident elements in the ruling family. These elements persuaded King Saud to place certain policy demands on Faisal which he was unwilling to accept. Faisal resigned and was replaced by a candidate from the dissident ranks. The new prime minister, Prince Talal, fell victim to jealous intrigues himself, some eight months after his rise to power. From 1962 to 1964, Crown Prince Faisal gradually reacquired his lost power and gained more, until he became the virtual ruler and Saud became a figurehead. This situation was finally resolved in November 1964 when Saud was deposed and Faisal made king. Saud died in exile in 1969.

King Faisal continued the close relationship between the United States and

Saudi Arabia, but for different reasons. Between 1964 and 1975, Faisal became increasingly bewildered and irritated by the United States' unconditional support of Israel. This developing tension between the two countries did not suffice to reorient Saudi policy toward the revolutionary Arab states or the Soviet Union. But it was undoubtedly instrumental in Faisal's decision to participate in the Arab oil embargo immediately after the 1973 Arab-Israeli war. This embargo, which shook the American economy, was indicative of a new Saudi attitude toward the U.S. and the U.S.S.R., an attitude that did not find substantial moral differences between the two antagonists. Saudi Arabia thus moved into Phase III of its foreign policy. In this phase relations were based more and more on the grounds of pragmatism and national interest. Thus, although Saudi Arabia participated fully in the 1973 oil embargo, it continued to have close economic and military relations with the United States. And Saudi Arabia, under Faisal and his successor, Khalid, attempted to substantially improve its independent military strength through the purchase of sophisticated armaments and training from the United States and elsewhere. In 1980–81, the Saudis sought to significantly upgrade their tactical air capabilities and to purchase sophisticated U.S. radar planes (AWACS). Israeli opposition to such transfers was vehement.

The assassination of Faisal in March, 1975, by a minor member of the royal family, ended the administration of this remarkable leader. He was succeeded in office by King Khalid. The transition was smooth and involved minimal administrative disruption. Of some importance from an elite perspective was the continued influence of Prince Fahd, whose influence on Saudi government continued unabated from the reign of King Faisal through the reign of King Khalid. Under Khalid, Fahd would assume even more direct control over the conduct of foreign policy.

Between 1978 and 1980, Saudi Arabia became even more disillusioned with U.S. policy in the Middle East. Saudi spokesmen such as Prince Fahd and Sheikh Yamani were openly critical of U.S. policy. In their view, a quid pro quo between the United States and Saudi Arabia developed shortly after the 1973 oil embargo. This agreement required Saudi Arabia to increase its oil production and oppose extreme price increases by the militant members of OPEC and OAPEC. In return, the United States committed itself to an even-handed Middle Eastern policy; it agreed to sell sophisticated military technology to Saudi Arabia and Egypt and pressured Israel to return the occupied territories and settle the Palestinian question. In the Saudi view, they were faithful to their part of the bargain, while the U.S. dragged its heels on armament sales and failed to bring the Begin government to implement the Camp David agreements regarding Palestinian autonomy.

The Saudi complaints have substance, but in fairness the Saudi elite probably overestimated the independence of the American president in the conduct of foreign policy. Israeli support in Congress was very strong, and the presidential election of 1980 made such a Middle Eastern policy a political liability of the first order. The August, 1980, Israeli proclamation of Jerusalem as the undivided capital of Israel brought a harsh response from King Khalid, who proposed a jihad against Israel.

What is clear, however, is that in the past twenty years Saudi Arabia has changed from being a grateful ally of the United States to a country pursuing its self-interest based on its growing financial and economic power. More and more, the elites of Saudi Arabia have turned away from dependent international alliances and toward independent national pragmatism. The events of 1979–1980 in Iran did much to undermine Saudi confidence in the ability of the U.S. to protect the Saudi monarchy and Saudi territory. Saudi Arabia can be expected to pursue even more independent foreign policy in the coming years, years that will see growing internal pressure on the Saudi elite. These internal pressures, combined with the potent forces of revolutionary Islam in the contemporary Middle East, could thrust Saudi Arabia into domestic and international conflicts.

As Saudi confidence in the ability of the U.S. to determine the outcome of Middle Eastern events waned, it became increasingly paternalistic toward its Persian Gulf neighbors, the U.A.E., Qatar, Bahrain, Kuwait, and Oman. Saudi Arabia saw these states as part of her defense perimeter and thus sought closer relationships. For the most part, these efforts proved successful, although the increasingly radical posture of Kuwait was worrisome to Saudi decision makers. An uneasy tension existed along the Gulf axis with Iran, especially given Khomeini's support of the Shiite minorities there. Oman became a primary focus of U.S. attempts to improve its position on the Gulf and the Straits of Hormuz; it also improved the scope and quality of its international relations with Saudi Arabia. Saudi Arabia has intervened in North Yemen whenever necessary since 1962, and there are no signs that this concern for Yemeni stability will abate, especially given the pressure on North Yemen from her Marxist adversary to the south. Saudi Arabia has taken the initiative in all of these relationships. As she asserts a greater degree of independence from the United States, it stands to reason that she will become even more aggressive.

Events in Afghanistan in 1979–1980 brought a heightened awareness of Soviet power in Western Asia. This new awareness produced cooperation from old adversaries. Iraq and Saudi Arabia, for example, tried to frustrate the Soviet-sponsored war of national liberation that was launched against Oman from South Yemen, and agreed finally to divide the "neutral zone" between them, a longstanding source of conflict. Healthy fear of Soviet penetration in the area had produced "discussions" between the conservative states of the Middle East and all but the most radical revolutionary states. Saudi Arabia was deeply involved in these developments.

Because of her perceived vulnerability in the emerging international order in the Middle East and because of its unique role in the defense of Islam, Saudi Arabia has become a center of pan-Islamic activity. Many conferences have been held in the past decade in Saudi Arabia that embrace a variety of questions confronting the Islamic world. Conferences on Islamic banking and finance, Islamic law, and economic development have been held in Riyadh, Mecca, Taif, and Dharan. In these conferences, the weight and prestige of the Saudi government have been prominent. The emergence of revivalist Islam as a potent force in the Middle East may have presented the Saudi elite with a counter-strategy against the revolutionary secular governments of the region. These possibilities and implications will be explored in the concluding chapter.

Iranian Foreign Policy

Iran's geopolitical position in the Middle East has always assured it of a central role in the international relations of the region and the world. Unfortunately, this has not always worked to its advantage. It has frequently been involved in the ambitious plans of stronger nations. In the nineteenth and twentieth centuries, Russia attempted to extend its influence in Iran or gain control over Iranian territory. Britain, the Ottoman Empire, and Germany tried to frustrate any Russian gains. These international pressures have been compounded by the complicated domestic makeup of Iran, composed as it is of many diverse cultures and nations. The Persian-Shiite core of Iran is surrounded by large concentrations of Kurds, Armenians, Baluchis, Turks, and Arabs, all of which nurture dreams of relative autonomy or independence. This makes for a political system of great complexity and potential conflict, inviting foreign intervention.

The rise to power of Shah Mohammed Reza Pahlevi in 1941 indicates the degree to which Iranian domestic politics have been influenced by international relations. The Shah came to power after his father, Reza Shah, was forced to abdicate by a combination of Soviet and British pressure. In deference to the pro-German sympathies of Iran's ruling class Reza Shah had tried to keep Iran neutral in World War II. Soviet and British leaders would have none of this, of course, and demanded his abdication.

The reorientation of Iran from neutrality to alliance with the West was accomplished during the war. A definite policy of pro-Western and anti-Soviet international relations was pursued deliberately by the Shah from that time on, often causing domestic opposition to the policy. The period of stress and disorder from 1951 to 1953, engendered by Premier Mossadegh's attempts to nationalize British oil holdings, is an example of the domestic opposition to the Shah's foreign policy.

From the immediate postwar period through the 1970s, the Shah of Iran pursued a foreign policy predicated on close, even intimate, relations with the United States, rabid anticommunism, and the systematic expansion of Iranian military power. The Shah envisioned Iran as the dominant political and military force in the Middle East that would police an area of growing economic and strategic importance. Associated with these goals were the recovery of Persian greatness and the transformation of Iran into a modern, industrial complex ruled by a beneficial monarchy. The petroleum reserves of Iran made such grandiose ambitions distinctly possible. Iran's sharing of a boundary with an increasingly powerful Soviet Union added the necessary note of urgency.

Iranian relations with the United States were not a one-way street. The United States played an important role in the Shah's return to Iran in 1953. Subsequent American aid under the Eisenhower administration, aid denied to Premier Mossadegh during his brief stay in power, helped stabilize the Shah's power. Shortly after this consolidation, American oil companies successfully negotiated entry to the Iranian oil concessions. The "love affair" between the Shah and the United

States was definitely reciprocal. A charter member of the Baghdad Pact, Iran was a major success in American strategy among the northern tier nations. Substantial aid and trade followed. Relations with the Soviet Union, already cool, cooled further.

The 1958 revolution in Iraq signaled the onset of strained relations between Iraq and Iran. The border became the scene of tension and frequent armed hostilities. The Kurdish minorities were exploited by each side in their attempts to embarrass or occupy the attention of the other. As the revolution in Iraq moved into its Baathist phase in 1963, relations became even more strained. Conflicting claims over the territory at the Shatt al-Arab of the Persian Gulf aggravated an already unfriendly relationship, as did the safety of Iranian pilgrims in southern Iraq. Both sides viewed each other's military growth with alarm. With the Soviet Union supplying arms and materiel to Iraq, and the United States fulfilling a similar role for Iran, the bipolar confrontation manifested itself in the regional politics of the Middle East.

Iranian relations with the United States were not unduly complicated by the Arab-Israeli conflict, at least not to the degree seen in the foreign policies of Egypt and Saudi Arabia. As a Persian rather than Arab nation, Iran did not share the rabid anti-Israeli sentiments of its neighbors, particularly Syria and Iraq. In fact, during most of the Shah's reign, Iranian relations with Israel were cordial and constructive, with Iranian oil fueling much of the Israeli economy. Cooperation also existed in other spheres, with both countries exchanging espionage and police technology. Iran, alone among Middle Eastern oil producers, declined to participate in the Arab oil embargo of 1973-1974 and continued to sell oil to the U.S. and Israel.

During Phase II, the Shah committed Iran to a series of major reforms that he called the White Revolution. These reforms were in part prompted by the international course charted earlier. Growing Iranian military and economic power necessitated a skilled population capable of managing the complicated machines of war and production. Predictably, the changes attendant on the White Revolution produced strains and tensions in Iran. These tensions, which included the growing alienation of the landed gentry from the Shah, the outrage of the Shiite ulema over the secular thrust of the reforms, and the political frustration of groups wanting social and economic modernization, prompted increased political repression. The instrument of this political repression was SAVAK, the Iranian secret police. SAVAK became a nightmarish fact of life in Iran, presiding over a pervasive network of spies and informants, utilizing the latest in surveillance and interrogation techniques. Widely recognized in Iran as a client of the U.S. Central Intelligence Agency and the Israeli Mossad, SAVAK killed tens of thousands of Iranians and tortured and mutilated many, many more. SAVAK became increasingly linked in the public mind with the Shah and the United States. These factors combined with other political forces to bring the revolution of 1978. Before the final act was played out, however, the Shah managed to acquire one of the largest military machines in the world.

It would be simplistic and incorrect to portray the Shah of Iran as a mere puppet of U.S. interests. Toward the end of his rule, particularly after the success of OPEC greatly increased Iran's oil revenues, the Shah pursued policies sometimes at odds with the United States. This is particularly evident where oil pricing was concerned. In this policy area the Shah pursued a course best described as militant, arguing for massive increases in the royalties paid the producing countries. The Shah was very aware of the limited nature of Iran's petroleum reserves and wished to use the remaining production to build a post-petroleum economy. Needless to say, the dramatic increases in petroleum prices he advocated were not perceived as in the U.S. interest, or in the interests of its European and Japanese allies. The Shah pursued the price increases vigorously, in spite of American discomfort and pressure. In point of fact, the Shah was one of the earliest supporters of OPEC and thus played a key role in ushering in the third phase of post-World-War-II international relations in the Middle East. The Shah, even given the most conservative assumptions about his rule, contributed greatly to the changing face of Middle Eastern politics.

In Phase III diplomacy, the foreign policy of Iran was increasingly influenced by domestic politics. After 1975, rising domestic opposition to the Shah's regime and to SAVAK repression prompted the Shah to pursue even more drastic measures to control his opposition. Many of the opposition were exiled or fled to Iraq, whose government lent support and a podium for verbal attacks. The success of these attacks contributed materially to the ultimate decline of the Shah's national prestige.

In this phase of its foreign policy, Iran became even more involved in the politics of the states neighboring the Persian Gulf. Iran sought close and amicable relationships with the smaller states of the Gulf as well as with Saudi Arabia. Iranian troops occupied three small islands near the Straits of Hormuz in 1971, thus giving it potential control over traffic in and out of the Gulf. When a Marxist-backed rebellion threatened the security of Sultan Qabus of Oman, Iranian troops were dispatched to Oman to help suppress it. All in all, from 1972 to 1978, Iran enjoyed something approaching a military hegemony in the Persian Gulf. This was the high point of Iran's international power and influence.

Nineteen seventy-eight saw the effective consolidation of the Shah's opposition, leading to a virtual state of anarchy in Iran's cities. On January 16, 1979, the Shah left Iran with his family. He would not return. Iran, under its revolutionary Islamic leaders, would enter a new age of Iranian diplomacy and foreign policy.

The Foreign Policy of the Iranian Revolution. Iranian foreign policy under Ayatollah Khomeini was nearly diametrically opposed to that of the Shah. The United States, instead of being seen as a steady and respected ally, became the personification of imperialism and decadence, rivaled only by the Soviet Union. The foreign policy of Iran was to be based on the principles of Shiite Islam, not the interests of Persian nationalism. Iranian ideology reflected an imperfect combination of Islamic social and political thought with the drives for political independence and nonalignment characteristic of Phase III developments in the region. Compounded by the irregular and intermittent leadership of Ayatollah Khomeini, it is no surprise that Iranian foreign policy would appear to its detractors as a mishmash of contradictory impulses and goals.

A low point in U.S.-Iranian relations occurred with the seizure of the U.S. embassy and the taking of its employees as hostages on November 4, 1979. The degree of complicity between the government and the students who seized the embassy was unknown, but the seizure was triggered when the United States admitted the Shah for medical treatment. Many in Iran believed that the United States, so instrumental in returning him to power once before, would attempt to do so again. The seizure of the embassy was seen by these groups as one way to forestall such an effort.

The seizure and continued holding of the hostages was contrary to international law in both its symbolic and pragmatic dimensions. Negotiation proved fruitless, especially as the Iranian regime connected the future of the hostages with the return of the Shah by the United States for trial. Traditional U.S. contacts with the Iranian elite had been obliterated by the revolution. In April, 1980, the United States attempted a military rescue of the hostages, but it failed. More and more, the situation began to resemble a classic no-win situation for both sides. The international prestige and patience of the United States were severely tested by the seizure. Iran suffered from the U.S.-imposed and inspired economic sanctions initiated in early 1980. The resolution of the conflict came in January, 1981, on the day of the inauguration of President Reagan, and some fifteen months after the hostages had been seized. Although both sides attempted to portray the outcome as a great victory, more sober judgments prevailed. As ABC correspondent Pierre Salinger concluded after his exhaustive analysis of the negotiations, it may have been a victory for the human spirit of the hostages, themselves; it was not a victory for the United States. Nor was it a victory for Iran. Both sides lost considerable prestige and influence in the exchange.

Although the hostage situation held the spotlight for most of 1980, other shifts in Iranian foreign policy could be observed. First, Iran became one of the rejectionist states in the Arab-Israeli conflict. Yasir Arafat met with Khomeini shortly after the latter's return to Iran in 1979, and the two pledged to work together for the liberation of the occupied territories and for Palestinian independence. The Israeli mission was turned over to the PLO.

Relations with Iraq did not improve. Armed hostilities along the joint border occurred in 1980 and continued in 1981. The Iranian government under President Bani-Sadr accused the Iraqis of fomenting discontent and revolution among the Iranian Kurds and Khuzistan Arabs. For its part, the government of Iraq viewed the antigovernment pronouncements of Ayatollah Khomeini as hostile and provocative. Iraq, the majority of its population being Shiite Muslims, was a logical focus for the next step in the Islamic revolution, as was southern Lebanon, another area of Iraqi concern. Saudi Arabia, with its Shiite population concentrated in its eastern oil fields, holds a similar posture toward Iran. For its part, Iran regards the Saudi leadership as hopelessly corrupt and venal.

The Soviet Union, while obviously enjoying the United States' predicament in Iran, was unable to capitalize on the Iranian revolution. Virulently anticommunist, the Iranian revolutionary elite was in domestic conflict with pro-Soviet elements, particularly in the cities and the oil fields near Abadan. As a consequence, Iran did little to reverse the Shah's anti-Soviet foreign policy. The Soviet Union, with large populations of Muslims bordering on Iran, contemplated the disorder in Iran with apprehension. The Soviet invasion of Afghanistan, in 1980, brought Soviet-Iranian relations to their lowest point since the fall of the Shah.

Iranian influence in the foreign relations of the Middle East are best thought of in moral and symbolic terms. The Islamic revolution in Iran, with its Islamic constitution and its stress on Islamic sources of social, economic, and political policy, is a dramatic demonstration of the revolutionary potential of Islam in the contemporary world. Coming as it did, during widespread disenchantment with the politics of bipolar confrontation, the Iranian revolution spoke to the ability of peoples in the Middle East to organize domestic and international politics on their own terms, in their own way. In short, the Iranian revolution demonstrated that minor players could seize the international initiative. This realization may have momentous consequences for the international system.

Israeli Foreign Policy

More than any other Middle Eastern state, Israel was formed in the crucible of international relations. The difficulties that afflicted the Jewish community in Europe in the early twentieth century produced the international Zionist movement. This diverse group of Europeans was able, against heavy odds, to establish a Jewish state in the Middle East. In the Zionist view, this state symbolized a return to the historical site of their religion and civilization. In the view of the Palestinians living there at the time, the state symbolized an aggressive invasion of their homeland by European colonists. Neither side perceived a middle ground between these two positions. Consequently, Israel's foreign policy is also its domestic policy. Domestic security in Israel has always been a function of her international position.

During Phase I of Middle Eastern diplomacy, the leaders of Israel were concerned with the physical establishment of the state. To accomplish this, they resorted to a variety of international efforts, legal and illegal. Above all, they sought international approval for their efforts, both unilaterally and bilaterally. In this they were successful, much more so than their Arab opponents. Unanimous great-power recognition of the state of Israel came virtually upon the announcement of sovereignty. The fledgling United Nations provided the necessary diplomatic midwifery. All of this, of course, occurred in the immediate context of Arab diplomatic and military opposition.

Support in the United States for the young Israeli state was widespread. In addition to formal U.S. aid, Israel received great infusions of financial and political aid from the American Jewish community. This private aid proved to be critical for Israel. Support for Israel assumed a mantle of inviolability in the U.S., particularly in election years. Opposition to increasing support for Israel was characterized as anti-Semitic or baldly fascistic. To say the least, Arab prestige was not high.

During Phase II, Israeli foreign policy was linked tightly to its domestic policy. Domestic development depended on safe and secure boundaries; domestic development would help provide those same boundaries. In this stage of Israeli policy, the governments of Israel sought to capitalize on their diplomatic advantages over their Arab neighbors. Thus, Israel moved enthusiastically and fully into the bipolar alliance structure of the postwar period. American arms and aid flowed freely into Israel from its founding until Phase III diplomacy necessitated an American reappraisal of the relationship.

In its relations with its Arab neighbors, Israel pursued a carrot-and-stick policy. The carrot in the relationship was the supposed benefit of bilateral negotiations with Israel—the carrot ultimately nibbled by Sadat at Camp David. The stick was Israel's undisputed military superiority. The statement that the best defense is a good offense was put into practice by Israel in the Suez War of 1956 and the 1967 war. In both instances, Israeli first strikes initiated the armed conflict. In addition, smaller Israeli military groups operated as necessary in the surrounding countries.

Although the Israeli military exercises were impressive for both their speed and effectiveness, the price was high. During this period, military superiority and preparedness began to take a higher and higher toll on the Israeli economy. This toll was reflected both in increasing levels of inflation and in the economic losses connected with the full mobilization of the Israeli military. Israel, possessing a small population, found it more and more difficult to sustain full military mobilization and a thriving economy simultaneously.

Repeated confrontations with Israeli military superiority made the Arab states reluctant to battle with Israel. Instead, the Arab states chose a strategy of diplomatic confrontation and isolation, a strategy that began to pay off first in the United Nations. The 1967 conflict, in which Israel occupied the West Bank and Golan Heights, produced U.N. Resolution 242, calling for the full restoration of those areas. Israel found itself increasingly isolated in the United Nations and relied more and more upon friendly vetoes from the United States. World public opinion began to turn and resulted in a repolarization of attitudes toward Israel.

This period of Middle Eastern history also saw the beginning of Palestinian organized terrorist activity against Israel. This activity was not confined to Israeli territory; it included many harassment actions such as hijacking commercial airliners, and horrifying acts such as the seizure and murder of Israeli athletes at the Munich Olympics in 1972. Israeli reprisals included assassination squads sent into Beirut, the machinegunning of Arab villagers ignorant of a newly imposed curfew, and the shooting down of a Libyan commercial airliner that strayed over Israeli air space.

By the mid 1970s world opinion had shifted markedly to a pro-Palestinian, anti-Israeli direction. In 1975, the U.N. General Assembly adopted a resolution condemning Zionism as a form of racism. Semiofficial "observer" status was extended to the PLO. Israel's treatment of imprisoned Palestinian Arabs was condemned by Amnesty International, and a similarly critical U.S. State Department report surfaced in the mass media. Israeli prestige, initially created and supported by the larger world community and the U.N., was now on the defensive in the same forums.

The same set of circumstances that ushered in Phase III diplomacy and resulted in a heightening of Arab prestige also signaled the growing diplomatic isolation of Israel. During this period, Israel became more and more protective of her special relationship with the United States. Simultaneously, the Nixon, Ford and Carter administrations became more even-handed toward the Middle East. The result was an inevitable and growing political strain between Washington and Tel Aviv. The United States, more and more dependent on Middle Eastern petroleum production, found unyielding support for Israel increasingly expensive.

The Camp David agreements of 1977 demonstrate one dramatic attempt to reconcile the security needs of Israel with the economic problems confronting the United States. The first section of the agreements, implementing a bilateral disengagement between Egypt and Israel, proceeded smoothly; section two, which would have established Palestinian "autonomy" on the West Bank and Gaza, made little progress. Prime Minister Begin, after the implementation of section one of the accords, began a policy of new Jewish settlement, a process referred to as "settlement thickening." Israel was determined to maintain an effective presence in the West Bank, regardless of what Palestinian autonomy entailed.

The inability of Egypt and Israel to make progress on section two of the accords was aggravated symbolically by the Knesset's decision in 1980 to make Jerusalem the undivided capital of Israel. Arab reaction was predictably strong to this action. As we have seen, King Khalid called for jihad to bring Jerusalem back under Arab control. Coming as it did from a leader who has cultivated an image of restraint and control, such a call was indeed a sign of the growing Arab irritation over the expansionist policies of the Begin government. The Palestinian Liberation Organization fueled these flames of discontent by increasing its terrorist raids against Israel. Israel responded with air strikes, commando raids, and a tightening of security precautions, all of which served to heighten the sense of urgency among the Arab states.

The Israeli elections of June 1981 injected yet another note of uncertainty into Middle Eastern politics. The elections were called after the Begin government found it increasingly difficult to control its parliamentary coalition. At the onset of the campaign, the Labor party enjoyed a healthy lead, at least as reported in national polls, but by the end of the campaign the Labor and Likud parties were in a virtual dead-heat. This turn of events was at least partially attributable to the prevailing atmosphere of international confrontation.

Two major conflicts dominated the period prior to the elections. The first involved Israeli expansion of its role and activity in Lebanon, including stepped up counter-Palestinian raids in southern Lebanon, air surveillance of virtually all of Lebanon, and strong financial and military support for right-wing Christian paramilitary groups. Syrian action involved increased pressure on the Christian units, particularly to the east of Beirut, and the introduction of a large number of Soviet supplied SAM antiaircraft missiles into eastern Lebanon and the Bekaa Valley. Prime Minister Begin vowed to remove the missles by force if Syria failed to withdraw them. A nasty diplomatic confrontration between Syria and Israel emerged. It is difficult and perhaps meaningless to try to determine the sequence of events that led to this confrontation. What is important is to recognize the seriousness of both sides in the conflict and its potential for widening the Arab-Israeli conflict. U.S. shuttle diplomacy, utilizing the talents of retired State Department official Philip Habib, focused on keeping the confrontation contained and resolved, using international diplomatic pressure. In this, Habib was at least partially successful.

The second, and much more dramatic, international action involved the Israeli raid on Iraq's nuclear reactor complex (OSIRAK) near Baghdad. The raid, using American built F-15 and F-16 fighters, succeeded in knocking out the reactor in what must be described as a flawlessly executed exercise. World opinion near-unanimously condemned the raid and the U.N. formally condemned Israel for the raid and asked for compensation to Iraq. Significantly, the U.N. resolution condemning Israel was a joint product of the U.S./Iraqi delegations to the United Nations, a collaboration unthinkable a decade earlier. Many saw in this reaction an increasing international isolation of Israel and growing resolve in Prime Minister Begin to go it alone, regardless of the consequences. For his part, Prime Minister Begin characterized the attack as defensive in nature, given the reactor's ability to produce weapon's grade plutonium, and argued that the raid was a moral imperative to avoid another Holocaust.

Controversy over these two actions—the confrontation with Syria and the raid on Iraq—polarized Israeli politics more than at any time in its political history. Many backed Begin for his firm handling of the Arab danger, and as many criticized him for unnecessary reliance on military action where diplomacy might have been successful. The virtual dead-heat between Labor and Likud doubtlessly found much of its cause in the internal division. The resulting fragile coalition majority for Begin will doubtlessly serve to limit initiative in Israeli international diplomacy, at least until new elections are held. And U.S./Israeli relations were again subjected to serious strain.

For its part, the U.S. substantially expanded its military and economic relationships with the Arab states, particularly Egypt, Saudi Arabia, and the Gulf emirates. Israel became deeply disillusioned when the United States delivered high-technology weapons systems to some of these Arab states. Consequently, Phase III Israeli diplomacy moved in an independent direction. Both Israel and its Arab opponents found their foreign policies predicated on pragmatic self-interest.

CONCLUSIONS

In the years since the end of World War II, the Middle East has been the scene of intense international exchange. The forces of great-power interests, emerging national self-interest, international economic interdependence, secular and Islamic revolutions, have changed the international relations of the Middle East. No longer reacting primarily to the bipolar strategies of the United States and the Soviet Union, the Middle Eastern states themselves now initiate international moves to which the great powers must respond. Pragmatic self-interest pervaded the policy atmosphere of Phase III diplomacy. This attitudinal change, together with the real financial power of the petroleum-rich Arab states, signaled the emergence of the Middle East as one of the several independent power centers that make up the multipolar world.

Future conflicts in this multipolar world will be settled by the principals involved and not by superpowers' consensus. Since the Middle East retains many points of open conflict, the potential for violence in the region remains high. Future scenarios of international relations, complicated by the introduction of nuclear weaponry into the area, persistently describe the Middle East as a tinderbox that is capable of setting off worldwide hostilities.

The resolution of the Palestinian question would release the Middle East from one of its worst conflicts. It might also prompt Arab states to fall back into the regional conflicts that were simply ignored during the confrontation with Israel. However this works out, the Arab states will be responsible and accountable for their own actions internationally. The same mechanisms that brought Israeli prestige from its height to its contemporary nadir can work against the Arab states as well. International power confers both independence and accountability. In a nuclear age, we can only hope that responsibility accompanies the exhilaration of power.

The assassination of President Sadat on October 6, 1981, served to emphasize the degree to which the U.S. and Israel had predicated their policies on the particulars of Egyptian policy. They, most of all, found themselves in the process of agonizing reappraisal of their foreign policies. In the main, these reappraisals centered on the question of whether or not the policies of Sadat would survive his administration or would fall victim to the new political realities likely to follow. The immediate assurances by vice-president Mubarak were comforting, but could not prevent the inevitable reassessment. The absence of Arab heads of state at Sadat's funeral emphasized the isolation of Egypt in the Arab world.

For the U.S., a number of interrelated policies were affected. For one thing, the highly touted Rapid Deployment Force, a creature of both the Carter and Reagan administration, designed to deliver effective force to the Persian Gulf in the event of threats to oil production there, was logistically hostage to Egyptian cooperation, particularly at Ras Banas on the Red Sea. For another, Congressional opposition to the sale of sophisticated AWACs radar planes to Saudi Arabia had been fierce and the events in Egypt firmed many Senators in their conviction that the U.S. should avoid such sales. Other senators, citing the possible difficulties with the Rapid Deployment Force, claimed greater urgency for the sale. Finally, fears were raised that the final implementation of Section I of the Camp David accord would be jeopardized by either Egyptian reluctance or Israeli mistrust.

For its part, the government of Israel found itself uncomfortably close to the deadline for the return of the last Sinai territory, territory with significant military installations and Israeli settlements. The specter of a newly hostile Egyptian government sitting once again on its exposed southern flank was understandably unsettling to a recently elected government with a razor-thin parliamentary coalition, and of course, the whole question of Palestinian autonomy had yet to be resolved.

For both the U.S. and Israel, the events in Egypt underlie the degree in which their diplomatic and military policies in the area had been dependent on Egyptian good will. In the aftermath, one can only hope that both parties will realize the necessity of broader involvement with the full range of Middle Eastern governments —a development that simply must be based on a just and lasting solution to the Palestinian problem.

12
The Islamic Revival
and the
Islamic Republic

Throughout this book we have emphasized the relationship between contemporary political conflicts and the historical and cultural settings that influence them. We have seen that various factors conditioned political encounters—factors such as geography, ethnic concentrations, economics, and Islam. Islam, a religion of radical universalism, has influenced all the countries in the contemporary Middle East. For all that, however, Islam has manifested itself in a number of ways over time, some of them apparently contradictory, some complementary, and others simply coexistent. Now, in the 1980s, new or newly militant movements in Islam are apparent.

The phenomenon to which we refer has been variously labeled "the Islamic revival," "the Islamic renaissance," "Islamic fundamentalism" "the Islamic revolution": and indeed, it is all of these things, and more. "Islamic modernists" contend intellectually with "Islamic conservatives." Some definition of terms is necessary here. By "Islamic revival," we refer to those individuals and movements that want to strengthen Islamic influences in political, economic, and social life. "Islamic fundamentalism," on the other hand, refers more specifically to individuals or groups that wish to see a return to what they perceive as a lost purity in religious practice which often entails the reimposition of the Sharia and Koranic education. "Islamic modernists," in contrast, believe that Islam can be adapted to the circumstances of modern life without losing the fundamental truths of Islam. In opposition to the fundamentalists who see the Koran as a strict and unvarying prescription for righteous behavior, modernists wish to preserve the spirit and intent of Islam in the modern context. "Islamic conservatives" generally wish to see little or no change from current practice, a position rejected by both fundamentalists and modernists. "Islamic renaissance" is a term that can be claimed by any or all of the preceding groups and denotes a rebirth of Islamic influence, albeit in a wide variety of forms, just as "Islamic revolution" entails the implementation of religious belief in political life. Many of these terms are not mutually exclusive. For example, it is possible to be an Islamic modernist committed to the Islamic renaissance. And it is equally possible for an Islamic fundamentalist to be a proponent of the Islamic revival, and in fact he usually is. We will refer to all these phenomena hereafter as the Islamic revival, emphasizing that the term is both exceedingly general and includes a variety of movements and philosophies. The Islamic revival is real and pervasive and raises challenges to most forms of constituted authority, whether modern bureaucratic, traditional, charismatic, democratic, or authoritarian. It is an orientation toward life that in the words of Ayatollah Khomeini desires "Islam, nothing but Islam, only Islam." Many groups fundamentally disagree on what this formula means.

THE ISLAMIC REVIVAL

The Islamic revival movement has some unusual characteristics. First and foremost, the movement appears to be a mass movement. It did not originate in the universities, mosque-institutes, or among the higher ulema. There has always existed a tension between Islam as it was explicated and elaborated in theology and philosophy and Islam as it was practiced at the "grass-roots" level by the pious but untutored masses. To some degree, Sufism and cults of local saints represent the popular side in the equation. Quite often Islam incorporated and maintained pre-Islamic and non-Islamic rites and customs. Although this was anathema to those acquainted with the "truth" of the Koran, the naïve practitioner was unaware of this conflict. This situation is not restricted to Islam, however. People who believe the wrong things for the right reasons have bedeviled all theologians and clerics throughout history.

Historically, the protectors of high, theological Islam have been associated with the state and its bureaucratic apparatus. The practitioners of folk Islam have been found outside the formal political arena—in the villages, towns, and farms, and deserts. Periodically, as in the case of the Muslim Brotherhood until its suppression, these religious feelings found political expression, but for the most part politics was the preserve of high Islam and its adherents. Now, however, fundamentalist political activity is so widespread that it must be called a movement. Virtually no country in the Islamic world is immune from such movements and their implications. Consequently, we should examine the motives behind the present Islamic revival and try to see what its political consequences are likely to be.

Contemporary Islamic fundamentalism seems to spring from a number of political and historical sources. First and foremost, the movement attempts to explain the terrible times into which the Umma has fallen: the subjection of Islam to foreign and then secular control; the apparent falling away from simple pious faith, particularly among the urban intelligentsia and ruling elites; the Western technological challenge to time-honored social conventions; the fall of Arab and Islamic influence to an all-time low. All this can be explained as the consequence of turning away from the true and uncorrupted revelation of Islam. Implicit in the movement, then, is the expectation that a return to Islamic purity will restore the Umma to its rightful place on earth and bring Allah's beneficence once again to his people.

This assertion of the potential role of resurgent Islam in restoring the Umma occurs in what some would call an ideological vacuum. None of the successful Middle Eastern political movements of the twentieth century was sparked by a coherent ideology. The Egyptian revolution, for instance, first seized power and only later turned its attention to the problem of program or justification. Baathism, despite its origin among Levantine intellectuals, has never clearly specified what sort of society it was trying to mold. Similar criticisms could be made of the Shah's White Revolution in Iran or the Turkish revolution under Atatürk. They did have this in common, however: they all treated Islam secularly, excluding it from the specifics of their ideology and policy. In so doing they denied one aspect of Islam that most sustained the pious masses—the unity of Islam as a system of belief and practice. Thus, in religious terms, the Islamic revival occurs in an environment in which the predominant political and social ideologies of the day have specifically and deliberately not addressed themselves to the problems of the pious and faithful and thus are inherently unsatisfying or inappropriate. Thus, a major force for legitimation has gone unused.

In addition, the modernization programs of these secular regimes were even further removed from the concept of Islamic unity than were their respective ideologies. Modernization in the Middle East in the 1960s and 1970s became increasingly a program of Westernization and technological development. In the educational systems, religious schools were replaced with secular government institutions. To its fundamentalist critics Westernization also appeared in the guise of increasingly immodest dress, profligate sexual behavior, the consumption of alcohol, and "corrupt" entertainment including motion pictures, television, pornography, and rock music. The growing wealth of many of the cities of the region magnified this image; and as the political and social elites consumed more and more of these Western products, the pious folk became more and more estranged from the elites of their societies.

The incredible growth of urban wealth, concentrated in the elites, has given rise to perceptions of a widening economic gulf between the rich and the poor. Such a gulf is particularly obnoxious to the pious Muslim who takes the Koranic injunctions regarding charity seriously. The failure of elites to support a more equitable distribution of national resources has become a rallying point of revivalist Muslim opposition demanding "social justice." In another sense, this reaction may also signify a resurgence of the radical equalitarian or democratic movements associated with Islam in its earliest forms. Either way, there is widespread dissatisfaction with the existing social structure, patterns of social relations, and most of all, the existing political authority.

These forms of "degenerate" behavior have long been connected with the European West. The argument is given strength and validity from the common memory of European colonialism. Thus, the Islamic revival often calls for the rejection and expelling of Western influences, influences logically seen as "Satanic" in origin. More and more, the proponents of an Islamic revival profess to see little difference between the social systems of the Eastern and Western blocs, a perspective of growing prominence among secular Middle Eastern leaders as well.

Groups espousing an Islamic revival have gained political power in Iran, Libya, and Pakistan. They are actively, if irregularly, advocating the inclusion of Islam in government—in short, they are trying to design an ideal Islamic Republic. Their progress has been uneven to date, and the obstacles to their programs are serious. These experiences notwithstanding, the movement gains strength in those countries ruled by traditional and modern bureaucratic elites. We will return to the problems associated with the implementation of the Islamic Republic in the concluding sections of this chapter. Let us turn now to a general survey of the Islamic revival in the major states of the region.

Revival in Egypt

The Islamic revival and Islamic fundamentalism combined early in this century in the movement known as the Muslim Brotherhood. The brotherhood's growth was based as much on its opposition to continuing foreign influence in Egypt as on its religious fundamentalism. The two combined, however, to produce a powerful movement with a substantial membership. It kept its operations secret, following a centuries-old pattern for Muslim organizations of this type. Variously in and out of favor with the Egyptian governments of this century, the brotherhood eventually ran afoul of Nasser and the Egyptian Revolution. Officially proscribed, the brotherhood went underground and exists to this day.

Many movements and trends advocating an Islamic revival or Islamic fundamentalism have developed in Egypt in the 1980s. President Sadat's increasing use of Islam as a potent symbol has greatly legitimized these movements. This has apparently encouraged the growth of groups and movements ultimately opposed to the secular government now in power. In fact, a growing minority is greatly dissatisfied with the government's inability to address successfully the problems of the economy and social justice. Sadat may be trading short-term gains for long-term liabilities.

One indication of the degree of popular dissatisfaction is the Sharia dress movement now popular among low- and middle-level government bureaucrats and university students and professors. This movement includes the substitution of more modest clothing for the provocative and seductive clothing of the West: for men, loose-fitting pants that conceal the outlines of the body, full shirts with long sleeves and high necks—all in dull colors; for women, tentlike costumes that cover the head, arms, and legs. Such clothing, while essentially Western in form, follows the Sharia injunctions against immodest dress. It also testifies to the political and religious orientation of the wearer. Dress of this sort is particularly prevalent among the older bureaucrats from the Nasser era, who feel compelled to act on what they perceive as an erosion of Nasser's commitment to social justice.

There are other signs of a growing Islamic revival in Egypt. Attendance at mosques is increasing. Merchants and bureaucrats are more likely now than before to interrupt official business for daily prayers. The government, responding to both international and domestic Muslim pressures, has prohibited the sale or consumption of alcohol except to non-Muslim foreigners. And Sadat's attempt to raise the price of bread was opposed by the masses partly because it was a sign that the government was neglecting issues of social justice.

The difficult economic circumstances of Egypt are likely to fuel the fires of Muslim fundamentalism. It is difficult to predict all the political implications of such change, but there are some probable consequences. First, it is likely that fundamentalist Islam will manifest itself in a political party, encouraged by the political liberalization programs under Sadat. It is equally likely that another Islamic modernist party may emerge, a party attempting to square the Koran and Sharia with the realities of technical life in the twentieth century. Both of these movements may emphatically reject the predominant secularism of Nasser and Sadat, and may seek to reintroduce the Sharia as the basis of law. This is likely to produce a potentially very disruptive conflict over the legitimacy and structure of the government. The Islamic parties, having gained legitimacy by participating in the representative process and by their opposition to the secular modernizing policies of the government, might launch an attack upon the modern bureaucratic assumptions that underlie the Egyptian constitution.

Revival in Saudi Arabia

As for Saudi Arabia, the problem is how to interpret an Islamic revival and Islamic fundamentalism in a state already dominated by one of the most puritanical of Islamic sects, the Wahhabis. In reality all things are relative: in Saudi Arabia, there are sufficient numbers of people relatively dissatisfied with the Wahhabi regime to oppose it on fundamentalist religious grounds. The most open challenge to Saudi political and religious authority came with the seizure of the Great Mosque in Mecca in January, 1980.

The group that seized the mosque was composed largely of Saudi Arabian tribesmen who were following a leader claiming to be the Mahdi. The force was sufficiently armed and large enough (around 100 plus their families) to resist the Saudi government's efforts to remove them for days. The government sealed off the mosque, removed as many pilgrims as possible, and then slowly dug the dissidents out, all with the support of the Saudi Arabian higher ulema. The ulema, significantly, recognized the necessity of a future Mahdi, but stressed that the Mahdi would come against a much more corrupt regime than currently existed.

The ulema's legitimizing of Saudi military action in the Great Mosque is one illustration of its role in Saudi government. The government and the ulema combine to maintain a conservative Sharia law (Hanbalite) and a conservative theocratic kingdom. Thus, although they have minor disagreements, the two forces try to maintain a fundamentalist Islamic system dedicated to Islamic revival.

The dedication to Islamic revival is very important to the Saudi elite and public. Saudi Arabia, as custodian of most of the important shrines of the Umma, has long claimed a special role in Islam. As a proponent of Muslim fundamentalism, Saudi Arabia has sought to make itself a center of international Islamic dialogue. Riyadh has been the scene of countless Islamic conferences that have been supported liberally by the Saudi government. Notable among them have been conferences on the organization and operation of Islamic banking. The yearly hajj brings to Saudi Arabia many of the religious and political elites of other countries; thus it offers diplomatic opportunities for the Saudi government to exploit. Saudi financial aid to Egypt has been explicitly tied to greater Egyptian faithfulness to Islamic injunctions, and the prohibition of alcohol under Sadat can be interpreted as a direct response to this Saudi concern.

The Saudi elite has been sensitive to the problems of its international image. Saudi reaction and opposition to the showing of a British film, *Death of a Princess*, on American television was intense. Official diplomatic complaints were lodged, asserting that the film placed Islam and Saudi justice in an inappropriate and inaccurate perspective. The film was shown in spite of this opposition. All in all, Saudi Arabia is a fundamentalist Islamic state pursuing a general Islamic revival. The forces of Islamic fundamentalism should continue to be a major element of support for the royal family.

There is one nagging problem, and that is the royal family's increasing wealth and habits of conspicuous consumption. If the perception of the royal family as dissolute and degenerate becomes widespread, the fundamentalist ulema and their followers could turn against them, as some of them did in the deposing of King Saud. The present staggering personal wealth of the royal family raises the possibility of just such a reaction. As Saudi Arabia acquires more and more modern communication systems and advanced technology, it will have to make a more effective commitment to social justice. To do otherwise will be to court disaster.

Revival in Iran

In Iran, the Islamic revival has progressed far enough to be called an Islamic revolution. The traditional leaders of Iranian Shiism now dominate the country's political, social, economic, and religious life. The enforcement of Shiite beliefs and practices in Iran may give us some insight about the implications of this movement for politics generally.

The Islamic revolution in Iran is definitely committed to fundamental Islamic practices. Social justice has been proclaimed a major priority of government policy. Sharia law has generally replaced civil law, and traditional criminal penalties have been reintroduced. Western clothing, conduct, and entertainment have been declared un-Islamic. Commerce and banking strive to conform to Koranic injunctions, particularly in the taking of interest. A new form of language, rich in its religious symbolism and its emphasis on the unity of the Islamic vision, has replaced the previous secular language of politics. This new language incorporates the historical, chiliastic imagery of Shiism with the demand for piety and anti-Western reform. It is a language confusing to Western ears.

One example that has been confusing to the Westerner has been the Iranian insistence on calling the United States the "great satan." The use of this term is derived from the Shiite commemoration of the death of the martyr Hussein at the hands of the arch-fiend, Caliph Yazid. The analogy of the U.S. for Yazid is a powerfully symbolic way of equating U.S. support for the Shah with the centuries old persecution of the Shiite faithful. Another example involves the timing of political acts to coincide with important dates in the Muslim calendar. For example, Ayatollah Khomeini introduced his new Islamic constitution at the beginning of Muharram, traditionally the month associated with the martyrdom of Hussein. Further, as the United States stepped up its pressure on Iran and moved its military might into the Indian Ocean, Khomeini expressed the Iranian opposition to any invasion in terms of the faithful's willingness to be martyred. Finally, the failure of the U.S. rescue attempt was specifically claimed as evidence of God's approval and support of the Iranian revolution. These symbols incorporate the historical Shiite experience into the contemporary political dialogue.[1]

Some ambiguity in the Iranian movement was engendered by the perceived role of Imam Khomeini, himself. Some groups openly professed that he was *the* Imam, who had returned to set things right. Others professed that he was the servant of the Imam, preparing the way for His eventual return. Still others saw him merely as a forceful, pious teacher. For his part, Khomeini occasionally rejected these claims, but not strongly enough to suit his critics. Some commentators assumed that Khomeini himself was confused on this issue; while he was supposed to interpret Allah's will, he did not clearly understand the limits of this role. At any rate, Khomeini's reputed status tapped a long-standing Shiite belief in a redeemer. It legitimized his leadership over a significant proportion of the Shiites in Iran.

There is a distinct international dimension to the Islamic revolution in Iran. The Iranian leadership, especially Khomeini, has called for Shiite populations abroad, particularly in Iraq and the states of the Persian Gulf, to rise up and throw off the corrupt rule of their corrupt oppressors. The urgency of this call was no doubt one of the several factors that prompted the Iraqi-Iranian war. Khomeini's call for revolution throughout the Umma also figured in the conservative Muslim states siding with Iraq in the conflict—states that included Saudi Arabia, Morocco, North Yemen, and the United Arab Emirates. The minority status of Shiism in the Umma and the perceived radical nature of the Iranian revolution have combined to minimize the effect of Khomeini's call to specific revolution and jihad against Israel. The call also legitimizes Sunni fundamentalist opposition, however, to oppressive, secular, or non-Islamic regimes. Thus, although the Iranian revolution probably cannot be exported, it may encourage similar developments in the populist Sunni groups of the Middle East. Khomeini and his revolution are widely admired, if not followed. Few doubt his personal piety, and many admire his activism.

Revival in Turkey

The Islamic revival in Turkey was sufficiently intense to prompt a serious political crisis in 1980. Conflict between Muslim fundamentalists, conservatives, leftists, modernists, and modernizing secularists resulted in growing levels of political violence, including assassinations and terrorist bombings. The inability of the government to deal with this internal stress and a deteriorating economy led the military to intervene in the interests of stability.

---

[1] For an extended treatment of the relationship between classic Shiism and the Iranian revolution, see Michael Fischer, *Iran: from Religious Dispute to Revolution* (Cambridge, Mass.: Harvard University Press, 1980).

Islamic revival movements in Turkey are numerous and diverse. Local and regional influences are strong, as are ethnic and historical factors. The result is a highly pluralistic system that is focused in different ways on the reassertion of Islam in political life. These groups have manifested themselves in conservative Islamic political parties and movements advocating individual piety that are suspiciously similar to earlier Sufi tariqah orders. There has been much public discussion of these hitherto "invisible" movements, particularly Shiism.

The agenda of Turkish revivalist groups is similar to those in other countries: a return to personal piety, the reestablishment of Sharia law, religious education, and a retracing of the historical roots of Islam. There is a revival of interest in the hajj, and Sufi and tariqah orders are on the upsurge, particularly in rural areas. More women (although by no means a majority) are adopting conservative religious attire.

The resurgence of Islam in Turkey has political consequences that are likely to be substantial. Resurgent Islam may well find expression in government institutions, which, in Turkey, are well established. At least, the Islamic revival in Turkey may proceed less disruptively than in its neighbor, Iran. Islam has not suffered the fate predicted by the secular modernism of Atatürk. It has reemerged as an important part of all areas of Turkish life. In a country in which secular Western values were so vigorously promoted, this must stand as testimony to the durability of Islam.

Revival in the Levant

Islamic revival movements have been less successful in Iraq, Lebanon, and Syria, but even here Islamic fundamentalist groups are more numerous and more visible than a decade earlier. The rural Shiite populations of Iraq and Lebanon, in particular, are attentive to the revolutionary message of Imam Khomeini. The area is honeycombed with the remnants of secret orders and lodges, all of which are potential partners in revolution. The tape-recorded sermons of Khomeini and other Shiite religious leaders are reportedly played surreptitiously to interested audiences. During the 1980 war with Iran, Iraq reportedly avoided sending Shiite troops into Iran for fear that they would defect. It is also claimed that the Iraqi government's fear of successful Iranian appeals to the Shiite community figured prominently in its decision to initiate the hostilities in the first place, hoping for a quick victory over an apparently disorganized Iran. In the long run, tensions between the Sunni government of Iraq and its increasingly agitated Shiite majority will probably increase. If the Iraqi regime fails to satisfy both its Sunni and Shiite populations, then religious strife is likely.

In Syria and Lebanon, the Shiite minorities are considerably smaller. Islamic revivalist movements exist in both countries but are not large enough to present serious problems. Syrian resentment toward Alawite rule embraces both the Shiite minority and the Sunni majority. Religious fundamentalism, however, while on the upswing, is at a disadvantage against Syrian nationalism and commerce, both of which at this point seem to have the upper hand. Islamic revival in Syria, then, is likely to manifest itself more in personal piety than in political opposition. On the other hand, there is evidence to suggest that the Syrian government views fundamental trends very seriously. The 1980 border tensions between Syria and Jordan were blamed on Jordanian encouragement of the Muslim Brotherhood in Syria. Although Jordan denied the allegation, and although the confrontation eventually simmered down, the fact that the movement merited public international discussion is interesting in itself.

Revival in Libya

Events in Libya are difficult to assess and describe. The efforts of Col. Muammar Qadaffi to radically reorganize Libyan society along Muslim lines suggest a strain of Muslim fundamentalism. But the leader of the Libyan revolution has substantially reinterpreted the Koran. In fact, some critics argue that Qadaffi is creating a wholly new Islam that is only disguised by the rhetoric of Islamic fundamentalism. At base, the changes in Libya are sweeping; the statements of Islamic belief mystify many observers.

In Libya, Islamic revolution proceeded from the top down. No widespread fundamentalist movement existed to demand a return to personal piety and the reinstatement of Sharia law. In fact, Qadaffi himself reinstated portions of the Sharia, but not in response to public demands. Moreover, he eliminated, modified, or liberalized many of the traditional Sharia criminal punishments. *Zakat*, or the alms tax, is now enforced by the government. Anti-Western sentiments are also prominent, and the government is trying to minimize Western influence on the Libyan population.

Qadaffi's personal leadership, however, has influenced the Islamic revival outside of Libya. He has been widely perceived in the Middle East to be a leader of integrity and personal piety, particularly by fundamentalist groups. Like Khomeini, his persistent and outspoken opposition to things Western justified his religious innovations and pronouncements. However, Qadaffi's insistence on his personal interpretation of the Koran, his rejection of custom and hadith, and his radical democratic political policies have lessened his appeal in some quarters. Like Khomeini, he is widely admired in the larger Sunni community; like Khomeini, he is not widely followed there.

THE ISLAMIC REPUBLIC

Although not nearly as pervasive as Islamic fundamentalism, a wave of concern over the design of the ideal Islamic Republic has swept over the Middle East. A Muslim government is any government by Muslims for a country largely Muslim in population. Thus, the government of Egypt, secular and modernist, is a Muslim government. An Islamic republic, by contrast, is a government of Muslims organized and operated on the basis of divine revelation of the Koran, the hadith, and the Sharia. It is the ultimate earthly manifestation of the unity of Islam. Numerous groups and governments in the Middle East are investigating the possibilities of instituting an

Islamic republic. Iran, Libya, and Pakistan are experimenting with rudimentary designs. In so doing, they have discovered quite a few difficulties in the art of state building.

One of the difficulties confronting the designers of the Islamic Republic is the lack of political discussion in the Koran. Remarkably detailed in certain aspects of revelation, the Koran says very little about government and how it should be organized. Indeed, the origin of much of the conflict in Islam can be found in the ambiguity of political order and succession. There is thus little detailed institutional guidance in the Koran for the designer of the republic.

A second difficulty involves the role of the ulema in government. Should the ulema become the government itself, as is apparently the case in the Iranian Republic? Or should it be given a secondary and supportive role, as in Saudi Arabia or Libya? Should it content itself with periodic moral opposition and avoid coopting the political process, as it has done traditionally in Muslim states? No readily ascertainable consensus exists on this subject.

Another difficulty arises over the question of modernization. There is some debate over the degree to which technological advance is necessarily a part of the Western social and political order. Some advocates of the Islamic Republic assert that Western technology can be adopted without cultural or moral contamination, and that therefore modernization can be pursued without compromising Islamic virtue. Others argue that modernization *is* Westernization and should be avoided at all costs. Iran has been willing to pay a high economic and political price for its revolution by retrenching on the Shah's technological programs. Libya has embraced modernization enthusiastically although selectively. There are doubtless other possibilities, but again there is no consensus.

On the role of the Sharia in civil law, there is some agreement. Regardless of their starting points and methodologies, the various schools of Sharia agree remarkably about what constitutes appropriate social and religious behavior. Thus, the adoption of portions of Sharia law has not been overly difficult. On the other hand, the Sharia, codified largely before the fourteenth century, does not anticipate many of the conditions of modern life. This necessitates complementary legislation and the creation of new Islamic law, presumably by an Islamic legislature operating according to the Koran. This is much easier said than done. One attempt to implement an arrangement of this sort failed in Pakistan in the 1950s due to fundamentalist outrage over such legislation. So far, the tendency has been for Islamic republics to enforce Sharia law as far as it goes, and then supplement it with selections from other civil codes governing, say, maritime or commercial law.

Theorists and practitioners of Islamic politics alike have had enormous difficulty applying the Koran to modern financial affairs. The Koranic prohibition against the taking of interest, in particular, has been troublesome. For the most part, elaborate fictions designed to obscure the reality of interest have been created—for example, dovetailed sales contracts in which a buyer (really the lender) agrees to buy an object for one price and the seller (actually the borrower) agrees to buy it back at a given date at another, higher, price. The difference between the two prices constitutes a profit, rather than the taking of interest. This unwieldy solution does not fundamentally eliminate interest from commerce, and therefore it does not satisfy thoughtful Islamic scholars.

Nationalism is another problem for the designers of the Islamic Republic. If the republic is to represent the unity of the Islamic revelation, then the particularist claims of national groups should be of no importance in the design of the system. Yet, there is no denying the importance of nationalist feeling in the twentieth-century Middle East. Theoretically, there should be *one* Islamic Republic, reflecting the unity of the Umma. Competing Islamic republics should be a contradiction in terms, a condition reflecting the fragmentation rather than the unity of the Umma. In the conflict between Iraq and Iran, Pakistani and Indonesian leaders attempted to mediate on behalf of the Umma. Saudi Arabia, Jordan, Yemen, and Morocco instead sided with Iraq as an Arab nation in confrontation with a Persian nation, thus demoting the Islamic theme to a secondary role relative to national or ethnic considerations. Libya and Syria jointly criticized Iraq for attacking another Muslim nation instead of concentrating on the greater enemy, Israel. This kind of thinking is disconcerting to the proponents of Islamic unity and Islamic government.

This list of obstacles to Islamic government could be extended indefinitely, showing that statecraft is at best a difficult and uncertain operation. This should not, however, blind us to the religious and intellectual implications of the effort, whether successful or not. Like Islamic fundamentalism or Islamic revival, the pursuit of the Islamic Republic signifies the Muslim determination to turn to their own traditions and their own ingenuity for solutions to their problems. It signifies the intent, if not the success, of turning away from the ideas, institutions, and policies of the West. Most particularly, it involves a rejection of Western secularism.

It is a truism of politics that it is easier to make a rebellion than a revolution, easier to challenge existing authority than to replace it with effective and functioning institutions. The proponents of Islamic revival, Islamic fundamentalism, and Islamic republican government have crossed the threshold from rebellion to revolution. This signifies a time of testing, experimentation, compromise, and confrontation. Above all it signifies the coming of another chance for Muslims to make their world responsive to their own needs and aspirations. It is a time for patience and for adopting the long view of history.

Political change, under most if not all circumstances, may be frightening and disconcerting. The Middle East has experienced change throughout its history. The changes seen during the rise of the West were, and continue to be, traumatic for Muslims. Now, changes in the Muslim world raise fears and anxieties in a West that is dependent on the uniform flow of petroleum from the Middle East. These fears and anxieties could lead to unwise efforts to reassert European, Soviet, or American control over the area, efforts which would be resisted bitterly. Instead, we might hope for future relations based on mutual understanding and the recognition of the circumstances of interdependence that underlie the human condition in the modern world. Such a recognition thrives on patience and good will. This hope cannot, of course, rest on the elimination of all conflict. It could, however, change the contexts in which conflicts are resolved. In our nuclear age, we cannot hope for less.

Country Profiles*

These brief sketches are designed to aid the student in gaining an overall picture of the main demographic, economic, and political characteristics of each particular country. The profiles and accompanying maps cover the Middle East in roughly a counterclockwise circle beginning with Libya and ending with Jordan.

LIBYA

(Socialist People's Libyan Arab Jamahiriya)

Area: 679,358 sq. mi.
    1,759,540 sq. km.

Population: 2,946,000 (1980E)

Per capita GNP (1977): U.S. $6,680

Major urban centers (1973C):
    TRIPOLI (551,477); BEN GHAZI
    (140,000); Misurata (103,302).

Official language: Arabic

Libya is located in North Africa, bordered by Egypt on the east, Algeria and Tunisia on the west, and sharing its southern borders with Chad, Niger, and Sudan. Most of Libya is barren desert, with the population concentrated in a narrow strip along the Mediterranean coast. Ninety percent of the people are Arabs, and nearly half the remainder are native Berbers. Sunni Islam predominates.

The economy of Libya is dominated by petroleum production. Since the 1950s when petroleum was discovered there, Libya has become one of the world's largest oil exporters. Agriculture, which produces barley, wheat, tomatoes, olives and dates, is far behind petroleum in economic importance. The development of agriculture is limited by the arid climate and by urban migration which has drained the rural areas of skilled farm labor, but the government is making efforts to promote increased production of cereals, dairy cattle, sheep, poultry, fruits, and vege-

---

*The demographic and income figures used in the country studies are taken from Banks, A. and Overstreet, W. Editors, Political Handbook of the World 1980. McGraw Hill: N.Y., 1980.

tables. A weak domestic market, uneven population distribution and lack of skilled workers have impeded the development of industry, but government programs have aimed at the development of various industries besides petroleum, including the exploitation of other mineral resources and the production of foodstuffs, textiles and building materials.

Libya was an Italian colony from 1911 until it was occupied by France and England in the Second World War. It became an independent monarchy in 1951 under Emir Muhammad Idris al-Senussi, but a 1969 military coup led by Col. Mu'ammar al-Qadaffi set up a revolutionary republic under the control of a Revolutionary Command Council. Since then the government has been reorganized several times. The constitution adopted in 1977 places the government under the nominal control of a General People's Congress assisted by a General Secretariat consisting of a General Secretary and three other members. As General Secretary, Col. Qadaffi is the head of state. The General People's Congress is made up of 618 members representing the Revolutionary Command Council, the "people's congresses," and the trade unions and professional organizations. The General People's Committee oversees administrative functions, and its chairman functions as prime minister. The judicial system includes a special People's Court to deal with administrative and political crimes.

Libya has avowed its strong commitment to the principle of Arab unity, and has made several attempts to unite with other Arab nations. Its petroleum politics and its stringent anti-Israeli stance have often brought Libya into conflict with more conservative Arab states, and relations with Egypt were cut off in response to Egyptian peace negotiations with Israel. In 1980 and 1981, Libya proposed political union respectively with Syria and Chad.

EGYPT

(Arab Republic of Egypt)

Area: 386,659 sq. mi.
1,001,449 sq. km.

Population: 45,724,000 (1980E)

Per capita GNP (1977): U.S. $310

Major urban centers (1975E):
CAIRO (5,921,000); Alexandria
(2,320,000); Giza (893,000); Suez
(381,000); Port Said (349,000).

Official language: Arabic

Located in the northeast corner of the African continent, Egypt is bordered on the west by Libya, on the south by the Sudan, and on the northeast by Israel. Egypt is an extremely arid country which depends on the Nile River for its water supply. About ninety-nine percent of the population lives along the fertile banks of the Nile, which constitutes only about five percent of the land area. Population densities in the settled regions are quite high, reaching 6,000 per square mile in the urban areas. Most Egyptians are Sunni Muslims, and the small non-Muslim population consists largely of Coptic Christians.

Traditionally the "breadbasket" of the old Muslim empires, Egypt still depends on agriculture as the foundation of its economy. Industry, particularly petroleum-related industry, is making significant advances. Farming methods are being modernized by means of mechanization, hydroelectric power, chemical fertilizers, and double cropping. Egypt's most important crops are cotton, wheat, rice, sugar, and corn; its most important industries, besides petroleum, include textiles and the processing of agricultural products. President Gamal Abdel Nasser (d. 1970) attempted to reduce foreign domination of the Egyptian economy by nationalizing financial institutions and major industries, but his successor Anwar Sadat encouraged private enterprise and foreign investment as a means of promoting economic development. One of the most difficult barriers to Egypt's economic development is its rapidly increasing population. The population increase, combined with massive rural-to-urban migration and the influx of refugees from Egypt-Israeli war zones has made urban centers like Cairo and Alexandria some of the most crowded in the world.

Egypt was granted nominal independence from Britain in 1922, but the British maintained a military force at the Suez Canal until 1956 when the canal was nationalized. The profligate King Farouk was ousted in 1952 by a coup headed by the "Free Officers" including Colonel Gamal Abdel Nasser and Colonel Anwar Sadat, and Major General Muhammad Naguib. Under the present government, executive power is held by a president nominated by the legislature and elected by popular vote to a six-year term. The president appoints vice-presidents and ministers, and he is empowered to rule by decree in the event that martial law is declared.

The People's Assembly is Egypt's unicameral legislative body. It consists of 250 members elected by popular vote for five-year terms, ten of whom must be Coptic Christians. Religious courts were abolished in Egypt in 1956, and the present judicial system is based largely on European legal concepts.

Egypt's foreign and domestic policies have been strongly influenced by hostilities with Israel, which have broken into warfare four times since Israel's formation (1948, 1956, 1967, and 1973). In addition to the disputes with the Israelis, Egypt was involved in Yemen's civil war and several serious confrontations with Libya. Relations with Israel improved as a result of the U.S.-sponsored Camp David talks leading to an Egyptian-Israeli peace treaty and the withdrawal of Israeli troops from the Sinai, but the future of this fragile peace rests on the unresolved issue of Palestinian autonomy. The peace treaty with Israel alienated Egypt from some Arab states which viewed it as an abandonment of the cause of Palestinian independence.

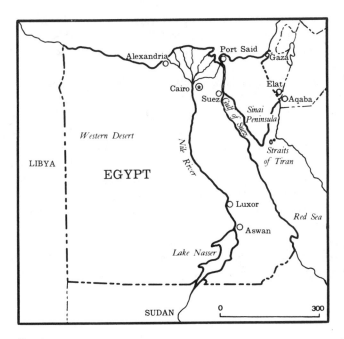

Egypt

SUDAN

(Democratic Republic of the Sudan)

Area: 967,494 sq. mi.
   2,505,813 sq. km.

Population: 17,867,000 (1980E)

Per capita GNP (1977): U.S. $300

Major urban centers (1973C):
KHARTOUM (321,666); Omdurman
(305,308); North Khartoum (161,278);
Port Sudan (123,000).

Official language: Arabic

Sudan is the largest country in Africa. It is bordered on the east by the Red Sea and Ethiopia. Working clockwise, it also shares borders with Kenya, Uganda, Zaire, the Central African Republic, Chad, Libya, and Egypt. Its outstanding geographical features are that both the White and Blue Nile transverse the country, meeting around Khartoum, and that the arid northern part of the country gives way to tropical forests in the south. Sudan's international relations in the region during the first half of the twentieth century were influenced by the fact that the Nile waters flow through it to Egypt.

Approximately seventy percent of the population lives in the north and is overwhelmingly Arab and Muslim. The southern population is largely black and adheres to tribal religions. This split has been a major concern of the government since Sudan became independent in 1956. Indeed, it was only in 1973 that a settlement was reached which ended southern insurgency by granting limited autonomy to the southern provinces.

The economy is primarily agricultural. Since both productivity and total agricultural output is relatively low, per capita income is also low. However, Sudan has only a small percentage of its arable land under cultivation. It has been estimated that the land between the White and Blue Nile could, with triple cropping and the application of modern agricultural techniques, double world foodgrain output. This has drawn the attention of the various Arab development agencies in the petroleum-rich countries and some funds have been granted to investigate whether the Sudan could indeed be the breadbasket of the Arab world.

The 1973 constitution allows for the president to be nominated by the single approved political party, the Sudanese Socialist Union, for a six-year term. The president has wide-ranging powers, including the right to appoint vice-presidents and the prime minister. The unicameral legislature is partially appointed. The Southern Region is administered by a vice-president and has considerable autonomy.

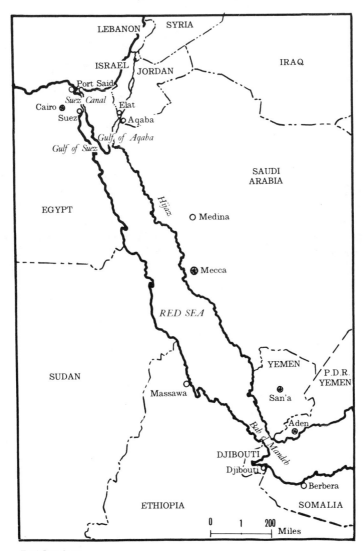

Red Sea Area

SAUDI ARABIA

(Kingdom of Saudi Arabia)

Area: 829,995 sq. mi.
2,149,690 sq. km.

Population: 7,665,000 (1980E)
(This includes
approximately 1,600,000
non-resident workers.)

Major urban centers (1975E):
RIYADH (450,000); Jiddah (375,000);
Mecca (250,000); Medina (100,000).

Official language: Arabic

Per capita GNP (1977): U.S. $4,980

Saudi Arabia is bordered by Jordan, Iraq, and Kuwait to the north. Moving clockwise, other adjacent territories include the Persian (Arabian) Gulf, the United Arab Emirates, Oman, the two Yemens, and the Red Sea. The country is mostly desert, with the only significant arable land being in the southwestern part of the country. Two of the most important cities of Islam, Mecca and Medina, lie along the old caravan routes parallel to the Red Sea.

Almost all of the population is Muslim, the great majority being of the conservative Wahhabi sect. A relatively small group of Shiites (about 300,000) are concentrated in the petroleum-producing areas of the northeast and therefore have been a source of concern to the government. About twenty percent of the population and one-third of the labor force is composed of non-nationals, the majority coming from Yemen. Large numbers of Saudis have studied abroad in recent years, mostly in England and the United States.

Saudi Arabia is the world's largest exporter of petroleum and holds the world's largest proven reserves—about forty years worth of petroleum at current rates of exploitation. Most petroleum production is in the northeast. Because of its premier position as a petroleum exporter, it has been the lynchpin on which the actions of the Organization of Petroleum Exporting Countries depend. It has been among the price moderates in OPEC because of its large reserves and rather low capacity to absorb yearly revenues for development purposes. The petroleum company was nationalized when majority control was purchased in 1974. Agricultural output and potential are very low. The extremely rapid growth of petroleum revenues during the seventies, however, allowed Saudi Arabia to launch significant development projects.

Saudi Arabia is an absolute monarchy with neither political parties nor legislature. The king also serves as prime minister and is the country's religious leader. In the past two decades, considerable effort has been directed at creating an efficient ("modern") administration of government affairs. From the formation of the country in 1932 through the early sixties, almost all significant affairs were handled personally by the king.

Both the pace of modernization and reports of deep-seated splits in the royal family suggest that the relative domestic calm Saudi Arabia has experienced in recent years may not last. Although Saudi Arabia has been the most important conservative Arab state in the Middle East with strong ties to the West, it has displayed more independence of action with respect to world events since the revolution of petroleum prices.

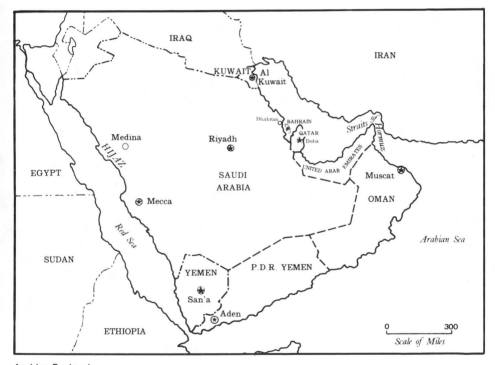

Arabian Peninsula

NORTH YEMEN

(Yemen Arab Republic)

Area: 75,290 sq. mi.
    195,000 sq. km.

Population: 5,751,000 (1980E)

Per capita GNP (1977): U.S. $390

Major urban centers (1975C):
SANA'A (134,600); Hodeida
(90,000); Taiz (80,000).

Official language: Arabic

The Yemen Arab Republic is bordered by Saudi Arabia to the north, the People's Democratic Republic of Yemen to the south, and the Red Sea to the west. Climate varies with the three general topographical areas: a coastal area, a desert-like strip adjoining it, and the mountainous interior. The mountainous regions have adequate water and sizable portions of the land are arable.

The overwhelming majority of the population is Arab. The Zaydi Shiites claim most of the northern population while the Shafi Sunnis are most numerous in the southwest. Although reliable figures are not available, it is known that substantial numbers of Yemenis work abroad, mostly in Saudi Arabia. Some estimates indicate that as much as fifty percent of the labor force works abroad.

Yemen is a very poor country and does not have good prospects for sustained growth in the future. The economy is dependent on agriculture and the remittances of Yemeni workers abroad. Although Yemen used to be self-sufficient in food production (and exported coffee), of late it has become a substantial importer. This has resulted from two major causes. First, the large number of Yemeni workers going to work in Saudi Arabia and elsewhere has reduced the size of the workforce. Second, the remittances have allowed the local population the finances to purchase imported foodstuffs and switch production to a preferred crop, Qat, a mildly narcotic plant. Industry is minimal.

For most of the twentieth century Yemen was one of the most inaccessible countries in the world due to the xenophobic policies laid down by its theocratic ruler. Although the government first established close ties with Egypt in 1958 in an unsuccessful attempt to join the ill-fated United Arab Republic (Egypt and Syria), it was not until a 1962 coup that a strong Egyptian presence was felt. The then revolutionary government fought against the Saudi-supported royalists for five years and had up to 70,000 Egyptian troops aiding them in the effort.

Yemen has experienced bewildering political instability in the past two decades. The government is headed by a president, vice-president, and prime minister who are chosen for their roles by the Constituent People's Assembly. Their major foreign policy tensions are with revolutionary South Yemen, although relations with conservative Saudi Arabia are not always smooth. The Yemen Arab Republic remains volatile and somewhat unpredictable.

SOUTH YEMEN

(People's Democratic Republic of Yemen)

Area: 111,074 sq. mi.　　　　　Major urban centers (1973E):
　　　　287,683 sq. km.　　　　　　ADEN (291,376).

Population: 1,948,000 (1980E)　　Official language: Arabic

Per capita GNP (1977): U.S. $320

The People's Democratic Republic of Yemen is bordered on the north by Saudi Arabia. Moving clockwise, it also borders on Oman, the Gulf of Aden, and North Yemen. The climate is most inhospitable, being very warm and dry, while the terrain is largely desert and mountains. The population is largely Arab and Sunni Muslim. There are numerous tribal groups in the hinterland which have effective autonomy from the central government on a large number of matters.

A great majority of the economically active population depends on agriculture. Since there is little rainfall, no irrigation to speak of, and poor soil to work with, agricultural productivity is low and the population is poor. The only industrial activity of any significance is the petroleum refinery at Aden, which itself has had difficulty operating efficiently in recent years. Prospects for significant economic development are bleak in the foreseeable future.

The British ruled South Yemen first as a part of British India, and then as a crown colony until independence was achieved in 1967. Although the British planned for the independent state to be a federation of the various, largely tribal, groups, the National Liberation Front waged active opposition and gained the leadership of the independent state.

The constitution of 1978 calls for a government formed along Marxist-Leninist lines with a single party and presidium. South Yemen's international posture reflects this orientation and has been the source of considerable tension between it and its conservative neighbors. It has received military aid from the Soviet Union and advisors from Cuba, and has provided refuge for the guerillas fighting in the Dhofar province of Oman. Relations with Saudi Arabia are strained.

OMAN

(Sultanate of Oman)

Area: 120,000 sq. mi.
310,800 sq. km.

Major urban centers (1975E):
MUSCAT (50,000); Salala (15,000)

Population: 900,000 (1980E)
(No census has yet been
taken, some estimates
range as high as
1,500,000.)

Official language: Arabic

Per capita GNP (1977): U.S. $2,520

Oman, formerly called Muscat and Oman, is located in the southeastern portion of the Arabian Peninsula. It shares borders with the United Arab Emirates to the northeast and, working clockwise, the Arabian Sea, South Yemen, and Saudi Arabia. Being located at the mouth of the Persian (Arabian) Gulf, Oman is of immense strategic importance, especially considering that a substantial amount of the world's petroleum exports pass through the narrow Straits of Hormuz. The climate is very warm and arid, and there is not much arable land.

There has never been a population census in Oman, and the available estimates are subject to wide margins of error. Much of the population outside the capital city, Muscat, lives in a quickly-changing tribal setting. The population is predominantly Arab and Sunni Muslim. There are, however, significant minorities, including Iranians, Pakistanis, and Indians. The number of foreigners in Oman increased substantially during the decade of the seventies; the foreigners appear to be filling an increasing percentage of skilled positions.

Although proven reserves of petroleum are rather modest in contrast with the major producers of the area, the income of the country is almost totally dependent on petroleum revenues. Production first started in 1967. Before the exploitation of petroleum, the country was based on agriculture (some products being exported), some cattle and camel raising, and maritime pursuits.

Oman gained independence in 1951. It is an absolute monarchy and does not have a constitution nor legislature. The sultan rules in a traditional fashion, depending on personal retainers for advice on the affairs of state. The southern province of Dhofar was in rebellion for many years until a truce (of sorts) was arranged in 1976. The Dhofar Liberation Front received refuge and material support from the People's Democratic Republic of Yemen, who, in turn, were supported by the Soviet Union, East Germany, and Cuba. The sultan received support from Saudi Arabia and Iran, among others. The substantial interest in the fate of Oman stems largely from its geographical position at the mouth of the Persian Gulf. The British had military installations in Oman until 1977; the desire of the United States to fill the gap for the West was demonstrated when the British left and, intensified after the Iranian revolution. U.S. troops have recently used Omani air and naval stations in military maneuvers in and around the Persian Gulf.

UNITED ARAB EMIRATES

Area: 32,278 sq. mi.
    83,600 sq. km.

Population: 760,000 (1980E)

Per capita GNP (1977): U.S. $14,420

Major urban centers (1975E):
    ABU DHABI (150,000);
    Dubai (70,000).

Official language: Arabic

The United Arab Emirates (UAE) is bordered on the north by the Persian (Arabian) Gulf and Qatar. Oman lies to the east, and Saudi Arabia lies along the southern and western borders. The UAE is a federation of seven emirates: Abu Dhabi, Dubai, Ras al-Kharima, Sharjah, Fujaira, Ajman, and Umm al-Qaiwain. The area is largely desert and the climate is very hot and dry.

The indigenous population is predominately Arab, but the majority of the labor force are non-nationals. Although about half of the non-nationals have no formal education, as a group they have significantly higher levels of education and hold the majority of skilled posts and government jobs.

The high per capita income figures result from significant petroleum production in Abu Dhabi and Dubai. These emirates are using petroleum revenues to diversify their economies, largely through the establishment of service industries such as the improvement of the deep water harbor at Dubai, banking facilities, and the like. Manufacturing is not well developed and the potential for agricultural expansion is quite limited although some progress has been made through the activities of an agricultural station.

The UAE gained independence in 1971 after attempts by the British to include Bahrain and Qatar in the federation failed. The government is superimposed on the conservative monarchies in the constituent emirates. The rulers of the emirates compose the Supreme Council of the UAE which elects a president and vice-president from its members. The fully appointed legislative body, the Federal National Council, has forty members. Since each emirate has substantial autonomy with respect to revenue and expenditure policy, and since Abu Dhabi and Dubai are the only significant producers of petroleum, relations in the UAE are dominated by these two emirates. Although there have been border disputes, the UAE generally has good relations with and maintains the same foreign policy posture as Saudi Arabia.

QATAR

(State of Qatar)

Area: 4,247 sq. mi.
11,000 sq. km.

Major urban centers (1975E):
DOHA (130,000)

Population: 107,000 (1980E)
(Does not include
non-native Qataris.)

Official language: Arabic

Per capita GNP (1977): U.S. $11,670

Qatar is located on a peninsula that juts northward from the eastern coast of Saudi Arabia into the Persian Gulf. The peninsula is largely sand and rock; the climate is warm and rainfall is sparse. The population is almost entirely Arab, but native Qataris constitute much less than a majority. The rest are predominantly immigrants from other Persian Gulf and Middle Eastern countries. Most of the people are Sunni Muslims of Wahhabi orientation.

Qatar was under British influence until 1971. Qatar attempted to join with Bahrain and the United Arab Emirates in a federation, but was not successful. In 1971, Qatar declared its independence as a traditional sheikdom, with the emir as an absolute monarch. The Basic Law of 1970 provides for a legislative Advisory Council of 20 members, three of whom are to be appointed and the rest elected. In 1975 the membership was increased to 30; most of these were appointed by the emir rather than elected. There is also a Council of Ministers headed by an appointed prime minister. The judicial system consists of five secular courts and several religious courts.

The economy depends almost entirely on petroleum production which has been in progress since the end of World War II. In 1976 and 1977, the government attained control of oil and natural gas production through agreements with Shell Qatar and Qatar Petroleum Company. Oil revenue is used primarily to provide broad social welfare benefits to Qatari nationals and to develop and diversify the economy. Industrial development projects include a steel plant, a petrochemicals complex, desalination plants, cement production facilities, a refinery for the liquefaction of natural gas, new electric power plants, and an enlarged port capacity at Doha. The desalinated water is being used to promote the development of agriculture, primarily fruits and vegetables. Shrimp fishing and processing has recently entered the economy.

The small size of the native work force has obliged Qatar to rely on immigrants and foreign nationals for most of its labor power. The government of Qatar does not grant the foreign majority the same benefits as it does its native citizens. Although this has not yet led to the political difficulties experienced by Kuwait, it is possible that a similar situation could develop.

BAHRAIN

(State of Bahrain)

Area: 240 sq. mi.
    622 sq. km.

Population: 292,000 (1980E)

Per capita GNP (1976): U.S. $3,790

Major urban centers (1975E):
MANAMA (150,000); Muharraq
(37,732); Rifa'a (10,000);
Hidd (5,500).

Official language: Arabic

Bahrain is composed of one large island (Bahrain) and thirty four smaller islands lying in the Persian Gulf between the coasts of Saudi Arabia and Qatar. As with the other nations of the Arabian Peninsula, the climate of Bahrain is hot and dry, and the land is largely desert.

The population is predominately Arab, with significant numbers of non-Arabs largely from Iran, India, and Pakistan. Non-nationals compose about one-fifth of the population and over one-third of the labor force. Bahrain's relatively long involvement in petroleum related activities has allowed both the finances and time necessary for Bahrainis to gain the know-how necessary to fill skilled positions in the economy. As opposed to such relative new-comers to petroleum wealth as Abu Dhabi and Dubai, Bahrain's nationals fill the majority of the skilled positions in the private and government sector. About half of the Muslims are Sunni, the remainder being Shiite. Both this split and the large number of foreigners in the country have been sources of tension.

Although petroleum finds have been modest compared to those of several close-by countries, the economy of Bahrain has long been dominated by petroleum since it was first produced for commercial sale in 1936. Petroleum production and reserves are now at very low levels. Significant efforts have been made in the past decades to diversify the economy, including the upgrading of Manama as a transit port, the building of an aluminum smelter, the construction of a causeway to Saudi Arabia, and the granting of tax exempt status to offshore banking so as to entrench Manama as a regional financial center.

Bahrain achieved independence in 1971 after British attempts to have it join the UAE were unsuccessful. The emir is head of state, and he is supposed to share power with a popularly elected legislative body. The legislature was dissolved in 1975 by the emir who (informally) substituted a fully-appointed Council of Ministers, the membership of which is dominated by members of the royal family. Bahrain's international posture generally is the same as the other conservative nations of the area, favoring the West.

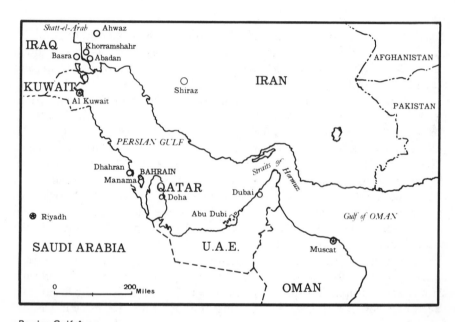

Persian Gulf Area

KUWAIT

(State of Kuwait)

Area: 6,880 sq. mi.
    17,818 sq. km.

Population: 1,482,000 (1980E)

Per capita GNP (1977): U.S. $12,700

Major urban centers (1970C):
    KUWAIT CITY (80,405); Hawalli
    (106,542).

Official language: Arabic

Kuwait is located at the northeast corner of the Persian (Arabian) Gulf, sharing borders with Iraq to the north and Saudi Arabia to the south. It has a hot and arid climate, has no major source of fresh water, and is almost totally dependent on petroleum revenues for its income.

The indigenous population of Kuwait is Arab and largely Sunni Muslim. However, non-Kuwaitis compose about half of the total population and three-quarters of the labor force. By far, the single largest foreign nationality represented are the Jordanians (including Palestinians) who account for about one-fifth of the total population. Kuwaitis generally are afforded better wages and working conditions, as well as more protection by force of law, than their foreign counterparts. The large Palestinian presence is cause for worry in Kuwait, and the Palestinians have been viewed by the Kuwaiti leadership as a disruptive force in the nation. Manpower projections indicate that the majority of the population will have to remain foreign if Kuwait is to sustain its economic growth.

The per capita income of Kuwait is the highest in the world due to the large petroleum supplies. Virtually the entire economy is based on petroleum, which has been exploited for four decades. Kuwait purchased majority control of the petroleum corporation in 1974. Kuwait has a very extensive welfare state for its citizens.

The 1962 constitution allows that the head of state, an absolute monarch, be selected from the Mubarak line of the Sabah family. An appointed Council of Ministers and a prime minister are in charge of the affairs of state. The constitution also calls for a legislative body, about one-quarter of whom are to be appointed. The legislature was suspended in 1975 following internal disruptions triggered by the Palestinian plight in Lebanon that year.

Although the political structure of Kuwait and the attitudes of its leaders put them in the conservative Arab camp, the large foreign Arab, especially Palestinian, presence has had a moderating effect on Kuwaiti policy with respect to Israel. Generally, their relationship with Iraq over the years has been one of controlled tension—Iraqis sometimes making the claim that Kuwait is rightly considered a part of Iraq.

IRAN
(Islamic Republic of Iran)

Area: 636,293 sq. mi.
1,648,000 sq. km.

Population: 37,064,000 (1980E)

Per capita GNP (1977): U.S. $2,180

Major urban centers (1975E):
TEHRAN (4,500,000); Isfahan
(680,000); Mashhad (620,000);
Tabriz (545,000); Shiraz (400,000);
'Abadan (335,000).

Official language: Persian (Farsi)

Iran is bordered on the north by the Soviet Union and the Caspian Sea, by Turkey and Iraq to the west, by the Persian Gulf to the south, and by Afghanistan and Pakistan on the east. Iran is predominantly an arid country consisting largely of elevated plains, mountains, and desert. The majority of the population, about two-thirds, is Persian; the remainder are mostly Turkish, Kurdish, or Baluchi. About ninety percent of the people are Shiite Muslims.

Iran was a seat of high civilization prior to the rise of Arab and Muslim power in the Middle East, and its traditions later came to influence the development of Muslim civilization. Iran remained an absolute monarchy until the revolution of 1979. Shah Muhammad Reza Pahlavi, who was overthrown in that revolution, had succeeded his father, the founder of the Pahlavi dynasty, in 1941. He survived many political intrigues during the 1940s, a coup attempt in 1953, and increasing unrest during the 1960s and 1970s. After the attempted coup of 1953 he initiated an ambitious "modernizing" program involving social and economic reforms, but power remained concentrated in his hands. In the "White Revolution," as his programs were called after 1963, there was a major expansion of petroleum-related and other industries; oil exports and industrial production assumed increasing importance at the expense of agriculture. The programs caused social upheavals including a shift of population to urban areas. Growing unrest culminated in religious demonstrations and rioting; in September of 1978 the Shah declared martial law in Tehran and eleven other urban areas in an attempt to restore order. Later in 1978 petroleum workers went on strike in response to the call of an exiled religious leader, the Ayatollah Ruhollah Khomeini. On December 21, the Shah appointed a new civilian government and left the country on an "extended vacation." On February 1, 1979, the Ayatollah Khomeini returned to Iran and his followers overthrew the government, proclaiming an Islamic Republic on April 1, 1979.

The Islamic Republic of Iran was initiated as an experiment in Islamic political and social organization. Based on the constitution adopted in 1979, the government is composed of a national religious leader (Faghi), a president with indeterminate executive power, and an assembly (Majlis) presided over by a speaker. The legislative majority is led by a prime minister. The legal system of Iran is officially based on the Sharia. Islam is recognized as the source of authority for foreign and domestic policy. The unsettled internal political situation in Iran has interfered with the establishment of clear lines of authority between the Faghi, the President, and the Majlis. The situation has been further complicated by Iran's foreign policy difficulties, including the seizure of U.S. hostages from November, 1979 until January, 1981, and a war with Iraq which started in September of 1980.

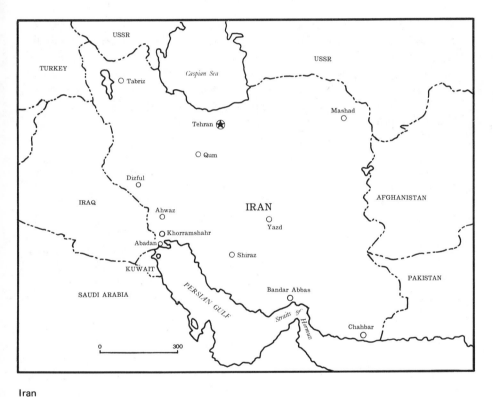

Iran

TURKEY

(Republic of Turkey)

Area: 301,380 sq. mi.
    780,576 sq. km.

Population: 48,636,000 (1980E)

Per capita GNP (1977): U.S. $1,110

Major urban centers (1975C):
ANKARA (1,699,000); Istanbul
(2,535,000): Izmir (636,000); Adana
(467,000); Bursa (346,000).

Official language: Turkish

Bridging Europe and Asia, Turkey borders on Bulgaria and Greece to the northwest, the Soviet Union to the northeast, Iran to the east, and Iraq and Syria to the south. North of Turkey lies the Black Sea, which joins to the Mediterranean via the Dardanelles Straits dividing the European and Asian portions of Turkey. Most of Turkey's land mass is on the Asian side of the Straits, including the Anatolian Peninsula, and is subject to extremes of climate. The majority of Turkey's population is ethnically Turkish, but there is a substantial Kurdish minority in the east and southeast as well as smaller groups of Arabs, Greeks, Circassians, Armenians, Georgians, and Bulgarians. Sunni Islam is the religion of ninety-eight percent of the population.

About seventy percent of the Turkish population is employed in agriculture, which produces grains, tobacco, cotton, fruit, and olives; sheep and cattle are also raised. Most industry is either owned or indirectly controlled by the government. Industrial products include iron and steel, textiles, processed food, paper, and cement. Turkey's natural resources include chrome, copper, iron ore, manganese, bauxite, borax, and some petroleum. A period of rapid economic growth following the Second World War has been slowed and recently the country has been plagued with inflation rates as high as seventy percent and up to twenty pecent unemployment. There is an urgent need for increased foreign exchange to defray the cost of the imported materials needed for continued economic expansion.

Turkey is the remaining core of the Ottoman Empire, which dominated the Middle East and parts of Eastern Europe until its decline and eventual dissolution after the First World War. Under the modernizing and secularizing leadership of Mustafa Kemal Atatürk, Turkey became a republic in 1923. In recent times the military has occasionally deemed it necessary to intervene in government. After two such interventions, in 1960 and 1971, the government was returned to civilian control. The third military intervention occurred in 1980, when martial law was declared in order to bring domestic violence under control.

Turkey's constitution provides for the election of a president by the legislature for a seven-year term. The legislature has the power to impeach a president and to override presidential vetoes. The prime minister, responsible for general administration, is presidentially appointed and is chosen from the majority party or coalition in the lower house of the legislature. The Grand National Assembly is a bicameral legislative body consisting of an upper house, the Senate, and a lower house, the National Assembly. One hundred and fifty of the 184 members of the Senate are popularly elected to six-year terms, fifteen are appointed by the president, and the remainder have life appointments as former holders of high government office. The National Assembly's 450 members serve four-year terms by popular election.

Turkey

IRAQ

(Republic of Iraq)

Area: 167,924 sq. mi.
434,923 sq. km.

Population: 13,197,000 (1980E)

Per capita GNP (1977): U.S. $1,530

Major urban centers (1973E):
BAGHDAD (2,800,000); Mosul
(857,000); Basra (854,000); Kirkuk
(559,000); Sulaimaniya (504,000).

Official language: Arabic, Kurdish

Iraq shares borders with Iran on the east, Turkey on the north, Syria on the west, and Jordan, Saudi Arabia, and Kuwait on the south. Most of Iraq's population is Arab, with a Kurdish minority in the northeast. The Kurds are Sunni Muslims. They, along with an Arab Shiite minority located in the southeast, have been the source of considerable internal dissatisfaction with which the Sunni Arab dominated government has had to contend.

Iraq has been a major farming region since ancient times, and agriculture still employs three-fourths of the work force even though it accounts for less than a quarter of the national income. Iraq's main crops are dates, barley, wheat, rice, and tobacco. Most of Iraq's export income and two-thirds of its gross national product come from the petroleum industry, which is dominated by the nationalized Iraqi Petroleum Company. Manufacturing industries, also largely nationalized, are undergoing rapid growth despite an unstable political climate and shortages of skilled labor. Iraq's other raw materials include phosphates, sulphur, iron, copper, chromite, lead, limestone, and gypsum.

Iraq became a British mandate under the League of Nations after World War I, and it achieved independence in 1932 under the Hashemite monarchy established during the mandate. Iraq became a republic following a 1958 coup led by Brig. Gen. Abdul Karim Kassem. After a series of political triumphs and defeats, the Baath (Arab Resurrection) Party came to power in a bloodless coup in 1968 led by Maj. Gen. Ahmad Hassan al-Bakr. Iraq has struggled under the burden of domestic instability resulting from conflicts within the Baath party and Kurdish demands for political autonomy. A 1974 amendment to the provisional constitution granted the Kurds limited autonomy, and in 1975 Iran agreed to cease aid to Iraqi Kurds in return for Iranian control of the disputed Shatt al-'Arab waterway. The agreement fell apart in 1980 when war broke out over the Shatt al-'Arab and adjacent lands. Iraq has pledged its support of Arab nationalism and was a signer of the 1978 "National Charter for Joint Action" calling for Iraqi and Syrian military unity against Israel. Tensions between Iraq and its neighbors, both Arab and non-Arab, remain an important factor in Iraqi politics.

Legislative authority in Iraq's government is held by the Revolutionary Command Council consisting of military and civilian members. A provisional constitution provides for a legislative National Council of one hundred members, but this body has not yet been convened. The Iraqi judicial system includes civil, religious, and revolutionary courts.

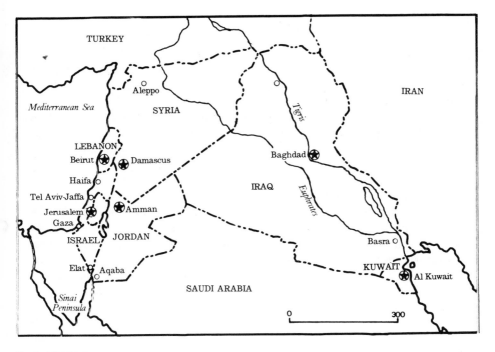

Central Regions

SYRIA

(Syrian Arab Republic)

Area: 71,586 sq. mi.
185,408 sq. km.

Population: 8,640,000 (1980E)

Per capita GNP (1977): U.S. $900

Major urban centers (1970C):
DAMASCUS (836,668); Aleppo
(639,428); Homs (215,423); Hama
(137,421); Latakia (125,716).

Official language: Arabic

Syria is bordered by Turkey in the north and, clockwise, by Iraq, Jordan, Israel, Lebanon, and the Mediterranean Sea. Although sizable portions of the southeastern and south-central parts of the country are mountainous, Syria possesses large tracts of arable land. The Euphrates river enters Syria from Turkey and flows through the central lands to Iraq.

Arabs make up about ninety percent of the population and Sunni Muslims constitute about the same percentage. However, minorities (Alawites and Druze) are important and have had influence beyond their numbers. Alawites, non-ortho-dox Shiite Muslim Arabs, dominate the government. This has been a continuing source of friction in Syria.

The economy of Syria is primarily agricultural; however, it is more diversified than most countries of the area. Although agricultural yields have been low, the source of the problem has been a lack of water; there are large tracts of potentially highly productive soil. The recently completed massive Euphrates Dam should offer substantial irrigation potential and thereby boost agricultural output. Since the Euphrates also supplies Iraq with water for irrigation, there has been considerable friction between the two countries concerning the amount of Euphrates water which Syria uses.

From independence in 1946 until 1971, Syria experienced considerable political turmoil, with the military always being involved, and since 1963 formally in control. The Arab Resurrection Party (Baath) a socialist and nationalist group with pan-Arab sentiments, first gained power in 1958. Its power was consolidated in 1971 when a group of military officers dominated by Alawites seized the govern-ment. Although internal strife remains a serious problem, Syria experienced more domestic political stability in the decade of the seventies than in any previous decade of the century.

Syria's foreign policy has been dominated by hostile relations with Israel and Baathist notions of anti-imperialism which generally have tilted against the West. Its regional alliances, while sometimes spectacular—joining with Egypt to form the U.A.R. in 1958 and the 1980 announcement of a proposed merger with Libya being prime examples—have been marked by reversals of policy towards neighbors, especially Iraq and Jordan, as events dictated. The bulk of the Arab Deterrent Force in Lebanon is made up of Syrian forces.

LEBANON

(Republic of Lebanon)

Area: 4,015 sq. mi.
    10,400 sq. km.

Population: 3,217,000 (1980E)

Per capita GNP (1977): U.S. $750

Major urban centers (1972E):
    BEIRUT (800,000); Tripoli (160,000);
    Zahle' (47,000); Saida (25,000).

Official language: Arabic
(French used widely.)

Lebanon is located north of Israel on the east coast of the Mediterranean Sea, sharing a border also with Syria on the north and east. The majority of its population is Arab Muslim, about evenly divided between Sunni and Shiite; Christians form a very large and important minority, and there is also a small but influential Druze minority. The Christian population includes Maronites, Orthodox Greeks, Greek Catholics, Orthodox Armenians, and Armenian Catholics.

Lebanon has a long history of commercial activity, and has enjoyed a high standard of living relative to other Middle Eastern countries, serving as a center of commerce, finance, tourism, and education. While agriculture employs the majority of the work force, it contributes only a small portion of the national income. The service sector, involved in such activities as banking, insurance, transit trade, shipping, petroleum pipelines, and tourism, are most important to the economy. Industries such as food processing, cement, and textiles also make a significant economic contribution.

Lebanon was a French mandate under the League of Nations after World War I, and became an independent parliamentary republic in 1941 although French troops did not actually withdraw until after World War II. According to the unwritten National Pact of 1943, the chief offices of the state were to be divided among Christians and Muslims, with a Maronite Christian as president elected by a two-thirds majority of the legislature, the prime minister a Sunni Muslim appointed by the president in consultation with political and religious leaders, and the president of the Chamber of Deputies a Shiite Muslim. The Chamber of Deputies, Lebanon's unicameral legislature, has ninety-nine members elected to four-year terms by universal suffrage. Seats in the legislature are proportionally allotted according to religious affiliation.

The delicate balance of religious groups in the government of Lebanon began to disintegrate in 1975, partly as the result of the presence of a large number of Palestinians. A substantial number of "leftist" and "rightist" groups identified with particular religious affiliations struggled for power, ultimately provoking the intervention of Israel in the south and Syria in the north. The destruction of Lebanon's fragile political balance led to catastrophic civil strife which has not yet resolved into a new and viable order.

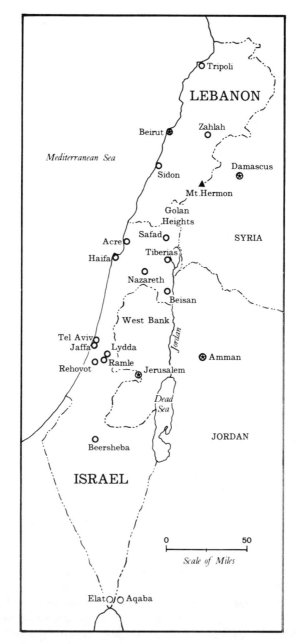

Israel and Lebanon

ISRAEL

(State of Israel)

Area*: 7,847 sq. mi.
20,325 sq. km.

Population*: 3,904,000 (1980E)

Per capita GNP (1977): U.S. $2,920

Major urban centers (1979E):
JERUSALEM (380,200); Tel Aviv/
Jaffa (345,600); Haifa (230,000);
Ramat Gan (200,120).

Official languages: Hebrew, Arabic
(English spoken widely.)

Israel occupies a narrow strip between Mediterranean Sea and its eastern neighbor, Jordan. It is bounded on the north by Lebanon, on the northeast by Syria, and on the southwest by Egypt. During the 1967 war with neighboring Arab states, Israel occupied the Sinai Peninsula and Gaza Strip of Egypt, the West Bank of Jordan, and Syria's Golan Heights. Control of the Sinai returned to Egypt in 1979–1981 as a result of the Camp David peace agreement between Israel and Egypt. The population of Israel (not including the occupied territories) is eighty-five percent Jewish, with Druze and Arab (Christian and Muslim) minorities.

The Israeli economy is exceptionally diversified by Middle Eastern standards. Agriculture remains a significant part of the economy, though diminishing in relative importance. The principal crops are citrus fruits, wheat, olives, rice, and tobacco. Israel's industries are rapidly gaining in importance; these include diamond cutting, textiles, food processing, military equipment, metalware, plastics, chemicals, machinery, electronics, and computers. Israel's hostile relations with neighboring Arab states necessitate high defense spending leading to inflation, an adverse balance of payments, and a shortage of labor in certain industries. The economy has benefited from U.S. aid, tourism, and financial contributions from Jewish residents of other countries.

Seventy-five to eighty percent of the urban labor force is unionized in the Israeli Federation of Labor, or Histadrut, an organization which involves both labor and management in decision-making processes. Much of the rural work force is organized in communal or cooperative arrangements including the Kibbutzim, or communal farms.

The state of Israel was formed out of the region formerly known as Palestine, which had become a British mandate under the League of Nations following World War I. From the turn of the century until the end of World War II, Palestine had seen growing conflict between Jewish Zionist settlers and Palestinian Arabs, each with strong nationalistic aspirations. The United Nations attempted to resolve the

*Area and population figures include the Old City of Jerusalem but not the Gaza Strip, Golan Heights, West Bank, or Sinai Peninsula. These areas total 27,000 sq. mi. (70,000 sq. km.), with a population of over one million.

conflict in 1947 by partitioning Palestine into independent Jewish and Arab states, but in the ensuing warfare between Israel and its Arab neighbors the Arab Palestinian State was demolished and its territories absorbed into Israel and Jordan; many Palestinian Arabs became refugees and remain so today. Chronic hostility with Arab states erupted into war in 1956, 1967, and 1973. These hostilities and the resultant problems of national security have greatly influenced Israel's foreign and domestic policies.

Israel has no written constitution but its laws provide for a president, whose duties are largely ceremonial, and a prime minister who functions as the head of state. The government is responsible to the Knesset, Israel's unicameral legislative body, whose members are elected for four-year terms by universal suffrage. The selection of candidates is based on proportional representation of the political parties, according to national party lists.

JORDAN

(Hashemite Kingdom of Jordan)

Area: 37,737 sq. mi.
97,940 sq. km.
(Including Israeli occupied
West Bank territory of
2,181 sq. mi.)

Major urban centers (1974E):
AMMAN (733,000); Zarqa' (270,000);
Irbid (140,000).

Official language: Arabic

Population: 3,060,000 (1980E)
(Including 800,000 under
Israeli military control
on West Bank.)

Per capita GNP (1977): U.S. $710

Jordan is bordered on the west by Israel, on the north by Syria, on the northeast by Iraq, and on the south and southeast by Saudi Arabia. It is completely landlocked except for a sixteen mile coastline on the Gulf of Aqaba in the Red Sea. Most of the country is high, arid plateau. The majority of the population is Muslim Arab, but there are many ethnic minorities. Sunni Islam is the predominant religion.

Agriculture, concentrating on fruits and vegetables, is the most important sector of Jordan's economy; nevertheless it is necessary for Jordan to import foodstuffs. The 1967 Israeli occupation of the West Bank, which includes the bulk of Jordan's farmable land, has substantially lowered production. Industry is restricted mostly to cement making, light consumer goods, food processing, and phosphate extraction. Refugees from the West Bank have contributed to urban overcrowding and high unemployment. In order to maintain a stable economy Jordan has had to rely on aid from the United States, Britain, and from other Arab states.

Jordan became part of a British mandate under the League of Nations after the First World War, and was granted full independence in 1946 as a constitutional monarchy under the Hashemite Emir Abdullah. The present king, Hussein, took the throne at the age of sixteen after his father's assassination in 1951. The king shares his authority with a legislative body, the National Assembly. He holds executive authority and serves as commander of the armed forces, and he is also empowered to appoint the prime minister and cabinet, to order general elections, to convene, adjourn or dissolve the legislature, and to approve and promulgate laws. The National Assembly has an upper house, the Council of Notables, and a lower house, the Council of Deputies. The legislature must approve all treaties and has the power to override royal vetoes. Following the recommendation of a 1974 Arab Summit Conference, Hussein recognized the Palestinian Liberation Organization as responsible for the political affairs of West Bank Palestinians (although not formally relinquishing Jordan's claim to the territory). The Council of Deputies was dissolved pending new elections, which have since been postponed indefinitely. In 1978, the King appointed a sixty-member National Consultative Council to advise the prime minister on legislative matters.

Jordan's relations with other Arab states have been strained by its pro-Western stance and its "moderate" position on Israel, and disputes between Jordan and Palestinian guerilla organizations operating from Jordanian bases have added to the friction. Jordan did, however, sever its relations with Egypt in 1979 to protest Egyptian-Israeli peace negotiations.

Glossary

Abbasids: An important Hashemite Arab family descended from Abbas, which founded the Abbasid Caliphate at Baghdad in 750. This dynasty saw the highest development of the Caliphate during what is recognized as the Golden Age of Islam.

Afghani: Jemal al-Din al-Afghani. A nineteenth century Egyptian school teacher who became one of the first modern nationalist writers and spokesmen. He traveled widely and was important in inspiring Middle Eastern opposition to European colonialism.

Alawites: A non-orthodox Shiite sect of Islam, found primarily in Lebanon and Syria. The Alawites dominate the Syrian government under President Assad, causing considerable internal resentment and tension among the Sunni majority.

Ashkenazim: The term generally used to describe Jews of European origin, but who are specifically from north central Europe.

Baath: The Arab Socialist Resurrection Party, a political party dedicated to Arab nationalism and socialism. Founded in Lebanon in the 1940s, Baath factions control both Syria and Iraq, sometimes pursuing mutually contradictory goals, particularly in foreign policy.

bedouin: Refers generally to Arabic-speaking camel nomads in the Middle East and especially in the Arabian peninsula.

Caliph: The title given to the successors of Muhammad as leaders of the Umma.

diwan: Originally this was a record listing those fighting for the Umma and was used to determine shares of conquered booty. This became the rudimentary bureaucracy of the early Muslim state.

djimmi: Refers to those religions given special status in Islam, particularly to the Jews and Christians, the "People of the Book." They enjoyed immunity from forced conversion but had to pay higher taxes than the Muslim. Also included, eventually, were Zoroastrians and Hindus.

Druze: Mystical non-orthodox Muslim sect, located in the south of Lebanon and Syria.

fellahin: (sing. fellah) Refers specifically to the peasantry, and occasionally to the manual laborer in an urban workforce.

fiqh: Islamic jurisprudence. Literally, an "understanding" of Sharia law. Different schools of fiqh were founded in the first centuries of Islam, most prominently the Shafi, Hanafi, Hanbali, and Maliki.

ghazi: Defender of the faith, usually as a soldier.

hadith: The collected reports about the life of the Prophet, which, along with the Koran, constitute the major authoritative sources of Islamic thought.

hajj: Refers to the pilgrimage to Mecca, one of the five pillars of Islam and the once-in-a-lifetime obligation of the faithful, given adequate health and finances. A successful pilgrim becomes known as "hajji" and enjoys significant prestige.

Hashemite: The family of the Quraish tribe to which Muhammad belonged, and which subsequently became influential in Muslim affairs. Traditionally powerful in the Northwest of the Arabian peninsula, Hashemites were established in power in Iraq and Transjordan following World War I.

Hijaz: A mountainous region of the Arabian peninsula adjacent to the Red Sea coast, including the cities of Mecca and Medina; the region in which Islam originated.

Hijira: The migration of those faithful to Muhammad's preaching, from Mecca to Medina (then called Yathrib), in 622. At Medina the full fruition of the political and social aspects of Muhammad's revelation took place.

imam: A religious teacher. Most often, the term refers to a leader of services in the mosque. In Shiism the term also refers to the leader of the Shiite community.

Isma'ilis: The followers of Isma'il, the seventh Imam of the Shiite tradition. Marked by a more esoteric and mystical emphasis than other branches of Shiism. Includes the Qarmatians.

Janissary: The slave-soldiers who eventually became the core of the Ottoman bureaucracy. Highly trained in special schools, in the early years they were denied the right to have children, thus eliminating hereditary claims to administrative office.

jihad: "Holy War," refers to the obligation of the faithful to extend the Umma and protect it from its enemies. Jihad has been variously interpreted as actual warfare or spiritual struggle.

Kaaba: A shrine dedicated to Allah, of great historical importance in Arabian history. Although of pre-Muslim origin, it was incorporated by Muhammad into the Islamic faith. Located in the Grand Mosque of Mecca, the Kaaba is the ultimate destination of the pilgrim (hajji). Maintenance of the Kaaba is very important to the wider Islamic community and to the government of Saudi Arabia in particular.

katib: The scribes, or recordkeepers, employed by the traditional governments, especially under the Caliphate.

Kharijite: An early puritanical movement in Islam; initially allied with Ali, this radically democratic group eventually turned against him and assassinated him in 661.

Koran: The word written of Allah as revealed through his prophet, Muhhamad.

madrasah: Schools of religion, sometimes independently supported by waqf endowments; often associated with a prominent urban mosque.

Mahdi: The messiah or redeemer in Islam, expected to come to earth in the final days to lead the faithful in their war against the infidel.

Mameluks: The slave-dynasty of Circassians ruling Egypt from 1250 to 1798. From 1517 until their destruction, they ruled Egypt giving only nominal allegiance to the Ottoman sultan.

Maronites: A monophysite Christian sect located primarily in Lebanon and Syria.

millets: The religious groups given official status in the Ottoman Empire. In matters of civil conflict among members of the same millet, the conflict would be resolved by the traditional authorities and processes of the respective millet. Thus a Christian was governed by Christian laws in his dealings with Christians regardless of his physical location in the Ottoman Empire.

miri sirf: State ownership of land with specified rights to the tenant farmer.

mosque: Islamic house of worship.

Muhammad Ali (also Mehmet Ali):   Ruler of Egypt from 1805 to 1849. He initiated major reforms in Egypt, many of which were blunted by a combination of European and Ottoman strategies. The economic and military power of Egypt were greatly increased by Muhammad Ali, who was also the first of the great modernizers in the Arab world.

Muharram: A month of the lunar year, dedicated in the Shiite community to commemorating Hussein's martyrdom. The commemoration is emotionally very strong for the faithful.

mujahid: Religious leader, preacher, and scholar. Shiite equivalent of Sunni ulema.

mulk: Private ownership of land.

Najd: The extremely arid north-central region of the Arabian peninsula.

Ottomans (Ottoman Empire):   Founded by the Turkish leader Osman, the Ottoman state gave rise to the last great Islamic caliphate. Centered in Anatolia, the empire lasted from its founding in the thirteenth century to the first decade of the twentieth century.

pir: A recognized master in a sufi tariqah or order.

Qarmatians: A long-lived communal movement within the Isma'ili sect of Shiism.

Quraish: One of the most important and powerful of the Arab tribes at the time of Muhammad, which controlled Mecca. As descendants of the Prophet's tribe, the Quraish have always been accorded a special respect in Islam.

Ramadan: One of the lunar months of the Muslim calendar. Fasting during the daylight hours of Ramadan is one of the five "pillars" of ritual obligations of Islam.

Riddah: Wars of apostasy, fought soon after the death of Muhammad, forcing rebellious Arab tribes to continue their allegiance to Islam.

sadaqua: Voluntary charitable contribution, bringing religious merit to the donor.

Sanussi: A Sufi order that became very influential in North Africa.

Sephardim: Generally, the so-called "Oriental" Jews of Spanish, African, Asian, or Middle Eastern origin. Specifically, the term refers to Jews from Spain.

shahada: The declaration of faith in Islam: "There is no God but Allah, and Muhammad is his Prophet."

Sharia: The Muslim legal code, founded on the Koran and Hadith (traditions of the Prophet) and codified by various systems of interpretation or *fiqh.*

sheikh: A term that can apply to high-level political, local, communal, or religious leaders.

Shiites: Muslims following the Caliph Ali and his successors, differing on various points of doctrine from the orthodox Sunni majority. Shiism, concentrated largely in Iraq and Iran, is divided into several different sects.

Sufism: A movement pervasive in Islam, based on mystical experience. The diverse Sufi orders, each with its own tradition of mystical teachings, have cultivated the inner, ecstatic aspect of Islam, and their appeal has greatly aided the spread of Islam in some parts of the world.

Sunni: The largest "orthodox" division of Islam.

suq: Bazaar; a place for commerce, comprised of a number of merchants selling a limited variety of wares. An important setting for social interaction as well as commercial exchange.

sura: Chapter in the Koran.

Tanzimat: Generally a series of attempted reforms in the Ottoman Empire from 1839–1876; at least partially a response to growing European dominance.

taqiyyah: Dissimulation, or the disguise of one's true religious feelings in order to avoid persecution. Widely used among Shiites in response to the many attempts to control or persecute the Shiite community.

tariqahs: Specific orders of Sufism, with specified secret paths to mystical ecstasy. After the decline of the Caliphate, tariqah lodges often filled many local social needs as well.

ulema: Refers to the Muslim scholars who take the place of priests in Islam. Unlike their Christian counterparts, the ulema are not organized into a clergy and claim no special powers of sanctity beyond their study of the documents of Islam.

Umayyad: One of the most powerful and important of the Arabic families at the time of Muhammad. The Umayyad Caliphate was founded at Damascus by Muawiya after his conflict of succession with Ali.

Umma: The worldwide community of Islam, which ideally commands a Muslim's loyalty above all considerations of race, kinship, or nationality.

Wahhabism: A religious movement founded in the late eighteenth century by Abd-al Wahhab. Wahhabites are a particularly puritanical Muslim sect that dominate Saudi Arabia.

wajh: Group honor, "face," a concept of great importance in the maintenance of group and individual prestige.

waqf: Religious endowments, usually made in perpetuity, which support a specific institution devoted to good works, such as a madrasah, a home for orphans, or a religious building. Waqf sometimes became a device for avoiding taxation.

zakat: One of the five pillars of the Islamic faith, obligating the faithful to support the unfortunate and the needy.

Suggested Sources
for Further Reading

This bibliography is designed to give the interested student a few additional sources in the subject matter of each of the chapters. Most of the works cited are intellectually appropriate to an undergraduate student audience. The student should note that there are many specialized books, monographs, and articles dealing with particular topics. This bibliography is not designed to include these works. Nor is it designed to include the most important books or controversial scholarly works. Rather it should be viewed as a "sampler."

GENERAL

Borthwick, Bruce. *Comparative Politics of the Middle East: An Introduction*, Englewood Cliffs, N.J.: Prentice-Hall, Inc., 1980.

Hodgson, Marshall G. S. *The Venture of Islam*, 3 volumes. Chicago: University of Chicago Press, 1974.

Holt, Peter M., Ann Lambton, and Bernard Lewis (ed.). *The Cambridge History of Islam*, Cambridge, England: Cambridge University Press, 1970.

Kahn, Margaret. *Children of the Jinn: In Search of the Kurds and Their Country*, New York: Seaview Books, 1980.

Legum, Colin, and Haim Shaked, *The Middle East Contemporary Survey: 1978–1979*, New York: Holmes and Meier, 1980.

Mansfield, Peter (ed.). *The Middle East: A Political and Economic Survey*, New York: Oxford Press, 1980.

Said, Edward. *Orientalism*, New York: Pantheon Books, Inc., 1978.

CHAPTER 1: TRADITIONAL CULTURES
OF THE MIDDLE EAST: THE CRADLE
OF CIVILIZATION AND POLITICS

Cole, Donald. *Nomads of the Nomads: The Al Murrah Bedouin of the Empty Quarter*, Arlington Heights, IL.: AHM Publishing Corp., 1975.

Coon, Carleton. *Caravan: The Story of the Middle East*, New York: Holt, Rinehart and Winston, 1966.

Fakhouri, Hani. *Kafr El-Elow: An Egyptian Village in Transition*, New York: Holt, Rinehart and Winston, 1972.

Patai, Raphael. *Society, Culture, and Change in the Middle East* (3rd ed.), Philadelphia: University of Pennsylvania Press, 1969.

CHAPTER 2: THE FOUNDATIONS OF ISLAM

Arberry, Arthur J. *The Koran Interpreted*, Volumes I and II. New York: Macmillan Publishing Co., Inc., 1955.

Gibb, Hamilton A. R. *Mohammedanism, an Historical Survey* (2nd ed.), New York: Oxford University Press, 1953.

Hodgson, Marshall G. S. *The Venture of Islam, Volume I: The Classical Age of Islam*, Chicago: University of Chicago Press, 1974.

Watt, W. Montgomery. *Islamic Philosophy and Theology*, Edinburgh: Edinburgh University Press, 1962.

Watt, W. Montgomery. *Muhammad, Prophet and Statesman*, London: Oxford University Press, 1961.

CHAPTER 3: THE POLITICAL LEGACY
OF ISLAM, 632–1800 C.E.

Hitti, Philip K. *History of the Arabs* (8th ed.), London: Macmillan, 1964.

Hodgson, Marshall G. S. *The Venture of Islam, Volume II: The Expansion of Islam in the Middle Periods*, Chicago: University of Chicago Press, 1974.

Lewis, Bernard. *The Arabs in History* (revised ed.), New York: Harper & Row, Publishers, Inc., 1966.

Shaw, Stanford. *History of the Ottoman Empire and Modern Turkey*, Cambridge: Cambridge University Press, 1976.

Tabatabai, Muhammad Hussein. *Shi'ite Islam*, Albany, N.Y.: State University of New York Press, 1975.

Von Grunebaum, G. E. *Classical Islam, A History 600–1258*, Chicago, Aldine Publishing Co., 1970.

Watt, W. Montgomery. *Islamic Surveys, Volume 6: Islamic Political Thought*, Edinburgh: Edinburgh University Press, 1968.

CHAPTER 4: WESTERN IMPERIALISM

Hodgson, Marshall G. S. *The Venture of Islam, Vol. III: The Gunpowder Empires and Modern Times*, Chicago: University of Chicago Press, 1974.

Holt, Peter M. *Egypt and the Fertile Crescent*, Ithaca, N.Y.: Cornell, 1967.

Lewis, Bernard. *The Middle East and the West*, New York: Harper & Row, Publishers, Inc., 1966.

Polk, William R., and Richard Chambers. *The Beginnings of Modernization in the Middle East*, Chicago: University of Chicago Press, 1968.

Rivlin, Helen. *The Agricultural Policy of Muhammad Ali*, Cambridge, Mass.: Harvard University Press, 1961.

Shaw, Stanford, and Ezel Shaw. *History of the Ottoman Empire and Modern Turkey*, Vol. II, New York: Cambridge, 1976–77.

CHAPTER 5: RISE OF THE STATE SYSTEM

Hodgson, Marshall G. S. *The Venture of Islam, Vol. III: The Gundpowder Empires and Modern Times*, Chicago: University of Chicago Press, 1974.

Issawi, Charles (ed.). *The Economic History of the Middle East 1800–1914*, Chicago: University of Chicago Press, 1966.

Lewis, Bernard. *The Emergence of Modern Turkey*, New York: Oxford, 1968.

Shaw, Stanford, and Ezel Shaw. *History of the Ottoman Empire and Modern Turkey, Vol. II*, New York: Cambridge, 1976–77.

CHAPTER 6: MODERNIZATION: AN OVERVIEW

Critchfield, Richard. *Shahhat: An Egyptian*, Syracuse, N.Y.: Syracuse University Press, 1978.

Esposito, John L. (ed.), *Islam and Development: Religion and Sociopolitical Change*, Syracuse, N.Y.: Syracuse University Press, 1980.

Fakhouri, Hani. *Kafr El-Elow: An Egyptian Village in Transition*, New York: Holt, Rinehart and Winston, 1972.

Hodgson, Marshall G. S. *The Venture of Islam, Volume III: The Gunpowder Empires and Modern Times*, Chicago: University of Chicago Press, 1974.

Lerner, Daniel. *The Passing of Traditional Society*, New York: The Free Press, 1958.

Mernissi, Fatima. *Beyond the Veil: Male-Female Dynamics in a Modern Muslim Society*, New York: Schenkman Publishing Company, Inc., 1975.

CHAPTER 7: THE DRIVE FOR SELF-DETERMINATION

Bill, James, and Carl Leiden. *Politics in the Middle East*, Boston: Little, Brown & Co., 1979.

Binder, Leonard. *Iran: Political Development in a Changing Society*, Berkeley: University of California Press, 1962.

Borthwick, Bruce. *Comparative Politics of the Middle East: An Introduction*, Englewood Cliffs, N.J.: Prentice-Hall, Inc., 1980.

Peretz, Don. *The Government and Politics of Israel*, Boulder, Co.: Westview, 1979.

Polk, William. *The Arab World*, Cambridge, Mass.: Harvard University Press, 1980.

Thompson, Jack, and Robert Reischauer (ed.). *Modernization of the Arab World*, Princeton, N.J.: Van Nostrand, 1966.

Zonis, Marvin. *The Political Elite of Iran*, Princeton, N.J.: Princeton University Press, 1971.

CHAPTER 8: THE ECONOMIC SETTING

Askari, Hossein, and John Cummings. *Middle East Economies in the 1970s*, New York: Praeger Publishers, Inc., 1976.

Birks, J. S., and C. A. Sinclair. *International Migration and Development in the Arab Region*, Geneva: International Labor Office, 1980.

Chenery, Hollis. "Restructuring the World's Economy," *Foreign Affairs*, Vol. 53, no. 1 (Jan. 1975), pp. 242–63.

Hansen, Bent, and Karim Nashashibi. *Foreign Trade Regimes and Economic Development: Egypt*, New York: National Bureau of Economic Research, 1975.

International Labor Office. *Manpower and Employment in Arab Countries*, Geneva, Switzerland: International Labor Office, 1976.

Michaely, Michael. *Foreign Trade Regimes and Economic Development: Israel*, New York: National Bureau of Economic Research, 1975.

Sayigh, Yusif. *The Determinants of Arab Economic Development*, New York: St. Martin's Press, 1978.

Sayigh, Yusif. *The Economies of the Arab World: Development Since 1945*, New York: St. Martin's Press, 1977.

Vernon, Raymond (ed.). *The Oil Crisis*, New York: W. W. Norton & Co., Inc., 1976.

CHAPTER 9: POLITICAL ELITES

Bill, James A., and Carl Leiden. *Politics in the Middle East*, Boston, Mass.: Little, Brown & Co., 1979.

Binder, Leonard. *In a Moment of Enthusiasm: Political Power and the Second Stratum in Egypt*, Chicago: University of Chicago Press, 1978.

Elon, Amos. *The Israelis: Founders and Sons*, London: Weidenfeld and Nicholson, 1971.

Frey, Frederic W., *The Turkish Political Elite*, Cambridge, Mass.: The M.I.T. Press, 1965.

Lenczowski, George (ed.). *Political Elites in the Middle East*, Washington, D.C.: American Enterprise Institute for Public Policy Research, 1975.

Tachau, Frank (ed.). *Political Elites and Political Development in the Middle East*, Cambridge, Mass.: Schenkman Publishing Co., Inc., 1975.

Zonis, Marvin. *The Political Elite of Iran*, Princeton, N.J.: Princeton University Press, 1971.

CHAPTER 10: POLITICAL LEADERSHIP
IN THE CONTEMPORARY MIDDLE EAST

Almond, Gabriel A., and G. Bingham Powell. *Comparative Politics: System, Process, and Policy*, Boston, Mass.: Little, Brown & Co., 1978.

Dekmejian, Richard Hrair. *Patterns of Political Leadership: Lebanon, Israel and Egypt*, Albany, N.Y.: State University of New York Press, 1975.

Dekmejian, Richard Hrair. *Egypt Under Nasser*, Albany, N.Y.: State University of New York Press, 1971.

Nasser, Gamal Abdel. *Egypt's Liberation: The Philosophy of the Revolution*, Washington, D.C.: Public Affairs Press, 1955.

Rustow, Dankwart A. *Philosophers and Kings: Studies in Leadership*, New York: George Braziller, 1970.

Sadat, Anwar. *In Search of Identity: An Autobiography*, New York: Harper & Row Publishers, Inc., 1978.

CHAPTER 11: INTERNATIONAL RELATIONS
IN THE CONTEMPORARY MIDDLE EAST

Freedman, Robert O. *Soviet Policy Toward the Middle East*, New York: Praeger Publishers, Inc., 1975.

Khouri, Fred J. *The Arab-Israeli Dilemma* (2nd ed.), Syracuse, N.Y.: Syracuse University Press, 1976.

Lenczowski, George. *The Middle East in World Affairs*, Ithaca, N.Y.: Cornell University Press, 1980.

Polk, William R. *The Arab World*, Cambridge, Mass.: Harvard University Press, 1980.

Quandt, William B. *Decade of Decisions: American Policy Toward the Arab-Israeli Conflict, 1967-1976*, Berkeley, Ca.: University of California Press, 1977.

Said, Edward W. *The Question of Palestine*, New York: Time Books, 1979.

CHAPTER 12: ISLAMIC REVIVAL
AND THE ISLAMIC REPUBLIC

Esposito, John (ed.). *Islam and Development: Religion and Sociopolitical Change*, Syracuse, N.Y.: Syracuse University Press, 1980.

Fischer, Michael M. J. *Iran: From Religious Dispute to Revolution*, Cambridge, Mass.: Harvard University Press, 1980.

Keddie, Nikki R. *Scholars, Saints and Sufis: Muslim Institutions in the Middle East Since 1500*, Berkeley, Ca.: University of California Press, 1972.

Mitchell, Richard P. *The Society of the Muslim Brothers*, London: Oxford University Press, 1969.

Rahman, Fazlur. *Islam* (2nd ed.), Chicago: University of Chicago Press, 1979.

Said, Edward W. *Covering Islam*, New York: Pantheon Books, 1981.

Shariati, Ali. *On the Sociology of Islam* (3rd ed.), Trans Hamid Algar, Tehran: Mizan Publishers, 1980.

Index